LEGACIES OF FEAR

Law and Politics in Quebec in the Era of the French Revolution

Legacies of Fear

Law and Politics in Quebec in the Era of the French Revolution

F. MURRAY GREENWOOD

The Osgoode Society

©The Osgoode Society 1993
Printed in Canada

ISBN 0-8020-0543-8 (cloth)

Printed on acid-free paper

Canadian Cataloguing in Publication Data

Greenwood, F. Murray (Frank Murray), 1935–
Legacies of fear : law and politics in Quebec
in the era of the French Revolution

Includes bibliographical references and index.
ISBN 0-8020-0543-8 (bound) ISBN 0-8020-6974-6 (pbk.)

1. Canada – Politics and government – 1783–1791.*
2. Quebec (Province) – Politics and government – 1791–1841.*
3. Law – Quebec (Province) – History.
4. France – History – Revolution, 1789–1799 – Influence.
5. Napoleonic Wars, 1800–1815 – Influence. I. Osgoode Society. II. Title.

FC2921.G744 1993   971.4'02   C93-094264-7   F1053.G744 1993

To the memory of my father,
Frank Edmund,
for his encouragement in my early years as a scholar

Contents

Foreword

THE OSGOODE SOCIETY

The purpose of The Osgoode Society is to encourage research and writing in the history of Canadian law. The Society, which was incorporated in 1979 and is registered as a charity, was founded at the initiative of the Honourable R. Roy McMurtry, former attorney general for Ontario, and officials of the Law Society of Upper Canada. Its efforts to stimulate the study of legal history in Canada include a research support program, a graduate student research assistance program, and work in the fields of oral history and legal archives. The Society publishes (at the rate of about one a year) volumes of interest to the Society's members that contribute to legal-historical scholarship in Canada, including studies of the courts, the judiciary, and the legal profession, biographies, collections of documents, studies in criminology and penology, accounts of great trials, and work in the social and economic history of the law.

Current directors of The Osgoode Society are Jane Banfield, Marion Boyd, Brian Bucknall, Archie Campbell, J. Douglas Ewart, Martin Friedland, John Honsberger, Kenneth Jarvis, Allen Linden, Colin McKinnon, Roy McMurtry, Brendan O'Brien, Peter Oliver, Allan Rock, James Spence, and Richard Tinsley. The annual report and information about membership may be obtained by writing The Osgoode Society, Osgoode Hall, 130 Queen Street West, Toronto, Ontario, Canada M5H 2N6. Members receive the annual volumes published by the Society.

Legacies of Fear is a compelling study of the evolving relationship between 'old' and 'new' subjects, English and French Canadians, during a critical period in the history of Canada – the era of the French Revolution and of the Napoleonic Wars. Focusing on the excitement caused by events in revolutionary France and the fear of the English-speaking minority of a French invasion, Professor Greenwood argues that this turbulent period of disturbances, riots, and apprehended insurrection, climaxed by a treason trial and the execution of David McLane, was characterized by a dramatic deterioration in English-French relations, and the development among the English-speaking group of a 'garrison mentality.' Placing the legal history of Quebec in the foreground of these dangerous and dramatic events, Professor Greenwood's account is a significant reinterpretation of Quebec and Canadian history.

R. Roy McMurtry
President

Peter Oliver
Editor-in-Chief

Acknowledgments

My editors and readers deserve my gratitude. Marilyn MacFarlane of The Osgoode Society was wonderfully supportive and clear-headed through many crises. Editor-in-chief Peter Oliver guided me well, and effectively insisted on cuts and more cuts, making the work, I believe, better than it once was. Laura Macleod of the University of Toronto Press showed intelligent tolerance in dealing with my many publishing problems, and the copy editor, Diane Mew, did a complex job very sensitively, so that the manuscript flowed in its final form. My official readers for The Osgoode Society – Evelyn Kolish, Peter Moogk, and Brian Young – were encouraging and moved me to make many major changes I judged to be worthwhile. Evelyn has also given freely of her great knowledge of the civil law in early Quebec/Lower Canada. Peter did a highly skilled line-by-line criticism as well as making professional 'macro' suggestions. There were also unofficial readers. DeLloyd Guth, Douglas Hay, and James P. Huzel read large portions of early manuscripts dealing with the 1790s. Their comments were much appreciated and in some cases prevented serious error. Barry Wright read an entire early manuscript, made many acute recommendations, and throughout the main period of writing was a knowledgeable and encouraging friend.

Of the dozens of librarians and archivists who have assisted in this project, two deserve special mention. For years Al Soroka of the Law Library at the University of British Columbia has fielded my arcane requests with skill and good humour. Patricia Kennedy of the National

Archives of Canada has learnedly advised me and retrieved obscure documents (often on her own initiative) for my use for almost twenty years. I thank my research assistants – Julie Boudreault, Christopher Greenwood, and Marty Logan – for much underpaid diligence and many inspired finds. I also thank Judy Cowling, Robert Cowling, and Judith Anne Greenwood for their patient help, many years ago, in my coining the short title 'Legacies of Fear.'

I must also mention the late Leslie Upton, who taught me how to recognize and sometimes avoid poor academic writing. Leslie encouraged me to pursue this unusual topic. At about the same time as Northrop Frye published an essay in which he used the phrase 'garrison mentality' to refer, brilliantly, to Canadians psychologically huddling together in response to formidable geography, Leslie and I independently coined the same term to explain the mindset of the English minority in Lower Canada from 1793 to 1811.

Finally, I thank my wife Beverley for doing it all – cutting with a scalpel, finding the unfindable, suggesting new insights, word processing, more word processing, encouraging when the horizon was bleak – with love.

Author's Note

A French-language pamphlet published in Quebec City in 1792 divided lay Canadien (that is, francophone) society horizontally into three general classes: 'Seigneurs and Nobles'; 'Merchants and Bourgeois'; and 'Habitants, Farm Labourers ... Artisans and Workers.' This classification faithfully reflected the language of class in the new mother country.

Late eighteenth and early nineteenth-century Britishers adopted a hierarchical tripartite division of society.[1] At the apex were the leisured landed gentlemen of the aristocracy and gentry (referred to sometimes as the higher rank, higher classes, higher orders, and the nobility). In the second rank were those people, not of the landed classes, who worked with their heads: merchants, bankers, professionals, lower clergy and shopkeepers, for example. These men were variously referred to as middling people, and middle ranks. The actual dividing line between the two upper ranks was never very clear. A physician who was the younger son of an impoverished squire, for example, would have been difficult to classify although his non-inheriting brother holding a commission in the army was certainly a member of the higher rank. At the bottom of the pyramid were the lower classes, the poor, the common people, or most commonly, the lower orders. Men and women of the lower orders depended on manual labour for their livelihoods and hence included farmers, farm labourers, artisans, urban labourers, and domestic servants. The precise dividing line between the lower and middle ranks was vague. It is not clear, for example, to which rank a pedlar, goldsmith, dancing

master, or surgeon should be assigned. Architects and school teachers –
even though neither group was organized by law professionally – were
probably thought of as in the middling ranks.

In the absence of any consensus among historians, I have chosen to
use this tripartite division because it was by far the most common usage
in Quebec/Lower Canada.[2] My three classes or ranks are: the seigneurial
class; the middling ranks, middle classes, or bourgeoisie; and the lower
orders (without pejorative connotation), working people, or workers. I
have 'down-ranked' an individual if there is serious doubt as to his or
her social status. Ownership of a seigneury is not the test of inclusion in
the seigneurial class. There were a number of Canadien seigneurs of very
modest social consequence (e.g., from artisanal or habitant families) who
were not of course admitted to the social circles of the Canadien lay élite
or the Chateau. Even lawyer Jean-Antoine Panet (1751–1815), a high-
ranking militia officer, a seigneur, and the son of a judge, did not qualify
as a member of the seigneurial class, at least according to Governor Sir
James Craig (who was expert in such assessments), since he came from
a 'new family which has risen in the law.'[3] My tests for inclusion in the
seigneurial class are either membership (including by marriage) in a
family of the nobility, or a commission in the British army, the officer
corps being a preserve of the higher ranks. In neither case is the ownership of a seigneury (although very common) deemed essential. Unless the
context indicates that I am referring to Canadien seigneurs as *owners of
land*, the words 'seigneurs' and 'Canadien seigneurs' refer to individuals
in the seigneurial class.

Population

According to the census of 1789–90, the total population of what would
soon become Lower Canada (east of the Ottawa River) was 161,311.[4] The
Canadiens then outnumbered the English approximately fifteen to one
and in 1811 (after much American immigration into the Eastern Townships during the early nineteenth century) by between nine and twelve
to one. The total population was probably near 275,000.

The Lower Canada of the early 1790s was largely undeveloped. Only
a quarter of its arable land was under cultivation. Even so, its demographic character was overwhelmingly rural, with more than 80 per cent
of the population living in the country, the vast majority in farming
families. The population of Quebec and its suburbs then numbered
about seven thousand and Montreal, perhaps six thousand. By 1805 and

1811 respectively each had a population of approximately nine thousand and twelve to thirteen thousand. These were the only 'cities.' Trois-Rivières, a minor market-administrative town probably had fewer than fifteen hundred in 1789, while William Henry (later Sorel) contained perhaps a thousand people, mostly the families of active army personnel and half-pay loyalist officers. These two cities and two towns made up the colony's modest urban areas. Dotting the countryside were a number of 'large' villages (there were numerous hamlets) of a few score souls. One of the most important commercially – St-Denis on the Richelieu River – had a total population of 169 in 1789 and 347 at the turn of the century.[5]

Habitant Literacy

Rural schools for Canadiens were almost non-existent throughout the period. Probably fewer than one in thirty farming adults could read and write with any degree of fluency as of 1789; fewer than one in ten could even write his or her name.[6]

Monetary Matters and Measures

The main currency used in the colony was called the Halifax currency or just currency, one pound of which was worth twelve-thirteenths of one pound sterling. Unless otherwise specified, a reference to pounds indicates sterling. Canadiens and those they dealt with often calculated prices in terms of the old French money of livres, sols and deniers. A livre was worth about one English shilling, that is, one-twentieth of a pound. There were twenty sols to the livre and twelve deniers to the sol.

It is probably futile to attempt to translate these monetary values into today's, and in any case I am not competent to try. Some idea of values may be gained from the following list of prices, wages, and salaries, dating from 1795, unless otherwise specified:[7] a) beef (per lb) about twopence; b) wheat, about six shillings a bushel; c) white bread (4 lbs, 8. oz), six pence (1792); d) single letter from Quebec City to England via Halifax, one shilling, eight pence (1792); e) annual rental (Montreal) of a house fit for a gentleman, about £30; f) meals and room in a quality inn (Quebec City) for one night, about four shillings (1797); g) man servant's annual wage (excluding room and board), about £12; h) wage of a labourer (male, summer), about two shillings, six pence a day; and i) annual salary of the governor, £2,000.

A square *arpent* was approximately five-sixths of an English acre. A linear *arpent* was about 192 feet. The French *minot* was a measure of volume equalling 1.05 English bushels.

A Note on Style

In accordance with contemporary usage, particularly among Canadiens, the term 'English' refers to all non-native persons who were not Canadiens and had not assimilated to the Canadien way of life (for example, as many disbanded Hessians had done). In particular, the term included those of Scottish or Irish origin and American loyalists. The term 'Canadien' ('Canadian' in English) was commonplace at the time, although the occasional usage of 'French Canadian' can be found.

Translations from French to English are mine unless otherwise specified or obvious (for example, quotations from the bilingual *Journals of the House of Assembly of Lower Canada*).

Citations for events occurring from 1 January to 24 March before the calendar change of 1752 are given for both years, thus 1461/62. For most sources in the Notes full citations are given only in the Select Bibliography.

Chief Justice Smith and His French Party Opponents

Chief Justice William Smith

Judge Adam Mabane

Judge René-Ovide Hertel de Rouville

The Early Governors

Sir Frederick Haldimand

Guy Carleton, Lord Dorchester

Leading Canadien Politicians

Jean-Antoine Panet

Joseph Papineau

Judge Pierre-Amable De Bonne

Legal and Political Representatives of the 'Garrison Mentality'

Chief Justice of Montreal James Monk

Chief Justice William Osgoode

Chief Justice Jonathan Sewell

Two Leaders of the English Party

Montreal merchant James McGill

Bureaucrat Herman Witsius Ryland

The Authoritarian 'Garrison Mentality' Governors

Sir Robert Prescott

Sir James Henry Craig

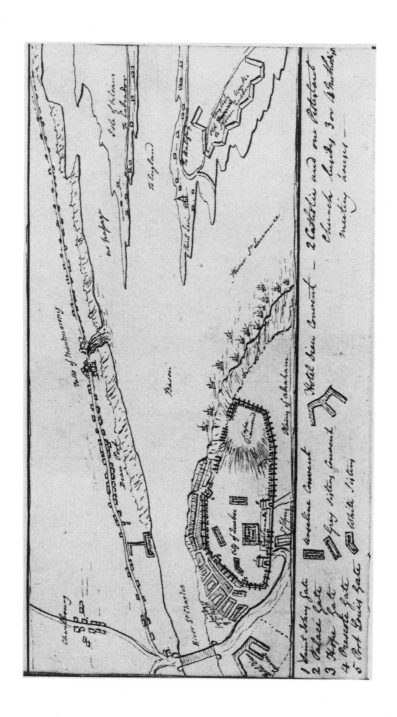

Plan of Quebec City and Environs, 1805, by Sempronius Stretton

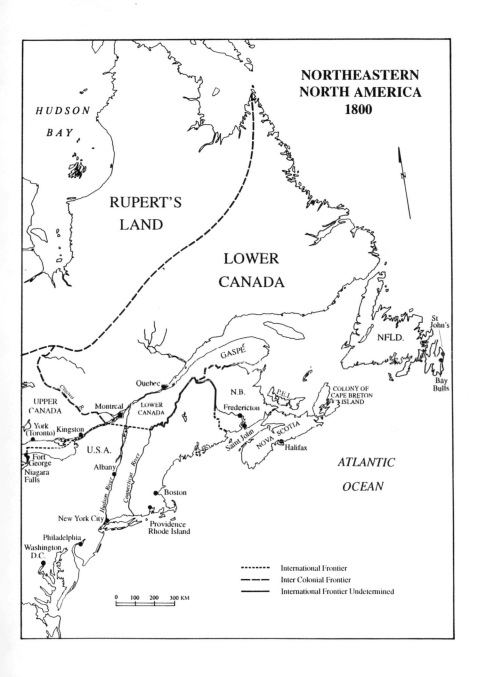

NORTHEASTERN
NORTH AMERICA
1800

HUDSON

BAY

RUPERT'S
LAND

LOWER
CANADA

GASPÉ

NFLD.

St
John's

Bay
Bulls

Quebec

N.B.

P.E.I.

COLONY OF
CAPE BRETON
ISLAND

UPPER
CANADA

Ottawa R.

Montreal

LOWER
CANADA

Fredericton

York
(Toronto)

Kingston

U.S.A.

Saint John

NOVA SCOTIA

Halifax

Fort
George

Niagara
Falls

Albany

Hudson River

Connecticut River

ATLANTIC

OCEAN

Boston

New York City

Providence
Rhode Island

Philadelphia

Washington
D.C.

0   100   200   300 KM

-------------   International Frontier
– – – – –   Inter Colonial Frontier
─────────   International Frontier Undetermined

This map replaces the one on page xxvii.
Errors on the original, created in typesetting, have been corrected.
University of Toronto Press regrets any inconvenience caused.

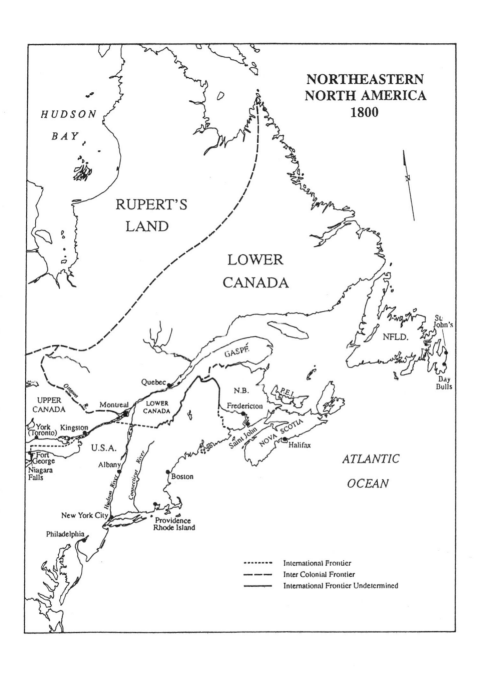

**NORTHEASTERN
NORTH AMERICA
1800**

*HUDSON
BAY*

RUPERT'S
LAND

LOWER
CANADA

NFLD.

St.
John's

GASPÉ

Quebec

N.B.

P.E.I.

Day
Bulls

UPPER
CANADA

Ottawa

Montreal

LOWER
CANADA

Fredericton

York
(Toronto)

Kingston

U.S.A.

Saint John

NOVA SCOTIA

Halifax

ATLANTIC

Fort
George

Niagara
Falls

Albany

Hudson River

Connecticut River

Boston

OCEAN

New York City

Providence
Rhode Island

Philadelphia

--------	International Frontier
— — —	Inter Colonial Frontier
———	International Frontier Undetermined

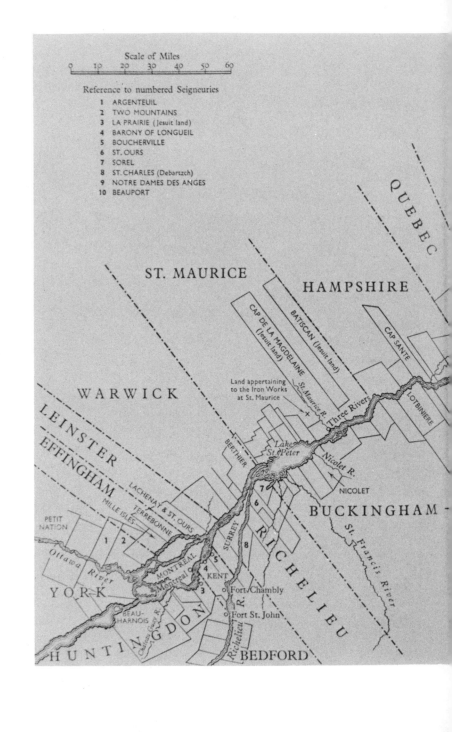

Scale of Miles

0   10   20   30   40   50   60

Reference to numbered Seigneuries

1 ARGENTEUIL
2 TWO MOUNTAINS
3 LA PRAIRIE (Jesuit land)
4 BARONY OF LONGUEIL
5 BOUCHERVILLE
6 ST. OURS
7 SOREL
8 ST. CHARLES (Debartzch)
9 NOTRE DAMES DES ANGES
10 BEAUPORT

QUEBEC

ST. MAURICE

HAMPSHIRE

CAP DE LA MAGDELAINE (Jesuit land)

BATISCAN (Jesuit land)

CAP SANTE

WARWICK

Land appertaining to the Iron Works at St. Maurice

St. Maurice R.

Three Rivers

LOTBINIERE

LEINSTER

EFFINGHAM

BERTHIER

Lake St. Peter

Nicolet R.

NICOLET

LACHENAY & ST. OURS

TERREBONNE

MILLE ISLES

PETIT NATION

1   2

Ottawa River

SURREY

7

6

8

RICHELIEU

BUCKINGHAM

St. Francis River

4
5
MONTREAL
Montreal

KENT

3

Fort Chambly

Fort St. John

YORK

BEAU-HARNOIS

Chateau Guay R.

Richelieu R.

HUNTINGDON

BEDFORD

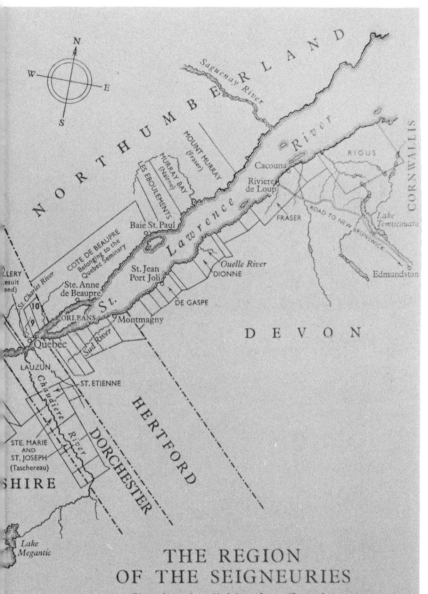

THE REGION
OF THE SEIGNEURIES
Showing the division into Counties
by Proclamation of the Lieutenant Governor, 1792

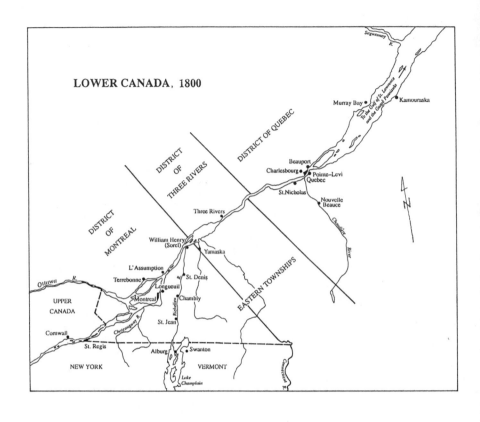

Based on 'A New Map of the Province of Lower Canada'
by Samuel Holland c. 1792

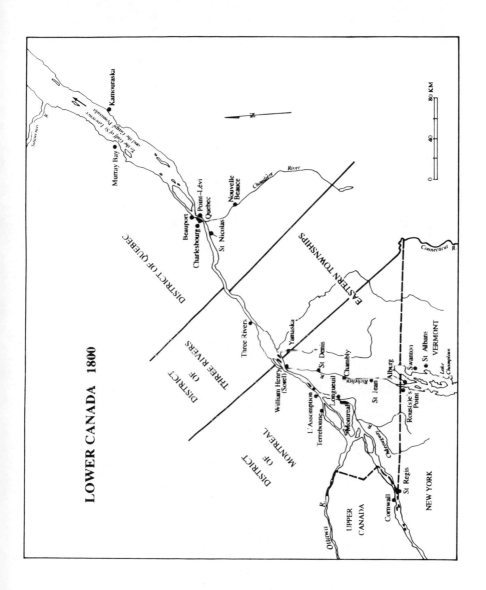

LOWER CANADA 1800

This map replaces the one on page xxx.
Errors on the original, created in typesetting, have been corrected.
University of Toronto Press regrets any inconvenience caused.

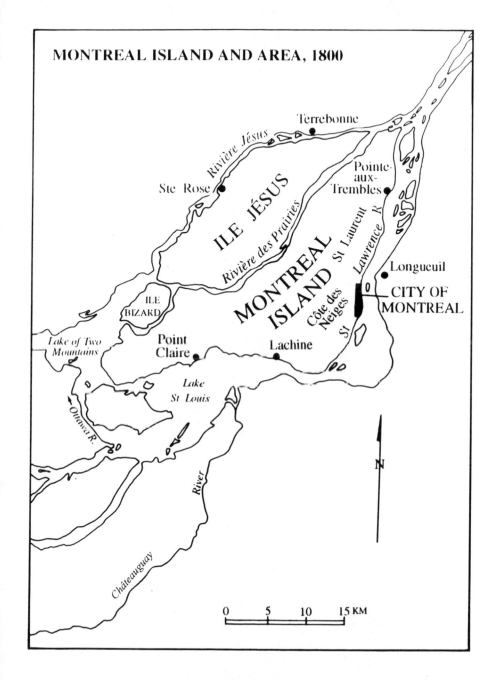

MONTREAL ISLAND AND AREA, 1800

Terrebonne

Rivière Jésus

Ste Rose

ILE JÉSUS

Rivière des Prairies

Pointe-
aux-
Trembles

MONTREAL ISLAND

St Laurent

Lawrence R.

Longueuil

CITY OF
MONTREAL

Côte des
Neiges

St

ILE
BIZARD

Lake of Two
Mountains

Point
Claire

Lachine

Ottawa R.

Lake
St Louis

River

N

Châteauguay

0   5   10   15 KM

This map replaces the one on page xxxi.
Errors on the original, created in typesetting, have been corrected.
University of Toronto Press regrets any inconvenience caused.

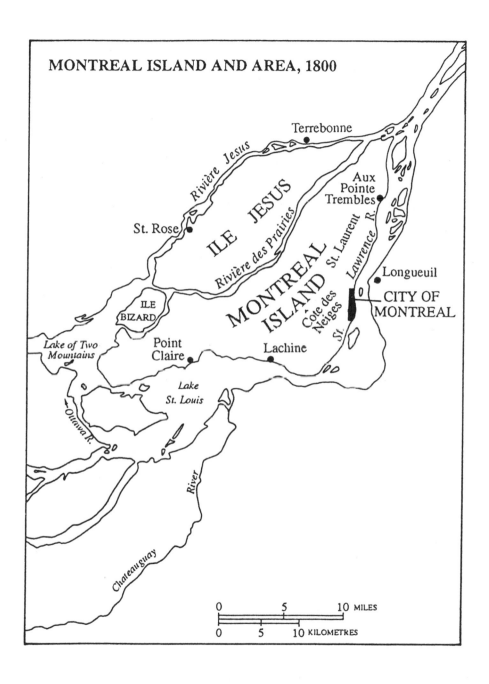

MONTREAL ISLAND AND AREA, 1800

Terrebonne

Rivière Jesus

ILE JESUS

St. Rose

Rivière des Prairies

Aux
Pointe
Trembles

MONTREAL
ISLAND

St. Laurent

Lawrence R.

Longueuil

ILE
BIZARD

Côte des
Neiges

St.

CITY OF
MONTREAL

Lake of Two
Mountains

Point
Claire

Lachine

Lake
St. Louis

Ottawa R.

Chateauguay

River

0   5   10 MILES

0   5   10 KILOMETRES

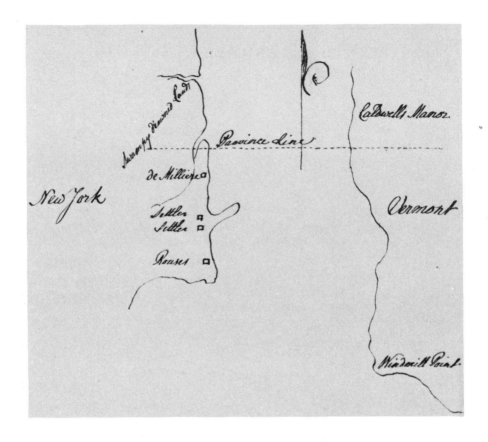

French base of espionage operations on Lake Champlain (1796), drawn by a government informer. Neighbour and experienced spy Jacques Rousse advised the man in charge, one General de Millière.

Legacies of Fear

Introduction

On a summer's day in Quebec City, 1797, a young American from Rhode Island stood high on a platform speaking to the crowds below. He was tall, handsome, dressed in virgin white. Women interrupted his address, screaming proposals of marriage. Many of them shed tears that 21 July, for David McLane was about to be hanged for high treason against His Britannic Majesty, George III. Minutes later it was done:

The body hung for five and twenty minutes and was then cut down. A platform ... was brought near the gallows, and a fire was kindled ... the head was cut off, and the executioner holding it up to public view proclaimed it 'the head of a traitor.' – An incision was made below the breast and a part of the bowels taken out and burnt; the four quarters were marked with a knife, but were not divided from the body.[1]

Many Canadiens then and later thought McLane was the victim of judicial murder. They had warrant for thinking so, although we now know for certain that the American was a fully fledged spy sent into Lower Canada by representatives of revolutionary France. The English élite in the colony generally applauded the execution, overlooking the many questionable proceedings at trial, as they had such draconian security legislation as the 1797 statute suspending habeas corpus and restricting civil liberty far more drastically than in contemporary Great Britain. Relations between Canadiens and English, particularly in the middle classes, were at a low point. The latter, imbued with what I call a 'garrison mentality,' feared a Canadien revolution supported by French troops and willingly accepted any authoritarian enactment, court proceeding, or executive action. The English élite would applaud again in 1810 when the governor sent the Canadien leaders of the elected Legislative Assembly to prison without right to bail or trial.

It had not always been that way. Just a decade or so before, the English merchants and Canadien bourgeoisie had worked in alliance for very liberal constitutional reform, seeking an elected assembly with the power of the purse, a judiciary independent of the executive – indeed isolated from partisan politics – and entrenchment of the right to habeas corpus. The alliance was also working to commercialize the French civil law. By 1797, if not earlier, it was clear that neither significant constitutional liberalization nor commercialization would come about in the near future. One of the major themes of this book describes the functioning of the bourgeois alliance, explains its ideology, traces its demise, and suggests the serious implications of that demise for the history of Lower Canada.

There are other themes. The impact of the garrison mentality on the operation of the constitution and the administration of justice in security cases are two. Closely related to the latter is what I call the development of a 'Baconian judiciary,' that is, one which overwhelmingly guided its behaviour and reasoning by the political needs of the governors. A further theme attempts to explain the serious riots among working people in the 1790s in terms of a long tradition in French Canada (from about 1700 to at least 1850) of 'rebellion à justice' – that is, resistance to law enforcement where the resisters thought their vital interests were in jeopardy. Another concern is the long-range impact of the French Revolution on Canadien civil law as it affected the family. Finally, I attempt to relate several legal and political issues of the period to later history and in particular to the Lower Canadian rebellions of 1837–8.

The new legal history of the last twenty-five years or so has emphasized the past interrelation of law and society. Legal historians now strive for sophisticated contextual explanations of their subject matter. They are not satisfied to restrict themselves to tales of self-evident internalist logic nor content to use only such legal materials as statutes, cases, parliamentary proceedings, and jurists' published works. Wherever useful and feasible they exploit other primary sources, including manuscripts preserved in various archives. These sources may bear directly on past law – eye-witness accounts of trials, for instance. They may also be used to illuminate the context – male attitudes to sexual offences in the nineteenth century, anti-orientalism in British Columbia, and illustrations of the garrison mentality, to give three examples.

The essential nature of the new legal history requires a catholic – and always tentative – definition of its ambit. In general, where law and society have significantly interacted in the past, there should the legal historian be. Thus the history of crime, at least where important changes in substantive law or enforcement took place, can fall under this rubric. I too adopt a wide definition. Security statutes and their implementation, court cases involving those accused of seditious or treasonable crimes, and related opinions of law officers are of course given detailed treatment. But I also include as legal history popular resistance to law enforcement, revealing attempts to change the law, although unsuccessful, and constitutional law in practice.

This book is meant to be a narrative with analysis, presenting new evidence or evidence seen in a new light and expounding various theses. It is not primarily intended as an historiographical work, although comments about previous writing on early Lower Canadian history appear from time to time in the text and notes. The most important of these comments relate to the Laurentian thesis of Donald Creighton and Fernand Ouellet, far and away the most influential interpretation of the period outside francophone Quebec.

In his magisterial book *The Empire of the St Lawrence*, first published in 1937, Creighton attributed English attacks on the Canadien way of life and Sir James Craig's so-called Reign of Terror (1810–11) to the frustrations of the 'progressive' merchants, harbingers of a Confederation based on 'natural' east-west trade routes, who in the early nineteenth century were engaged in exploiting the commercial empire of the St Lawrence, including the Great Lakes area, Ohio country, and the Saskatchewan and Fraser river systems.[2] Creighton suggests that English attitudes were significantly conditioned by structural changes in the economy during the first decade or so of the new century. Earlier, when the fur trade had provided the main source of mercantile income, the two nationalities had lived in reasonable harmony, both being vitally interested in the trade. With the growing importance of profits derived from grain and especially timber exports – which could be maximized by encouraging immigration, increasing agricultural production, establishing a chartered bank, and facilitating the transfer and improvement of land – the seigneurial system, civil law, clerically controlled education, traditional backward-looking farming methods, and the anti-commercial stance of the *parti canadien* began to appear as intolerable brakes on economic development. The merchants were driven to justifiable and outspoken fury.

Creighton dates the commencement of overt political antagonism from the 1805 Gaols Act crisis when the *parti canadien* successfully voted down the merchants' amendment to tax lands and imposed additional import duties to finance prison building. From that year down to the rebellions of 1837–8, he interprets the political history of Lower Canada mainly as a contest between 'commerce' and 'agriculture' represented by a *parti canadien* desirous of preserving a seventeenth-century rural arcadia on the banks of the colony's magnificent but under-exploited highway of trade. Of importance here is his assertion that Sir James Craig's behaviour, particularly in attempting to crush the *parti canadien*, was that of an ideological ally seeking to advance the merchants' political aims. Creighton also concluded that the main components of the Canadien way of life were not seriously called into question by the English. Provided the merchants could have realized their economic reforms – for example, changes to the land laws – there would have been little further demand for anglification.

Creighton's interpretation was elaborated by Fernand Ouellet. Ouellet accepted explicitly or by distinct implication most of Creighton's major points, although many are presented with skilful nuance – for example, giving due weight to Pierre Bédard's constitutional ideas, the psychological malaise of the *parti canadien*, and Craig's authoritarian character. Ouellet interprets Lower Canadian politics during the French Revolutionary War (1793–1802) as reflecting a Canadian version of an 'age of good feelings.' Economic prosperity during the apogee of the fur trade and revulsion towards France 'favoured social peace and encouraged ideological accord' among all segments of the Canadien and English élites. More than this, even the 'peasants ... who had not forgotten their former motherland shared in the glorification of Imperial solidarity.' The general tone was one of calm and harmony. Unfortunately the 'opening of the nineteenth century would almost completely overthrow this fine edifice.'[3]

The Laurentian thesis is a major tool with which to interpret Lower Canadian political history from 1805 and particularly in the 1820s and 1830s. But as applied to the period 1793 to 1811, it should not be given greater importance than the security danger as perceived by the English élite – their garrison mentality. The latter contributed mightily to embitter and ethnicize politics almost beyond repair, well before the Gaols Act, during the revolutionary war of the 1790s, which was anything but a period of harmony. Nor was Craig the political arm of the merchants. His highest priority was to ensure the colony's security and in so attempting, he several times acted out the garrison mentality. Indeed, he can be portrayed as the leader of the garrison. Finally, the anglicization desired by the English élite was virtually total (with some qualification in the case of religion). Safety was in issue, not merely economic progress. These and other criticisms of the Laurentian thesis appear in the text.

A radically different, sophisticated, neo-nationalist interpretation of the period is offered by Jean-Pierre Wallot, whose interest is primarily to explain the crises under Governor Craig in the years 1808–11.[4] Wallot argued that the Craig crises were virtually inevitable given the near-impossibility of two distinct nations sharing the same political territory in peace, nations which differed in so many areas: language, religion, laws, land tenure, ethnic feeling, participation in high commerce, and so on. He takes strong issue with Creighton and Ouellet on timing, utterly rejecting 1805 as a critical date and arguing that there were serious ethnic tensions dating back almost to the Conquest, providing concrete documentation, however, only for the period 1799–1804.[5] Wallot presents a great deal of persuasive evidence and his essays are, as always, rich in insight. I believe, however, that serious ethnic disharmony began to surface only in late 1792–3, at the very time the garrison mentality was emerging. It must be conceded that differences between the nationalities made serious political conflict along ethnic lines probable at some time. But was such permanent conflict inevitable? Did it not rather require some profound historical experience to bring it about? I contend that the reactions of the English élite to the perceived security problem provided that experience. I suggest that all three interpretations are necessary to understand the period and leave to readers and future scholars questions of precise weighting.

There is no need to outline the writing on Lower Canadian legal history in the early years. There is as yet no significant debate on any of it and it is only very recently that first-class scholarship has become available with Evelyn Kolish's studies of the civil law and Jean-Marie Fecteau's work on criminal and administrative law. As for the law relating to internal security, the field has hardly been touched upon. I hope this book helps fill the gap and in doing so illuminates from yet another angle the depth of Canadians' penchant to support authority, with little heed to the rule of law.

1

Justice and Order: The Legal Setting

In the Quebec of the 1780s hiring a horse could be a risky undertaking. So a man named Mackenzie found. While dining en route he discovered that another traveller had appropriated his transport, later learning that the 'borrower' had driven the animal so hard that it died. The owner of the horse sued the innkeeper – who else? Out of curiosity Mackenzie, who was not a party to the suit, wandered into the Montreal courtroom, where seigneur René-Ovide Hertel de Rouville – a judge renowned for his authoritarian tendencies, not to mention his choleric and chronic intoxication on the Bench – presided. After the evidence was complete, de Rouville spotted the ill-fated Mackenzie, announced that the man who had hired the horse obviously bore legal liability for the loss, and had judgment immediately entered against him.[1]

This vignette captures the essence of civil justice in Quebec during the years 1784–91. Its grossly uncertain nature owed much to the absence of professional training of those appointed to the colony's two main civil courts, the Common Pleas for the Districts of Quebec and Montreal.[2] Evelyn Kolish has convincingly demonstrated, too, that the change in legal metropolis after the Conquest resulted in two legal systems vying for supremacy in the political arena and the courtroom, as well as judges of a British cultural background (in the case of the chief justice and of most judges appointed after 1791, training in the common law as well) attempting to administer the unfamiliar civilian system restored by the imperial Quebec Act of 1774.[3] And that 'system' encompassed a bewildering array of sources: Roman law; the *Coutume de Paris* and provisions from other *Coutumes*; legislation emanating from the French kings, the intendants, and the post 1774 council; judicial decisions in France and New France; and learned commentaries on the *Coutumes*. Other causes of uncertainty were the usual class frictions between gentry and bourgeoisie, and the thorough politicization of the judiciary.

The so-called French party dominated the Common Pleas Courts up to 1792 and the appointed Legislative Council. This political grouping, consisting mainly of Canadien seigneurs and certain highly placed English government officials with pretensions to aristocratic status, stood for authoritarian government, that is 'le système des généraux' implemented by Governors Sir Guy Carleton (1775–8) and Sir Frederick Haldimand (1778–84) during the American Revolutionary War. The system of the generals included hostility to the very notion of habeas corpus and to political dissent; secrecy in government, including the legislature; and determined opposition to an elected assembly which was being pressed for in these years by reformers. The French party also looked upon the Quebec Act as a 'sacred Charter' granting Canadiens cultural autonomy and as a brilliant political stroke guaranteeing the security of the colony, as had been proved early in the war. The act had to be protected in the courts and the legislature from any significant change, particularly in relation to feudal land tenure and the traditional civil laws.

Despite its name, the French party was led, in Council and on the Bench, by a Scot, Dr Adam Mabane, a former army surgeon who had been a judge in Quebec City since 1764. He was Carleton's most trusted councillor in the 1770s and Haldimand's virtual 'prime minister.' Not surprisingly, this protector of Canadian feudalism pursued an aristocratic lifestyle, entertaining 'quality' at his landed estate of Woodfield in Sillery and, as Mrs John Graves Simcoe of Upper Canada remarked, living 'what is called most hospitably, far beyond his fortune.'[4] Mabane exercised power behind the scenes, in Council and from the Bench, where he gave dozens of conservative decisions which he used from time to time to attack legal and political reformers. The Montreal Bench included two French party activists: John Fraser, Mabane's lieutenant on the Council, and de Rouville, a leader in the political campaign against the introduction of an elected assembly and English commercial law. On the Quebec court sat merchant-councillor Thomas Dunn, a party supporter except on certain matters to do with commercial law.

In 1786 Mabane's former patron, Sir Guy Carleton, now Lord Dorchester, returned as governor. No longer certain the Quebec Act represented eternal verity, he tended to take a passive role in politics and on the colony's legal and constitutional future. Despite losing influence at the Chateau, the French party continued, with some effect, to fight legal reform of any kind, especially those initiatives pressed by the new chief justice, Loyalist William Smith (1786–93), who had held the same position in the old colony of New York. With a view to attracting American immigration, Smith attempted among other things to abolish seigneurial land tenure, introduce English law for English litigants, and establish a non-sectarian university. Until the end of 1791 the French party and Smith's supporters on the Council (such as the deputy postmaster general, Hugh Finlay) were at constant loggerheads in that body, whether sitting in its legislative capacity, or as the colony's Court of Appeals.[5] The latter, dominated by Smith's adherents, and the Courts of Common Pleas were virtually at war until Mabane's death in early 1792.

The English merchants (with varying degrees of support from their reformer allies among the Canadien middle class, depending on the issue) fought in Council, in the newspapers, in petitions to the king and by lobbying Parliament to eradicate the anti-commercial features of the traditional law as embodied in the main source, the *Coutume de Paris*. They were irked by the restrictions on making oral proof of debt, the absence of what they considered adequate bankruptcy provisions, short prescriptions in commercial matters (usually six months or a year), the rules of estate administration which allegedly favoured heirs over business partners and creditors. Most vitriol was directed against secret hypothecs (akin to mortgages) which arose automatically from notarial deeds specifying debt (for example, a marriage contract promising a monetary payment after death) and could not be registered as there were no land registry offices, despite the merchants' continual campaign for them. In all this there was some justification, but also some prejudice and definite insensitivity to the high value Canadiens tended to place on protecting the vulnerable, whether debtors or family members. Prejudice also helps explain the merchants' insistence that the French *Code Marchand* of 1673 was not in force, since it had not been registered by the Sovereign Council of New France – a dubious legal position, but one more often than not adopted by the courts and lawyers in the colony and much later sanctioned by the Judicial Committee of the Privy Council.[6] The *Code Marchand* had greatly facilitated business practice, for example by enacting tough pro-creditor bankruptcy regulations and enunciating reasonably clear rules with regard to commercial paper. The merchants, perhaps influenced by Lord Mansfield's judgments, believed the code was out of date and in any case acceptance would undermine their prime political goal of having Parliament introduce the familiar commercial laws of England *in toto*.

A few concessions had been wrung from the Council. In 1777 an ordinance enacted that the English law of evidence would govern in commercial matters and introduced imprisonment for debt. A law of 1785 provided for optional jury trials in cases of delict (akin to tort) and contracts 'of a Mercantile Nature only, between Merchant and Merchant.'[7] These changes hardly satisfied the merchants. Jury trials were not available, even in commercial matters, where one of the parties was not a merchant. French party judges severely restricted the scope of the evidence rule and, unlike England, imprisonment was not generally available, but depended on the plaintiff swearing an affidavit that his or her debtor was about to abscond.[8]

The English merchants and their Canadien allies were incensed by the uncertainty of the laws governing business transactions and the grossly unprofessional, partisan conduct of the judges. Both were revealed in great detail during the inquiry into the administration of justice conducted by Chief Justice Smith in 1787, assisted by a bellicose Attorney General James Monk acting as the merchants' counsel. London did nothing with the thirteen thick volumes of damning evidence, except to fire Monk in 1789 (he returned to office in 1792). These volumes and dozens of letters to the newspapers in this period provide the basis for judging the merchants' complaints about the Common Pleas.

Instances of judicial misconduct were legion. Until 1787, when compelled to do so by ordinance, the judges of Common Pleas seldom gave reasons for their decisions. Delays were inordinate, parties arbitrarily denied hearings, French party lawyers favoured *ex parte*. The judges frequently exhibited personal, political, and class (pro-gentry) bias. A telling incident involved Judge Fraser, who refused to accept merchant James McGill's offer of an account book as proof that he owed no money to retired Colonel John Campbell. In Hilda Neatby's words, Fraser, 'taking from his pocket a letter from the plaintiff, a personal friend, assured the court that Colonel Campbell was incapable of a dishonourable action.'[9]

Inconsistency in decision-making was almost a daily experience in litigation. The courts regularly contradicted each other or themselves on procedure, bills of exchange, evidence, seizures before judgment, insolvency, and much more. The judges in any given case might accept arguments based on the *Coutume* (even where not appropriate), Roman law, English law or, above all, personal notions of equity. Incoherence often characterized the Quebec court, but the situation was utterly chaotic in the District of Montreal. Judge Fraser angered the merchants by insisting that virtually all cases, even those involving proof of business transactions, were to be decided by the *Coutume*. Judge Edward Southouse proclaimed in court that 'he had no occasion for a knowledge of French laws ... as his conscience ... guided his judgments.' In one case Southouse, unable to understand the arguments, had the defendant's lawyer draw up his written decision![10] Mr. Justice de Rouville's legal learning has been sufficiently illustrated.

The Court of Appeals afforded no relief. Until Smith took control in late 1786, it applied Canadien or English law to similar cases, depending on whether the Bench was controlled by the French party (which was usual) or by reformers on the Council. Smith only exacerbated matters when in his first major judgment, the case of *Gray* v. *Grant* (1786), he distorted the Quebec Act to mean that in any civil litigation between old subjects (that is, the English) English law was to prevail. This decision assumed that when the act referred to '*all* Matters of Controversy' or '*all* Causes' it didn't really mean all and that without express words Parliament had resurrected the complex pre and early medieval system called 'personality of laws' (as opposed to territoriality). The Courts of Common Pleas, led by Dr Mabane, adamantly refused to follow *Gray* v. *Grant*, and as a result reversals on appeal became commonplace. Ironically, these included several instances where the verdicts of English juries, applying the *Coutume* in a manner satisfactory to the merchants, were overturned.

Litigating was akin to Russian roulette. Loyalist lawyer William Dummer Powell, who had a large and long-standing mercantile practice in Montreal, always confessed to clients he had no idea what legal rule, if any, the judges would pull out of a hat. Quebec City attorney Thomas Walker had 'frequently seen the event or success of a suit decided among the advocates by the turning up of a piece of money, or the drawing of straws.' By 1789 it had become even more incontrovertible to the English merchants and their Canadien allies that constitutional reform – with particular emphasis on the courts and the judiciary, as well as an elected assembly – was urgent and required imperial legislation.

The Seigneurial System

The Quebec Act directed that in matters of controversy relating to property and civil rights recourse was to be had to Canadien law. One of the most important areas of Canadien law related to the system of land tenure known as the seigneurial system. Important in the daily lives of the vast majority of the population, it is also crucial to the themes pursued in this book. The operation of the regime was not only a major grievance for the bulk of the population and a theme of French revolutionary propaganda during the war, but a major stimulus to the garrison mentality of the English élite.

Like the *Coutume de Paris* in general, seigneurial law reflected humane values appropriate to a pre-industrial society imbued with feudal concepts, Christian notions of equity, and paternalistic ideals that vulnerable members of society deserved legal protection against the avaricious. Socio-political stability, and personal honour, rested partly but importantly in preserving the link of a family to its traditional lands, an absolutely central concern of pre-revolutionary French law.[11] Seigneurial law was manifestly anti-commercial, particularly with regard to land speculation and the extension of credit. Sales of farms or *rotures* outside the line of succession, for example, were subject to mutation fines known as the *lods et ventes*. This charge, payable by the purchaser to the seigneur, amounted to one-twelfth of the sale price. In addition, a member of the vendor's family, by means of the *retrait lignager*, could repossess, within a year and a day of the sale, by tendering the purchasing price and the buyer's basic costs. Widows and their children were favoured by the customary dower, which prevailed in the absence of contrary provisions in a marriage contract. Dower consisted of the widow's life interest in (and the children's ultimate ownership of) half her husband's real estate, whether seigneurial or *roture*. These rights had preference over ordinary creditors' claims and could not be renounced by the wife after marriage (for example, in a contract of loan) – a rule which restricted the extension of credit by merchants to married men. Under Canadien or French law at this time, married women's property interests were far better protected against their husbands than in England, where an atrophied form of dower prevailed and the husband became the virtual owner of his wife's property. In Quebec the standard marital arrangement (unless varied by marriage contract) was community of property. Although administered by the husband, the community assets (chattels and most real estate acquired after marriage) were owned in common.

Aside from the *lods et ventes*, fees for pasture, exploitation of his private or domain farm, and the annual *rente* (examined in detail later), the seigneur's economic rights related to his *banalités* or monopolies and the private corvée. No one but the seigneur could erect a grist mill on the seigneury and the *censitaires* (farmers) were bound by law to have the grain required for domestic consumption ground at the banal mill, paying one-fourteenth of the grain processed. Another monopoly was the exclusive right to fish, which was included in many title deeds granted by the crown and often delegated to the *censitaires*, provided they remitted a certain portion of the catch – usually between one-twentieth and one-tenth. Private corvées of one or two days labour on the domain or otherwise for the seigneur began to appear as additions to rent in some concession deeds early in the eighteenth century. After complaints by a number of habitants, the intendant in 1716 declared such clauses illegal. While this ruling was not universally obeyed (for instance, in the seigneury of Beauharnois from 1733 to 1759), Cole Harris estimates that stipulated private corvées were a minority before the Conquest.[12]

The Canadien seigneurs did not own the unconceded lands to rent or sell as they saw fit. Louis XIV's Edicts of Marly (1711), applicable to New France alone, made the seigneurs holders of those lands in trust for potential settlers.[13] The landlord was obliged not only to rent them to suitable applicants, but to do so at the rent and on the conditions prevailing in the seigneury. Thus in New France (but not in France) a form of rent control applied to *roture* land. Unfortunately for the habitant, such control survived the Conquest mainly in theory. This subject, of crucial importance to the security issue in the 1790s, requires special treatment.

Illegal Exactions

Annual rents in New France for a ninety-*arpent roture* varied from a low near three livres (three English shillings) to a high of about nine. To cite but one example, a 1757 deed of concession in the seigneury of Beauharnois set the rent for such a farm at one and a half *minots* (French bushels) of wheat (a *minot* being then worth about two and a half livres) and four and a half livres.[14] Rents by themselves formed a modest tribute, normally amounting to less than 10 per cent of a farmer's annual wheat production.[15]

From time to time the intendants ordered the seigneurs not to charge new *censitaires* more than the rate customary on the seigneury. While abuses were not unknown, disputes over rents or the interpretation of concession deeds were few. Where they occurred, the farmer had a free and speedy recourse by appealing to the intendant. Although the law relating to rent control in the French regime is subtle to the point of obscurity, the leading jurists in the colony of the 1790s – including the law officers and Chief Justice William Osgoode – thought it beyond question that raising rents payable by new grantees or old ones without deeds (and of course old ones with deeds) had been and still was illegal under the Edicts of Marly.[16]

This was not the view of the seigneurs generally, particularly the English seigneurs. In many cases the latter had purchased their properties in the 1760s or early 1770s when the Royal Proclamation of 1763 was in effect. That document could be interpreted as introducing English land law and hence freeing rents except where existing farmers had deeds of concession.[17] According to Attorney General James Monk, these early purchasers asserted 'a legal right to concede how and on what Terms they thought proper.' This attitude continued down to the 1790s, despite the passage of the Quebec Act.

The intendant's office had not been re-established after the Conquest and his powers to police the land system had passed (if at all) to the courts where litigation was expensive. Most habitants were naturally loath to risk their patrimony by applying to such a forum, especially since most of the judges seemed likely to favour the seigneurs. As a result, by the 1790s the rents in a majority of seigneuries had doubled or even tripled from those prevailing at the end of the French regime. This was the considered judgment of Monk in 1794 and numerous sources corroborate it. There is also evidence that in the 1790s the seigneur's miller often contrived to take one-tenth rather than one-fourteenth of the grain ground for the farmers.[18]

The main offenders were the English seigneurs, who looked upon their land not only as a source of social status, but as private investment property. While a small minority adhered to the older notion of lands held in trust for the farming community,[19] most Canadien seigneurs, including clerical ones such as the Quebec Seminary on Ile Jésus and the Sulpicians in Montreal, indulged in significant rent-raising. Some, such as Antoine Juchereau Duchesnay of Beauport, rivalled any of the English landlords with their exactions.

Although largely unpoliced, the seigneurial regime probably protected the farmers' monetary interests better than a system of outright ownership would have done, or so prominent members of the Canadien élite believed in 1791. There was probably a serious point to this claim. The sale of unconceded land (which would have been a burden to cash-poor habitants) was illegal and to make new or old grantees pay in rent or other exactions what the market might truly bear was to risk a test case, rent strikes, physical retaliation, and/or embarrassing petitions to the governing authorities.

In a worst-case scenario, illegal rents and milling charges would have deprived the typical, middle-income farmer of approximately six *minots* of wheat (out of about two hundred produced) in a normal crop year. This might not seem very much, but it was the yearly bread ration for a small child, or a day-labourer's winter wages for three weeks. It should be remembered, too, that rents, tithes, and milling fees were not the only forms of tribute which the farmers paid. There were also annual pew rentals, payments from time to time of *lods et ventes*, and recurrent assessments for the building or repair of the parish churches. Indeed, Alan Greer estimated that feudal and clerical dues in 1765 'deprived the Lower Richelieu peasantry of a substantial portion – probably more than half – of its agricultural surpluses.'[20] Rent and milling charges were not the only causes of conflict or grumbling. Others included evictions for non-cultivation, the collection of the *lods et ventes* on alienations other than by sale,[21] tree-cutting for firewood, and the ownership of streams. Several post-Conquest deeds of concession imposed new conditions such as a day's corvée or money payment equivalent (presumably at the seigneur's option), reservation of all wood (even for commercial manufacturing) or all mill sites, establishment of a sawmill monopoly, extension of the gristmill monopoly to all grain with provision for heavy fines and/or forfeiture, and so on.

In most cases, rising wheat prices because of British demand during the war and increased cultivation after 1763 offset the increasing seigneurial exactions. Indeed, some habitants during the 1790s developed a taste for European manufactured goods, particularly clothing.[22] This rising income suggests that in most years during the 1790s, the farmers' grievances against the seigneurs were more matters of annoyance and fear for the future direction of exactions than explosive anger or a sense of excessive deprivation. Resentment could easily come to the fore, however, during a poor crop year like that of 1795–6 when deficits were the norm, every *minot* exacted increased debt, and adverse conditions increased the need for charity and the possibility of malnutrition.

While the operation of the seigneurial system provoked complaint throughout the colony, its functioning in two areas near Montreal illustrates the nature of the problem, particularly where the landlords were English and hence less respectful of custom than some Canadien counterparts. For years James Cuthbert Sr, seigneur of Berthier, carried on a running dispute with his tenants, who insisted on following the custom of cutting trees on one of the seigneury's islands. In July and August

1793 he announced via the *Montreal Gazette* that he would now prosecute these refractory 'Vassals' under a statute of George I. Convicted offenders could expect three months imprisonment and a monthly whipping in public. In January 1794 about a hundred *censitaires* of Berthier responded by complaining to Dorchester about the 'odious despotism' Cuthbert had exercised for twenty years. The immediate issue was Cuthbert's refusal to allow the habitants to repair a bridge over what he claimed was his private river. Since they were too poor to proceed through the courts, they petitioned the governor for justice.[23]

A month later the government considered a petition signed by sixty-four *censitaires* of the Barony of Longueuil.[24] Originally drafted in March 1793 and addressed to the House of Assembly, it complained of the oppression of David Alexander Grant, a seigneur so unpopular he had been defeated by the votes of his *censitaires* (Kent) in the general election of 1792. The gravamen of the charges against Grant indicates that not only new grantees but even established settlers with concession deeds had something to complain about:

That in defiance of the ordinances of the old Kings of France, he has arbitrarily raised the rents for the lands he has conceded since he has been seigneur ... [and that] without regard to the ancient title deeds, which several of petitioners possess, he has threatened and [still] threatens them daily with legal suits and uses all kinds of vexatious means to force them to change their modest rents to those more burdensome [trans.].

Solicitor General Jonathan Sewell reported that in his judgment the *censitaires* had an unimpeachable case by virtue of the Edicts of Marly which clearly showed the 'Intention of the Legislator of the day [1711] to compel the seigneurs to grant their unconceded land to the Inhabitants ... at the then customary rent.'[25] And of course the rent specified in deeds could 'never be increased by the Seigneur under any pretence whatsoever.' To Sewell the real problem lay in the cost of litigation, particularly because, in seigneurial disputes, future rights were always in issue. Hence, these cases, however small the actual amount in question, could invariably be appealed to the Plantations Committee of the Privy Council in London, but 'the enormous Expence attending an Appeal to His Majesty in Council ... deprives them of the possibility of obtaining Justice compels them to abandon their cause and throw themselves upon the mercy of their Antagonist who ... grants a new deed of Concession upon his own terms.'

In a lengthy report to Secretary of State Henry Dundas, Monk agreed with Sewell that increases in rents were illegal and fingered the high cost of litigation as the root of the problem. The complaining 'peasants' had often been 'told "the Courts were open. Justice was free." But the French King's protection was *not* continued ... The Roturier found a contest with his seignior, an enterprize of Ruin, and submitted to the hand of power.' Monk went on to note that there had been a few cases brought by the habitants, but the courts had expressed doubt whether they possessed the intendant's power to compel a seigneur to grant lands at the customary rent. The farmers perceived this as grossly unfair, since the courts were used by the seigneurs – Cuthbert was one – to enforce those portions of the edicts dealing with forfeiture for insufficient cultivation. Indeed, evictions seem to have been commonplace at this time, reflecting in part the habitants' tendency to accumulate land in advance for eventual cultivation by their sons.[26]

CHURCH AND STATE

The Quebec Act of 1774 granted the Canadiens 'free Exercise of the Religion of the Church of *Rome*' but made the grant 'subject to the King's Supremacy.' The doctrine of the royal supremacy over all ecclesiastical practices in the realm and the dominions dated back to the Tudors and in particular to Elizabeth I's Act of Supremacy of 1559. Had it been fully implemented in Quebec/Lower Canada, the colonial government would have controlled the seminaries; priests would have been able to marry; the bishop would have been chosen exclusively by the crown and confined to using the title 'Superintendent of the Romish Church'; he would have been prohibited from communicating with Rome and unable to create parishes; the governor would have appointed priests to their parishes or other clerical offices; and much more.[27] But this was not to be.

True to his policies of ruling through the clergy/seigneurs and conciliation, Governor Carleton informed Bishop Jean-Olivier Briand in early 1775 that reference to the Supremacy had been included only as a public relations gesture to ensure passage of the Quebec Act and would mean very little in practice.[28] Thus began a fundamental political bargain between the state and the Roman Catholic Church. If the latter used all its efforts to keep the people loyal, the crown would, *de facto*, allow the bishop autonomy in running ecclesiastical affairs. The 'contract' was reiterated by Carleton's successor, Sir Frederick Haldimand, in 1780.[29] With the exception of the years 1800 to 1811 (and then only in Quebec

City, not London) the crown adhered to its terms ever afterward. The
church fulfilled its duties with a fidelity born of its vulnerability and
the profound belief that God allocated territory among monarchs. Sove-
reigns were His chosen lieutenants on earth and Roman Catholics were
religiously bound to support the established political power. Although
unsuccessful more often than not, the Roman Catholic clergy of Que-
bec/Lower Canada expended great energy propagating these notions
during the American Revolutionary War, the French Revolutionary War,
the war against Napoleon, the War of 1812, and the rebellion period of
1837–8.

The hands-off policy of the state had exceptions. Until the Revolution,
recruitment of European priests, especially French ones, was heavily
restricted, for instance. More significant was the involvement of the
crown in the choice of a bishop's successor. This official, known as the
co-adjutor bishop, automatically succeeded his superior on the latter's
death or retirement. Upon such a succession, the question immediately
arose as to the choice of his own second-in-command. At that point (or
when a co-adjutor died) until the 1830s, the state exercised its control by
requiring the governor either to make an appointment or assent to it.
Such control ensured that the heads of the Quebec diocese and their co-
adjutors were men of unstinting and active loyalty.

But far more revealing of what Marcel Trudel has called the church's
servitude at this time – which he judged more thoroughgoing than in
New France – concerns the use made of the parish priests as representatives of the provincial government. On innumerable occasions during the
period under study the bishops hastened to comply with the governors'
desires for political or administrative action in the parishes. Letters were
sent out to the curés, for example, instructing them to inculcate loyalty
by various means; to take the censuses of population and grains; to help
organize the militia; to post laws; and to publicly read statutes, orders,
or proclamations.[30] This visible link to a government, Protestant and
British, worked to undermine the moral authority of the Roman Catholic
clergy, particularly among Canadien working people. The priests' manifestly fragile influence in matters outside spiritual matters and personal
morality would be revealed clearly and be of momentous importance
during the war against revolutionary France.

THE FRAMEWORK OF THE CRIMINAL LAWS

The criminal laws of England, administered by the Quebec courts from the beginning of civil government in August 1764, were continued in force by the Quebec Act, a decision grandiloquently justified by reference to their great 'Certainty and Lenity' and the satisfaction sensibly felt over nine years by Britain's new subjects. Modern scholarship, using comparisons with old and New France, has shown the criminal laws of England as hardly lenient, the murderous capital code and the absence of a state-financed investigation of the facts being particularly noted. Nor were these rules any more established than other areas of the notoriously uncertain common law. Nor again had many of their elements (private initiation of prosecution, jury trials, and so on) recommended themselves to the honour-conscious Canadien seigneurs, as Douglas Hay convincingly demonstrated.[31] Genuine acceptance by educated Canadiens of the English criminal law as an improvement dates only from the mid-1780s.

The Criminal Law Statutes

The criminal laws were amendable in the colony but local legislation of any substance was very rare. The main concern was to add penal clauses (fines and/or short terms of imprisonment) to statutes of administrative regulation, applying to such things as the militia, road maintenance, stray cattle, and unqualified medical practitioners. The criminal laws, then, essentially consisted of judicial decisions in the mother country, juristic writing by authorities such as Blackstone, and an untidy mass of parliamentary statutes dating back to the Middle Ages. Certain pre-1774 criminal law statutes enacted by Parliament, so precisely tailored to conditions in England as not to be readily transportable across the sea, were not in force. A rare example was Charles II's Habeas Corpus Act of 1679, discussed below.[32]

It did not matter in the slightest that the vast majority of the pre-Quebec Act criminal law statutes had been framed without the colonies in mind; by virtue of the Quebec Act they were 'received' statutes enforceable by the colonial courts. Thus, despite references in it to the 'realm,' Edward III's Statute of Treasons, 1351/52, was part of the criminal law of Quebec/Lower Canada. This act, central to many themes pursued here, limited high treason to seven cases proved by 'open deed,' of which the three most important were plotting the king's death, rebelling in arms, and adhering to the king's enemies during a state of war. Treason occurred, in the words of the statute, '... when a man doth compasse or imagine the death of our lord the king, of my lady his queene, or of their eldest sonne and heire ... or if a man doe levie warre against our lord the king in his realme, or be adherent to the kings enemies in his realme, giving to them aid and comfort in the realme or elsewhere.'[33]

Parliamentary enactments on the criminal law passed after the Quebec Act did not apply to the colony unless it was referred to or the statute was made applicable to all colonies or to a group of which Quebec/ Lower Canada was one. There does not seem to have been any notion of 'necessary intendment' at that time, which explains the status of the Treason Act of 1795.[34] That statute contemplated persons (including those resident in the colonies) committing the widely phrased treasons thereby enacted 'within the realm or without.' It also described one of the treasons as conspiring to deprive the king of any 'of his Majesty's dominions or countries.' The act, however, neither contained an application clause referring to the colonies, nor directed the colonial courts to enforce its provisions. Whatever might be the modern view as to the statute's geographic reach, Canadian judges were clearly of the opinion it formed no part of the law of either of the Canadas.[35] This is an important point to bear in mind when assessing the 'royalist' interpretations of the law of treason handed down by the judges of Lower Canada: they had no warrant to base them on the wide-ranging provisions of the 1795 act.

The Criminal Courts

Throughout this period, unpaid justices of the peace staffed the lower criminal courts. By contrast to England, where these prestigious offices were reserved to the gentry and aristocracy, the Magistrates' Bench in Quebec/Lower Canada contained not only seigneurs of both language groups, but of necessity the more successful of the middling ranks of society (especially merchants, but also professionals to a limited degree), Canadien as well as English. The justices (appointed by district) sat in quarter sessions every three months in Quebec, Montreal, and Trois-Rivières, and two of their number held petty sessions weekly in those centres. The latter dealt summarily with the more trivial offences such as public drunkenness and enforced the police regulations enacted by the justices (e.g., bread pricing). The quarter sessions, complete with grand and trial juries, handled the more serious offences under local statutes (e.g., the Militia Acts) and the less heinous misdemeanours, particularly common assaults and petty larcenies. Punishments took the form of one or more of fines (usually under one pound), short jail terms, burning in the hand, the pillory, and the lash.

The supreme court of criminal justice was the King's Bench, which had

jurisdiction over all offences. In practice it dealt almost solely with treasons, felonies (capital crimes), and the more serious non-capital misdemeanours such as manslaughter, perjury, receiving stolen goods, aggravated assaults, riots, and seditious offences. Prior to 1795 the King's
Bench was a single court for the whole colony, exclusively concerned
with criminal matters and held before the chief justice of the province or
commissioners appointed for executing his office. This arrangement was
altered by Attorney General Monk's Judicature Act of 1794 which replaced the Courts of Common Pleas by Courts of King's Bench with both
civil and criminal jurisdiction. The two new courts were presided over
by the chief justice of Lower Canada (Quebec District) and a chief justice
of Montreal. Three puisne judges assisted each chief justice. The courts
held two criminal sessions (or terms or assizes) a year: in early March
and September for Montreal; in the last ten days of those months for
Quebec, with the governor having express statutory authorization to issue
special commissions of oyer and terminer and general gaol delivery for
hearing criminal cases at any time out of term. The act did not come into
force until 1795.[36]

Procedure

The system of criminal procedure and evidence was essentially that of
England: indictments by a grand jury (by a vote of twelve out of twenty-
three), structure, challenges to and functioning of the trial jury, the reasonable doubt test, exclusion of hearsay, and so on. Juries could and
sometimes did recommend mercy, which was almost always taken into
account by the governor. As in the mother country, there was no right to
counsel in felony cases. Defence lawyers were allowed *ex gratia* to examine and cross-examine witnesses, argue points of law, and object to the
admissibility of evidence. But they could not address the jury. So we
have what today would be the extraordinary example of an illiterate man
tried in Quebec for murder in 1801 offering what the newspaper account
reported as a one-sentence summary in defence of his life.[37] In the cases
we are concerned with in this book, however, persons charged with
misdemeanours, including the seditious offences and, by virtue of the
Treason Act of 1695,[38] accused traitors, could make full defence through
counsel. Differences from the English procedural model, of course,
existed. Jurors could be, and often were, drawn from the lower levels of
society.[39] Collegiality on the Bench (that is, two or three judges sitting)
seems to have been more common than in the Old Bailey and the ac-

cused was entitled to have at least six of the twelve trial jurors competent in his or her language if English or French.[40] More important, in Quebec/Lower Canada the law officers invariably prosecuted before the two juries, while in England full private prosecution from complaint before a magistrate to judgment was the norm, the principal exceptions being treason trials and selected sedition cases.[41]

Capital Punishment

Capital punishment was at the theoretical centre of the criminal law system. Death by hanging was the penalty for over two hundred offences in the England of the late eighteenth century, ranging in seriousness from treason and murder through rape, highway robbery, cattle stealing, burglary, and buggery to shoplifting (five shillings or more), larceny in a dwelling house (forty shillings or more) and pickpocketing. Lower Canadian juries, following the lead of those in the mother country, were very reluctant to convict for capital property offences.[42] Acquittals were frequent, as were partial convictions which reduced the offence to the non-capital category. Juries often artificially found the value of the goods stolen from dwelling houses to amount to thirty-nine shillings or less, that the pickpocketing had not been done 'privily' (that is without the immediate knowledge of the victim), and so on. Juries in other words exercised considerably autonomy of judgment and could by no means be relied upon to see a case through the eyes of the prosecuting law officers or the Bench.

Even if convicted of a capital offence the prisoner was unlikely to hang. As in England, the idea of the governing élite was to inculcate terror by a limited number of executions and to reap the political-social benefits of gratitude and deference by extending mercy through the royal prerogative. Douglas Hay estimates that during the first decade of civil government in Quebec the actual rate of execution was approximately one per year per 100,000 population, almost identical to that on the western circuit in England in the latter half of the eighteenth century. My own research suggests this rate was not exceeded in the 1790s, while in 1810 British traveller John Lambert reported 'a singular proverbial saying among the people, that "it requires great interest for a man to be hung in Canada"; so few in that country ever meet with such an ignominious fate.'[43]

Judicial and Law Officers' Behaviour

One point which will become clear later is the contrast between the behaviour of the provincial law officers and judges in dealing with persons accused of ordinary crimes and their treatment of alleged political offenders. In the case of the latter, the prisoners' rights were often ignored, the law stretched to obtain the result desired by the crown, and leniency extended or a highly punitive attitude enforced, whichever was politic. In ordinary cases – our concern here – judges articulated the reasonable doubt test; law officers accepted that penal laws had to be interpreted restrictively; and both must have been influential in maintaining a low ratio of executions to capital convictions. Without doubt, as in England, acquittals or convictions for reduced non-capital crimes owed something to the Bench turning a blind eye to the 'pious perjury' so often practised by juries in property cases.[44]

Specific examples strengthen these propositions. Chief Justice Smith, who found the capital code barbarous unless regularly relieved by the prerogative of mercy, intervened in 1792 to save the life of a Canadien convicted of incestuous rape. Although the jury had been in no doubt as to guilt and the conviction was popular, Smith had serious misgivings about the weight of evidence. In 1793 Osgoode privately expressed revulsion at having to perform the duty of sentencing prisoners to death. As attorney general, Jonathan Sewell ensured that a Montreal man convicted in 1803 of burglary with violence was spared, despite embarrassment to himself. He admitted he had been wrong in law to have argued at the trial in favour of admitting a certain piece of damning evidence, urging successfully that the prisoner be given the benefit of the doubt. Private letters to his wife and the *Mémoires* of a former articling student indicate that Sewell personally abhorred capital punishment, the incidence of which he attempted to reduce legislatively in the 1820s. On the Bench as chief justice, he often strove to protect the prisoner from the noose and was even thought by certain members of the bar to be too lenient on criminals.[45]

HABEAS CORPUS

A major focus of this book is the writ of habeas corpus ad subjiciendum, which allowed the legality of imprisonment to be tested in the courts. In the two decades separated by the Quebec Act, most government officials on both sides of the ocean agreed that the 1679 statute of Charles II, which enacted stiff procedural sanctions to make the common law right effective in criminal matters, was not in force in the colony.[46] This conclusion was based on the assumption that the Habeas Corpus Act was 'merely local, and confined to England.'[47] At the time of the Quebec Act, the ministry decided not to extend to the colony the advantages of Charles II's statute and government supporters easily defeated a motion in the Commons to introduce it.

A strong case can be made, as British Solicitor General Alexander Wedderburn believed in 1772 and the practice of the older colonies suggested, that the common law right to habeas corpus existed as part of the public law introduced by the Conquest or the Royal Proclamation of 1763 and, at least in criminal matters, had survived the passage of the Quebec Act.[48] During the American war, however, the common law right was largely irrelevant to state security cases since an act of Parliament, first passed in 1777 and annually continued to 1 January 1783, suspended bail and trial for any persons 'who are or shall be charged with or suspected of the crime of high treason, committed in any of the ... colonies' in America.[49] From 1779 on Governor Haldimand interned some twenty-five individuals suspected of collaboration with the American revolutionaries. Most internees indeed sympathized strongly with republican ideals, but concrete proof of treason was usually lacking and sometimes extremely flimsy. Among those imprisoned for lengthy terms without bail or trial were the radical Frenchman, Fleury Mesplet, a freethinking Montreal journalist who would later found the *Montreal Gazette*; Montreal merchant, polemicist, and constitutional reformer Pierre Du Calvet, a Huguenot native of France; and cooper-timber merchant Charles Hay, a resident of the capital.[50]

The internments were tested at least twice in the Quebec courts. In 1780 Charles Hay's wife Mary applied for a writ of habeas corpus. She had a strong case, for the internments had been effected through military warrants, while the act of 1777 required committal to be 'by any magistrate having competent authority.' Her application was nevertheless dismissed by the King's Bench sitting in commission for the absent Chief Justice Peter Livius and consisting of French party judges, Dr Mabane, Dunn, and Jenkin Williams. This unanimous decision received Haldimand's hearty approval as one which 'very much Strengthened the hands of Government.'[51] Two years later Pierre Du Calvet's application for the writ was dismissed by the same Bench, this time on the ground that, as Justice Williams explained orally, 'since the establishment of the French laws in the province all matters of property and civil rights [1774] ... the English laws concerning the writ of Habeas Corpus were not in force.'[52] The judges had thus shifted position, presumably to immunize military warrants from legal attack – a difficult task had they had to rely on the 1777 suspending act. The common law right to the writ, apparently, did not exist even in criminal matters. The governor's precise reaction is unknown, but he did appoint Williams solicitor general of Quebec at £200 per annum. After the war, Haldimand, under increasing pressure from London, finally accepted that a local habeas corpus ordinance should be passed – a directive which had been included in the royal instructions for nine years. Led by wealthy merchant William Grant, the legal reformers on the Legislative Council succeeded, over Mabane's strenuous opposition, in having the Council enact such a law.

The habeas corpus ordinance was essentially Charles II's act tailored to Quebec conditions.[53] By means of fines and forfeitures the ordinance attempted to prevent such abuses as refusal to issue the writ in vacation, delay by judges or jailers, secreting the prisoner in another jail, transporting him or her out of the jurisdiction, and immediate rearrest. The main purpose of these provisions was to ensure that a person imprisoned on a misdemeanour charge – including one for any of the seditious offences – who was improperly refused bail by the committing justice of the peace could speedily enforce the right to obtain bail pending trial. The prisoner or anyone acting on his or her behalf, by making a *prima facie* case by affidavit or otherwise, could get the issue into the Court of King's Bench, usually within a few days. The amount of bail and the number of sureties demanded were within the discretion of the court, but the English Bill of Rights of 1689 and the ordinance itself specified that the bail should not be excessive.[54] Persons accused of felony had no right to bail and in general were refused it by the committing magistrate. Accused traitors could not be bailed by the justices. Both accused felons and persons imprisoned on treason charges could apply to the Court of King's Bench (although not by the habeas corpus procedure) to be allowed pre-trial bail, but their chances of success were slight.

The second main purpose of the ordinance was to ensure that accused felons and traitors received a speedy trial.[55] In these cases the prisoner (or anyone on his or her behalf) could insist by petition or motion that he or she be indicted by the grand jury during the first criminal law session or assizes following committal, or failing that to be granted bail immediately. Unless the crown could show it had been impossible to produce the prosecution witnesses, the court was bound to grant bail. An accused thus refused bail was liable to have imprisonment continue until the subsequent session. If not indicted and put on trial at that time, he or she was to be immediately discharged.

Although not dealt with in the ordinance, the writ of habeas corpus, by virtue of the common law, could also be used to test the legality of imprisonment where no criminal charges had been laid. The writ had been employed successfully in eighteenth-century England, for example, to enable persons held in madhouses to obtain a medical review and to have the Court of King's Bench declare that English law did not recognize slavery.[56] Despite the Quebec Act, habeas corpus procedure was used in Lower Canada (1798–1800) to destroy slave-holding and to free persons arbitrarily detained by the military (1791).[57] Habeas Corpus had failed, in practice, as a weapon against imprisonment by Charles I for reasons of state, but the Petition of Right, 1628, as retroactively sanctified by the Glorious Revolution of 1688–9, made the writ available in such cases. Similarly, it would be available if a person were imprisoned merely on suspicion of high treason, for no stated cause, or for no crime known to the common law. In such cases, being criminal, the act of 1679 or the 1784 ordinance applied.

Despite being what William Blackstone called 'another Magna Carta,' the habeas corpus procedure was regularly suspended – not explicitly, but by denying bail and trial and justifying internment of persons detained on mere suspicion of treason. These suspensions, effected by temporary parliamentary statute, occurred on those occasions when the government strongly feared insurrection or invasion or both and were usually justified by the notion of giving up some liberty to save the constitution as a whole. There were about a dozen such cases from the Glorious Revolution to 1794. The ease with which governments obtained suspensions troubled the Quebec reformers. They strove to combat it, but failed, with serious consequences for the administration of justice during the war against revolutionary France. In Lower Canada the writ was suspended for political cases in every calendar year but two from 1793 to 1811.

JUDGES IN POLITICS, 1791–1811: A COMPARISON WITH THE ENGLISH BENCH

The Bench under Charles II and James II embodied, if in caricature, the judicial role which Sir Francis Bacon as James I's attorney general had so forcefully articulated. Judges, Bacon claimed, were 'lions under the throne, being circumspect that they do not check or oppose any points of sovereignty.'[58] It was important that the king and his judges consult often on matters of state so that judges could better perform their duty of supporting the government. Impartial analysis of the law came second to that duty. Bacon's great rival, Sir Edward Coke (successively chief justice of the Common Pleas and King's Bench) gave pride of place to impartial interpretation, even where it might damage the short-term political interests of the crown and his own career (as it did in 1616 when he was dismissed). It was Coke's view that triumphed in the revolutionary settlement of 1688–9. The idea of a Bench genuinely autonomous of the executive received the approval of Parliament (1701, 1760), George III, constitutional experts such as Blackstone and Jean-Louis De Lolme, popularizers like William Paley, and judges as various as advanced liberal Sir John Holt (1693) and the politically conservative Lord Mansfield (1784).[59] With some qualifications and exceptions, the Bench in England was at least as Cokean as Baconian during the reign of George III. Yet the Lower Canadian judges were thoroughly Baconian. Why?

The answer might lie in the simple fact that the Lower Canadian chief justices (appointed by London) and the puisne judges (appointed by the governor) held their offices at the crown's pleasure, rather than on good behaviour, as was the case of the common law judges of England from 1689. Although judges held office at pleasure, their tenure was not particularly insecure. Thus, when Chief Justice William Osgoode pressured the lieutenant-governor, Sir Robert Shore Milnes, in 1800 to remove Pierre-Amable De Bonne from the Bench because of his involvement in a scandalous double adultery and repeated absences from court sittings, De Bonne had no legal position from which to argue. But he was able to convince Milnes that his valuable services in the Assembly made it politic to overlook these failings.[60] Even where a governor was indifferent or hostile, though, the tenure of a judge was not entirely subject to political whim, since he was guaranteed a hearing in London. When, for example, Quebec Chief Justice Peter Livius was dismissed by Carleton in 1778 – officially for political rather than judicial failings – the Plantations Committee of the Privy Council restored him to office.[61] Moreover, it is very unlikely that the imperial authorities would have dismissed a colonial judge merely or primarily for decisions rendered from the Bench, however unpalatable they were politically. The principle of judicial independence, a cornerstone of the Glorious Revolutionary settlement, was becoming so thoroughly entrenched in British constitutional thinking, that any such blatant interference could be undertaken only at considerable risk. In the entire history of Quebec/Lower Canada, from the introduction of civil government to the Rebellions of 1837–8 no judge was dismissed for handing down an 'incorrect' decision.[62]

were candidates for the bench overlooked because of "incorrect" beliefs? This is the more important query.

While the Bench was likely influenced in security cases by considerations of tenure, salaries, pensions, promotion, and increased political consequence, this relationship to the executive does not offer a satisfactory answer for its Baconian cast of mind. Many of the judges were far from weak-willed men, easily intimidated. Osgoode, for example, fought with three successive governors over matters of policy and in one case threatened Lord Dorchester with repercussions from the Bench.[63] Although a schemer for influence and office, Monk had risked his career in 1787 and enjoyed a reputation for independence of mind. Seconded by his colleagues on the King's Bench, he rendered decisions between 1798 and 1800 which effectively abolished slavery in Lower Canada, despite the protests of slave-owners and with but marginal support from the text of law.[64]

An additional factor in the judicial mindset was the heavy involvement of the judges in partisan politics: supporting the governor in his relationships with the Legislative Assembly and the citizenry, and in the factional feuding which occurred in the Executive Council from time to time. Osgoode aptly observed in 1798 that the 'Canadians universally' and even many of the English 'naturally connect the Ideas of will and power when speaking of ... a Judge.'[65]

The judges of Lower Canada were far more active politically than the common law judges of England – that is, the twelve men sitting on the courts of Common Pleas, Exchequer, and King's Bench.[66] Rarely was one of the British judges a peer qualified to sit in the House of Lords. The judicial element of that body consisted mainly of the lord chancellor and former lord chancellors.[67] From 1792 to 1811 there were almost always three or four judges in the Legislative Council, where they entered into debate on all variety of issues. By analogy to the role of the lord chancellor, the chief justice of the province acted as the Council's Speaker. In his absence the chair was usually assumed by one of the other judges on the Council.

By virtue of resolutions passed by the House of Commons in the seventeenth century, the twelve common law judges were excluded from membership in the Commons. The original ground for this incapacity was that the judges were summoned by royal writs to assist in the deliberations of the House of Lords, meaning that they should be prepared to advise on points of law if requested.[68] The more modern notion of isolating the Bench from partisan politics appeared later, probably by the early eighteenth century.

Whatever the rationale in England by the 1790s, it did not apply in

Lower Canada. Judges were eligible to sit until 1811. None was elected in 1792 but two years later Dorchester attempted to consolidate his control of the Lower House by appointing MPPs to the Bench. In January–February 1794 the hitherto independent-minded and anglophobic seigneur, Pierre-Amable De Bonne, the 'democratic' Assembly Speaker Jean-Antoine Panet, and James Walker, already a government supporter, were named judges. When Panet refused to accept a posting to Montreal, his commission was revoked and the position given to his cousin Pierre-Louis Panet, a Tory anglophile and indefatigable government propagandist in the Assembly. In the general election of 1796 Panet (who believed it improper to campaign personally) did not stand and Walker went down to defeat. De Bonne waged a vicious, wholly partisan campaign in Hampshire against notary Joseph Planté and shopkeeper François Huot. The Judge portrayed Planté as a low-born, 'obliged to scour the country after any little business' and Huot as a man who 'kept the public Scales upon the Market and fought every day with the country people.' De Bonne had the local militia officers 'order' votes for the government and spread rumours that batteaux would come to conscript those electors who did not do so. Although many farmers took to the woods in fear, they were not collectively seduced, and the judge had to settle for a safe seat in Trois-Rivières. From 1797 to 1810 the seigneur-judge was a pro-government floor leader in the House and the virtual campaign manager for the administration. In the various ridings he contested between 1796 and 1808, he did nothing to counter widespread fear that to vote against him would bring retaliation if the elector ever appeared in his court as a party to a civil suit or an accused in a criminal trial.[69] De Bonne was joined in the Assembly in 1801–4 by Panet – who in 1801 was known as 'a kind of prime minister and even takes the Governor (Milnes) by the Button'[70] – and in 1804–8 by the provincial judge at Trois-Rivières, Louis-C. Foucher, formerly solicitor general.

With the exception of the lord chancellor, judges in England did not become ministers of the crown. From the Glorious Revolution to the year 1806 only one common law Judge sat in the inner or 'efficient' cabinet: Lord Mansfield, chief justice of the King's Bench, in the years 1757–65. While the terse record of the debates makes if difficult to determine whether his double tenure was questioned in Parliament at the time, it was definitely criticized outside by the Wilkesites and roundly attacked in Parliament some years later, in 1775. During this debate Mansfield tacitly admitted the incompatibility of the twin roles and in the very year he left the cabinet, Sir William Blackstone pronounced that nothing 'is more to be avoided, in a free constitution, than uniting the provinces of a judge and a minister of state.'[71]

When in 1806 Lord Chief Justice Ellenborough was named to the 'ministry of all the talents,' the opposition Whigs marshalled convincing arguments to show the conflict of such dual office holding with an impartial administration of justice, especially were the country to face another round of sedition and treason trials. Cabinet ministers took refuge in legal technicalities and unpersuasive precedents, while Secretary of State Charles James Fox virtually gave the game away when he assured the House of Commons that should possible state trials be discussed in cabinet, the lord chief justice would naturally absent himself. Although the government easily won the Commons vote, informed opinion outside Parliament generally condemned this break with past traditions. Lord Ellenborough was cowed by the strong public reaction into adopting a very low political profile and apparently came in time to accept the opposition's case.[72] His appointment was the last of its kind in England.

From 1792 to the end of 1811 judges were a major and active presence in the Executive Council of Lower Canada, with the proportion of one-third to total members usually maintained. The judicial appointees did not confine themselves to appeals or even to issues of a technical legal nature. Rather they participated fully in helping the governor define the whole gamut of executive policy: education, public accounts, land granting, import-export regulation, entitlement to fees, internal security, and much more. Factional fights in the Council were not uncommon and here too the judges were prominent. During the dispute over Governor Sir Robert Prescott's attempts in 1798 to curtail speculation in crown lands, Monk and De Bonne actively supported the governor while Osgoode, representing the majority, opposed him. Judges could achieve a predominant political influence, as Monk and De Bonne did for a while in 1798 and Panet in 1801. The chief justice of the province, however, was much better positioned to succeed.

The sources of influence enabling a chief justice to approach an apex of power were many. In the Upper House he was the governor's man, appointed by him to the Speakership and responsible for defending official policy in debate. He also acted as chairman of the Executive Council when it sat in Committee of the Whole. Such a function enabled Smith and his successors to exercise some control over agenda and to ensure that Committee reports recommending executive action reflected their own ideas. It was almost inevitable that the chief justice was either the governor's client, as Smith was, or could draw on multiple threads of influence in Whitehall, as in the case of Osgoode and later Jonathan Sewell.

His contemporaries considered the chief justice as the head of a government department.[73] The concept clearly implied a general political mandate, analogous to that of the lord chancellor to oversee the functioning of the law, in its administrative, legislative, patronage, and political aspects. But the chief justices in the 1790s and early 1800s invariably aspired to more – to become as Judge De Bonne put it, 'the second person in Government.'[74]

Given his multiple sources of influence, the way was open for a chief justice to become 'prime minister.' Smith was that to Dorchester and Lieutenant-Governor Alured Clarke in the early 1790s, defining government policy in such areas as higher education, disposal of crown lands, conversion of seigneurial tenure, and implementation of the new constitution. The office under Smith was, in fact, so potent, Monk argued that the establishment of a second chief justiceship was necessary to achieve a political balance.[75] Osgoode bitterly resented Dorchester's studied refusal to consult him on most matters of state, which he found inexplicable on constitutional grounds and against which he retaliated by opposing many of Dorchester's Council initiatives.[76] He later regretted losing influence at the Chateau because of his opposition to Prescott on the crown lands issue. Milnes's penchant for taking advice from persons other than Osgoode may well have precipitated the judges's resignation.[77] But for a period of some months in 1796 and 1797 he achieved the position of a 'prime minister' eulogized by Prescott.[78] Osgoode himself described the relationship – in the third person – this way: 'At this period another person [other than Monk] was known to possess the unlimited Confidence of the Governor. The whole management of the Civil affairs of the province and the patronage connected therewith were in his Hands.'[79] Chief Justice Jonathan Sewell would hold a similar position under Governor Craig in 1810–11 – a role which even the lord chancellor could not attain in England.[80]

Extra-judicial Opinions in England

One of the ways in which the Stuarts manipulated the Bench was to insist that the judges render extra-judicial opinions on politically sensitive questions which might later come before them in court. The possibilities for abuse were considerable, especially since most of the judiciary held office at the king's pleasure. The objectionable features of the practice are several: the temptation to give the desired answer, thus committing the judges in advance; the secrecy of the proceedings; the lack of testimony; and the absence of counsel and at times even the need to give reasons. Early illustrations are provided by *Peacham's* case (1615) in which the accused was convicted of treason on account of passages found in an unpreached sermon, and by the opinion on the legality of ship money (1635) which condemned Hampden in advance and which Charles I promulgated in 1637 in order to foreclose litigation on its validity.[81] In *Gregg's* case, 1707/8, the judges of England handed down an *in camera*, now provably unreasoned opinion,[82] which put the law of treason onto several routes inimical to an accused: enemy aliens resident in the realm owed allegiance; sending intelligence was 'adhering' to the enemy, even though the intelligence was intercepted and Edward III's Statute of Treasons, 1352 could be interpreted to require giving effective aid; and more.

Early critics of the practice, such as Sir Edward Coke, had little effect. Indeed, extra-judicial opinions continued to the end of George II's reign, when in 1760 the judges, led by Mansfield, pronounced that Lord George Sackville could be tried by court martial for dereliction of duty at the Battle of Minden, even though Sackville had since been dismissed from His Majesty's service. But this opinion indicates that the judges were becoming hostile to the practice – not surprisingly since it was incompatible with an independent judiciary and had been roundly condemned in 1748 by such an authority as John Lord Fortesque in his case reports.[83]

In his covering letter to the lord keeper, enclosing the certificate, Lord Mansfield stated in the most general terms that the judges 'are very averse to giving extra-judicial opinions, especially where they affect a particular case; but the circumstances of the trial now depending ease us of difficulties upon this occasion.' The reference was, almost certainly, to Sackville's repeated and public insistence on being tried by a court martial. In the opinion itself, the judges expressly reserved the right to change their minds should the matter be raised before them in court.[84] Later hostile authorities can be readily found. Most useful is that of the distinguished legal historian Francis Hargrave, in his edition of *Coke upon Littleton*, first published in the 1780s:

... however numerous and strong the precedents may be in favour of the king's *extra-judicially* consulting the judges on questions in which the Crown is interested, it is a right ... to be exercised with great reserve; lest the rigid impartiality so essential to their *judicial* capacity, should be violated. The anticipation of *judicial* opinions on causes *actually depending*, should be particularly guarded against; and therefore a wise and upright judge will ever be cautious how he *extra-judicially* answers questions of such a tendency.[85]

Thus by the 1780s and 1790s, extra-judicial opinions furnished to the executive power had become an anomaly, justifiable only in exceptional cases, and only on the understanding the judges retained entire discretion to change their minds. It is significant that the Sackville case of 1760 was the last documented instance, in England, where such extra-judicial advice occurred, although the occasional covert individual opinion was not unknown thereafter. The nineteenth-century jurists continued to condemn the practice and by the early twentieth century it appears clear without any qualification that it had become contrary to constitutional convention, unless authorized by statute (for example, authorizing reference cases).[86]

Extra-judicial Opinions: Lower Canada

In Lower Canada after 1800 extra-judicial opinions were commonplace, particularly on issues affecting internal security. In 1810 Chief Justice Sewell, for example, advised on the legality of arresting members of the Assembly and on the law in relation to various anglicizing proposals. The first known collective opinion was rendered in 1803 when all eight King's Bench judges advised, by a five-to-three decision, on the application of English law on descent and dower in relation to lands held under free and common soccage. Not one of these respondents hinted at any possible impropriety or reserved the right to change his mind, despite these matters having been before the courts. It was Chief Justice John Elmsley, not Lieutenant-Governor Milnes, who had conceived of this reference to the judiciary, an amazing aspect of a remarkable incident, since the Lower Canadian judiciary was well aware of Mansfield's 1760 correspondence with the Lord Keeper.[87]

2

The Struggle for Constitutional Reform, 1784–1792

By autumn 1784 the reformers of Quebec City had organized themselves into two committees, English and Canadien, to draft a petition for constitutional change. The former consisted of seven merchants, among them Adam Lymburner, a dominant force in the seal fishery and a polished, dedicated politician in the mercantile interest.[1] The Canadien Committee then consisted of sixteen men. Two were from the seigneurial class (Antoine Juchereau Duchesnay and Philippe de Rocheblave, son of a French noble and outspoken opponent of the seigneurs who sat on the Council). The remainder, drawn from the bourgeoisie, included lawyer Jean-Antoine Panet, merchants Louis Dunière (grain trade, fisheries), Pierre-Nicolas Perrault (known as Perrault l'aîné [furs]), and several shopkeepers. Montreal soon organized similar committees with the English group of seven or so, featuring some of the leading names in the fur trade: southwesters Richard Dobie and James McGill; nor'westers Benjamin Frobisher and Simon McTavish. English government officials, even those favouring legal reform, remained aloof, leery of an elected assembly.[2] The Canadien Committee of about nine was composed mainly of prominent merchants such as Pierre Foretier (real estate, formerly in furs), but did include two professionals: notary Jean Delisle and notary-surveyor Joseph Papineau.[3] The latter was a brilliant intellectual and rivetting orator whose artisanal origins, squat build, unpretentious language, and homely dress made him seem 'a man of the people,' and a very dangerous one to his political opponents.

The two Quebec committees drafted English and French versions of a petition to the king dated 24 November 1784.[4] A public meeting called by the Montreal committees ratified the petition, which remained the basis of reformer demands until 1791. In February 1785 all four committees published an explanatory French-language pamphlet entitled *Aux Citoyens et Habitants des Villes et des Campagnes de la Province de Québec.*[5] These are the main sources for the reformers' ideas, which provide important insights into the deadening impact of the French Revolution a few years later.

The petition asked for the repeal of the Quebec Act except for the rights granted therein to Roman Catholics. The new legislature was to consist of the governor, a representative Assembly without any religious qualification, and an appointed Upper House or Council. It requested that the criminal law of England and the Canadien laws respecting 'landed Estates, Marriage Settlements, Inheritances and Dowers' be maintained,[6] but that the 'Commercial Laws of England be declared to be the Laws of this Province, in all Matters of Trade and Commerce, subject to be Changed by the Legislature of Quebec.' The petition also sought the extension of jury trials not only for commercial disputes in which one of the parties was not a merchant but for all civil cases.

The French party countered the reformer offensive immediately. A group of seven men of the seigneurial class formed themselves into the 'Committee of Seigneurs, Gentlemen, Principal Tenants and Citizens of the Province of Quebec.'[7] Among its members were Judge de Rouville and Pierre-Amable De Bonne, soon to prove the most active of the committee. These men prepared written rebuttals, published in December 1784, including an anonymous French-language circular letter drafted by De Bonne, and a humble address to the king, known as the counter-petition.[8] The counter-petitioners very likely had the sympathy of most of the Roman Catholic clergy – an elected assembly sat badly with the divine right of kings and hierarchical values generally – but they remained, in general, uninvolved publicly.[9]

For almost seven years the reformers and the French party engaged in a battle for signatures to their petitions and support from British officials and politicians. In London the French party relied heavily on the influence of former Governor Haldimand and conservative Under-Secretary Evan Nepean and were initially successful. The four reform committees chose Adam Lymburner in 1787 as their joint agent to the imperial authorities. Lymburner proved indefatigable in rallying the British merchants trading to Canada, recruiting liberally minded MPs to the cause and lobbying cabinet ministers. In 1788 and again in 1791, during the debate on the Constitutional bill, he appeared in the House of Commons to read papers outlining the reformers' case. Despite his activity, though, Lymburner's influence on imperial policy was negligible.[10]

The other details of the campaign for representative government and legal change, have been exhaustively studied elsewhere and need not detain us. Four features, however, bearing on the themes pursued in this book, do require some brief comment.

The Alarmist Tactics of the Counter-petitioners

Opponents of electoral institutions stressed the supposed danger to the traditional laws and religion and of greatly increased taxation. In De Bonne's letter, for example, the counter-petitioners associated an assembly with 'the abolition of your laws' as well as new taxes. According to the reformers' 1785 pamphlet, their opponents were telling the people the House of Assembly would 'impose duties on your lands, on your animals, on the windows of your houses, and on your heads.' In the areas near the cities, where the De Bonne forces actually campaigned, it appears that these scare tactics had a definite effect among farmers and villagers. In February 1785 the two Montreal reforming committees and the Quebec Canadien Committee informed the British merchants trading to Canada that 'credulity, the eldest daughter of ignorance, has made rapid progress among the lower class of people.' They had been taught that reform meant new taxes and the alarm generated by this falsehood 'has given the opposing party a great many crosses instead of signatures' on their petition.[11] About three and a half years later, the two Quebec committees complained to Lord Dorchester that 'it has been held out to them [the habitants] that their Religion was in danger of being abolished, that a House of Assembly was requested only for the purpose of imposing numerous and oppressive taxes and of destroying the Ancient Laws of the Country relative to real and personal property.'[12]

A Conflict of Class

Between 1784 to 1791 political divisions over the constitution and the laws were based primarily on class, not ethnicity. Both parties were bi-ethnic coalitions, made up of the politically active bourgeoisie and those who defined themselves to be of the upper ranks.

In letters, speeches, and published propaganda, the French party hammered away at the theme that the reformers had no status – they were not landed gentlemen – to speak for the colony.[13] During the stormy legislative session of 1787, seigneur Jacques-François Cugnet typically complained that everyone, even a merchant or lawyer 'from the Third Estate fancies himself entitled to give advice to the Council.' If the reformers succeeded, they would try to reduce the seigneurs to the level of their 'vassals.'[14] A French party pamphleteer informed his British readership in 1790 that while the individuals on the Quebec Canadien Committee, holding such modest positions as advocate, notary, carpenter, merchant, shopkeeper, and a 'person who furnishes dinners or entertainments ... may be very good men in their respective stations ... they cannot come under the denomination of the most respectable of the Canadiens.' It seemed obvious to the writer – and the American Revolution was his stated example – that a Quebec House of Assembly could easily become an instrument 'in the hands of designing men, of sedition and revolt.'[15] Almost identical reactions can be found among English supporters of the French party. Montreal physician Charles Blake, for example, expressed shock that the gentlemen of the colony had not been consulted and that a group of 'Twenty-Two Merchants, and not with a Foot of Land in Canada was to Dictate laws to the Throne,' while in Council Judge Fraser confidently dismissed the English reformers as 'rich folk of low birth who seek to rise in society by causing a change in the province.'[16]

Middle-class resentment of seigneurial pretension had many echoes in the campaign for representative government. Notary-surveyor Joseph Papineau did not spare the feelings of his 'betters' when he appeared as a witness during the 1787 justice inquiry. The seigneurial bloc on the Council, he claimed, which was not counterbalanced by anyone representing the interests of the people, prevented all efforts to protect the farmers against abuses resulting from the seigneurs' greed or indifference. Damning correspondence from French-language subscribers of liberal persuasion regularly appeared in Mesplet's Montreal Gazette. These letters attacked the seigneurs for their feudal arrogance, despotic cast of mind, lack of brains and education, living beyond their ludicrously meagre means, for their contempt of the habitant who provided rent from honest toil, scorn for the skilled artisan who served them and so on. Letters, both English and French, published in the Quebec City papers likewise satirized the gentlemen of the French party as claiming a divine right to misrule. Although many of these self-styled grandees read nothing and others had no landed income to speak of, they nevertheless pushed themselves forward with 'pomp and a mighty parade of title, calling themselves the Canadian nation, and arrogating ... feudal honours.'[17]

It would be the impact of the French Revolution after 1792 that gradually divided the language groups along political lines. One casualty would be the bourgeois alliance; with its demise, opportunities to liberalize the constitution and commercialize the laws were lost for decades.

The Strengths and Weaknesses of the Reformers' Alliance

The ethnic factor at times weakened the alliance of reformers, but did no irreparable harm. Both groups, after all, were ideologically united in favour of a liberal constitution, shared an interest in the commercial development of the province, and had a common class enemy – the Canadien seigneurs and those English residents who associated themselves with the landed interests. At the beginning, during the months of circulating the 1784 petition and preparing the pamphlet, all was camaraderie.[18] This harmony would be severely tested in 1787 and again the next year.

The principal problem lay in the English Committee of Quebec's increased demands for legal reform. Encouraged by Chief Justice Smith's attitude as revealed in Gray v. Grant, the merchants of Quebec requested from the Commerce Committee of the Legislative Council in January 1787 changes in the laws which went well beyond the recommendations contained in the petition.[19] The merchants requested that the laws of England be introduced, not only for commercial matters, but for all contracts and delicts as well. These new demands appeared to the Canadien reformers as the serious beginning of an all-out assault on their traditional laws, which outside the area of commerce they cherished as much as the French party.

The two Quebec committees were soon at loggerheads over the merchants' January report. In 1788 Juchereau Duchesnay wrote Perrault l'aîné explaining he would never agree to the unrestricted introduction of English commercial law since that would 'ruin the points in our laws which protect the widow and minors.' Montreal Committee member Joseph-François Perrault had a similar reaction to this perceived attack on the Coutume. Although he did not resign as Duchesnay had done, Perrault became convinced that the Canadien committees should choose their own agent to represent them in London since there was reason to believe Lymburner 'would favour the English in the differences between them and us.'[20]

No second agent was appointed. However, separate instructions were issued to Lymburner in the autumn of 1787, with the Quebec English Committee requiring its agent to use the January report as a basis for recommendations.[21] In October 1788, when Lymburner was again preparing to leave the colony for London, the two Quebec committees tried to arrive at common instructions. Problems arose over a list of new demands from the Canadien group, which sought, *inter alia*, that the royal supremacy be relaxed and that government patronage be distributed on the basis of population figures for English and Canadiens. The English Committee would not initially agree to any of the Canadien proposals and the dispute meant that the ship on which Lymburner had booked passage sailed without him on 25 October. Within days a workable compromise was reached, however, as recorded in separate instructions issued by the two Quebec committees. The English document dropped any demand for the laws of England in non-commercial cases. The Canadien instrument, omitting the constitutional points, expressly demanded the introduction of the commercial laws of England as absolutely imperative in the interests of trade. Through the ability to compromise the alliance was able to survive severe strains and the four groups would continue to work in relative harmony until the passage of the Constitutional Act and indeed until at least June 1792.[22]

It is clear that the Canadien reformers were willing to commercialize the civil law. True, they would have resisted wholesale repeal of rules protective of the family and of the seigneurial system of tenure. But, had the alliance been maintained through our period, compromise might have permitted changes such as maintaining customary dower but permitting married women to renounce it, and modifying estate administration to give somewhat greater protection to creditors and partners of the deceased. Again, one can imagine trimmings to the system of tenure which would not importantly affect the family or be contrary to the interests of the habitants. In the early years of the French Revolution, feudalism was not in particularly good odour among Canadien reformers and therefore there was some room for movement.

In other areas, where the family was only indirectly an issue, a contemporary observer would have expected change if the bourgeois alliance were to dominate the Assembly: proof in commercial cases, juries where the defendant was not a merchant, negotiability of commercial paper à la Lord Mansfield, a pro-creditor bankruptcy law, longer prescriptions and even – though this is much less certain – a carefully drafted land registry statute, in which costs were minimized, notaries' interests taken into account, and family privacy protected.[23]

Much of the preceding analysis is speculative. But there can be no doubt the Canadien reformers wanted a major commercialization of the civil law. The French-language pamphlet of 1785 characterized the *Coutume* as made for an outdated feudal society and lauded the English laws as those of 'the greatest commercial kingdom in the World.' Commercialization of the civil law, however, was not to be until well into the nineteenth century.

The Constitutional Radicalism of the Reformers

Excepting the proposed franchise and property qualifications for the Assembly (which would restrict membership to males of the middle and upper ranks), the reformers were radical in their constitutional demands, when compared with the existing governments of New Brunswick and Nova Scotia, the actual system established by the Constitutional Act of 1791, and the constitution of Lower Canada down to 1840.

In the first place they asked for a legislature with the exclusive power of taxation, thus requesting the repeal of the Quebec Revenue Act, 1774 by which the imperial Parliament had imposed import duties on liquor and established licence fees for any person keeping a house of public entertainment or retailing strong drink. This, the executive's main revenue source in Lower Canada down to 1831, helped the governors avoid having to seek supply from the Assembly. (Deficits were paid from a secret account for the British colonial garrisons known as the army extraordinaries or military chest.) Several sources, including the petition, distinctly imply, and one (Pierre Du Calvet's influential reforming pamphlet published in 1784) explicitly urged that the power of appropriation be lodged in the Assembly and not with the governor. The issue of control over public spending would, of course, precipitate severe constitutional crises in the 1820s and 1830s and would be resolved in favour of the elected representatives only after responsible government was conceded in the late 1840s.

A second area of democratic liberalism was the administration of justice. Sheriffs – who executed court judgments on real estate, struck jury panels, and were responsible for running the penal system, including capital punishment – were to be nominated by the Assembly and approved by the governor. This reform was never realized. Article 7 asked that jury trials be granted, at the option of either party, in *any* civil case. Had this request been acceded to, civil procedure would have been drastically anglicized, since in the Canadien system judges were arbiters of fact as well as law. Eighteenth-century commentators praised jury trials in civil suits as a protection of the ordinary citizen against the rich and powerful. The 1785 pamphlet proclaimed that such trials 'are rightly regarded in England as a bulwark of fortune and honour against the scheming of placemen [officials] and all writers say that they have preserved the liberties of the British Empire.'

The petitioners asked in articles 9 and 12 that judges be appointed 'during Life, or their good Behaviour.' As it was also important to insulate judges as much as possible from political influences, article 12 asked they 'be rewarded with Sufficient Salaries, so as to confine them to the functions of administering Justice.' The distinct implications, I believe, were that judges should be ineligible for election to the Assembly, should not advise the governor on executive policy, and should not sit in the Council as legislators. According to an entry in the State Minute book, less than five years before, the merchant George Allsopp had protested in Council (6 March 1780) against judges who acted as legislators and advisers of the governor. Allsopp quoted Montesquieu: 'according to the Great Author of the spirit of the Laws [*De l'Esprit des Lois*] ... All would be lost if the same man or group ... were to exercise these three powers: that of making the laws, that of executing public resolutions, and that of judging the crimes or disputes of individuals' (trans.). The pamphlet, characterizing these articles as 'of the highest importance,' summarized the reformers' position as follows: 'the independence of English judges does great honour to England and has gained ... the respect of all of Europe; in effect it would require a judge, who has sufficient renumeration and is shielded from *all* extraneous influences, to be of a highly depraved and corrupt character, if he were to fall from the path of virtue and be governed by political and biased motives.' This statement is but one indication of the great stress the reformers placed on guaranteeing an independent judiciary, which was not, however, achieved, even in embryo, until the 1840s.

Article 6 aimed at entrenching the right to habeas corpus by including it in an imperial statute. This would put repeal or drastic suspension beyond the power of the colonial legislature – a reform which has not yet been achieved in Canada. What the reformers had in mind was contained in an abortive bill one of their British lobbyists, Thomas Powys, put before Parliament in 1786. The bill allowed suspension of habeas corpus where there existed 'a Rebellion or ... Invasion ... by a foreign Enemy *but in no other Case whatsoever.*'[24]

During the 1784 Council debate on habeas corpus William Grant proposed that 'the Common and Statute Law of England in so far as the same is favorable and productive of personal Liberty, Safety, and Security, is the Right of all His Majesty's faithful Subjects ... in this Province ... whereby to decide every case ... not provided for by the present ordinance.' After bitter debate, Mabane's men defeated the motion by nine to seven.[25] Had Grant succeeded, Quebec/Lower Canada would have received a quasi bill of rights in the nature of an Interpretation Act provision creating a legal presumption in favour of personal liberty – which might, for example, have brought about an end to slavery in the 1780s rather than in 1800.

There were many other forward-looking ideas in the reformers' minds. The petition, for example, asked that elections be triennial, rather than septennial as in England. (The Constitutional Act imposed annual sessions and a four-year term.) Lymburner recommended paying MPPs and objected strongly to the governor's power to appoint returning officers as contrary to the 'Freedom and Independence of the Legislature.' English reformers writing to the *Quebec Herald* made no secret of their support for Thomas Erskine's position that juries were entitled to return general verdicts in seditious libel cases.[26] This constitutional radicalism – especially on the part of the English reformers – would quickly fade as the fear of the French Revolution grew.

THE FRAMEWORK OF THE CONSTITUTION OF 1791

With the appointment in June 1789 of the energetic William Grenville as secretary of state, the imperial government began to take the Canada issue seriously. The major decisions were to divide the Old Province of Quebec into Upper and Lower Canada along the Ottawa River and to grant each new colony an elected assembly. The first was motivated mainly by a desire to avoid ethnic dissension in a single legislature, and the second principally by a desire to reduce the Quebec deficit.[27] Because of the complexity involved in distinguishing which common law rules were and which were not examples of 'commercial laws' and of reconciling the former with traditional Canadien legal values, commercialization of the civil law was left to local legislation. The *Coutume* therefore remained in force except that, as in 1774, outside the region of the seigneuries (for example, the Eastern Townships) grants of land could be and, after 1791, invariably were made according to English tenure. Grenville was not opposed in principle to security of tenure for colonial judges, but concluded that 'the present state of legal information, [expertise] or of Judicial Character, in the province' did not justify taking such a step in the immediate future.[28]

The Theory of Balance

Lord Grenville and Prime Minister William Pitt aimed at creating in the Canadas a version of the British balanced constitution, eulogized by William Blackstone, Jean-Louis De Lolme, and many other authorities, as well as virtually every prominent politician of the day, from Pitt down.[29] The balanced constitution, as described by Blackstone, consisted of the king (representing the safety and reassurance given by hereditary monarchy; also unity of executive command), the House of Lords (representing landed aristocracy with a substantial stake in the country; also wisdom), and the House of Commons (representing democracy, humane sentiment, and, despite the highly restricted franchise, the mass of the nation). Each organ of Parliament acted as a check on the other two and all functioned together in a marvellous, almost mystical equilibrium. If the constitution were to become unbalanced, the result would be regal tyranny reminiscent of James II, a landowners' oligarchy, or mob rule. The theory did not envision organized opposition parties dedicated to removing, much less replacing, the king's ministers. Opposition to the executive was the function of either house as a whole (or both), but any part thereof and was supposed to be directed to individual measures, not men. In any case, until well after 1800 parliamentary opposition was commonly tarred by the brush of disloyalty based particularly on the memories of the Jacobite uprisings of 1715 and 1745. Nor did the balanced constitution idea encompass the notion of responsible cabinet government – although for a variety of reasons (for example, the king's growing need for supply and Pitt's authoritarian tendencies) it was embryonically evolving during this period. Blackstone, for instance, did not even mention the cabinet in his lengthy description of British government. Until the late 1820s all political factions of Lower Canada, whether of tory or whiggish inclination, used the language of the balanced constitution, Blackstone and De Lolme, like the Bible, being easily interpreted to support the position at hand.

While the Constitutional Act and ancillary instruments attempted to provide each of the Canadas with a balanced constitution, in the British empirical way principles were not enunciated and much detail was left for the future. Nothing was said, for example, about parliamentary privilege or official language(s). Of course, the act would disappear in the violence of the 1837 rebellion. But serious conflict, especially if politics became ethnicized, was likely from the outset, as there were no obvious means of harmonizing the various organs of government. Such problems might have been mitigated if the bourgeois alliance had held together and had cooperated with the governors at the same time as seeking a gradual liberalization of the constitution.

The Governor

At the apex of the system in the lower province was the royal governor[30] who was supposed to act in accordance with His Majesty's commission, standing instructions, and any specific directives from the secretary of state. When present in the colony he was at this time also commander-in-chief of the regular forces in British North America and had overall responsibility for Indian policy in both Canadas and in relation to Indians on the northwestern frontier of the United States.

The governor (and in his absence the lieutenant-governor) was given the usual balancing powers of summoning, proroguing, and dissolving the Legislature. He could also reject the Assembly's election of a Speaker, although the constitutional propriety of doing so was debatable, and he appointed the Speaker of the Legislative Council. Unfettered patronage power was limited largely to minor officials but he did name the justices of the peace, the puisne judges, and his civil secretary who largely controlled official correspondence and access to the Château. His recommendation influenced London's appointments of the chief justices, law officers, executive councillors, and legislative councillors, but he was usually not even consulted in its naming of officials responsible to British departments: the receiver general, collector of customs at Quebec, deputy postmaster general, surveyor general, and Anglican bishop, who reported to the Archbishop of Canterbury. The governor was entitled to veto any bill and occasionally did so.[31]

The Councils

An Executive Council, appointed in London, advised the governors. During the early years, numbers varied from nine to fifteen, with the

English in a majority, and it was composed mainly of government officials of both language groups (including three or four judges) and a few English merchants. At any given time about half of the councillors sat in the Upper House, but except in the few government safe seats they found election very difficult. The law required Council's advice be taken only in a very few cases, such as granting public lands. For the rest, the governor could consult or not as he saw fit. Only a fare executive action required council's consent.

The notion of accountability to majority opinion in the Assembly would have been considered by all as sansculottic and certain to bring anarchy. De Bonne (appointed in 1794), for example, was utterly condemned by and excluded from the Lower House in 1810 but retained his seat on the Council until his death in 1816. While seats in the Council were legally at pleasure, they were normally held for life. This arrangement contrasted with the British practice of reconstructing the cabinet to reflect changing Commons' opinion. However, considering the powerful patrons the councillors could usually call on and the absence of any pressing need for the executive to obtain supply, such life tenure was understandable.[32]

The Legislative Council or Upper House was to consists of not fewer than fifteen British subjects of the age of majority, resident in the colony and appointed by the king. Certain sections of the act aimed at enabling the councillors to act independently of the governor. They were to hold their seats for life, the only specified causes of removal being prolonged absence without official permission, swearing allegiance to a foreign power, and conviction for high treason. As office-holders were not prohibited from membership, at any given time during the period approximately 40 to 50 per cent of the members were also executive councillors and a large majority of others held offices on the civil list. All these posts were held at pleasure, and gave the governor considerable influence in the Upper House.

As Lord Grenville had desired, the act made provision for a future hereditary council of local aristocrats, to be modelled on the House of Lords. These arrangements – unsuited to a frontier, commercial colony – were never implemented. But the idea of an aristocratic upper house was reflected in the appointments made to the Council. Throughout the period two groups dominated: Canadien seigneurs, and a slightly larger contingent of English officials, including the chief justices and puisne judges. The English appointees were either landed gentlemen of real or apparent substance, or clients of powerful aristocratic patrons in England, or both. Significantly, not a single merchant then actively engaged in commerce (aside from money-lending and supervising investments in real estate), sat in the Upper House during the period, although several businessmen were executive councillors.[33]

Given the composition of the Council and the equal legislative role of the Lords in Great Britain (outside public finance), the members of the Upper House naturally interpreted their mandate in the widest manner. Several important bills originated in the Council[34] and it often opposed Assembly initiatives à l'outrance, doing so, for instance, in 1795 with regard to lowering admission requirements to the Dai. Even in the area of public financing the Council demanded an equal role, going far beyond the pretensions of the contemporary House of Lords, where money bills were seldom even discussed. Predictably, given its make-up, it was prepared to support the governor in every serious dispute with the Assembly.[35]

The Assembly and Elections

The fifty-man Legislative Assembly, enjoying only the negative powers of protest and legislative veto, was elected (publicly) by twenty-seven ridings, all but four of them returning two members.[36] The urban areas (Quebec, Upper and Lower Town; Montreal, East and West Wards; Trois-Rivières, and William Henry), were entitled to eleven members. There were no property, linguistic, religious, or literary requirements for membership – a more liberal arrangement than that common in the United States or in France under its 1791 constitution (with regard to property) and than that of Great Britain (as to property and religion). In the rural counties, as was the case for England, all adult landowners with estates having an annual net worth of forty shillings or more could vote. Urban owners of dwelling houses of at least £5 annual value and tenants paying £10 or more in rent per year were electors. The Lower Canadian franchise was one of the most democratic in the world, with virtually all habitant farmers, a majority of artisans (but not labourers, domestics, or soldiers) and even women being able to qualify as electors.[37] Not surprisingly this franchise, which was far more liberal than that of Great Britain with its numerous 'nomination [rotten and pocket] boroughs,' began to terrify the English élite as revulsion to the French Revolution deepened in 1792 and after.

Operating through his patronage secretary and the first lord of the Treasury, George III (who controlled a civil list of £800,00 per annum) exercised a decisive influence over more than 200 of the 558 members who comprised the late eighteenth-century British parliaments. There was nothing comparable to this hegemonic electoral system in Lower Canada. Gaspé, where a handful of persons employed by the British fishing concern, Robin & Co., controlled elections in favour of the government, was the only pocket riding in the province. The electorates in the other constituencies were simply too large to be effectively and consistently manipulated by patronage,[38] even had the governors' resources been substantially higher than they were. In addition to the Gaspé, there were only eight seats (in five ridings) which the governors could count on as 'safe,' that is, which returned pro-government candidates 80 per cent or more of the time at the seven general elections held in the period.[39]

Legislation in early Lower Canada was a modest affair, the number of statutes per session from 1793 to 1811 averaging slightly fewer than eleven. Hardly any acts exceeded thirty sections. One of the exceptions, the Militia Act of 1794 ran to thirty-five; the present National Defence Act contains 306.[40] Although not unknown, delegated legislation was rare. Only about 20 per cent of the statutes began as unambiguous government bills being recommended to the legislature by the governor. Governments then were not expected to have legislative programs and even executive recommendations that the two houses legislate in a certain way did not sit well with the theory of the balanced constitution.[41] Over 20 per cent of the statutes were simple continuances of temporary acts. Statutes which lapsed, unless continued, after a year or two were commonplace, but the technique was not exploited sufficiently by the Assembly – two taxation acts of 1795 were perpetual, for example – to gain power at the expense of the executive. The imperial government could refuse assent to bills reserved by the governor and disallow acts. Although entirely unfettered by convention, these powers were not exercised during the years 1792 to 1811.[42]

Assessment

Pitt's and Grenville's confidence that the balanced British constitution could be smoothly transplanted to Lower Canada was unrealistic. The principal factors enabling the three branches of Parliament to work in harmony – the great extent of royal patronage, the archaic electoral system dominated in the 'boroughs' by tiny voting élites, and the political influence of the landed classes in the rural counties where electorates were too large to be easily manipulated – were simply lacking. The governors could and sometimes did use their limited patronage resources in attempts to win over or consolidate support from members of the provincial Parliament. Although spectacularly successful in De Bonne's case, this technique was in general of very limited value in a system where only 18 per cent of the Assembly seats could be controlled or strongly influenced from the Château. The absence of pocket boroughs meant that the governor had no assurance that his appointee could be re-elected.[43] And there was always the possibility that a Canadien MPP put on the civil list would prudently refrain for electoral reasons from supporting the governor in the House.[44] Because of their pretensions, their close association with government, and their tendency to raise rents illegally, the Canadien seigneurs, with a few exceptions, were unpopular with the habitants and had no social, governmental, or financial position analogous to that of the British landed classes, a point which Grenville missed completely. The habitants, moreover, held their land in perpetuity. If they performed their obligations, they were not liable to eviction (unlike many British tenant farmers who qualified as electors in the counties) if they voted against the seigneur or his nominee. After initial success in the election of 1792, the Canadien seigneurs were eliminated as a significant political force in the Assembly. With their demise and the breakdown of the English and Canadien bourgeois alliance, any hope for a harmonious balanced constitution died.

THE CONTINUANCE OF THE BOURGEOIS ALLIANCE

When the contents of the Constitutional bill and later the act became known in Lower Canada, the English reformers expressed momentary outrage at the division of the colony and the absence of any provision introducing the commercial laws of England.[45] Still, there was always hope, particularly as the alliance with the Canadien bourgeoisie remained. John Richardson in Montreal and the then moderate reformer Jonathan Sewell in Quebec were both confident that the first fruits of the new legislature would include a healthy dose of British jurisprudence. Lymburner thought the legislature would enact a statute providing for the voluntary conversion to English land tenure, if the governor recommended it and the public had a chance to suggest amendments before the bill was introduced.[46]

By December 1791 the English reformers of Quebec had decided to make the best of things. On Boxing Day bi-ethnic celebrations of the act coming into force were held at Franks Tavern in the Upper Town and the

Merchants Coffee House in the Lower Town. Twelve managers, six English (including English Committee member John Jones, an auctioneer) and six Canadiens organized the Upper Town gathering. That held in the Lower Town seems to have been more representative of political activists. The president was George Allsopp of the committee, and the vice-president, merchant Louis Germain fils – a signer of the 1784 petition and soon to be a candidate for election to the Assembly. Of the five delegates chosen to repair to their brother reformers up the hill for a joint toast, Jean-Antoine Panet and merchants Charles Pinguet, John Painter, and Mathew Lymburner (Adam's brother) were of the committees. If we are to judge by such Lower Town toasts as 'Prosperity to the Trade and Navigation of the two Provinces,' 'abolition of the Feudal system,' and 'Reformation to the laws of Canada' the alliance was still alive and well. Hope was in the air.

The Franks Tavern meeting generated such interest in the new regime that by mid-January 1792 about sixty who had attended met again to form a Constitutional Club to stimulate and disseminate knowledge of the British constitution both in its imperial and colonial manifestations. The first president was the doughty reformer William Grant, with seigneur Charles-Louis Tarieu de Lanaudière the first vice-president. By the beginning of February the club numbered at least eighty-three members and many more people would join in the next few weeks. In the late winter and spring of 1792 such topics as 'The Rights of Canadian Citizens,' the education of youth, the optimal qualifications for election to the Assembly, and the nefarious continuing campaign of the Canadien seigneurs against representative government were debated.[47]

THE ELECTION OF 1792

With one very important exception, treated in chapter 4, the alliance remained firm during the election, which saw six of the eight city seats taken by English merchants. Jean-Antoine Panet publicly supported the candidacy of Adam Lymburner in Quebec's Lower Town[48] and in a widely publicized anti-seigneur speech to the Constitutional Club, notary Alexandre Dumas appealed to Canadien electors to vote for capable liberal men of good judgment 'regardless of their ... nation and religion.'[49] Successful candidates William Grant (Upper Town) and James McGill (Montreal, West Ward) drew significant voting support from the Canadien middle class.[50] In the county of Montreal, Joseph Papineau and lawyer (later judge) James Walker, running as joint candidates, were returned unopposed, while Jacob Jordan's election in Effingham was warmly welcomed by Fleury Mesplet in his *Gazette*.[51]

The tone of the Montreal city elections had been set early on in May, when a number of prominent citizens of both nationalities advertised a slate of four candidates, all of whom were leading English fur merchants: Alexander Auldjo, Joseph Frobisher, McGill, and John Richardson. The nominators included three members of the local Canadien Committee: real estate developer Pierre Foretier, merchant Dumas Saint-Martin, and Papineau. At the end the same harmony prevailed with the election of Richardson and Frobisher in the East Ward by a very large and hence bi-ethnic majority – the cause of much celebrating at Dillon's Tavern, in which Canadien and English supporters joined in alcoholic *bonne entente*.[52]

The main force for constitutional liberalization and commercialization of the law had survived the passage of the Constitutional Act which made the English a small and seemingly permanent political minority. It also survived the first electoral campaign and the initial period of hostile reaction to the French Revolution. The alliance would not survive the later and more profound reaction to the Revolution and would begin to unravel in the winter of 1793.

The Election Results

A few words should be added here, if only to explain the ease with which the Château controlled the first legislature in 1794 and after, and to set the stage for the dramatic election results of 1796. The successful candidates fell into three major groups: the English group of fifteen, including several prominent merchants who had struggled for representative government (for example, Grant, John Young, Richardson, McGill) and a number of government officials. The Canadiens of the seigneurial class, numbering about fourteen (all but one in rural seats), had obviously succeeded with their scare tactics and appeals to the aristocratic right to govern.[53] The great majority of the seigneurs had, of course, opposed representative government, but the group also included the local 'Mirabeau,' Philippe de Rocheblave from the Canadien Committee.

Seventeen members represented the Canadien middle class, of whom fourteen were elected in rural ridings. This group included one surveyor, two lawyers, a notary-surveyor (Papineau), two notaries employed as court officials, and the remainder merchants. The majority were drawn from the upper levels of the bourgeoisie. Examples include lawyer Jean-

Antoine Panet, prominent grain exporter Louis Dunière, merchant-seigneur Hubert-Joseph Lacroix, JP, prosperous country merchants such as François La Roque, seigneur Pierre Legras Pierreville, accepted into the exclusive Canadien social set of Boucherville, and René Boileau, JP, a friend of the de Salaberry family. Two or three had opposed representative government, but the large majority had supported the idea. Some members, such as J.-A. Panet, Dunière, and Papineau, had sat on the Canadien committees.

Such was the composition of the Assembly as elected. It would be but slightly changed through by-elections held in February 1793. The high social status of most members – seigneurial class or upper bourgeoisie – stands out. Twenty-one members, for example, held the respected office of justice of the peace. Not surprisingly, then, despite the initial constitutional orientation of a majority of members, the first Assembly of 1792–6 would not resist the reaction against the French Revolution after the September Massacres of 1792 and would become a deferential, docile instrument in the hands of the governor.

ANGLICIZATION AND 'SURVIVANCE,' 1784–1793

Most of the English, of course, hoped the colonized subjects would lose much of their Canadien identity in time. There was no dearth of assimilating projects. Hugh Finlay, for example, wanted to 'make the people entirely English by introducing the English language. This is to be done by free schools, and by ordaining that all suits in our Courts shall be carried on in English after a certain number of years.' Loyalist lawyer Isaac Ogden advocated an almost identical plan in a document published in 1788 in the *Quebec Herald*.[54] Chief Justice Smith had worked out a grand design consisting of a secular university, the abolition of the seigneurial system, and the application of the common law to His Majesty's old subjects, all with the object of attracting massive immigration of American settlers – a proposal Mabane and friends fought unrelentingly. Smith hoped his cherished reforms and a federation of British North American colonies would create a strong, prosperous British dependency which would overshadow, and perhaps ultimately absorb, the United States.[55] A large proportion of the merchants were inclined to favour the abolition of the seigneurial system, as those who were seigneurs would become outright owners of the unconceded lands under freehold. Moreover, freehold would open vast tracts to American settlers, who had an ingrained aversion to anything resembling feudalism. The English merchants in general undoubtedly agreed with Lymburner that 'Nothing remains of the old feudal System that can render it advantageous to the Government or beneficial to the People.'[56]

Many in the colony, too, shared the interpretation of the American Revolution which had become standard among some loyalists and those British politicians and officials who concerned themselves with colonial affairs. According to this view, the differences in the colonial constitutions from the British model, the absence of a landed aristocracy, and the weakness of the Anglican Church had greatly facilitated the work of the revolutionaries.[57] The more a colony's institutions of all kinds were patterned after the British model, and the more colonial residents culturally resembled the citizens of the mother country, the more secure the imperial tie. Monk was only stating this conventional wisdom when he wrote that failure 'to change the language or manners of the people' so they could understand the value of British citizenship led to the loss of Minorca in 1756.[58]

While many English favoured assimilation, the question was not one of great urgency, as evidenced by the incompleteness of projects. Chief Justice Smith in *Gray v Grant* was willing to allow the Canadiens their civil laws outside the realm of commerce and this appears to have been almost universally conceded by the English élite.[59] No one apparently suggested the enforcement of the supremacy. The merchants may have wished for assimilation in all the laws but they were preoccupied only with ensuring the introduction of the British commercial rules.[60] In the petition of November 1784 – which remained the basis of their constitutional and political claims throughout the later 1780s and early 1790s – they specifically requested that the French civil law in general and the seigneurial system in particular be retained. And it is important to bear in mind that anglicization did not become the policy of the colonial government in the years prior to the French war.[61]

Restrictions imposed on the merchants by their political alliance with the Canadien bourgeoisie kept assimilating pressures in check. Also there was little economic need for assimilation. The fact that a majority of Canadiens were French-speaking, illiterate, Roman Catholic *censitaires* did not affect profits derived from the fur trade. The diplomatic situation, moreover, was such that Canadien cultural particularism did not appear as any great liability.[62] During the American Revolution the French Ministry of Foreign Affairs had decided that France must abandon any idea of reconquering Canada and this policy remained the orthodoxy until after 1792. As a result France showed little interest in Quebec during the mid and late 1780s, although an occasional rumour of such interest circulated in the colony.,[63] From 1789 to mid-1792 France, in the throes of revolution, appeared impotent to undertake any war, which indeed the revolutionaries had renounced as an instrument of policy.

On the other hand the American Revolutionary Army had invaded the colony in 1775–6 and American negotiators at Paris in 1781–2 had attempted to have Quebec included as a part of United States' territory. The series of acrimonious disputes over such things as unpaid loyalist claims and Westminster's refusal to surrender the western forts in American territory severely strained relations between Britain and the new republic. Thus in the late 1780s and early 1790s the United States rather than France appeared to pose the greater threat to security (reflected in extant documents),[64] and the repeated assertion of the French party that the Canadiens, because of their 'Religion, Language [,] Laws & Customs are the class of men the least likely to coalesce or unite with the Neighbouring States of America' made definite strategic sense. This consideration had convinced some of the English, Finlay regretfully noted, that 'the natives of this Province ought ... to be kept unmixed and unconnected with the other Colonists, to serve as a strong barrier between our Settlements and the United States.'[65] In summary, while most English in the late 1780s and early 1790s were predisposed to the idea of assimilating the Canadiens, few felt it an urgent question. It was not government policy and an influential minority contested the whole concept.

Most Canadiens appear to have had no clear sense of a permanent cultural destiny distinct from the English. Observers noted that a number of seigneurs were becoming anglified in language, dress, and manners. In one extreme case, dating from the 1790s, young Charles-Michel de Salaberry (later the hero of Chateauguay) wrote letters to his father in English.[66] No one yet glorified the agrarian way of life as a means of resisting assimilation. While the term 'la nation canadienne' or some variation was in common usage, it did not then imply, as it would in the years 1808–11, the preservation inviolate of the language, laws, and religion as a Canadien's highest secular duty.[67] On the contrary, a significant portion of the lay upper and middle classes supported the idea of a non-denominational, bi-national university. Some prominent Canadiens, such as constitutional reformer de Rocheblave, hoped a common school system and a liberal British System of government, in contrast to the despotic rule of New France, would dissolve differences between the two ethnic groups. The Canadien committees for representative government advocated the introduction of English commercial law and the English jury system (not to mention a British constitution). A number of leading Canadien politicians assumed that in due time the English language would, quite properly, become predominant throughout the colony.[68]

In summary, the continual confrontation between all-out anglification and rigid 'survivance' would be a later development stimulated in significant part by the French Revolution and the war and the reaction of the English élite to those events.

3

From Promise to Paranoia: The Impact of the Early French Revolution, 1789–1793

Bliss was it in that dawn to be alive,
But to be young was very Heaven! ...
When Reason seemed the most to assert her rights
When most intent on making of herself
A prime enchantress...
William Wordsworth, *The Prelude*, Book XI

One might as well think of establishing a republic of tigers in some forest in
Africa, as of maintaining a free government among such Monsters.
Samuel Romilly on the French revolutionaries,
September 1792

On 14 July 1789 the Bastille fell to the Paris crowd and the French Revolution began in earnest. When the news, some two and a half months later, reached Quebec, French- and English-speaking residents noticed the event: some with respect for the passing order, others with hopes of a better life for mankind, but all with wonder. No one, though, had the faintest inkling of how the startling events in far-off France would affect the people living in the valley of the St Lawrence. Unknown to contemporaries, a turning point in the history of Canada was at hand.

For constitutional liberals and persons favouring an equal, enlightened relationship between French- and English-speaking Canadians, the experience of the impact of the early French Revolution on Quebec/Lower

Canada is one of the saddest chapters in our history. The opportunity was lost for both ethnic groups to truly tolerate each other, as was the opportunity for the middle classes of each to gradually democratize the constitution and to reconcile paternalism with the needs of commerce. For the most part French affairs were initially seen through Words-worthian eyes: enlightenment and justice were promised to the whole world, regardless of background. This included French and English speaking, Roman Catholic and Protestant Quebeckers/Lower Canadians. Indeed, some expressed hope that the Revolution would do away with national and religious prejudices altogether – a hope which obviously encompassed the disappearance of the remaining animosities between old and new subjects as all became rational 'citizens.' By the onset of war in 1793 all such yearning, as well as aspirations for constitutional liberalization and commercialization of the civil law, were nearly doomed.

THE NEWSPAPER RESPONSE TO THE FRENCH REVOLUTION (1789–1792)

From the time it became evident towards the end of 1788 that Louis XVI would convoke the Estates General, the French Revolution was the major news story in Lower Canada.[1] The staggering variety of material published on the Revolution in its early months – forcing even British happenings into a poor second place – reflected public interest. Subscribers regularly supplied items on France to editors William Moore and Fleury Mesplet of the *Quebec Herald* and *Montreal Gazette*, with both remarking in February 1790 that the Revolution dominated conversations in Quebec and Montreal. The coverage and interest waned somewhat in the summer of 1790, but remained considerable until the second peak of fascination occurred after the September Massacres of priests and others in 1792.

Until that point the news was overwhelmingly favourable. Seventeen eighty-nine had apparently ushered in an era of liberty, equality, fraternity, and reason for all. The capture of the Bastille – tomb of untold Frenchmen – the surrender by aristocrats of their feudal rights, and the women's march to Versailles were celebrated in thousands of words. A letter written from France to a Montrealer, and published by Mesplet on Christmas Eve, 1789, claimed the key to scientific legislation had been found: 'All Friaries and Nunneries ... are seized in order to be sold for the good of the nation ... A total abolition of feudal rights ... An entire change in the civil and criminal laws. The administration of justice gratis. All kinds of tithes to be abolished ... Entire liberty of conscience throughout the kingdom. In short a thousand good laws for the happiness of Frenchmen.' As these glorious principles spread to the Low Countries, Spain, the Germanic nations, Poland, and Russia, national prejudices were apparently disappearing and soon the whole world would be under their sway.[2] One news item in the *Montreal Gazette* in February 1790 even predicted that within a decade the entire continent of South America would likely be freed from the tyranny of kings, nobles, and priests.

The euphoric coverage reflected, in part, the heavy reliance of the newspapers on reprints from journals in London and other British cities. And in England, during the first two years of the Revolution, opinion was very positive.[3] Many of the middle class saw in the Revolution the means to their own political enfranchisement at the expense of the aristocracy, the rationalization of the legal system (for example, Chancery delays, capital code, game laws) and, in the case of dissenters, the destruction of the privileges of the Church of England. Even the landed classes, including government ministers and senior officials, took a tolerant view of developments across the Channel. The revolutionaries were clearly emulating the Glorious Revolution of 1688–9. In any case, France had been reduced to impotence, a thoroughly just result in view of the Bourbons' support of the revolting Americans in 1778 and after. The local newspapers in Lower Canada reported these viewpoints, usually in the form of reprints from the English press.

The laudatory treatment owed a great deal, too, to the personal opinions of Moore, Mesplet, and Samuel Neilson of the *Quebec Gazette*, all of whom were constitutional liberals, enlightenment intellectuals, and – whether for Protestant or deistic reasons – adamantly opposed to the Roman Catholic Church. The editors' opinions were reflected in occasional comments, the choice of headlines, and material reprinted, and the selection of letters to publish.[4] Most interesting of all such examples was the sarcastic letter composed on the 'aristocratic couch' of one 'Horrificus de Maledissimus' which was published (in French only) by Neilson and reprinted by Mesplet in the early summer of 1791. This fictitious seigneur revealed massive ignorance and arrogance and in his letter propounded the view that 'the social order requires that nine tenths of the people be slaves of the other tenth.'

OTHER OPINION

The Early Proponents

Judging from the newspaper response to the early Revolution – and the total absence of critical comment in letters to the editor or pamphlets published in the colony – most of the politically interested population was favourable to or at least tolerant of Parisien developments.[5] It is even likely that government officials looked upon the Revolution with some benevolence.[6] Many doubtless shared the English landed classes' view that France was trying to imitate English constitutional history. One landowner in the Quebec City region who called himself 'Old Country Fellow' stated in 1793 that 'at the beginning of these affairs in France, I was a great admirer of the reformers: they seemed to me to be copying us, which appeared wise.' Many also must have welcomed the apparent weakening of France as just revenge on the Bourbons for aiding the American Revolutionaries. Writing in the context of the Bastille's capture, Montreal merchant John Richardson claimed his circle rejoiced in Louis's discomfiture: 'The Grand Monarque seems in a woeful plight – The Devil help him say we all here.'[7]

English and Canadien reformers were naturally predisposed to welcome news of the early Revolution. After all, they advocated constitutional liberalization, freedom of thought, and the march of science. Many resented the privileges accorded the Canadien seigneurs, seeing their opponents as advocates of despotic government. Reformers writing letters to the newspapers often used allusions and vocabulary sympathetic to the Revolution and in attempts to persuade Canadiens to support the campaign for representative government, explicit use was made of it. One 'Junius,' representing the English merchants, had drawn the connection in May 1789 and returned to the theme early in the next year. In the *Herald*, he attacked the narrow-minded selfishness of those who had supported the counter-petition. Citing reduced clerical stipends, less poverty, better education, and a spirit of industry, he advised his readers to concentrate on developments in their old mother country: 'You must be aware of the good effects felt by the enlightened people of France from the proceedings of the National Assembly.' In March 1790 Adam Lymburner, then in London, sent the English and Canadien committees for constitutional reform a packet of newspapers containing 'all the proceedings of the French National Assembly.' As he informed the secretary for the Quebec Canadien group, Lymburner had 'no doubt that the Committee will find lots of material appropriate to publish in order to show Canadians what is happening in France.'[8] And at a meeting held by the Montreal Société des Patriotes at the end of the year, the club's president rhapsodized on the theme of 'a renewed France, a people freed from oppression, a purified religion ... and an end to nobility, except of the heart and of deeds.' The members toasted Lafayette, Mirabeau, and 'a House of Assembly for this province and its supporters.'[9] Mesplet published the proceedings in the French section of the *Gazette* to insure wider publicity.

The Society, consisting mainly of young Canadien reformers, met from time to time to sing patriotic songs, discuss French news, particularly in relation to local politics, and to study the works of the *philosophes*. From this last pursuit a strong streak of anti-clericalism developed. According to one of the leading lights, Henri Mezière, the society numbered more than two hundred by 1792.[10] Mezière, son of a conservative Montreal lawyer and a printer at Mesplet's *Gazette*, was eighteen years old in 1790. Soon after graduating with honours from the Sulpician College he had come across the startling works of Rousseau, Mably, Montesquieu, and other 'friends of the truth':

I devoured their works, which taught me my duties and my rights and gave me a hatred of civil and religious tyranny. For the first time I was happy to be alive.

The French Revolution, which dawned at that time, completed what my reading had begun. From that moment all my affections, all my desires had to do with Liberty. The idea of it obsessed me day and night, my only regret being that I could do no more than love it.[11]

Mezière also boasted of having turned the *Montreal Gazette* into a 'vehicle of reason.' Among the products of Mesplet's press which his young printer likely composed or solicited was a pamphlet provocatively entitled 'Bastille of the North,' which unmasked the tyranny practised by Canadien militia officers at Trois-Rivères, who had imprisoned three English residents for insubordination.[12] More controversial was a fero-cious attack on the Roman Catholic clergy taken from a French pamphlet printed in the *Gazette* towards the end of 1790. The extract, which Mesplet announced had the approval of the Société des Patriotes, made liberal use of Voltaire to expose the clergy as hypocrites, swindlers, eunuchs, perpetrators of atrocity, and so on, and called for the establishment of Deism in a 'RELIGION NATIONALE.' Such rampant anti-Catholicism went beyond the tolerance of Mesplet's Canadien readers. To pacify the many complainants he hastily promised not to print articles which struck at the basic dogmas of any religion, a promise honoured mainly in the breach.

The reaction to the French Revolution in Lower Canada was largely a safe middle-class one of words, not actions; of detached intellectual appreciation, not emotional involvement. There was nothing comparable to the earnest letter writing, publications, petitioning, and mass meetings of the francophile societies in Great Britain. This was probably due to the fundamental irrelevance of the Revolution to the middle and upper class in Lower Canada, where most careers and honours were open to talented persons of the middle ranks (at least those with contacts), where establishment of an elected Assembly was in the works as early as 1789, where religious freedom was greater than in the old country, and where the seigneurial system was usually seen as a pale replica of French feudalism. In terms of self-interest the English merchants were concerned most with the introduction of common law in commercial matters. This had nothing to do with developments in France, and the Canadiens of the middle class saw their social elevation in representative government. Not surprisingly, neither group exhibited much resistance when opinion began to turn strongly against the Revolution.

THE CONSTITUTION OF 1791 AND THE FRENCH REVOLUTION

Because of the coincidence in time and the appeals made to the example of France by pro-assembly Canadiens, it might be thought that Britain granted representative government to Lower Canada in order to inoculate the Canadiens from the contagion of the French Revolution. Such an interpretation has been advanced more than once. It seems to have held favour in young Mezière's circle of enthusiastic francophiles.[13] This idea has cropped up at various times among political radicals and even among professional historians. Indeed, the most detailed scholarly analysis of the impact of the French Revolution on Lower Canada interpreted the 1791 reform in terms reminiscent of Mezière. According to Claude Galarneau, the speed with which Grenville acted on the Canadian constitutional morass 'is explained by fear of the contagious effects the French Revolution might have on the Canadiens.' London granted an elected assembly 'in large part because of worry lest the Canadiens become aroused by the inspiration of the Revolution triumphant.'[14]

Not a shred of hard evidence is offered to support this viewpoint and many objections to it seem insuperable. The architect of the Constitutional Act, William Grenville, opted for assemblies primarily as a mean of reducing the financial deficit. True, the secretary of state was also convinced that constitutional change was essential in the interests of security. But the groups he was hoping to appease were English, not Canadien, and the revolutionary influence which disturbed him was that of 1776, not 1789. As Grenville perceived the state of colonial opinion, the pro-assembly Canadiens were a small minority. There were indeed 'some of the Canadian, or French inhabitants, who have signed the [reform] Petitions,' he wrote in 1789, 'but ... the Habitants or Farmers who compose the Bulk of the Community are unacquainted with the nature of the Question, & indifferent to it.' The clergy, moreover, had remained neutral and the natural leaders of the society (in Grenville's view), 'the Canadian Gentry or Noblesse, in general, oppose it.'[15] This is hardly the language of a man concerned to undermine the dangerous influence being exerted on Canadiens by the Declaration of the Rights of Man.

The English merchants led the agitation for an assembly, Grenville thought, and the loyalists sooner or later would become allies of that dissatisfied group. The 'neighbourhood of the American States' and the predictable growth of the English in wealth and numbers made it 'impossible that the people of Canada should acquiesce for any considerable length of time, in continuance of a system at all resembling that under which they are now governed.' It was, he believed, 'a point of true Policy to make these Concessions at a time when they may be received as matter of favour ... rather than to wait 'till they shall be extorted from Us.'[16] All this was written in the typical accents of those many politicians still haunted by the American Revolution. Republicanism was indeed perceived as a dangerous malady. But it was a North American malady and one that had not then travelled to France. There, centuries of kings made it difficult, initially, to see beyond crown and sceptre and almost all shades of revolutionary opinion remained monarchist until Louis XVI's abortive flight to Varennes in June 1791.

Neither Grenville nor other British cabinet ministers could have been alarmed at developments across the Channel during the period of Canadian constitutional policy making (August 1789 to June 1791). This was a time when the landed classes in England tended to look upon the French Revolution as a flattering imitation of Britain's constitutional monarchy. Official circles, moreover, viewed the uprisings as having drastically and conveniently weakened France, a viewpoint fully shared by Pitt and his secretary of state. In the one known document relating to the Canadian constitution in which the secretary referred to the French Revolution he expressed this same conventional wisdom: 'Your Lordship [Dorchester] will perceive, by the different accounts, which you will receive from Europe, that the state of France is such, as gives Us little to fear from that quarter in the present moment. The opportunity is therefore most favourable for the adoption of such measures as may tend to consolidate Our strength, and increase our resources, so as to enable Ourselves to meet any efforts that the most favorable event of the present troubles can ever enable her to make.'[17]

Developments in contemporary France undoubtedly influenced the British government, as represented by Grenville, in its Canadian constitutional policy. The chaotic plight of the French court obviously encouraged the secretary of state to embark on a far-reaching restructuring of government in Canada in order to press Britain's advantage over its rival power. Moreover, French happenings, because they were at first so favourably interpreted, made it politically very difficult at home to withhold electoral institutions from Quebec.[18] In the late summer or early autumn of 1789 Grenville wrote that 'considering the general temper of the present moment' it would hardly be possible to 'maintain with success' the denial 'to so large a body of British Subjects, the benefits of the British Constitution.' Perhaps the secretary was concerned that democratic ideas emanating from France might strongly reinforce the reform demands of the English merchants, but if so he did not mention it in the relevant documents. Fear that the Canadiens might be encouraged to revolt, to riot, or even to petition in embarrassing numbers if representative government were denied probably never entered his thinking.

The Early Opponents

Not everyone in Lower Canada, of course, welcomed the early Revolution. In a widely publicized address to the Quebec Grand Jury in November 1789, Chief Justice Smith likely expressed the dominant viewpoint of his fellow Loyalists and of those government officials who supported legal reform, but were concerned about the introduction of representative government. It was the 'prayer of our common humanity,' he said, that France would emerge as the enlightened nation the revolutionaries aimed for. But at the moment 'their miseries teach us a lesson' and that was a simple one: the two nationalities should cease all squabbling and blend into a single people, the unspoken premise being that the Canadiens should do more of the blending. To bolster his thesis, Smith found new and benevolent meaning in the British conquest of New France:

... if there is an ancient Canadian alive, that has heretofore repined at his separation from his original flock, let him, now the curtain of divine providence is drawn, lift up his hands with thanksgiving, that this country escapes the complicated afflictions and sorrows, which involve all branches of that empire.

Canada was conquered – but conquered into liberty, and engrafted into such a constitution as the French admired; and which after a deluge of blood, they may never be able to erect and establish for themselves...
All praise therefore to the arbiter of the Universe!

As Leslie Upton aptly noted, it was Smith in 1789, not the Canadien clergy in the 1790s, who invented the providential interpretation of the Conquest. The chief justice would regularly reiterate his thesis until his death in 1793.[19]

The overwhelming majority of the Canadien clergy were suspicious of the Revolution at least from the time news arrived that the First Estate of France had been submerged in the National Assembly, a body dominated by freethinkers. Suspicion soon became hostility with the abolition of feudal dues and tithes, toleration of Protestantism, the suppression of monasteries, the drafting, enforcement, and papal condemnation of the Civil Constitution of the Clergy (providing for the election of priests), the confiscation of valuable properties held in France by the Seminary of Quebec and other clerical bodies, and the stripping of powers from His Most Christian Majesty – an affront to believers in divine right. And the local political situation suggested an unholy alliance of anti-clerical Canadiens and Protestant merchants attempting to bring the Revolution into the valley of the St Lawrence. As Henri-François Gravé, superior of the Quebec Seminary worried: 'those who in my opinion think a little are very angry about this change [passage of the Constitutional Act], since there are several of our bumped up Canadiens and many English, admirers of the National Assembly, who already talk of making the Rights of Man the basis of legislation.'[20] While hostile, the Canadien clergy, doubtless recognizing the prevailing favourable opinion, did not openly condemn the early Revolution.

Although the evidence is thin, most Canadien seigneurs and English officials in the French party probably reacted with suspicion or hostility to the early Revolution. This was almost certainly so by the first months of 1790, when news of bloody peasant uprisings against the noblesse reached the colony. Also, during the last weeks of 1789 the correspondence received from relatives in France by some of the most prominent seigneurs had begun to take on the apprehensive, critical tone, which would deepen as the months passed.[21] And it was only too apparent that the energy of their detested political opponents was being stimulated by developments in France. Hard evidence of negative attitudes dates, however, only from the first half of 1791. While the French party supporters continued their prudent silence in print, at least in speaking with their friends they portrayed local francophile advocates of an Assembly as dangerous incendiaries. However, the French party leader, Judge Mabane, referring to the Constitutional bill submitted by the Pitt government to Parliament, wrote unambiguously in June 1791: 'Those who had been most forward in making Applications for a new Constitution as it is called, appear the most dissatisfied with the one proposed, and I make no doubt will by their Conduct evince that they wish for no Government at all, and that they are as much infected with a Rage for the Abstract Rights of Man as the most enthusiastic or most daring of the National Assembly of France.'[22] Edmund Burke, it appears, had made his first convert in Quebec.

Mabane and people who thought like him represented a mostly silent minority. In these early years the French Revolution acted as a potential force for ethnic harmony in Lower Canada. Religious tolerance, dissipation of natural prejudice, assessment of institutions such as the whole corpus of law on a rational rather than ethnic basis, and a shared appreciation that France, the motherland of the Canadiens, was taking its place among the most enlightened nations of the world seemed to promise much along these lines. Perhaps the bi-national dinners held at the end of December 1791 in Quebec's Upper and Lower Towns to celebrate the coming into force of the Constitutional Act best reveal that promise. Several of the toasts, implicitly or expressly lauded developments in France, as well as liberal highlights of British history and expressed hope that ethnic differences and the terminology of old and new subjects could be swept away in a common status of Canadian citizens.[23] But these interesting attempts to change the language of political and personal discourse soon floundered. It was evident even before the end of 1791 that opinion was becoming less favourable to the Revolution.

THE INITIAL PERIOD OF REACTION, NOVEMBER 1791 TO SEPTEMBER 1792

In the wake of Louis's flight to Varennes, the growth of republicanism in France, and the popular disturbances of 1791, opinion in Britain among the landed classes and upper levels of the middling ranks began to shift. A similar reaction occurred towards the end of that year in Lower Canada, particularly among the more affluent English reformers. In November 1791 John Richardson, who only two years before had accepted the Revolution with serenity, expressed the hope, which he claimed was shared by other Montrealers, that the first fruits of the new legislature would be the introduction of English laws. This was so, he explained to a correspondent, because 'we must confess ourselves enemies to every thing à la François, both as to their old & new systems, we mean tyranny & licentiousness.' As for Quebec, Neilson reported that public opinion was becoming seriously divided by the Revolution.[24]

The celebrations in Montreal and Quebec City to greet the inauguration of the constitution on 26 December 1791 neatly illustrate the changing attitude to France among reformers. According to the historian François-Xavier Garneau, a number of young Canadiens (presumably Mezière's group) met in Montreal to celebrate the new order, with toasts to the abolition of feudal tenure, civil and religious freedom, liberty of the press, and the French and Polish revolutions. The English merchants of the city, by contrast, held no celebrations at all. In Quebec's Lower Town Canadien and English campaigners for representative government toasted 'The abolition of the Feudal system' and 'The French Revolution, and true liberty to the whole world.' In the Upper Town the celebrants were less forthright. Some of the toasts indeed seem to have been influenced by the late events in France, such as: 'May the New constitution speak the will ... of the people' and 'May all civil distinctions among Men be founded on public utility.' But there was no explicit reference to the French Revolution, the safe Glorious Revolution of 1688–9 being honoured instead. Other signs of the times included rule sixteen of the Constitutional Club, which the members unanimously adopted on 21 January 1792: 'No subject whatever, relating to Religion, or the late Revolution in France, can be debated in this Club.'[25]

While the reaction had begun, there remained a minority strand of pro-Revolution opinion. Liberally minded Canadiens especially continued to applaud the Revolution, which is not surprising as they were less influenced by developments in England than their English confrères. On New Year's Day of 1792 the Quebec sculptor-woodcarver François Baillargé recorded in his journal that '1792 is the first year of liberty for the country' and decorated the entry with two drawn heads, on one of which was the symbolic Phrygian cap.[26] Another illustration is a speech made to the Constitutional Club by notary Alexandre Dumas in May 1792, denouncing the continuing attempts by the French party to blacken the new constitution. If perpetrators of these lies were to succeed in their aim of convincing the habitants to refrain from voting, Dumas contended, they would deprive the Canadiens of a free government, 'which the most enlightened peoples of Europe desire and seem disposed to acquire at the price of their blood and their fortunes.'

During the election campaign of May–June 1792 a fascinating French-language pamphlet appeared, entitled *Dialogue sur l'Intérêt du Jour, entre plusieurs Candidats et un Electeur libre et indépendant de la Cité de Québec* and published by a group calling itself 'une Société d'Amis de la Patrie et de la Constitution.'[27] Although printed by William Moore, it emanated almost certainly from a radical minority of the Constitutional Club. This group had as its leading figures Dumas and two Canadiens from France: Dr Timothée O'Connor and innkeeper Alexandre Menut. Menut had grown up in France, while O'Connor had studied medicine in that country before setting out for Quebec in 1786, where he soon married a Canadienne and set up shop as an apothecary, surgeon, and physician. All three detested the Canadien seigneurs and had given speeches to the club on that point.

Eschewing all ethnic distinction the *Dialogue* made a Jacobin-type appeal against the social élite (Canadien and English), broadly defined to include the middling ranks. Speaking in the vocabulary of contemporary Paris, the pamphlet bristled with references to 'Citizens,' the 'General Will,' 'natural rights,' 'equality,' the Deist 'Supreme Being,' and so on. After listening to the seigneur who represented feudal privilege, a black-habited and lugubrious advocate who robbed widows and children, and a gambling merchant who caused famines, the elector promised one vote to the artisanal candidate and one for the habitant, since these men alone were useful producers who could properly represent the General Will. The pamphlet concluded by insisting the 145,000 working people of Lower Canada should rule the 5,000 bourgeois and seigneurial parisites, not the other way round.

The *Dialogue* represented the high-water mark of positive, public reaction in the colony to the French Revolution. And it would be many generations before any document so critical of the Canadien élite would be published by Canadiens in French Canada.

REVULSION, OCTOBER 1792 TO MAY 1793

With the imprisonment of the king in August 1792, the September massacres, the abolition of monarchy, the fraternité decree of 19 November promising aid to republican revolutionaries abroad, the execution of Louis (21 January 1793) and the growing menace of war (finally declared by the Republic on 1 February 1793), opinion in Britain towards the Revolution became ever more unanimous in vociferous denunciation. Except among artisans, labourers, and a few intellectuals, the Revolution was now seen as an experiment which degraded man, fostered anarchy, and posed a dangerous threat to the British social order. Liberty, equality, and fraternity were chimeras or, worse, pretexts for a redistribution of wealth through mob rule, at which Thomas Hardy, Horne Tooke, and their associates in the reform societies clearly aimed.[28] The radical Whig Charles James Fox was heartbroken about the descent into violence in France, while a shocked Pitt began to gear the country for war. The law reformer Samuel Romilly had been purely Wordsworthian in his ecstasy over the promise held out by the early Revolution. Now, in September 1792, he gave vent to visceral hatred in a passage which might have been written by thousands of his countrymen:

How could we ever be so deceived in the character of the French nation as to think them capable of liberty! wretches, who, after all their professions and boasts about liberty ... employ whole days in murdering women, and priests, and prisoners! ... the cold instigators of these murders, who, while blood is streaming round them on every side ... reason about it, and defend it, nay, even applaud it, and talk about the example they are setting to all nations. One might as well think of establishing a republic of tigers in some forest in Africa, as of maintaining a free government among such Monsters.[29]

The news as printed in the *Quebec Gazette* from mid-October and in John Neilson's *Quebec Magazine – Le Magazine de Québec* which had begun publication shortly before, mirrored dominant opinion in the old country. Gruesome and condemnatory accounts were given of the September massacres and Louis's execution. In Montreal Mesplet resisted the reaction for some time, but began to wobble in the second week of December. By mid-May he finally declared his new colours, characterizing the revolutionaries as 'monsters' and 'wild beasts' whose sole aim was the bloody overthrow of peaceful societies everywhere in the world.

The depth of reaction was not confined to the newspapers. As in England, Lower Canadians increasingly came to view the Revolution as a rising of the unpropertied rabble against wealth, rank, respectability, and all law. This viewpoint was reflected by several persons who wrote letters to the papers. 'A Citizen of this town' decried the 'glorious fruits of modern Philosophy, and of that spirit of innovation ... which instead of attempting with prudence the Reform of abuses ... cut up every thing ... even ... the ancient and ever respectable foundations of the social and Religious state.' Others, who had also read their Burke and their Hobbes (including a much chastened 'Old Country Fellow') flailed away at the dangers of allowing inherently selfish human beings undue liberty and of promoting an equality of property. The application of these abstract principles would bring any country to economic ruin, political anarchy, and endless crimes of violence. The British way of life, with its graded social ranks, true equality before the law, respect for religion and governmental authority, carefully confined specific liberties, and the balanced constitution (proof against mob rule as well as executive tyranny), stood in brilliant contrast to the benighted nation across the Channel. These letters also reveal the beginnings of a conspiracy interpretation of the French Revolution. To 'Britannicus,' writing to the *Quebec Magazine* in February 1793, for example, the revolutionaries were properly described as 'those pretended Apostles of peace and good will to Society, but real Apostles of Sedition and treachery.'

The September massacres, in which over a thousand alleged counterrevolutionaries imprisoned in Paris (including dozens of priests, among them two Canadian-born) were murdered by rampaging crowds, – elicited utter disgust.[30] In January 1793, for example, seigneur Chartier de Lotbinière told the Assembly that modern Frenchmen had taken to human slaughter 'with a ferocity and barbarity worthy [only] of the cruellest of cannibals.'[31] The execution of 'His Most Christian Majesty' was even more staggering, particularly to the Canadian seigneurs and clergy for whom Louis was God's appointed ruler of the once great country of their origin. 'Infamous beasts! They have guillotined their king,' cried the seigneur Pierre-Ignace Aubert de Gaspé when he first learned the news. One priest wished that the clergy of France had enveloped the king with their bodies and died at his feet, rather than emigrating as they had done,[32] and Montreal merchant Samuel Gerrard wrote in late April that the 'Inhumanity and barbarity of France is the general theme of conversation in this place' – even the news of war was 'almost forgotten in the dreadful detail of the French King's murder.'[33]

The Assembly's proceedings during the first legislative session (December 1792 to May 1793) clearly reveal the rejection of the French Revolution. Given that the majority of members had supported the reformers' far-reaching constitutional program, one might have expected such proposals as bills to establish the independence of the judiciary, to emulate Fox's Libel Act and provide for the election of sheriffs, as well as petitions to entrench habeas corpus, make legislatures triennial, and repeal the Quebec Revenue Act. Nothing was done along these lines. The sole constitutional initiative of the house was an assertion of financial privilege as against the Legislative Council. On 28 March, Richardson moved that the house legally enjoy the same exclusive privileges as the House of Commons in originating tax and supply bills. This was defeated seventeen to sixteen but in early April Richardson managed to convince the house to lay aside bills from the Council on the debatable ground that imposing fines amounted to levying a charge on the public.[34] This would be the last clear assertion by the Assembly for over a decade of a privilege in new or contestable areas and the last such initiative supported by the English parliamentary contingent throughout the period under study. Indeed, within two years the Assembly, led again by Richardson, would abandon its position on the Council's originating (or amending) bills imposing fines.[35]

More representative of opinion in the first session was the fate of proposed legislation dealing with the selection of returning officers. The Legislative Council sent down a bill providing that these officials be chosen by the voters, only to find the elected house determined not to interfere with the royal prerogative![36] As an added sign of the times, almost all members refused to be called 'democrats,' which meant admirers of the French Revolution and had been an honourable title only two years before. As early as March 1793 'Anglo-Canadien' – obviously a radical Whig – complained in the *Quebec Magazine* that the great majority of members thought that using the appellation would be a disgraceful breach of the spirit of the constitution. The word was taking on connotations of social envy and treachery in the interests of a foreign power.

A few individuals such as 'Anglo-Canadien' resisted the trend. In Quebec the Constitutional Club for a few months in 1792 – discussed French affairs and sang patriotic songs at its infrequent meetings. The *coup de grace* was administered upon the outbreak of war when government officials let it be known that membership in such organizations would bring charges of sedition. 'Scepticus' was another resister. In early April he complained to the *Quebec Gazette* that in conversations many people expressed opinions on the Revolution 'as illiberal as they are ill founded, given out with all the arrogance and self-sufficiency of Aristocratic insolency or ignorance,' and concluded 'I am convinced that the French Revolution, however it may turn out, must be of advantage to mankind, by kindling a spirit of inquiry among men, into the various truths, errors, and prejudices by which they are governed.' Such sentiments would not again appear in the Lower Canada newspapers for as long as the French Revolution lasted. And at the time of publication they must have horrified the colonial élite, particularly the English portion of it.

GROWING NERVOUSNESS AMONG THE ENGLISH ÉLITE

By the late autumn of 1792 important segments of the English élite feared that the French Revolution might exercise a dangerous attraction among the Canadiens, now furnished with an elected house which they could control. Writing from Quebec in December 1792, the Duke of Kent described for a friend the judgment of 'the most sensible and experienced people here,' who remembered that the American and French revolutions had been provoked by representative assemblies. The 'situation in France,' he wrote, 'having occasioned such a general fermentation ... may sooner or later work on the minds of the people here, and be productive of consequences which can be paralleled only by those, thro' which England unfortunately lost the American colonies.' These same people quite naturally now thought 'that the new constitution was not perfectly well timed.'[37] The nervous saw clear confirmation in the bitter debates over language in the first session.

The details of these disputes need only be touched on.[38] Principally, the issues involved the election of Jean-Antoine Panet as Speaker, even though he was then not perfectly fluent in English, and whether English should be the sole official language of the legislature, particularly of statute law.[39] Acrimonious debates divided the Assembly along ethnic lines. Merchants John Richardson, William Grant, John Lees, James McGill, and John Young took the lead on one side and were opposed by an ad hoc alliance of Canadien seigneurs such as De Bonne, Gabriel-Elzéar Taschereau, and de Lotbinière with such bourgeois members as Panet, Papineau, and young Quebec lawyer, Pierre-Stanislas Bédard. While the view was commonly expressed by Canadien speakers that the future spread of the English language was to be welcomed, all but lawyer-seigneur Pierre-Louis Panet adamantly resisted its immediate establishment as the sole official language. If this were to happen, said Taschereau, 'our liberty becomes an illusion proving our slavery.' De Bonne was even more acerbic. According to Quebec merchant John Painter, De Bonne 'said that the Constitution was given for the express benefit of the Canadians' and that if 'the few old subjects inhabiting here ... did not like the mode which the Canadians might think necessary to adopt in enacting laws, they might easily retire from the Country by the same road they enterd [sic] it.'[40] The Assembly ultimately adopted resolutions that the Journals be kept in both languages, motions and bills be translated, and that the official texts of bills/statutes be English in the criminal law area and French in civil law matters. The colonial secretary quickly undermined this by instructing Lord Dorchester to assent only to English versions of bills.[41]

Many of the politically active among the English interpreted the Canadien stance on the language issue as the selfish response of ingrates.[42] Others adopted a more sinister construction. Richardson thought his Assembly opponents were divided into two factions: the Canadien seigneurs and the middle ranks. The latter group, consisting of men such as Papineau and Panet, was particularly to be feared: 'there are two Parties amongst the French – one obnoxious to the New Constitution, as they opposed our procuring it – the other more dangerous as being infected with the detestable principles now prevalent in France.' James McGill likewise attributed Canadien recalcitrance on the language question to the fact that the 'French revolution and Mr Paines Book on the rights of man have turned peoples Heads.'[43]

THE ONSET OF WAR

On 25 April 1793 Lieutenant-Governor Alured Clarke informed the legislature that war against Great Britain had been declared by the 'persons exercising the supreme authority in France.' The Assembly responded by passing a unanimous address expressing horror at Louis XVI's execution, 'the most atrocious Act which ever disgraced society.' The address also promised to make any changes needed in the militia laws to protect the province from His Majesty's enemies, but none was in fact made until the subsequent session.[44]

In the first few weeks after the declaration of war, government officials must have drawn confidence from the appearance of loyal unity. The legislature could be counted on to cooperate in the war effort, the francophile societies had been suppressed (in the next year or so several determined radicals, including Mezière and O'Connor, would emigrate to a safer political climate in the United States) and the English community was no longer divided politically.It seemed likely, too, that the Canadien clergy and seigneurs, although French in origin, would lend all support to the crown. This proved to be the case.

Attitudes of the Clergy, Seigneurs, and Bourgeoisie

During the war against revolutionary France the clergy worked in a great variety of ways to foster internal security. The hierarchy sanctioned the practice of refusing the sacraments to persons suspected of republican sentiments[45] and the clergy were active in attempting to make the Canadien working people obey the militia and road laws. More important, they devoted countless hours sermonizing, addressing, and privately indoctrinating their parishioners in the need for loyalty. Obedience to the established secular power and the monstrous happenings in the old mother country were emphasized, as were the providential thesis and the many positive benefits of British rule: the religious section of the Quebec Act, a civilized criminal law, prosperity, limited militia duty, and much more. Some of these communications – particularly those delivered in the Quebec Cathedral in June 1794 by Joseph-Octave Plessis on the death of Bishop Briand and celebrating Nelson's Victory of the Nile (in 1799) – were theologically sophisticated.[46] Others were not. According to one usually reliable source, by early 1794 many curés were telling their flocks that modern Frenchmen thought it permissible to murder one's parents if they became a nuisance.[47]

Besides giving unquestioned support to the government in the legislature, the Canadien seigneurs, in general, could be relied upon to report the doings of suspicious characters, to instruct their tenants on French atrocities, and voice utter disgust with the principles of 1789.[48] Referring to Canadien society in 1795, a British traveller named Guillemard wrote that the 'upper class, consisting of the seigneurs and men attached to the English government, hate the French Revolution in all its principles and seem on this point more extreme than the British Ministry itself.'[49]

While some of the English suspected political activists among the Canadien bourgeoisie to be dangerous francophiles, the evidence suggests that in general the Canadien middle class was loyal, one indication being the unanimous condemnation of Louis XVI's execution by the Assembly. Appalled by the violence in France, the bourgeoisie, like the clergy and seigneurs, could contemplate a French reconquest only with horror. As Guillemard put it, the 'second class of Canadians, [politically] opposed to the seigneurs and gentry, applaud the French Revolution for its principles, but detest the crimes it has spawned.'[50] By the end of the century the Canadien bourgeoisie were moving beyond what Guillemard noted in 1795 to condemn the Revolution in principle. To cite but one example, poet-playwright Joseph Quesnel composed a satirical drama script (1800 or 1801) on Robespierre's republic, which had bequeathed to mankind, not liberty, equality, and fraternity, but licentiousness, bloody dictatorship, and divorce.[51]

The observation that the Canadien bourgeoisie formed an opposition party was substantially accurate, although Guillemard exaggerated its importance at the time. By 1794, though, the unnatural alliance of seigneurs and middle-class Canadiens, operative during the official language dispute, was on the wane. An identifiable group of opposition MPPs, numbering six core members (but attracting others from time to time) and following the lead of Joseph Papineau and Jean-Antoine Panet, had emerged and seemed determined to replace the seigneurs as the political spokesmen for French Canada. They were of the middle ranks, with the exception of de Rocheblave.[52] It seems perfectly proper to refer to these men as the *parti canadien*, even though that term has usually been reserved to the majority grouping under Pierre-Stanislas Bédard after 1800.[53] By early 1795 the *parti canadien* was already at work organizing against the seigneurs in the rural constituencies and the behaviour of its members in the house was calculated to drive home the message that neither the government, the English élite, nor the Canadien landholders were to be trusted. In 1795-6 they attempted to bring the simmering discontent with illegal seigneurial exactions to a boil, opposed new road corvées, and fought the punitive Engagés bill aimed at voyageurs. The opposition politicians failed in these endeavours, but such stands contributed greatly to their growing popularity, which would be evident in the general election of 1796.

Few have noticed that Papineau, Panet, and their lieutenants were the first constitutional liberals of note in Canadian parliamentary history – that is, after the introduction of representative government – an honour usually reserved to Bédard and his followers a decade or so later. During the first legislature the *parti canadien* manifested a clear inclination to protect the individual against the state and the Assembly against the executive at a time when Tories and moderate Whigs, at home and in the colony, insisted that all right-thinking men embrace the royal prerogative. In 1794, for example, the group attempted to amend bills so as to provide for a politically independent judiciary, to establish trial by jury in all suits involving the crown, and to prevent internment of suspected traitors for more than eight days.[54] The next year they tried – again without success – to enact into law the principle that supply voted to the governor should be periodically subject to review by the legislature.[55] Although often called democrats by opponents, they were Whiggish reformers, not revolutionaries, not even republicans. Panet might remain convinced of the noble sentiments in the Declaration of the Rights of Man, but didn't dare say so publicly. Papineau might write privately in 1796 that the General Will is 'the most just and the voice of the people is in effect the voice of God'[56] but in public popular sovereignty meant to him only the right to advance the interests of the voters politically and to protect the powers of the Assembly in the balanced British constitution.

On learning that hostilities had broken out, Samuel Gerrard explained to an unknown correspondent 'the disagreeable situation into which this Country is involved by the declaration of War.' The loyal sons of Britain were surrounded by erstwhile citizens of France and they were Frenchmen still at heart: 'mark the partiality of the Canadians to their former Government, many, nay the greatest part of whom, can scarcely be pursuaded [sic] that the great and mighty King of the French had been put to Death by his own Subjects.'[57] Even though the danger did not seem immediate, two questions must have been pondered by many of the English élite that spring: would France make an attempt on its former colony? and if so, what would be the response of the Canadien working people? These two questions would continue to be posed throughout the war.

4

The Security Danger, 1793–1798

Lower Canada twice experienced severe security crises in the years 1793–7. Both featured plans by revolutionary France to invade the colony – undercover activity by enemy agents (foreign and domestic) or 'emissaries' in the jargon of the times; and serious province-wide rioting, which revealed the grave difficulties of maintaining order in the days before professional police. Both also featured paranoid alarm – the 'garrison mentality' – among the English élite of merchants, seigneurs, professionals, and government officials, including judges. The garrison mentality in turn resulted in draconian security legislation and a manipulation of the courts.

THE EXTERNAL DANGER, 1793–1794

Citizen Edmond Genêt, appointed as French minister to the United States, was nothing if not an optimist. This young Girondist ambassador revelled in his instructions to press the Americans for a joint expedition to unite the 'beautiful star of Canada' to the 'American constellation.'[1] When President Washington declared neutrality on 23 April 1793, Genêt enthusiastically reinterpreted his mission. To bring the truth of regenerated Frenchmen to their brothers, to help them escape from British oppression, the minister wrote in June, would be his crowning glory. Using New York as the base, Genêt soon established a powder magazine, arsenal, and barracks and recruited an irregular army of about twenty-five hundred (mainly American adventurers and Irish and French residents of the city). He also hoped to recruit Vermont frontiersmen for an attack down the Richelieu River and to make use of the French West Indian fleet, then at anchor in New York. At one stage, this irrepressible young man intended using these fifteen or so ships to destroy British fishing stations in Newfoundland, recapture St Pierre and Miquelon, burn Halifax, seize the fur convoy from Hudson Bay, liberate the Canadiens, destroy the Nassau base of British privateers, and capture New Orleans from Spain. All this would succeed, he thought, because of the surprise factor!

A kindred spirit, Henri Mezière, who in May 1793 had walked from Montreal to Philadelphia to offer his services to the French minister, assisted in formulating Genêt's Canadian policy. Mezière soon prepared a memorandum on Canada, revealing a mind where enthusiasm made short work of facts.[2] But Genêt used Mezière's ideas and some of his own to draft an inflammatory document entitled *Les Français libres à leurs frères les Canadiens*, which attributed the callous abandonment of Canada at the Conquest to the evil Bourbons, outlined the revolutionary paradise, and promised that enlightened France would help her former subjects to find it should they rebel.[3] The pamphlet dealt with such arcane subjects as free trade, the royal veto on legislation, an elected clergy, civilizing missions to the Indians, and careers open to talent, as well as more understandable matters such as the abolition of clerical tithes, corvées, and other seigneurial rights, establishment of a republic and political independence in alliance with France and the United States. By late summer Mezière, ensconced at Lake Champlain in upper New York State, sent Jacques Rousse, an expatriate Canadien, into Lower Canada with 350 copies of *Les Français libres* and a variety of other propaganda. In February 1794 Rousse reported that he had circulated the pamphlet, together with copies of revolutionary songs, American newspapers, a justification of Louis's execution, and Thomas Paine's democratic *Rights of Man*, in all parishes of the province. He had made contact with local sympathizers who agreed to ensure Canadiens would not take up arms if France attacked.[4]

By October 1793 Genêt had toned down his strategic extravaganza, dropping the southern campaign and the visit to Quebec. The officers of the French fleet at New York considered even this scheme excessive and after a council of war at sea, sailed back to France. Thus disappeared Genêt's only realistic weapon to test the effect his emissaries were having on the Canadiens. Thus disappeared, too, Henri Mezière who had been attached to the admiral as Genêt's political officer. The minister himself retired from his duties in February 1794 choosing to avoid a Jacobin guillotine by remaining as a gentleman farmer in the United States.

Rousse had made disciples, especially in the cities. The main francophile agitators in Montreal were one Jean-Baptiste Colombe, who read aloud *Les Français libres* outside a church door; Canadien François Duclos of Eagle Island, a former lieutenant in the American revolutionary army; carpenter Stephen Storey, of American origin; and a tailor named Costille.[5] Duclos had allegedly publicized the coming French-American attack, predicted its success since the Canadiens preferred French rule, and gloried in the prospect of a redistribution of wealth through plunder. Storey had pledged his support for the invasion, boasting he would 'then mark out the Judges and Justices and Mr. Thomas Walker the Lawyer.' Storey was also in cahoots with Costille, who had been busy circulating copies of *Les Français libres* and telling listeners that six hundred armed men and women north of Mount Royal had risen and were ready to assist the invasion.

In January and February of 1794 Rousse had spent about five weeks in Quebec's working-class suburb of St Jean, exhorting all not to take up arms against the American and French liberators. Some listened. Jean La Cosse, a wig-maker turned pedlar, carried the message to many parts of the colony. Tinsmith Augustin Lavau of St Jean made copies of the *Les Français libres* for circulation and read the document to illiterate *confrères*. He also worked effectively to undermine martial spirit in the Quebec militia. Joiner Louis Dumontier (from the Upper Town) did the same, citing thirty-four years of oppression, and exhorted visiting habitant relatives and friends they must not support the British militarily. Alexandre Menut, who kept a popular tavern, spread the word to artisans, workers, and farmers living near the city, claiming that the invincible French would give Canada a proper constitution. Revolutionary meetings, composed mainly of artisans, were held that winter and spring of 1794 in the St Jean house of roofer Louis Fluet. Of the dozen or so Quebec residents implicated as subversives and identifiable by occupation in depositions or voluntary examinations (out of about twenty in all), ten were artisans or labourers and two were shopkeepers. Genêt was clearly stimulating some response among the working people of the capital. The idea of not bearing arms fell on fertile soil.[6]

In his speech closing the first session of the legislature in May 1793, Lieutenant-Governor Clarke had referred to the war as a nasty but far-off event and expressed confidence in the 'loyalty and faithful attachment of his majesty's subjects of the province.' No particular legislation seemed to be immediately required.[7] The government confined its propaganda effort to partially subsidizing John Neilson's production of an engraved illustration (with a short propaganda text) of Louis XVI about to be guillotined. This cool assessment of the colony's security situation remained the norm for several months, not only in official circles but among the English élite generally.

The reasons for calm are easily found. Until the autumn there was no evidence that France intended an attack on the colony nor that French undercover agents had entered it. The United States had declared its neutrality and during these months France suffered a number of serious reverses, particularly the outbreak of formidable royalist insurrections in La Vendée on the west coast. Such setbacks encouraged the English élite to conclude that the war would shortly be won, with John Richardson deducing that 'the Game will soon be up with those Monsters of iniquity – the National Convention.'[8]

Towards the end of 1793 and in the first months of 1794 that calm confidence turned into serious concern. This was stimulated principally by well-grounded suspicions that Citizen Genêt was planning an invasion of the Canadas and had sent agents in to circulate written propaganda and tamper with the people. The first indication of the new climate was the treatment of General Galbaud, deposed governor of Saint-Domingo (Haiti), his aide-de-camp, and a French sergeant who entered the colony as supposed refugees in September 1793. On Clarke's orders the three men were arrested and escorted to Quebec as prisoners of war. Galbaud and his aide eventually escaped to the United States, while the sergeant was sent to Britain. Clarke and Dorchester, who resumed his governorship in late September, believed the visitors were agents of Genêt. While at Montreal Galbaud and the sergeant were thought to have spread revolutionary principles and to have attempted to establish clubs among the working people. The governor reported that labourers, artisans, and even some middle-class youth provided a ready audience for 'modern French principles.' By October, English Montrealers, worried about the departure of the Royal Navy's West Indies and North American Squadron, became so suspicious of revolutionary intrigues that most of Mezière's friends were afraid to write to him.[9]

In November the government mobilized its 'public relations' resources against the enemy. Chief Justice Smith warned the grand jury of the perils inherent in French 'Levelism' or 'Equality of Property,' urging it to hunt out the seditious. A Dorchester proclamation which referred to insidious alien enemies lurking in the province, ordered everyone, in and out of authority, to inform on any person attempting to 'excite Discontent ... [or] lessen the Affections of His Majesty's ... Subjects.' Bishop Jean-François Hubert's circular letter worried that rural residents, 'struck by the name *French*, would not know how to behave' if the fleet arrived. Priests must teach their parishioners that modern Frenchmen had murdered their virtuous Sovereign and given way to a spirit of 'irreligion ... of anarchy, of parricide.'[10] Two bills dealing with security followed these propaganda initiatives during the 1794 legislative session. One gave the government tighter control over the militia. The other, known as the Alien Act, provided means of keeping foreigners under close surveillance, subjecting them to summary deportation whenever the governor saw fit, and suspended habeas corpus for political offences. But before these bills even reached the statute book the province experienced its first popular disturbances of the war.

THE RIOTS OF 1794

The first sign of popular unrest occurred in April shortly after the Montreal Quarter Sessions condemned a canoeman named Joseph Leveillé to the pillory for having obtained advances from two rival fur-trading firms. A Canadien crowd, chiefly voyageurs to the Indian country, prevented execution of the sentence by hurling the pillory into the St Lawrence River and threatening to storm the prison. These developments so unnerved the magistrate, merchant Joseph Frobisher, that he promised to intercede with Lord Dorchester for a pardon. The sheriff, finding it prudent not to attempt to carry out the sentence again, released the prisoner some days later. Four arrested ringleaders were soon bailed and no one, it seems, was ever punished for the incident. The government eventually decided, in the circumstances, to issue a pardon to Leveillé.[11] Although a modest affair, the canoemen's rising and its aftermath were to play a significant role during the militia riots which broke out a month later.

In anticipation of war with the United States over the western posts, Lord Dorchester called for the selection by lot of two thousand unmarried militiamen for active service on the frontier. This was certainly a risky proceeding. The État Major of the Trois-Rivières District did not exaggerate in 1790 when it claimed that habitant heads of households would rather give up half their possessions than see their sons drafted for military service.[12] Probably, the 1790s farmers would have defended the province against invasion by Americans (uncomplicated by French involvement) if the invasion had been actual and service confined to the province.[13]

Dorchester's order of 5 May met intense resistance throughout the colony. The English contingents, to be sure, hastened to the flag, but a mere seventeen of the 222 Canadien companies were willing to comply. While a few companies which refused would have accepted the more traditional direct order to muster and march, the vast majority made it clear they would take up arms under no circumstances whatever, believing 'that should they ballot ... they would thereby be enlisted as [regular] soldiers [or sailors] and sent to the West Indies, or out of the Province, and subject to military discipline.' In some places stories flew about that service would be for life or that the British were embarking on a second Acadian deportation: conscription order would follow conscription order until 'the country loses all its people.'[14]

Other motives can be detected. Stories circulated in Quebec that the militia order had been concocted by half-pay officers (mainly Canadien seigneurs) for base monetary reasons. Attorney General Monk found that the operation of the seigneurial system had stiffened resistance. As he reported to Henry Dundas, secretary of state, the illegal exactions of the seigneurs were compared by French agents 'to the Kingly Government of France' and farmers' grievances fomented 'to the utmost, as the best means of detaching' them from loyalty and inducing them to 'aid a Revolution.'[15]

Many in the colony believed that French troops would soon appear, with or without the Americans. Evidence, including the militia returns made by the États Major following the riots, indicates the working people were generally loath to shed the blood of kin. The Duc de La Rochefoucauld-Liancourt learned from some British officers who had been stationed in Lower Canada during the balloting that resisters had often shouted words to the effect that if it 'were [really] against the Americans we would march no doubt to defend our country, but these are Frenchmen who are coming and we won't march. How could we fight against our brothers?'[16]

Resistance faded by the end of May, though actual and rumoured disturbances continued sporadically through the summer. The riots had not approached insurrection, nor had they required troops for their suppression. But much talk of violence, dangerous assemblies of the disgruntled, and rhetoric which sounded sympathetic to revolutionary France had surfaced.

Violence, threatened and actual, flared in many rural parishes, but most dramatically at Charlesbourg, a village just north of Quebec. For several days and nights up to three hundred habitants, armed with muskets, pikes, pitchforks, and hunting knives, formed patrols to defend themselves against an expected armed attack of city folk bent on enforcing conscription. Some of the farmers, by their own sworn admission, also thought this might prove a good time to bash 'les Anglais.'[17] The idea of patrols had been initiated by mob oratory outside the captain's residence, when habitants Jerome Bédard, Pierre Chartré, and Charles Garnaud threatened those who did not join in defending the community. Armed resistance, they claimed, was justified in the name of the people 'who are above any King.'[18] These farmer-revolutionaries warned any who might not support the popular cause that the people would have to 'kill and disembowel all those ... cowards' and 'mount their heads on pike-ends.' Threats of house and barn burning were commonplace near Charlesbourg that May and, according to Monk, so were boasts by the locals that 'they have no occasion for the clergy nor confession.' In other rural areas near the capital curés who attempted to ensure the militiamen did their duty were often threatened with physical injury.[19]

In the District of Montreal an armed mob of perhaps five hundred assembled in early June at Côte des Neiges to resist the militia order. According to Sheriff Edward Gray, these people, mainly farmers, had met for mutual defence in the belief that 'the Military were ordered to go into that part of the Country to disarm the Inhabitants & force them away from their families.' When in due course the troops did not appear the crowd had 'dispersed without committing Any Act of Violence.' Shortly after this incident Jonathan Sewell reported that the whole District, was in 'a state of allmost [sic] universal and alarming disaffection.' Such was popular hatred of the authorities that the Canadien magistrates in the city refused to prosecute offenders against the militia laws. If the English justices alone had to do the job, the result could well be disastrous.[20]

On the heels of Sewell's pessimistic opinion came another from Michel-Eustache-Gaspard-Alain Chartier de Lotbinière, pro-government Speaker of the Assembly, seigneur of Vaudreuil, Rigaud, and Lotbinière, who habitually kept a close political watch on the farmers of his neighbourhood northwest of Montreal. The heads of families still believed that the government intended 'to conscript their children for life, that it wants to send them to the Caribbean islands or to England and ... they will never see them again.' The farmers contended that the authorities 'had not punished those who threw the pillory into the river' during the Leveillé riots or those who had revolted at Côte des Neiges. Therefore, they too, if united, would escape punishment for preventing their children becoming soldiers. Lotbinière insisted the government take no precipitate action, but only make examples of indisputable ringleaders at a time when it was certain of obedience. Otherwise, there would be 'a violent flare-up, a considerable insurrection and perhaps the loss of the colony.'

Chartier de Lotbinière's letter encouraged Lord Dorchester's policy of extreme caution. Although punishing the rioters was important, the timing was wrong – foreign and domestic emissaries of France might stimulate serious rioting which could get out of control – especially if the United States declared war. As a result, no special commissions were issued for the speedy trial of political offenders, and the arrest of the ringleaders at Côte des Neiges was delayed until September. Dorchester put the best face on matters when he informed Dundas that the 'course of justice is advancing cautiously and with circumspection, to preserve if possible the Laws from again being insulted and to avoid all occasion of violence.'[21]

POPULAR UNREST, 1796–1797

French Intrigues

The Jacobin Committee of Public Safety, seeing France desperately dependent upon the United States for grain supplies, wished to prevent any diplomatic rupture between the two republics. Thus the new minister, Jean-Antoine-Joseph Fauchet, was instructed to drop Genêt's expeditionary projects and as a result took little interest in the Canadiens.[22] Only after the Directory took power in November 1795 was the policy of conquering Lower Canada revived.

In 1796–7 the French government again interested itself in liberating Lower Canada. Paris officials of the Directory, the French minister to the United States, Pierre-Auguste Adet, his subordinates, and the near-bankrupt 'Green Mountain Boy,' Vermont land speculator and soldier of fortune Ira Allen, worked out various plans of invasion.[23] This was part of a grandiose political strategy to encircle the rear of the United States. After Jay's Treaty of 1794, Paris viewed it as a renegade republic allied to the enemy, providing Britain with food. Louisiana would be restored to France by Spain – now an ally – and British North America would be conquered. By controlling the Mississippi and the St Lawrence, France could dismember the frontier areas of the American union. The end result envisaged two puppet regimes under French hegemony, 'United (or in some versions 'New') Columbia' in the north and the United States in the south. A host of other benefits was anticipated from the conquest of British North America, and France would finally fulfil its obligation to forsaken nationals, who were assumed to be yearning for liberty. As J.-A.-B. Rozier, French consul at New York put it, France 'having become free, will hasten to repair the crimes of its tyrants; she will never remain dead to the cries of her new world children who hold out their arms, begging for her help.'

The main provisions of the official invasion plan can be reconstructed from a report drafted by the French foreign minister Charles-Maurice de Talleyrand, in 1798[24] and memoranda prepared for the Directory by Ira Allen in the late spring or early summer of 1796.[25] The French government agreed to finance the purchase of twenty thousand muskets and bayonets and two dozen light artillery pieces, worth in all 500,000 livres (about £25,000). A transport fleet carrying three or four thousand French regulars and accompanied by two ships of the line and four or five frigates would reach Halifax in August 1797, attempt to take the town, and capture the British merchant fleet from Lower Canada. It would then proceed to join up with Allen's forces near Quebec City. Simultaneously with the naval attack on Halifax the Vermont irregulars would capture St Jean, assisted by armed men previously infiltrated into the area on one of Allen's timber rafts. From there Allen and his men would proceed to Quebec, on the way raising the Canadiens whose francophile political sentiments would meanwhile have been cultivated by emissaries. The combined forces would have no trouble in taking Quebec and then forcing the remaining enemy troops out of British North America.

From other sources additional elements of strategy can be reconstructed. French agents would contact the Indians in Upper Canada to ensure their neutrality, or if needed, participation. Serious consideration was given to a diversionary attack on Upper Canada by way of the Mississippi, likely consisting of American frontiersmen, Indians, and French and Spanish troops. Almost certainly a body of Allen's forces and perhaps some from the New York side of the St Lawrence were to attack Montreal. The fleet, it appears, was to stop temporarily at a point near Kamouraska, east of Quebec, where proclamations would be distributed to agents for circulation among the Canadiens. The terms of these proclamations were to include a call to armed insurrection, a guarantee of private property and freedom of religion, a prohibition of violence except against persons in arms against the Republic, the promise of prompt payment in cash for goods and services, the abolition of the tithe and seigneurial dues, and the establishment in former British North America of New or United Columbia.

To expedite matters, Adet and his subordinates sent numerous agents into Lower Canada to sound out Canadien opinion, distribute propaganda, recruit sympathizers, and obtain military intelligence. About mid-September 1796 two engineering officers in the Armée française d'outre mer (French Overseas Army) named De Millière – a general – and Ianson established a base in upper New York State on the Canadian border to gather information and organize a spy network. Ianson left for Paris shortly after. Later in September De Millière sent two Canadiens into the colony: Montreal tailors Jean-Baptiste Louisineau and Joseph Ducalvet.[26] Both were commissioned as second lieutenants. Crossing the border openly near St Jean on 27 September with inflammatory addresses signed by Adet and blank army commissions stitched into Ducalvet's breeches, they held a meeting the next day with sympathizers. Government officials apparently identified only three persons attending that meeting: Jean-Baptiste Bizette of Côte des Neiges and Ducalvet's uncle and grandfather Étienne and Joseph Girard dit Provençale, both gardeners in the employ of the Seminary of St Sulpice. Ducalvet also attempted distribution of literature promising liberation from British slavery by France, denouncing the forced labour required by the recently passed Road Act, outlining the advantages of the Revolution, and predicting that the cry of 'Vive la République' would soon be heard throughout the province.

Ducalvet quit the province at the end of September leaving his own commission behind at his uncle's. About two months later Richardson, having intercepted a letter requesting its return, organized a fictitious correspondence and misinformation campaign designed to entice Ducalvet to return home from his refuge in Vermont. Warned off at the last moment, the tailor-spy went underground and later attempts by Robert Liston, British minister to the United States, to have him extradited fell on deaf ears. The sentiments expressed in the intercepted letter gave government officials something to ponder long after he had disappeared: Ducalvet was ecstatic, he wrote, that the Canadiens in general entertained 'the best principles of liberty' and wanted all his relatives to know that 'I will have the pleasure of seeing them in the spring when we shall make the English dance the carmagnole. Vive la liberté.'[27]

By the end of 1796 Citizen Adet must have been supremely confident that the invasion plan would succeed. That summer the British blockade of the French navy at Brest had proved porous and the discontent of the

Canadiens with their lot had been manifest in a bitterly contested election. In the autumn his spies had brought him roseate predictions of success – and not surprisingly, since the colony had then experienced the most violent unrest since the war had begun.

The Election of 1796

This little studied election took place in a period of economic depression. A modest wheat crop of 1794 had been followed in 1795 by the worst harvest of the decade, producing only between one-third and one-half that of the year before. Marginal farmers faced starvation or charity. Inflation hit the urban dwellers hard with the price of wheat, flour, oats, beef, butter, and eggs steeply rising in 1796. Shortages were so severe that the government proclaimed an embargo on the export of foodstuffs, despite lobbying by the leading mercantile houses. As Osgoode explained to the under secretary of state in early August, 'From the disposition of the minds of the people much was to be apprehended had anything in the shape of Provisions been suffer [sic] to go out of the province.'[28] Seventeen ninety-six was indeed a painful year for the great majority of Canadiens.

The election results indicate a general alienation from the policies of government, including those of the Assembly. Dozens of habitants, artisans, and labourers, for example, had been arrested in 1794 and resentment lingered on two years later.[29] The consumption taxes – new duties on wines, spirits, coffee, salt, tobacco, and sugar – of 1795 must have been unpopular, as the traveller La Rochefoucauld-Liancourt claimed.[30] The Engagés Act of 1796 would have been resented, particularly in the Montreal region. This statute, responded to longstanding complaints of merchants by criminalizing what had been mainly a civil law field,[31] compelled canoemen, batteauxmen, guides, and winterers to enter into notarial deeds, and authorized summary imprisonment of those who did not fulfil their contracts without provable cause. But the issues which probably sparked the most resentment among working people were the failure of the Lower House to reform the seigneurial regime in 1795 and the passage of the Road Act in 1796.

Early in the 1795 session Philippe de Rocheblave moved to have the Committee of the Whole House inquire into the 'legal or customary rates of ... rentes and other ... burthens on ... concessions [of lands] before the conquest, compared with what have been exacted since.' Jean-Antoine Panet, wanting to stimulate popular opinion, moved in amendment that the committee be empowered to sit anywhere in the province and to subpoena witnesses or papers as it saw fit. The amendment was overwhelmingly defeated and the main motion was submerged in lengthy discussions of tenure in general. It came to nothing. Undoubtedly these manoeuvres strongly contributed to the almost universal unpopularity of the Canadien seigneurs.[32] Their standing sank further during the session of 1795–6.

In response to demands from Montreal merchants, Quebec magistrates and members of his own class, seigneur Gabriel-Elzéar Taschereau, highways commissioner for the District of Quebec, introduced a bill in November 1795 to improve the deplorable state of the roads. The *parti canadien* strenuously opposed it by moving that the bill be printed for public information, by withdrawing from the House so that proceedings were suspended for want of a quorum, and by arguing that the forced labour imposed on the people established a dangerous precedent justifying the enactment of land taxation. All these efforts failed and the bill became law on 7 May.[33]

The Road Act of 1796 was obviously designed in the interests of the urban upper classes, rural seigneurs, and those speculators hoping to open up crown waste lands for settlement. Unprecedented, unpaid corvées abounded. The District highway commissioners and locally elected overseers (a novelty) could require the joint labour – up to twelve days a year – of the neighbouring residents to open or repair roads through difficult terrain or unsettled areas, including unconceded seigneurial and crown lands. Roads leading to the seigneurs' grist mills were to be divided into fourteen equal parts, of which one was to be maintained by the seigneur and thirteen by the habitant heads of household. The repair of the streets in Montreal and Quebec was the responsibility of all males, eighteen to sixty, who resided in the cities or adjacent rural areas. Thus the farmer could be forced to work not only on the roads in his parish but also on the city streets he seldom used except in going to market. In the French and early British regimes the obligations of rural owners and occupiers were largely confined to maintaining the roads adjacent to their lands. Under the new act, those who could afford to do so were permitted to offer a payment in lieu of any imposed statutory labour.

The electoral campaign clearly featured many appeals against social and political authority – much more so than in 1792. A letter from 'A Good Citizen,' printed by the semi-official *Quebec Gazette*, castigated the anarchy being fostered by opposition candidates: '*Bad Men*' who were attempting 'to raise themselves and serve their own private interests.'

These social *parvenus* were doing everything possible to persuade 'the unthinking, that a certain class of their fellow citizens, who ... wisely oppose *their aims*, can triumph over the laws of the Country, and betray the people who may entrust them with the important Guard over *Public Liberty.*'[34] Alienation ran so deep in some places that the voters returned members who had been imprisoned for seditious offences or on suspicion of high treason, such as master shipwright John Black, illiterate farmer and Charlesbourg rioter Louis Paquet (Quebec County) and Quebec merchant Nicolas Dorion (Devon). Quebec tavernkeeper Alexandre Menut (Cornwallis) had been described as a subversive by two deponents.[35] There may well have been other cases, for Osgoode commented that such was the spirit of the people that 'any Person who had been accused was sure of being elected.'

The election results dealt a devastating blow to the colony's political and social élites, as they immediately perceived.[36] One statistic alone tells much of the tale: seventeen of the Canadiens elected in 1792 had been justices of the peace; in 1796 one Canadien magistrate ran successfully. It is true that the English contingent in the house almost maintained its numbers, dropping from sixteen at dissolution to fifteen, but this figure is highly misleading.[37] The real turnaround, though, occurred in the social rank of the elected Canadiens.

In 1792 the electorate had chosen about fourteen Canadiens of the seigneurial class – all but one in rural constituencies and only three considered safe for the government. In 1796 just three of this class succeeded – two of them in safe seats, and one, oppositionist de Rocheblave, in Surrey. The big winners came from the Canadien bourgeoisie, whose numbers increased from about seventeen after the first election to twenty-three four years later. The working people raised their representation from two to four in 1792 to nine in 1796. Typically, the newly elected and re-elected Canadiens from the middle class were professionals and shopkeepers far removed from the upper reaches of the middle ranks. Lawyer Bédard was the son of a baker, while notary-surveyor Joseph Papineau's father had been a cooper. Two seigneurs of the noblesse had held Dorchester County at dissolution; now the constituency would be represented by Charles Bégin, a tavernkeeper at Pointe-Lévi, and Alexandre Dumas, a bankrupt merchant turned notary.[38]

There is evidence of strong anti-government feelings held by Canadien voters and of the demise of the bourgeois alliance. Obscure notary Joseph Planté and shopkeeper François Huot, son of a farmer, bested De Bonne (Hampshire). In Surrey the sycophantic, 'patriotic' schoolteacher Louis

Labadie (who expended much energy in the years 1793–8 attempting to inculcate a reverence for British rule into his fellow countrymen) was decisively defeated by de Rocheblave and Olivier Durocher, son of a rural doctor and a committed follower of Papineau. Incumbent Judge James Walker, abandoned by Papineau, his 1792 running mate, lost Montreal County to merchant Jean-Marie Ducharme and law student Étienne Guy. Walker's brother Thomas, a lawyer, was beaten in Montreal West when his co-candidate, merchant Pierre Foretier, formerly of the Canadien Reform Committee, withdrew from the race in favour of Papineau and his cousin Denis Viger, a carpenter. Overall, the *parti canadien* won and the government clearly lost the election. In the 1797 legislative session, Executive councillor John Young (Quebec, Lower Town) was defeated as proposed Speaker by a vote of twenty-seven to fourteen, with Panet winning a second poll, twenty-nine to twelve. Soon government supporters failed to block debate on amendments to the Road Act.[39]

The Road Act Riots

On 26 August 1796 Quebeckers and inhabitants from the adjacent countryside were summoned to repair the city's streets. Cheered on by rowdy spectators, including many who had paid to avoid their statutory labour, the conscripted workers took the wheels off their carts, gave three cheers, and went off. Four or five ringleaders were seized and taken to the jail, in Osgoode's words 'notwithstanding the menaces of 500 Women.' This broke the resistance and those summoned the next day and thereafter went submissively to work. To the authorities that vigorous, early enforcement of the law entirely solved any problem of discontent in the District.[40] They had grossly underestimated the general detestation of the act.

What would prove to be far worse troubles broke out in Montreal a few doors from Ducalvet's revolutionary meeting, at a time when Ducalvet was still in the province and when his sympathizers were attempting to circulate the address with its reference to the Road Act as symbolic of Canadien oppression.[41] Late in September one Luc Berthelot, who lived on Mount Royal, was fined for following the general pattern of refusing to labour or pay. On 2 October constable Jacob Marston tried to arrest him. Five or six men in Berthelot's house, egged on by his fiery wife, Scholastique Mathieu, battered Marston. According to Sewell, the constable was 'happy to escape with his life.' Berthelot was arrested but as the attorney general described the scene, 'he had not been in the Sheriff's Custody above five minutes when he was forcibly and most violently rescued by a mob in the *Place d'Armes*.'

Anarchy loomed. Activists in and about Montreal planned a mass protest meeting, dispatching couriers to advertise it, and encourage continued resistance to the act. Many habitants of the Longueuil area on the south shore urged their neighbours to withhold all foodstuffs from the Montreal market in order to provoke, as one of them urged, 'un petit revolte' in the city. At the church in L'Assomption the farmers walked out of a sermon, after a parishioner warned the curé to remain 'within the Sphere of your Clerical Duty' and not 'interfere in Politicks.' In Pointe-aux-Trembles and Point Claire the massacre of the English became a topic of tavern oratory. Killing the most vigilant English magistrates was talked of in the city.

Sometime shortly after the Berthelot rescue the Montreal magistrates Bench, prompted especially by the Canadien justices, agreed with a citizens' delegation that enforcement of the act should be suspended for a few days until the governor responded to a request to summon the legislature for an emergency session. The magistrates claimed that for the time being enforcement was beyond their means: 'Emissaries have been dispersed through the different parishes to foment the general dissatisfaction ... [which has] risen to such a pitch of popular Frenzy as to render ... the Civil Power insufficient to compel obedience.' The governor refused to compromise, ordering the magistrates to compel obedience to the law. This they found difficult in the extreme. On 24 October the unlucky Marston, attempting to levy a fine on one Latour, a ringleader in the 'free Berthelot movement,' failed when Latour and several friends threatened musket fire. The justices thereupon suspended all further efforts to enforce the act.

In early October startling news reached the colony. The previous August French Admiral Richery, with seven battleships and some frigates, had escaped the British blockade at Brest and sailed to Newfoundland. In September the fleet destroyed some houses, fishing boats, and stores at Bay Bulls before returning home. Rumours flew in Lower Canada that St John's was taken, Halifax seriously threatened and, most certainly, the admiral would soon be ascending the St Lawrence to free his former countrymen.[42] These developments 'produced a Sensation throughout this Province,' as Prescott put it, with people everywhere excitedly speculating on the likely reaction of the Canadiens, particularly those in the distant parishes along the lower St Lawrence.[43] While it is difficult to gauge the popular response, it was sufficiently francophile to alarm the governor and the chief justice.[44] Coadjutor Bishop Pierre Denaut, then in Longueuil (where mass protest assemblies and starvation plots were commonplace), was also pessimistic: 'The news from Quebec of a French invasion ... has given joy to the greater number ... We are approaching ... a revolution similar to the one in France ... [That one] history tells us was begun by a mob of inflamed women; what then is not to be feared from men who have lost their heads.'[45] Richery's appearance, the apparent welcome he would receive if he did attack, and the impotence of the civil power in Montreal convinced the government that determined action was vital.

Sewell was sent to Montreal with a new commission of the peace. Two Canadien magistrates were dismissed and a number of hardliners, such as John Richardson, added to the Bench. Sewell offered justiceships to two popular politicians of the area: Joseph Perineault, MPP for Huntingdon, and Joseph Papineau. The latter had taken a prominent role in the resistance from the beginning, acting as adviser to many who were drafted for road duty. Refusing to labour or pay, not only had he headed the delegation of citizens who convinced the magistrates to suspend enforcement but had promised the people that Canadien members of the Assembly would effect the repeal of the offending statute. Papineau had also helped spread the idea that the Road Act was illegal – on the not unreasonable ground that the Legislative Council had only numbered thirteen during the session, two short of the mandatory minimum established by the Constitutional Act. Neither MPP agreed to serve. Back in Quebec, Sewell reported that Papineau had told him there would be serious trouble, perhaps even rebellion, if any Canadien blood were spilled and the government could have peace only if all fines were remitted and all attempts at implementation ceased.

General Prescott counter-attacked. On 30 October the government issued an order-in-council under the authority of the Alien Act.[46] After an obligatory recital of French wickedness, the order directed all Frenchmen who had entered the colony since 1 May 1794 to depart within twenty days. This initiative, accompanied by a proclamation urging reports on seditious conversations, instructed the magistrates to make appropriate arrests.[47] Again Bishop Hubert's resources were called upon. On 5 November 1796 he denounced the latest French intrigues as manifested by the riots, supported the measures of 30 October, and instructed his priests to emphasize that the faithful owed allegiance to George III, must obey laws punctually, and put aside any spirit of 'rebellion and independence' which had 'worked such sad havoc [among us] these last few years.'[48]

To reinforce the capital and probably to avoid looting, virtually all the gunpowder in the king's magazines at St Jean, Chambly, and Montreal was sent to Quebec. Prescott also dispatched two regiments to Montreal which, according to Sewell, restored the 'Consequence of the Magistrates and gave Energy to their Proceedings.' One such energetic proceeding was to serve an order on Papineau to perform his road duty or be fined. Accompanied by a huge crowd of retainers, the accused submitted a far-fetched argument based on his supposed parliamentary privileges. After Papineau's subsequent conviction, fine, and humbling, resistance to the enforcement of the Road Act crumbled in the Montreal region.

During these troubles the Quebec District had remained overtly passive, except for an incident in the suburb of St Roch. There, in October, a meeting of the Road Act overseers ended in rioting. A magistrate who attempted to disperse the crowd was assaulted and threatened with his life. Arrests restored order – but only temporarily. Rumours circulated that the elected overseers had been granted unlimited powers of oppression and were about to impose the dreaded class-based land tax of old France known as the *taille*.[49] Despite Bishop Hubert's admonitions, violence again flared, this time in St Joseph-de-Pointe-Lévi, across the river from the capital. In January angry farmers re-enacted scenes from the Stamp Act riots and the recent Whisky Rebellion in upper Pennsylvania by compelling overseers to renounce their offices. The ringleaders, arrested some days later, were being escorted to the city by two sheriff's officers, when eight habitants with bludgeons effected their rescue, informing the officers to forget about arrests, since 'we have three hundred men in arms ready to support our Determination.' Prescott responded by sending more than a hundred troops with two field guns to Pointe-Lévi, an action sufficient to frighten most of the rioters against whom warrants had been issued to surrender voluntarily.[50]

The Road Act riots were over, but for some months the habitants remained surly about road duty and the statute continued as an explosive political issue.

ANALYSIS AND EVALUATION OF THE THREATS TO LOWER CANADA

The External Threat

The external threat to Lower Canada from 1793 to 1798 was imaginary as it turned out, and modest even if the French had ordered a naval invasion and had recruited and dispatched an irregular army to proceed down the Richelieu. President Washington had immediately declared neutrality, despite the festering sore of Britain's retention of the western posts. After Jay's Treaty in 1794 the United States became an undeclared ally of Great Britain. True, the French-Irish-Vermont irregulars might have escaped American vigilance and been able to enter the colony through the frontier woods. But lack of discipline and the lure of plunder would have reduced greatly their military worth. The British naval blockade at Brest was generally effective, even though the French fleet did occasionally escape it.

Only once did senior officials of the French government, absorbed by more urgent priorities in Europe and well aware of the difficulties involved, plan an invasion. Genêt's farcical attempts had not been authorized by Paris and partly for that reason were rejected by the French West Indian fleet at New York. The attack force projected for August 1797 might conceivably have reached the colony, but the plan had been undermined months before. In December 1796 Ira Allen and his cargo of munitions, sailing from Ostend to New York aboard the ironically named *Olive Branch*, had been captured on the high seas by a British man-of-war. Allen spent much of the remainder of his life vainly attempting to convince a sceptical imperial government that he entertained no hostile intentions against the Canadas.[51] With the seizure of the *Olive Branch* the Directory lost interest in the idea of invading Lower Canada, not regaining it even when the British navy experienced serious mutinies in the spring of 1797.[52] No final decision to abandon the idea, however, was taken and French officials in the United States continued for several months to assume an attack might be made.

Had a French fleet landed a few thousand marines in Lower Canada, would the attack have succeeded? Although the British would have had the decided advantage of fighting defensively, the colony's means of protection were far from overwhelming. The Canadien militia could not be counted on. Regular troop strength in the Canadas during these years varied from about 2,600 to 3,500 all ranks.[53] This was hardly sufficient protection for the lower colony, let alone the vast exposed frontier of Upper Canada. Not surprisingly, the desperate need for reinforcements was an anxious *leitmotif* of official correspondence.[54] Nor were the regular soldiers entirely reliable. The proximity of the American border often proved an irresistible temptation for men subjected to the harsh discipline and Spartan conditions of eighteenth-century military service. In the winter of 1792–3, for example, a planned mutiny followed by mass desertion in Prince Edward's regiment at Quebec was barely averted at the eleventh hour by the arrest of the ringleaders.[55] Desertion was a recurrent lament of military commanders throughout the war.[56] Still, it seems unlikely that three to four thousand French marines could easily have defeated about an equal number of British troops (supported by English militia) in defensive positions – unless, of course, there was a Canadien insurrection.

Contemporary expert opinions during the period, such as those of David Alexander Grant and the Comte de Maulevrier (both former army officers) and General John Graves Simcoe Lieutenant-Governor of Upper Canada, agreed that the colony was highly vulnerable to French invasion.[57] Prescott estimated that with the troops at his disposal there was almost no chance of winning if the smallest French attacking force landed and if the Canadiens, as was likely, responded by rising in arms.[58] All these pessimistic opinions were based on a common and crucial assumption: that the working people of Lower Canada would rise *en masse* to aid the French. Was this likely?

Loyalty of the Urban Workers

To incite a revolt in the cities, French agents and their local sympathizers could try to exploit four themes: inflation and consumer taxes in the years 1793–7; the attractiveness of the principles for which revolutionary France stood; pure ethnic prejudice; and resentment of the well-to-do. This last theme owed its existence to the fact that the annual income of Canadien seigneur-officials and those English in the higher reaches of the public service was often over twenty times that of unskilled labourers lucky enough to be employed for the whole year. The immense wealth of the leading merchants was apparent to all. Simon McTavish, for example, left an estate valued at more than £125,000 and James McGill's was comparable. The higher economic status of the English is reflected in the fact that they occupied almost 45 per cent of the single-family dwellings in Quebec's Upper and Lower towns, although amounting to only slightly more than 20 per cent of the population of those two districts in the city.

Several reforms introduced by the French Revolution, moreover, had the potential to generate positive response among Canadien urban workers: careers open to talent, the Declaration of the Rights of Man, *fraternité*, the abolition of hereditary titles, the entry of the sansculottes into politics, stringent price-fixing (1793) and the elimination of food consumption taxes in the French capital (1791). How did the working districts of Montreal and Quebec perceive these changes and other news from France?

Artisans and labourers had been exposed to pro-French propaganda, and not only by *Les Français libres* which had some circulation. Those who could read had been taught by the newspapers from 1789 to late 1792 that the heroic doings in France were to be applauded. Others learned the same by word of mouth from literate artisans or those people working for the Canadien committees for constitutional reform. Montreal's Société des Patriotes was very active from 1790 to 1792 and in September of the next year Galbaud's revolutionary doctrines had some impact. In Quebec the few middle-class radicals such as Dumas, Alexandre Menut, Nicolas Dorion, Dr O'Connor, and Bezeau attempted to spread their message among urban working people.

One cannot discount, either, sympathy for France (largely of a non-ideological nature) which was manifest in these years. Rousse, an intelligent spy who made balanced judgments, reported to Mezière in September 1793 that 'Nothing is so common, even in the country, as the cry of *Vivent les Français!* "We hope to see our brothers," the townspeople tell the peasants, and these, as if they feared that what was said was intended to tease them, reply: "But is it really true that we shall see *Nos bonnes gens*," and tears of regret furrow the cheeks of the old people.'[59] Bits of proof support Rousse's assessment. Lévesque's shout of 'vivent les Français' at the Quebec parade in May 1794 must have been made with confidence that his fellow militiamen would be responsive. Adet's agents Ducalvet and David McLane operated in Montreal without being informed on by Canadiens. More incredibly, Rousse spent about five weeks doing undercover work in Quebec's St Jean suburb without disclosure to the authorities.

The potential disloyalty of the urban workers should not however, be exaggerated. Early approval of the French Revolution circulated easily. But from late 1792 the newspapers were full of critical comment emphasizing atrocities. Rousse reported in September 1793 that Mezière's friends had not yet distributed *Les Français libres*, 'for, as they observed, with a people wholly plunged in the dense shadows of ignorance and slavery, it is not fitting to suddenly ... shine the Sun of Liberty at noon.'[60]

While resentment of the well-to-do, ethnic hostility, and a sentimental regard for France certainly existed, it is not clear how influential these feelings were. Emotional attachment to France was not nearly as deep among the younger generation (particularly if they had attended school) as among those who had been born in New France. Dumontier's rage over thirty-four years of injustice under the British was not shared by his apprentices. When Dumontier's teenage son, then studying at the Quebec Seminary, dared suggest that Lower Canada had the mildest of governments and on another occasion praised Prince Edward for his success in the Caribbean theatre, he was told to shut up by his father.[61] Although there were men in the cities prepared to risk punishment by working for revolutionary France, their numbers were very small. In 1794, after exhaustive investigations, including the use of an agent -provocateur, the authorities were able to implicate only about ten Canadien workers of Quebec who had furthered the aim of Genêt, Mezière, and Rousse.[62] And at the time the city and its immediate environs included more than five hundred male Canadien artisans and skilled or semi-skilled labourers, exclusive of domestic servants.[63] Evidently few urban workers would have risked much to assist revolutionary France if it invaded the colony.

Habitant Loyalty

A fundamental point to be borne in mind when assessing the habitants' loyalty in this period is their strong resistance to propaganda. Most could not, of course, read Les Français libres or Adet's pamphlet of September 1796, and minatory local élites restricted rural circulation. In 1793–4 and 1796 distributors on horseback were often forced to throw copies through open windows and gallop off and the government discovered but one instance of Les Français libres being read publicly after divine service. During the Road Act riots the authorities traced Adet's tract to only ten recipients, all of whom claimed to have immediately burned them.[64]

Revolutionary agents and sympathizers from the cities undoubtedly tried to communicate orally a vision of the modern French paradise, but there is no reason to believe they were effective. Occasional francophile slogans emerged in the countryside at times of popular unrest. In 1794 a few habitants at Charlesbourg talked of popular sovereignty and heads on pikes, while during the election of 1796 two young hotheads from the south shore east of Quebec were arrested after shouting 'vive la liberté, we are from the National Convention [of France] and will smash everything in our way.' Such examples are very rare and are not representative. Monk, it is true, remarked in 1794 that many farmers had come to refer to Les Français libres ironically as 'le Catechisme.'[65] Since the principles of 1789 were not of obvious relevance to them, this was likely a bemused comment on zealots spreading the new mysteries with the same assurance as those who purveyed the old.

Careers open to talent in the public service could have made no appeal to farmers whose main aim in life was to find farms for their sons, a goal often realized in the 1790s. The free trade argument of the physiocrats would have been understandable to few rural dwellers, while popular sovereignty, republicanism, abolition of the royal veto, and an elected clergy were ideas alien to those who had known only monarchy and whose daily life was infused by the hierarchical authority of the family, the church, the militia, and the seigneurial system. Significantly, too, during the militia riots a number of habitants in the Quebec District thought they were justified in resisting an order which they had been told came from the illegitimate Assembly and not the king.[66] As late as 1838 – after three decades of liberal democratic agitation – many a habitant wanted to make Louis-Joseph Papineau king.[67]

Some revolutionary promises had appeal, particularly the abolition of seigneurial dues and tithes. In January 1794 Alexander Fraser, half-pay officer, seigneur of Beauchamp just south-east of the capital, remarked in alarm that talk of the coming American-French invasion had induced his *censitaires* to expect a quick end to their obligatory payments: 'they have got into their heads, that their friends the New Englanders has [*sic*] joined the french, and they are to be a free people, and have no rent, nor nothing to pay, such was the opinion of the greatest part of the inhabitants ... here.' Shortly after the 1796 election Osgoode commented that several successful candidates had promised their constituents 'to abolish all Rents and all Tithes.' At the time when Richery's fleet was expected and the Road Act riots were in full sway, the chief justice returned to the theme. Ignorance among the common people was so general and profound, he wrote, 'they firmly believe that ... under French or American Government they should be exempted from the Payment of both Tythes & Rent.'[68]

This assessment by Osgoode should not be taken at face value. Of the dozens of depositions, voluntary examinations, government reports, and other extant documents bearing directly on the militia and Road Act riots none refers to abolition as a factor motivating rural rioters. The social and political situation perhaps explains why.

The Canadien farmers of the late eighteenth and early nineteenth centuries shrewdly protected their interests. Dogged, skilful litigators in disputes with the clergy over tithes, pew rentals, location of churches, or other parochial matters, they were adept at nullifying, at least tempor-

arily, laws they considered oppressive. Letting lands recover their fertility
in alternating fallow years in the 1780s and 1790s, rather than engage in
the toil of clearing, rotating crops, and fertilizing was arguably intelligent.
Detailed alimentary pensions (in kind) exacted by parents as they turned
over the family farms to inheriting sons often exceeded notarial shrewd-
ness.[69] And it was intelligent, also, to ignore the promptings of the legislature, the government, and an assortment of experts, from 1790 on, to
invest in the growth of hemp – a crop difficult to cultivate and not assured of an imperial market.

Those farmers who thought about the elimination of seigneurial dues
may have wondered what would happen to the vast amounts of
unconceded land. If these were to be retained by the seigneurs as private
property or auctioned off (as had occurred in France with regard to
confiscated real estate) how would they obtain lands for their sons as
cheaply as before? In 1791, during a highly publicized conflict in the old
Legislative Council over a change in tenure,[70] prominent Canadiens –
senior clergy, seigneurs, bourgeoisie (including seven to ten members of
the city's reforming Canadien Committee) – defended the interests of the
farmers. The latter were represented as utterly opposed to outright ownership of land and, despite the abuses, favourable to the seigneurial
regime, which provided them with the valuable 'right ... of obliging him
[the seigneur] to grant lands 'at easy rates.'[71] The Canadien élite was
nearly united in favour of the existing land law, as reformed to prevent
abuse. This included members of the *parti canadien*, who became the
political mentors of the farmers in the years 1794 to 1797.[72]

The potential security danger in the countryside lay not only in the
operation of the seigneurial system, but also in the farmers' anglophobia
and their resistance to pro-British propaganda. The farmers' anglophobia
was manifest in many ways: their aversion to 'scientific' agriculture,
willingness to believe stories that their new masters were capable of
almost any oppression and so on. A particularly telling example occurred
during the general election of 1792 in Quebec County. Seigneur Louis de
Salaberry won easily. The real contest was for the second seat, with the
margin extremely close between lawyer Berthelot d'Artigny and clerk of
the peace David Lynd, a reformer. According to depositions sworn to by
resident farmers, Jean-Antoine Panet campaigned vigorously for his
confrère. After mass he announced, outside the Charlesbourg church that
'if he could get Mr. Berthelot into the House of Assembly they would
trample the English underfoot.' The next day Panet addressed a crowd,
saying 'my friends, you must elect a man of law, Mr. Berthelot, to join

me; we are a hundred against one and if you put him with me, we will throttle the English.' When the polls closed a few days later with Lynd slightly ahead, Berthelot's supporters (some of whom had not voted) almost precipitated a riot. Only a patriotic appeal to king, constitution, and ethnic harmony delivered by de Salaberry's close friend, Prince Edward, defused the tension.[73]

During the early war years the Lower Canadian government financed publications designed to show Canadiens the manifold evils perpetrated by their former countrymen. Among them were two Burkean assaults on abstract reasoning. These made no impact whatsoever among the farmers.[74] But the local notables did try to teach the simple facts about the outrages in the old mother country. Philippe-Joseph Aubert de Gaspé recalled his parents assembling their habitants to explain the sufferings of the French royal family – for whom the farmers retained a warm affection – as constantly reported in the newspapers. On each occasion the listeners 'would shake their heads, maintaining that it was all a fiction invented by the English.'[75] Several contemporaries substantiate de Gaspé's recollection. Count Colbert de Maulevrier, a French emigré visitor in 1798, has left perhaps the most graphic and persuasive description of habitant opinion. Their ignorance was such, he wrote, that few

want to believe in the death of the King of France. He's hidden, they say, and he will reappear; he has the power to make himself invisible. In general they don't want to hear a word about the Revolution's atrocities. The good French people – or as they say OUR FATHERS – aren't capable of that. These are lies that English spread for a purpose. Some priests who have tried to speak to them about the Revolution and the crimes it has spawned, have become suspect in their eyes.[76]

The Loyal Association Campaign, 1794

The idea for this campaign, originating with Attorney General Monk, was to identify the disaffected, teach the Canadiens about the horrors of revolution, and discourage agitators who might be inclined to violence when the militia rioters were brought to trial.[77] Parent associations (under the patronage of Lord Dorchester) in Quebec, Trois-Rivières, and Montreal circulated declarations execrating revolutionary France and eulogizing Britain. Citizens could prove 'loyalty' by signing or affixing their marks to these manifestos. English merchants and government officials largely controlled urban associations, but Canadien seigneurs, priests nominated by Hubert, and middle-class men such as Papineau and Panet played an active role. Working through the curés, resident seigneurs, and the Canadien MPPs, the parent societies attempted to organize associations in the rural parishes. The local notables were instructed to collect signatures to the Quebec Association's 1794 declaration of thanksgiving for British rule and to set straight the ignorant who were presumably guided to adopt those anarchistic opinions which had desolated France. The newspapers gave the campaign enormous publicity and the local notables of all varieties gave it every support. Several curés delivered speeches explaining the divine right of kings, and contrasting the benefits of British rule with the dark days of Intendant Bigot – no confiscation of grain, no military service outside the St Lawrence valley, protection of religion, and a free constitution.

Initially in the countryside there was opposition to signing. Over fifteen letters indicate that the early efforts of the priests were unsuccessful in varying degrees. The reasons for refusal were not often articulated but it is likely that illiterate farmers feared putting their mark to a written document which might impose onerous obligations (such as hypothecs or compulsory military service). In the County of Warwick the farmers feared that signatures would make them soldiers to fight in foreign lands, that the French, if they became the new 'maîtres,' wouldn't approve, and that priests would say anything to please the government, even if it meant throwing the people away. Explanations by the local élites that the militia law generally prohibited out-of-province service,[78] that the document bound signers to nothing specific, and that the consequences of refusal could be severe, contained the opposition.

About two-thirds of potential endorsers province-wide actually signed the declaration. Rural area signatures were proportionally lower than the overall average, but allowance must be made for the fact that many live-in adult sons of farmers did not sign, on the ground that the head of household alone made political decisions. The Montreal Association even claimed the Canadien working people would defend the province against revolutionary France, while the Quebec organization asserted that the 'ignorant and deluded part of the community' now understood that unspeakable atrocities inevitably flowed from modern French principles. These claims are not convincing. The minatory atmosphere of the campaign – lists kept of non-signers; habitants, labourers, and artisans in jail or threatened with imprisonment; the vocal and united local élites – ensured that most heads of farming households would subscribe to the declaration. Neither did the signatures or marks prove the signers believed what was in the document. Over sixty letters from rural loyal associations have been preserved, but only one clearly indicates that the farmers had any glimmering of the atrocities occurring in France, then at the height of the terror.[79] That they had not bound themselves to remain politically docile or obedient to law was made clear two years later, when the Road Act riots erupted.

As such contemporaries as Monk and De Bonne noticed, the 1790s riots were instances of a longstanding tradition in French Canada, known as 'rebellion à justice,' that is, rioting or threatening violence to prevent enforcement of the law. That tradition, which had come into being by the early 1700s, helps explain the 1837 rebellion. It would endure at least until 1850, if not up to the conscription crises of the two world wars. The important point here is that the working people could be goaded to riot, but only in a defensive way. They would not storm the prisons in 1794 or starve Montreal in 1796.

The Riots and Revolutionary France

Limited though the riots were, one wonders if they could be attributed to the machinations of revolutionary France. The answer is mixed but mainly negative. Rousse and the Canadiens working to further his aims helped stimulate the militia riots in and around the cities by spreading word that the French would attack, urging Canadiens not to fight their brothers, and presenting conscription as a malign English plot. But this is not to suggest that sympathizers with revolutionary France could bring people to riot at will. The issue was tailor-made for agitators, given habitant detestation of militia service (especially at or near sowing time) and the government's failure to explain the law. Without any effort by francophiles whatever, resistance would likely have been widespread – it occurred all over the province, beyond areas accessible to the urban-based sympathizers. With regard to the Road Act riots, the evidence is ambiguous. The first disturbances, in August 1796, occurred before emissaries were sent into the colony and it is highly unlikely Ducalvet and those he recruited would have advocated rioting in the Montreal area. Some agitators believed they were fostering the interests of France, but detailed proof is lacking. In any case, they again had a tailor-made issue (corvées in or shortly after the harvest period, failure of the government to explain the law) and again refusal to work was general throughout the colony.

The evidence makes it abundantly clear that the disturbances were not initiated by French diplomatic officials in the United States. The militia riots began about three months after Genêt had left office and when his successor, Citizen Fauchet, was following instructions from the Jacobin Committee of Public Safety not to become involved in subverting Lower Canadian government. In the fall of 1796 it would have been the height of folly for French officials to have fostered rioting or insurrection. The naval attack was projected for the next summer and early provocation would have resulted in British reinforcements and/or discouragement on the part of potential supporters. Ambassador Liston, who kept a close eye on happenings in the French embassy at Philadelphia, informed Prescott in January 1797 of 'the great Anxiety discovered [revealed] by Mr. Adet and his Associates here (on hearing of the Disturbance that took place at Montreal respecting the High Roads) lest an Insurrection should break out before their Plans were brought to maturity.'[80]

The Extent of the Danger

If French forces had invaded the colony, they would probably not have received widespread support. Revolutionary ideals remained foreign to Canadiens and working people were without educated leaders. Despite a general pro-French feeling and a general expectation of invasion at some time, working Canadiens did not prepare to aid their former countrymen. No cache of arms and no domestic plans for a rising were ever found by the Lower Canadian authorities. The working people normally did not inform on emissaries operating for France, but no coherent underground of known sympathizers, accumulating intelligence and prepared to help spies, was ever constructed.

The popular response, of course, would have depended partly on circumstances. French atrocities against the clergy, refusal to pay for provisions, or treatment of the Canadiens as country bumpkins would quickly have turned opinion against the invaders. Had the government at Quebec foolishly attempted general conscription, the result would surely have been disastrous for it too. Such extreme cases aside, I think the common response would have been a prudent neutrality in action (at least until the military issue was no longer in serious doubt), with the manifestation of national sentiment in favour of the French extending only to non-military aid, such as provisions and military intelligence. This was the opinion of emigré Jules Le Fer, a spy employed by the government at Quebec in the summer of 1798. Le Fer spent many weeks incognito in the towns and countryside gathering information for his report. According to Governor Prescott, Le Fer found the Canadiens

in general (he had not indeed found any Exceptions) very desirous that this Country should be regained by France: but he had not discovered that they had made any actual Arrangements for lending the French any regular Assistance in arms: and although their Wishes were very strong in Favour of France he did not think it likely, so far as he could discover, that any very considerable Number would join the French in Arms immediately ... [but] that the generality of them would be disposed to be mere lookers on at the first, while Matters might remain doubtful; but should the French succeed so far as to make themselves [potential] Masters of the Country in a short time ... the Canadians would then join them in great Numbers.[81]

The English élite, alas, did not see it in that balanced way.

5

The Garrison Mentality

'I found myself in a French Colony with an English Garrison'
Charles Inglis, Anglican Bishop of Nova Scotia
writing to the Archbishop of Canterbury about Quebec, 27 August 1789

By late 1793 a pattern to English élite perceptions of security emerged, which would prevail until 1812. The English entertained exaggerated fears of the external danger posed by France and magnified the insurrectionary potential of the Canadiens, who were French in culture, recently conquered, and formed the great majority of the colonial population. These fears – the garrison mentality – were linked. Contemporaries invariably assumed French invaders would meet with a strong, positive, armed response from the new subjects. In the few assertions of apprehended insurrection not directly implying that the rising would be sparked by a previous French landing, the writer almost always made one of two assumptions: that there would be such a previous landing, or that, sooner or later, there would be a French attack to support the rebels if their uprising was at all successful. Occasionally contemporaries expressed the view that Canadien insurrection without French military assistance was a solvable problem. Deputy Paymaster General John Hale even wrote in 1803 that there was not 'much fear of Rebellion, for a single Battalion would frighten the whole Province.' He went on though to claim that if 'a French Armament appear, they will be joined by every man in the Country.'[1] While the term garrison mentality is used to cover a variety of fears of external and internal danger, its pure expression can be summed up thus: in the event of a French invasion, the Canadien artisans, labourers, habitants, and middling ranks would rise *en masse* in supportive rebellion, with English heads targeted for Jacobin pikes. One English resident in the fall of 1793 decided to quit the colony because, as his American brother-in-law explained to Genêt, he was 'sure the moment a Descent was made by the Republicans of France that the French Inhabitants would Cut the throats of all that they thought to be in the British interest.'[2]

ANALYSIS OF THE GARRISON MENTALITY

External Danger

In October 1793 Dr John Mervin Nooth, superintendent of hospitals, remarked on the extraordinary 'Bustle' in Quebec City designed to frustrate an expected 'attack from the French.' A few years later, in 1797, John Richardson credited a report that Admiral Richery's recently elusive fleet, with up to thirty thousand troops (!), would attempt a landing in the spring. 'No man,' he wrote, 'can doubt of a contemplated invasion, to be aided by exciting a Revolt.' These are but two of dozens of such opinions expressed by government officials and other English élite members in the 1790s. Genêt's plans, the Directory's encirclement plot, Ira Allen's part in it and the activities of enemy agents in the province were known through extensive intelligence efforts, soon after the event, even to the general public, who were bombarded with war propaganda emanating from the governor, the Roman Catholic bishop, the Loyal Associations, the courts, the newspapers and the Legislature.[3]

The Seigneurial System

Reflecting on the petition from the *censitaires* of Longeueil, the normally unflappable Dorchester worried that agitation against the seigneurial regime might explode into a 'Party distinction of Aristocrat and Democrat,' with all that implied when hundreds of nobles were being guillotined in Paris.[4] Equally concerned, Monk inserted into his Judicature Act of 1794 a section explicitly granting the Intendant's regulatory powers to the Courts of King's Bench and urged the colonial secretary to direct that the attorney general represent the *censitaires* in all future litigation.[5] While nothing substantive came of these initiatives, the fact they were made at all indicates how seriously the threat was perceived at the Château. In addition, de Rocheblave's abortive motion of 1795 on illegal exactions and Panet's proposal in amendment for a peripatetic committee temporarily panicked Osgoode, who thought this 'Formidable Question' would 'necessarily produce a great Conflict between ... Landlords & Tenants throughout the Country.'[6] In the same session English members unsuccessfully attempted to eliminate the main feudal features of the land tenure system, painting a graphic picture of the security dangers it presented, as well as its restraints on commerce.[7]

The Riots and the Election of 1796

The militia riots thoroughly unnerved the English. Although initially unperturbed, Lord Dorchester informed the secretary of state in June that the upper classes in Lower Canada feared they might well 'experience a similar fate with Persons of their own description in France.'[8] Seigneur David Alexander Grant, among several others, thought if the French, the Americans or both attacked the colony 'it is *Gone*; The Canadians are either disafected [sic] or indifferent,' having been successfully tampered with by persons, working for the French or the Americans, who had industriously circulated rebellious pamphlets.[9] Monk, shocked 'to find the same savage barbarity [talk of disembowelling, heads on poles, and other horrors] exercised in France ... so early manifest itself in the present stage of Revolt,' asserted that only the 'effective exertions ... made by Magistrates and others' in Montreal had averted possible rebellion in that district during September.[10] Certainly his opinion was shared.

Endorsed by the magistrates, rumours of a *jacquerie* to liberate the Montreal prisoners in mid-September 1794 quickly spread panic among English residents. Writing on the 15th, Judge James Walker informed Osgoode that the town had been in a state of constant tension for days and had the revolt not been 'strangled in its birth' the district would have suffered all the calamities 'of a civil war.'[11] Magistrate Thomas McCord had quickly organized volunteer defences. Lawyer Stephen Sewell, who imagined the whole district had risen in revolt, and merchant James Ogilvy were assigned the task of making cartridges. Sewell informed his brother that fears had intensified when a group of priests entering the city on ordinary business were mistaken for clerical refugees fleeing from Jacobin insurgents. In the end, however, the impending attack proved to be a phantom: 'Most assuredly during Saturday and the night following we were in an alarm but had they come even with six hundred men they would have shared the worst but thank God it seems now to be entirely subsided and ... we begin to think there never were more than twenty men throughout the whole Country who had serious intentions of an attack on the town.'[12]

Of course, the election of 1796 was interpreted as a Canadien vote for treason and a revolt of the lower classes. To Osgoode, Prescott, and others, several elected Canadiens were 'Democrates' or 'Sans Culottes.'[13] More than three decades later merchant-historian John Fleming recalled the second general election with horror, writing that many of the 'successful Candidates ... were political fanatics, fired by the perusal of the doctrines of the French Republicans.'[14]

The same signs of political hysteria surfaced during the Road Act period, with Prescott believing almost all Canadiens disloyal and partial to the principles of the French Revolution.[15] Officials in the capital shared his views. Osgoode harped on the 'Ignorance and Disaffection of the whole [Canadien] Race,' concluding that 'open Resistance to all Civil subordination is prevented merely by the presence of the Troops that are quartered among us.' Sewell and Executive councillor John Young believed the riots had been intended as a full-scale insurrection, orchestrated by Adet through Ducalvet, a plethora of unidentified French emissaries, and some local revolutionaries.[16]

English Montrealers were equally alarmed. Loyalist Isaac Winslow Clarke, the deputy commissary general, compared the shadowy goings on to the activities of the secret committees of correspondence in the Boston of 1775. In February 1797 John Richardson, who suspected Papineau of being behind the Montreal riots, advocated the declaration of martial law in order to protect persons of property from 'all the horrors of assassination.' According to Montreal merchant William Lindsay, it was revealing and sinister that the 'spirit of licentiousness, both in Town and Country, rises, in propropotion [sic], to the success of our Enemys abroad.' Like many others, he believed a voluntary armed association was required to protect Montrealers from the democrats, should the regular forces be withdrawn to Quebec. On one point he was absolutely certain: only Prescott's dispatch of the troops to the city had frustrated the 'Junto in this neighbourhood' which had been and perhaps still was 'planning the destruction of the English within the walls.'[17]

These tensions had a deleterious effect on relations between the nationalities in the cities. John Neilson, editor of the *Quebec Gazette*, informed his mother in 1797 that he, like others, had married a Canadienne but had run into 'monstrous prejudice between the natives and Europeans' which he concluded was 'hurtful to their respective interests and even dangerous to their safety.' And at the height of the Road Act riots Sewell reported to Prescott that while there had 'always subsisted among the Canadians and the English settled at Montreal a certain degree of Intimacy and Friendship,' at the moment 'there is no Intercourse and the most ancient and established Friendships appear entirely interrupted.'[18]

Opportunism and Representativeness

Many historians consider the English expressions of alarm during the wars against revolutionary and Napoleonic France not genuine, believing them uttered or written to serve some ulterior purpose.[19] For the years of the French revolutionary war (1793–1802) the alleged motives include the law officers' desire to increase their fees by prosecuting a multitude of 'dangerous' offenders; the governing clique's wish to enhance its importance, political influence, and access to patronage; and the desire of the English élite generally to resist constitutional liberalization, to further monetary self-interest by abolishing the seigneurial regime, and to establish government-controlled elementary schools. For the later period (1803–11) opportunism has been also explained as a rationalization for attempting to suppress the local Roman Catholic church, as an electoral tactic, as a means of destroying the *parti canadien* or even representative government, and as a way of promoting anglification for commercial reasons.[20] Similar suggestions have been made with regard to the Rebellions of 1837–8, the repression of the Winnipeg General Strike, 1919, the internment of the Japanese Canadians in the Second World War, and the handling of the October Crisis of 1970.

Attorney General Monk's reaction to the militia riots is a revealing case study. In late May he adopted two subtly different versions of events. For Dorchester, who initially attributed the riots to 'a long disuse of military services, rather than ... disloyalty' Monk prepared careful reports.[21] No reliance could be placed on the militia and more serious rioting was certainly not out of the question, although from his best judgment of the Canadien character, Monk did not 'think there is much to be apprehended of insurrection, and open rebellion by force of arms, to effect a revolution in the government.' But the attorney general was also awaiting word from his patron, Henry Dundas, the British secretary of state, that he had been appointed chief justice of Montreal, a new position created by the Judicature Act of 1794 which he himself had drafted. To Dundas, far from the scene, he warned in chilling terms that the habitants, in hatred of seigneurs, Canadien as well as English, were preparing for a *jacquerie*, complete with disembowelling and heads on pikes.[22]

By June Dorchester had joined in the general alarm and Monk's reports then took on a new urgency Writing consciously to give his patron ammunition with which to gain favour with the imperial government, Monk detailed what he was doing to save the province: leading the effort to establish loyal associations, arresting dozens of suspects, and so on. In his private letters to Dundas written from May to November 1794 the attorney general stressed the need for a powerful, repressive judicial presence in disaffected Montreal, asked for £1,000 a year, and pressed for the chief justiceship of the province at the next vacancy.[23] Monk was soon appointed chief justice of Montreal at £900 per year. This is a clear case of a man consciously exaggerating the danger of insurrection to advance his own career and line his pockets. Such types can be detected during most security crises. Monk, however, was exceptional and even he believed the habitants, artisans, and labourers could turn to political insurrection if emissaries and local democrats were allowed a free hand to work on supposed grievances.[24] He had no self-interested reason to urge Dundas in the spring of 1794 that additional troops (to bring the total to five thousand) be sent to the Canadas to guarantee their defence.[25]

Most who expressed fear genuinely believed all they said. It is impossible to think, for example, that Stephen Sewell, in letters written to his brother Jonathan outlining the latest emergence of the Cloven Hoof would hypocritically exaggerate his true feelings. There are many other, extant private letters of influential men expressing alarm. There is, moreover, the argument from collective behaviour. When in September 1794, for example, prominent English Montrealers stayed up the night fortifying the town to repel a rumoured attack by armed habitants, they were surely not indulging in a charade for manipulative purposes.

Even believing their own alarming statements, the English, of course, could exploit the security danger for a variety of self-interested purposes, such as resisting any increase in the powers of the Assembly, promoting anglification through a new school system,[26] or seeking the abolition of seigneurial tenure – a prospect which many English seigneurs and merchants found financially alluring. Attracting government patronage was obviously one such purpose. Jonathan and Stephen Sewell, for instance, were ultimately rewarded for their energetic loyalty by being appointed provincial chief justice and solicitor general respectively. An excellent example of the exploitation of fear is provided in a letter written by

William Lindsay to John Young in May 1797, just after Adet's agent David McLane had been captured in Quebec. Lindsay outlined the threat posed by emissaries lurking about and 'our *Faithful* Brethren, the Canadians,' complained that no armed association had been formed and hoped his enclosed December letter to Sewell would 'bring about, at this critical juncture, an establishment [of defence], that may prove solid.' Lindsay then suggested that 'If you conceive that your putting the enclosed ... into the hands of the Chief Justice ... may be the means of strengthening my Interest with that Gentleman, youll [*sic*] then do me that favour.'[27] Lindsay made it onto the civil list in 1797 as comptroller of customs and guager at St Jean, his appointments (at £45 per annum) having been dated to begin on 1 May.[28]

Self-interested purposes there were, but they did not generate the fear. Their existence, of course, made it unlikely that the assumptions on which the fear was based would be undermined by critical examination. One further and simple point should not be forgotten: the perceived security threat provided a perfect vent for cultural prejudice. Stereotyping of the Canadiens became commonplace after 1792. Brilliance of mind did not prevent Jonathan Sewell from expressing this opinion in May 1797: 'Ignorance, profound Ignorance is too surely the characteristick of the Canadians and certainly renders them liable to be imposed upon by the grossest assertions.'[29] A few months earlier Osgoode had condemned 'the whole Race' as stupid, while Colonel John Nairne, seigneur of Murray Bay, wrote of folly and ingratitude being 'ingrained in these people.'[30] To Nairne, David Alexander Grant, and many others the Canadiens were pampered cry babies who should be taught a hard lesson in the interests of security.

There were individuals in the English élite, like Monk, who were not fully imbued with the garrison mentality. By 1795, a year of tranquillity, Lord Dorchester (and some other officials) concluded that Monk had 'excited Apprehensions to assume the merit (at Home) of having appeased them.'[31] In the wake of the Loyal Association campaign and again immediately following Prescott's use of troops in Montreal and in Pointe-Lévi, there were private letters written suggesting an end to the crisis.[32] These few exceptions pale by comparison to the dozens of expressions of fear, often by opinion leaders such as senior government officials in Quebec and prominent Montreal merchants or merchant-magistrates. It seems reasonable to conclude that the garrison mentality was representative of English élite opinion generally, at least during the main periods of perceived crisis.

Some features of the garrison mentality require no further explanation: for example, the fear that feudalism would prove as exploitable a grievance as it had in France, or the apprehension of a French attack, or the belief that massacre of the English was in store if the revolt succeeded. The newspapers, after all, continually poured out French atrocity stories and these exercised a horrible fascination for the English, as revealed in their private letters.[33] But some aspects of the garrison mentality require additional comment.

Perception of the Parti Canadien

By late 1793 the merchant George Allsopp, who had recently campaigned for an Assembly with extensive powers, was lecturing his son Carleton – an admirer of French republicanism – about the dangers of elected legislatures. 'Sour malcontents,' he wrote, 'are to be found in every country & it is the great satisfaction to such to raise murmurs and discontents and to stir up the disaffected with or without cause.'[34] This reaction to the new constitution, widely shared, is hardly surprising. Assemblies after all had led the agitation resulting in both the American and French revolutions and in Lower Canada the house would inevitably be controlled by a Canadien majority, beholden to a largely illiterate, often anglophobic electorate. The English feared the 'demagogues' who outspokenly defended the political interests of the lower orders. These 'malcontents' were able to excite the people and use the Assembly to promote grievances. Even a minor issue such as the replacement of Montreal's crumbling fortification wall caused Prescott and Osgoode to fret about demagogic manipulation.[35] The *parti canadien* attempted to liberalize the constitution even if that meant opposing, at least temporarily, the passage of security legislation. When it is remembered that in contemporary Britain the Whig rump under Charles James Fox was often castigated as treasonable, it is not surprising that the *parti canadien* leaders were thought of as cherishing Jacobin principles or likely working for French officials in the United States. The concept of a loyal opposition was a generation away in England, almost two in British North America.

The destruction of the Canadien seigneurs as a significant electoral force in 1796 must have seemed to many in the English élite as the classic forerunner to revolution. The Canadien contingent in the new Assembly would be composed mainly of lawyers and notaries of humble social origins, shopkeepers, artisans, and habitants. The English reaction followed Edmund Burke's famous analysis of the French National Assembly and particularly his claim that among the leading revolutionaries were low-born small town attorneys. 'The fomenters and conductors of the petty war of village vexation,' he had written, had nothing to lose by revolution and indeed had a natural interest in promoting it to 'lay open to them those innumerable lucrative jobs which follow in the train of all great convulsions ... in the state.'[36] Burke had also asserted that the illiterate peasants and petty shopkeepers in the Assembly were 'more formed to be overborne and swayed by the intrigues and artifices of lawyers than to become their counterpoise.' Understandably then in 1797 government officials worked to enact legislation enabling them to intern the leaders of the *parti canadien* as traitors. By a precipitate prorogation Prescott cut off all debate on amendments, pushed mainly by Dumas, to the Road Act.

The Physical Situation and Fragility of the Social Order

The physical situation was alarming. The colony's means of defence were barely adequate to repulse even a minor assault, while apprehending emissaries sent into the province by Genêt and Adet proved extremely difficult. As the many riots of the 1790s demonstrated, the rudimentary system of police provided only minimal protection. In the cities this force consisted of unpaid, part-time magistrates assisted by a handful of unsalaried constables (paid from fees) whom they appointed or reappointed annually.[37] In the countryside the distrusted captains of militia were responsible for law enforcement. But the single most threatening aspect of the physical situation lay in simple demography. The English were outnumbered about fifteen to one by former subjects of the enemy, the large majority of whom, possessed of hunting guns, lived along the St Lawrence and Richelieu rivers – the two principal avenues of expected attack. Prescott expressed the thoughts of many in the English élite when he informed the secretary of state in October 1796 that the situation would be critical if French troops managed to reach the colony, since 'His Majesty's English Subjects here ... are not in a greater proportion than as Seventy to Two Thousand.'[38]

Part of the mental make-up of the English élite can be expressed in the phrase 'deep sense of the fragility of the social order,' – meaning a belief that rioting, if not speedily and vigorously repressed, could easily turn into rebellion or revolution. One can cite several loyalists with such a sense: Chief Justice Smith, Stephen Sewell, and Isaac Winslow Clarke to name a few. Let Jonathan Sewell speak for this group. As a boy of eight in 1774 he had watched from inside his father's house in Massachusetts as it was attacked by one of the revolutionary crowds. After relocation to England in 1779, he must have shared his father's reaction to the Gordon riots the following year in London – disgust but not surprise.[39] At the outset of the Road Act disturbances, Sewell characteristically warned his subordinate, Solicitor General Louis-C. Foucher, that any serious 'opposition to the laws of a Country, if not timely checked may end in perfect Anarchy and the Destruction of the government.'[40]

The sense of the fragility of the social order was shared by many non-loyalists. David Alexander Grant, Monk, Richardson, Colonel Nairne, William Grant, Judge James Walker, Osgoode, George Allsopp, and other men of the time had witnessed the American Revolution as well as the loyalists.[41] Some had done so actively: Nairne, Richardson, and Allsopp had fought against American revolutionaries, while Monk had been active in creating loyal associations in Nova Scotia. The sense of the fragility of the social order, then, was not a loyalist preserve; it was a widely held assumption based on the American Revolution, to be sure, but above all a response to the French Revolution, where the Paris people had brought the age-old and formidable Bourbon monarchy to its end.

The Efficacy of Conspiracy

The garrison mentality was also nurtured by a belief that a small number of plotters had the potential to manipulate the people almost at will. In 1794 Attorney General Monk was forever trying to pierce to the heart of the conspiracy which lay behind the militia rioting. He also credited Sewell's appraisal of the situation in Montreal. As paraphrased by the attorney general, Sewell had reported: 'That it is discovered, that some leading Character is at Montreal who guides the Canadians to their disloyalty ... and is relied upon "That the French are coming" ... The person not yet discovered [and never was].'[42] In writing to Sewell, Richardson expressed shock that no one had voluntarily come forth to denounce the circulation of Adet's pamphlet, and he was 'persuaded there is hardly a Common Canadian in Town or a Democrat of the higher Order, who did not know of them, and the Commission.' Such lengthy and widespread secrecy might merely indicate political neutrality; more likely it marked 'the extent of the conspiracy.' Richardson was almost certain Ducalvet had made contact with influential democrats of the middle class and believed that, if he wished, Papineau could make a 'disclosure of the whole plot.'[43]

Belief in conspiracy as an explanation for shattering events has always been a temptation. The eighteenth century was no exception. Indeed, belief in the efficacy of conspirators was then more understandable, for it was grounded in commonplace ideas of historical causation. There was little attempt in the eighteenth century (Gibbon and Voltaire excepted) to relate historical change to broad political, social, or economic factors. Contemporaries tended to accept the simplest explanations, ascribing events approved of to Providence or Reason and those disliked to divine retribution or the nefarious activities of a small group of self-seeking conspirators. The prevalence of the conspiracy interpretation in the latter half of the century is well illustrated by the reaction of individuals, on both sides of the issue, to the events leading up to the American Revolution. The soon-to-be revolutionaries interpreted British policies from 1763 on as carefully planned steps in an elaborate conspiracy of British ministers gradually to enslave them with the establishment of the Anglican Church, commercial monopolies, ever-increasing taxation, and the elimination of representative government. British Tories and many American loyalists, on the other hand, ascribed the Declaration of Independence to a well-thought-out plot of Samuel Adams, John Hancock, and a few other men originating as early as 1764.[44]

Pointing the finger at secret subversive schemers remained commonplace through the 1790s. American Federalists, for example, often convinced themselves that Thomas Jefferson and his Republican colleagues were plotting a French Revolution of the lower classes, while leading Republicans worried about the supposed conspiracy of Washington, Hamilton, Adams, and other Federalists to restore the monarchy. In his *Reflections on the Revolution in France*, Edmund Burke wrote of a conspiracy of social upstarts. And in 1797 there appeared in London two books which claimed the French Revolution was the work of one Adam Weishaupt, a power-mad Bavarian professor who with a few henchmen had worked through his secret German societies known as the Illuminati and the French Masonic lodges to undermine piety and deference to authority, and to manipulate men such as Mirabeau, the Abbé Sieyès, Condorcet and others.[45] Weishaupt had orchestrated the election to the Estates General, had corrupted the Gardes Françaises at the time of the Bastille, and had financed the October 1789 march of the women on Versailles. He was the power behind the Girondins, the Jacobins, and finally the Directory. His secret tentacles spread throughout the world. These books, by an emigré priest, Abbé Augustin Barruel, and Edinburgh chemistry professor John Robison, had a brisk sale in London and considerable influence in Britain and Lower Canada at the turn of the century.

Belief in the capacity of conspirators meant that a small group of men could easily convince the Canadien masses, despite their privileges as British subjects, to resist law enforcement and might even be able to manipulate them to revolution as had happened in the thirteen colonies and in the Paris of 1789. For those who believe in secret conspiracies, failure to prove the plot or catch the plotters is likely to be interpreted simply as 'evidence' that the conspiracy is very well organized indeed. During the Second World War the American OSS and army intelligence concluded Germany was on the verge of producing the atomic bomb. The reasoning which led to this conclusion is neatly stated by two historians of secret intelligence: 'What was the evidence for it? None: the fact that no concrete evidence could be found was considered solid evidence that the program was so secret, no trace of it could be found. Therefore, the Germans had taken extraordinary measures to hide it; the high priority such a massive undertaking required indicated that the Germans were close to the bomb.'[46]

Lack of proof, after months of inquiry, did not prevent Jonathan Sewell from concluding in March 1797 that there was 'in the Province a systematic Intention of exciting a Rebellion, and ... the Road Act has been used as an Instrument for that Purpose.'[47] Had not Ducalvet's meeting and Berthelot's resistance occurred near each other in time and place?

6

The Garrison Mentality and the Administration of Criminal Justice, 1794–1797

The government responded to perceived security needs in 1794 by passage and enforcement of the much misunderstood Alien Act. The principles had been decided largely on the advice of Attorney General Monk, by the early winter and the bill was introduced into the Assembly on 15 May by recent political convert, Judge De Bonne. Although not provoked by the Leveillé or militia riots, its enactment was undoubtedly made smoother by those events. The only opposition came from a few supporters of the *parti canadien*, the most prominent of whom were de Rocheblave and Jean-Antoine Panet. According to Monk, the latter 'who is considered a Democrat .... at first declared his design to oppose some parts, particularly the suspension of the hab. corp. act,' but eventually backed down. In the end the bill passed with only three dissenting votes, an early example of the ease with which Canadians have enacted drastic security legislation in times of apparent crisis. Two days later it was accepted without amendment by the Legislative Council and on 31 May assented to by Governor Dorchester. The act was to be in force for one year only.[1]

The portions of the act dealing with aliens, drawn largely from a British statute of 1793, established elaborate regulations governing the registration of aliens and British subjects who since 10 June 1789 had lived in France or had made certain investments there. Aliens had to

carry with them certificates of their status. The governor was authorized to deport foreigners simply by issuing a warrant to a peace officer
to escort them across the frontier or place them on board an outbound
ship. By proclamation the governor-in-council could also order groups
of foreigners, however law-abiding, to depart the province on pain of
imprisonment. These provisions enlarged the scope of the royal prerogative, which already enabled the crown to evict enemy aliens summarily.

The Alien Act also suspended rights to bail and speedy trial and,
hence, to the writ of habeas corpus in the case of persons 'who are or
shall be charged with or suspected of the crime of high treason.' No
judge or justice of the peace could bail or try such persons without a
special warrant from the governor-in-council. Internment was possible
without charging a prisoner, a very convenient arrangement for the
government since it might have found itself under some moral obligation
to try some of those formally charged with treason. In case of persons
charged with seditious offences the right to bail (and it was a right if the
sureties offered were sufficient) was severely restricted. It could not be
granted by a magistrate but only by and at the option of the governor,
the chief justice, a puisne judge of the King's Bench or two or more
justices of Oyer and Terminer. The act also included an elastic definition
of seditious crimes.

As in modern times, sedition in late eighteenth and early nineteenth-
century Britain was a collective term embracing three offences: manifest-
ing a seditious intention either by means of a written libel, or spoken
words, or conspiracy.[2] The essence of seditious intention was characterized in 1793 by Lord Chief Justice Kenyon as one 'calculated to put the
people in a state of discontent' with the way in which they were governed.[3] The object, then, was to protect government – not at this time
classes of His Majesty's subjects – and to do so by preventing the spread
of disaffection.

The rationale behind punishing these offences was that if unchecked
they would lead to popular disturbances, and the charges in sedition
cases almost invariably referred to the accused with some such phrase as
'having no regard ... for the public peace and tranquillity,' or having
intended 'to disturb and disquiet the happy state ... of this kingdom.'[4]
But there was not the slightest hint that the accused must have directly
incited violence. Such a requirement would not be clearly established in
Canada or the United Kingdom until the middle of the twentieth century.
In the period we are concerned with courts were free to condemn a

publication or utterance if it was merely *conceivable* that sooner or later the masses might be aroused to direct action. As was said in *Burdett* (1820), the test was whether 'the people *may* be set in motion against the Government.'[5]

The bare freedom to criticize cabinet ministers or public servants was recognized by the courts. In *Cobbett* (1804), Lord Ellenborough conceded that it had always been the right of the British subject, 'to exhibit the folly or imbecility of the members of the government' and an 1810 decision held that advocacy of a wholesale change of ministers and measures was not, in itself, seditious.[6] But such criticism was to be addressed to reason, not passion. Critics could point out honest errors or condemn unintelligent policies, but were not to impute criminality, corruption, desire to oppress, gross bias, or self-interest to the powers that were, including either house of Parliament. If, as Lord Kenyon put it in 1789, the people 'should ever conceive their governors are so inattentive to their duty, as to exercise their functions only to keep themselves in power, and for their own emolument, without attending to the interests of the public, government must be relaxed, and at length crumble to dust.'[7]

In the 1792 trial of Thomas Paine for writing and publishing *Rights of Man*, Thomas Erskine took a strong stand in defence of academic freedom. Citing Milton, Locke, and other speculative writers to show the extent to which disputatious tracts on constitutional fundamentals had been sanctioned, he argued that every Englishman had the right to attempt the enlightenment of others on any subject, provided the author tried to tell the truth, did not advocate disobedience to the laws, and did not calumniate living officials. Neither the court nor the jury accepted Erskine's plea and in the following two years there was a spate of successful prosecutions against persons who, like Paine, praised Lockean ideas of trustee kingship and the right of revolution or extolled popular sovereignty or republicanism. Even advocacy of parliamentary reform – limited mainly to extending the franchise, but evoking fears of French equality – was deemed seditious.[8] The rulings were often justified by the excitement of the lower orders under the influences of the reform societies and the French Revolution and the supposed existence of French agents working among them.

During the first thirty years of George III's reign conflicts between juries and judges over verdicts in seditious libel cases were endemic. Stimulated by defence counsel such as Erskine and a host of pamphleteers, juries tended to resist restrictive instructions from the Bench, from

Lord Mansfield in particular. These instructions denied the jury any right to deliver a general verdict of guilty or not guilty; instead they were to confine themselves to deciding if the accused had in fact published the work in question and whether the innuendoes were to be taken as the crown interpreted them. Such a holding by Mansfield in the *Dean of St. Asaph's* case (1783–4) – the jury had found 'guilty of publishing only' after Erskine had delivered one of his timeless arguments – greatly intensified the battle.[9] A strong pro-Erskine consensus soon emerged in the House of Commons, resulting in Charles James Fox's famous Libel Act of 1792, the last significant liberal constitutional reform enacted for a generation. Juries were empowered to return a general verdict in all libel cases, after listening to the judge's instructions on the law.

Although the conviction rate in British sedition cases during the decade after Fox's Act was well over 50 per cent, a number of accused owed their acquittals to the new power enjoyed by juries to ignore judicial instructions.[10] Juries tended to excuse constitutional reform advocacy, inflammatory words uttered in a state of drunkenness, and even intemperate attacks on cabinet ministers.

Fox's Libel Act did not refer to the colonies and hence did not become part of the criminal law of Lower Canada. In the 1780s and very early 1790s, English reformers in Quebec, self-interestedly perhaps, had been solidly on the side of Erskine in the Erskine-Mansfield debate.[11] But hostile reaction to the French Revolution undermined their radicalism. There would be no legislative initiatives on the subject of seditious libel trials during the first session of representative government and the Alien Act remained silent on the issue. The failure to legislate left the law unclear. The judges of England had advised the Lords in 1792 that Mansfield's contention was correct, but the Libel Act itself, although ambiguous, arguably declared what the common law had always been. The punishment for sedition, as with other misdemeanours, was imprisonment and/or a fine, the length and amount being within the entire discretion of the court.

Section 31 of the Alien Act condemned any person who uttered or printed seditious words or spread false news. Any of these activities was made seriously criminal if it tended 'in any manner [to] disturb the peace and happiness enjoyed under his Majesty's Government.' The words 'in any manner' and the conjunction of 'happiness' with 'peace' would seem to have dispensed with any idea that physical disturbances in the future had to be at least conceivable. Presumably a writing or utterance which disturbed the peace of mind or contentment supposedly enjoyed by deferential subjects, by suggesting that life in Lower Canada fell short of human perfection, would have been seditious.

Clearly Monk wished to remove any argumentative weapons which defence counsel, citing British authority, might employ in sedition cases. Henceforth it would be seditious merely to criticize government policy in moderate tones, to call for constitutional reform, or foster ill will against the propertied classes. Section 31 would *a fortiori* also foreclose any appeal to the curiously limited definition of these crimes Chief Justice Smith had offered to the November 1793 assizes at Quebec. The criminal law, he had then declared, 'interdicts all Writing, Printing, and even speaking in derogation of the Civil Constitution of the Country, with an intent to subvert it.'[12] Although probably not intended, this interpretation might well have allowed defence counsel to argue that the emphasis on constitutional subversion left residents free to indulge in even vituperative attacks on individual officials, particular policies such as those suspending habeas corpus or constitutional arrangements differing from the British model (for example, the dependence of the judiciary, limited financial powers of the Assembly).

Monk had successfully eliminated any problems which might arise from the substantive law and naturally he did not extend to the accused the benefits of Fox's Libel Act. The penalties were severe. For a first offence, fine and/or imprisonment were to be applied. Second offences would bring sentences of transportation for any period up to life. But court convictions were probably a secondary concern to the attorney general; he now had the basis for a round-up and internment of persons deemed politically unreliable by the law officers or magistrates. The expanded meaning of sedition and the restriction of the right to bail in sedition cases enabled this to be done with effect and without fear of criticism based on the few liberal strands in the common law. These arrangements would also ensure that a host of informers would come forward.

Monk's statute, then, went beyond contemporary British restrictions on personal liberty. It was also far more authoritarian than the United States' Sedition Act of 1798 which required proof of malice, allowed truth as a defence, explicitly sanctioned the principle of Fox's act, did not suspend habeas corpus, and limited punishment to fines of $2,000 and imprisonment for two years.[13]

Under the Alien Act suspicious individuals were dealt with vigorously to the point of deportation. Nevertheless, control at the main inland point of entry at St Jean was far from perfect. Persons not suspected of being foreign agents could safely enter as disguised Canadiens. Even where emissaries were expected and descriptions available, enforcement was difficult. In 1797 Colonel de Bernière, commanding at St Jean, expressed regret to the governor's military secretary that despite his 'best endeavours in preventing the admission of the disguised Enemys of our Country into it, and preventing the escape of those who have been within it ... they are very inadequate ... The multitude of passengers makes it an easy matter for a disguised Person, speaking the language to escape detection.' And as the colonel also pointed out, emissaries could often enter clandestinely by way of a little-used road east of St Jean.[14]

By early 1794 Dorchester was refusing all requests from Frenchmen wishing to immigrate or visit the colony, unless they carried British passports. Such passports he urged London in July 1795 should be issued only by the secretary of state and not by the military authorities in the West Indies, as had recently occurred. It was quite impossible to discriminate safely among Frenchmen and some of these supposed royalists might well 'Excite an Interest among Certain Classes of the People, pregnant with dangerous Effects.' For that reason he had refused an application made from Upper Canada by the well-known traveller and emigré the Duc de La Rochefoucauld-Liancourt, even though the duc was received by the Simcoes in Upper Canada and carried letters of recommendation from Portland, Simcoe, and the British minister to the United States. La Rochefoucauld-Liancourt, it should be recalled, had been a supporter of the early French Revolution and remained favourable to many of its principles. Dorchester's successor, Sir Robert Prescott, continued the policy.[15]

The sections in the Alien Act authorizing internment were immediately applied by the attorney general. From May to November 1794 between fifty and one hundred persons were imprisoned for varying periods. Those arrested included the prominent and the humble: Paul and Nicolas Dorion, prosperous Quebec City shopkeepers, and illiterate habitant Louis Paquet of Charlesbourg, for examples. The Dorions and Paquet were never tried. Nor was the shipbuilder John Black. Because of his knowledge of colloquial French and contacts with the working people, Black had been employed by Monk to ferret out the disloyal among the artisans of Quebec and the habitants of the adjacent rural parishes. He apparently overplayed his hand as a sympathizer with revolutionary France and was himself arrested on suspicion of treason. For reasons which are obscure, Monk failed to intervene and Black languished in jail for some weeks. Although they had never suspected his loyalty, Black's merchant clients – except for his main patron, John Young – turned from him and his flourishing business was ruined. As he later complained, 'I passed for a disturber of publick peace & villen an Enemy to my King and Country the scoff & reproach of the times.'[16]

An American visitor remarked of Lower Canada in the late summer of 1794 it was 'a crime to think as a republican and high treason to speak as such.' The atmosphere had come to resemble that of a witch-hunt. Although perfectly innocent, the young Whig John Neilson, then a printer-editor at the family-owned *Quebec Gazette*, feared he might be arrested. Accompanied by a Canadien friend, Alexandre Menut Jr, Neilson fled the colony in early September and took up residence in New Jersey. On returning at the end of May 1795, he explained that his flight had 'proceeded entirely from his apprehensions of being imprisoned, as Mr Monk then Attorney General had threatened to have him punished for a bad translation in the *Gazette*.' Monk had warned that 'if such a thing happened again he would put him & all about him in a Dungeon, or words to that purpose.' Neilson had taken this threatened attack on the press very seriously. He was but one of dozens, during this period, who escaped the clutches of the attorney general by fleeing to the United States.[17]

THE ASSIZES OF 1794–1795

During his stay in Upper Canada the Duc de La Rochefoucauld-Liancourt learned that the English in both colonies thought the Canadiens should be much more harshly treated than was the case: ' "The French", they say, "beat them, starved them, and put them in irons; they should therefore be treated by us in the same manner".' There was certainly a great deal of regret over the supposed consequences of leniency and it is not difficult to find colourful quotations to the effect that lenity to the new subjects, whether in the administration of criminal justice or otherwise, was a policy so wrongheaded as to invite calamity. In July 1794 David Alexander Grant wrote Simon McTavish, then in London, to inform him the colony would certainly be lost if the French or Americans were to attack before reinforcements arrived. This state of affairs was easily traceable to the new subjects: 'Had coercive measures been taken with them ... it might have answered ... but over mild measures ... since under our Government has induced them to think that ... [these decisions] proceed from fear & want of power to put the Laws in force – you know the nature of the beast, therefore can conceive the above reasoning to be

just ... being founded on the ingratitude & ignorance of the Canadians ...'
With reinforcements and some highly punitive examples, he concluded,
'we might still hold our ground.'[18] But Grant and those many who
thought like him were not to be satisfied by the punishments meted out
by the Court of King's Bench. In Montreal sentences ranged from £5 and
one month, to Duclos's punishment of £20, security for seven years, and
twelve months in prison. This was the stiffest sentence meted out to any
rioter in 1794–5 or again after the Road Act riots. At the end of the
session Osgoode delivered a tirade against Duclos which went down
very well with the English spectators.[19]

At the November criminal term in Quebec five Charlesbourg rioters,
including farmers Jerôme Bédard and Pierre Chartré, were indicted by
the grand jury for high treason under Edward III's Statute of Treasons.
The precise count was for levying war against the king. The trials were
continued because acts of William III (1695) and Anne (1708) required that
a person accused of treason receive copies of the indictment, the jury
panel, and a list of proposed crown witnesses (with residences and
occupations in both cases) at least ten days before arraignment.[20] The
grand jury also indicted seventeen men for misdemeanours related to the
militia riots: sixteen Canadiens and John Black. Due largely to a juryman
falling dangerously ill, only four verdicts were delivered, the other trials
(including those of Black and Dumontier) being continued to the subsequent term. A leader of the rioting at Nouvelle Beauce (where crowds
had imprisoned their officers), Gervais Lambert dit Champagne was
given twelve months' imprisonment (plus £5 and security for two years).
One resident of the capital named Jean-Baptiste Vocel dit Belhumeur, a
carpenter, who had helped circulate Les Français libres, was sentenced to
two months and fined a shilling. Carpenter François Le Droit dit Perche,
an instigator of the Quebec city militia rioting, and the tinsmith Augustin
Lavau were acquitted, Monk attributing this to politically inspired perjury on the part of Canadien witnesses – a phenomenon which, he
claimed, had also appeared in the Montreal trials.

The threatened lawlessness following the arrest of the Côte des Neiges
ringleaders just after the September assizes and the urging of legal
advisers convinced Dorchester that a mild penal policy was essential
to ensure against further rioting or even insurrection. As the Montreal
1795 March term approached the governor issued firm instructions to
Sewell with regard to political offenders. 'His Lordship directs me to
say,' wrote civil secretary Herman Ryland, 'that in cases of this nature he
wishes all the lenity to lie that the peace & tranquility [sic] of the Country

will permit.' The governor 'therefore desires you will drop all such prosecutions as do not appear necessary for example & good order.' In compliance with this directive Sewell did not bring the tailor and supposed traitor Costille to trial. All thoughts (which Monk had entertained) of prosecuting the Côte des Neiges trio for high treason were given up. They were convicted of riot and each sentenced to three months in prison.[21]

One major political trial was that of a Canadien named Pascal P___, charged with uttering seditious words and indulging in seditious practices at a review of militia held (probably at Point Claire) in August 1794. Unfortunately the only record discovered of this case is a torn letter written by the accused's counsel, David Ross. According to the letter Ross obtained an acquittal against all expectation and owed his victory to arguments made famous by Thomas Erskine in the *Dean of St. Asaph's* case. Ross must have argued in favour of the jury's right to make up its own mind whether the words or practices were seditious – a courageous position considering the times and the fact that Monk was presiding over his first assizes as chief justice of Montreal. The latter, it appears, did not take kindly to the plea: '... our Chief has not yet efaced [sic] from his mind or forgot his having been Atty Genl. his charges in general press hard on the prisoners.'

A few days later the governor ordered the entry of *nolle prosequi* in all political cases pending in the District of Quebec, a decision the local *Times* praised as but one more example of that 'lenity which distinguishes his humane government.' Sewell explained in court that His Excellency had concluded the militia disturbances were due to error, not disloyalty and that further, punitive examples were unnecessary. Osgoode reminded the accused that the crown's magnanimity 'calls loudly for a grateful ... conduct on your part,' adding that 'under any other government, some of you would not now be living.'[22]

One strong impression emerging from a study of the assizes of 1794–5 is the obvious reluctance to indict Canadiens for treason and when so indicted to try them. The evidence of high treason against Dumontier, Lavau, Duclos, and Costille was very strong, but they were not indicted for that crime. Nor were the three Côte des Neiges rioters imprisoned in September 1794, despite Monk's belief that they were guilty. The five Charlesbourg habitants against whom true bills for levying war had been found were pardoned. Part of the reason for such leniency may have been concern that, helped by perjured witnesses, juries would not convict, thus embarrassing the government and reinforcing a general sense of immunity among the working people. Probably more important was the governor's longstanding policy of governing the Canadiens with a light rein.

Lord Dorchester's name is of course associated with the conciliatory policy of the Quebec Act. Less well known is that from the outset he had adopted a very lenient approach in the administration of criminal justice as it applied to the ethnic majority. When, during his initial administration in Quebec from 1766 to 1770 as Guy Carleton, the first new subject was condemned to death after the introduction of civil government, the lieutenant-governor took propaganda advantage of the occasion by issuing a commutation to the offender and announcing it by royal proclamation as an example of general policy: 'Now know ye that we be willing to give a proof of our Paternal Affection and Regard to our ... new Subjects and of our Disposition to extend our Royal Clemency towards them whenever it is in our power to do so.'[23] Certainly he was true to his word. During his last administration, from September 1793 to June 1796, for example, he had to deal with the cases of at least four Canadiens convicted of crimes carrying the death sentence: two burglaries, one incestuous rape and one offence against the Stabbing Act of James I. In all these cases the governor pardoned the offender on condition of banishment. The only known executions in this period were of English residents: a Samuel Thorpe for sacrilege in the Cathedral church of Quebec and one Charles Cavanaugh for murdering his wife.[24]

Thus Dorchester would not make capital examples of Canadiens if he could possibly avoid it, since he worried lest any rigorous enforcement of the law spark renewed rioting. If a Canadien were convicted of high treason, it was not of course inevitable that he would be executed. But the governor was not vested with the royal prerogative of mercy in cases of treason (or murder). Hence the convict would have remained in jail for several months, awaiting trial, then word from the secretary of state. Assuming mercy was extended, the most likely punishment would have been banishment for life or transportation. Among the family-conscious Canadiens even banishment might have been viewed as provocatively severe. Dorchester, I believe, wanted to take no such chances, but to exploit mercy as a political tool which clearly he did at the March 1795 assizes in Quebec.

The overriding notion of the criminal law punishment system in the 1790s was to combine terror by public execution of a few with the political benefits flowing from royal mercy. In the vast majority of cases capital sentences were commuted by the crown to lesser punishments such as transportation to New South Wales or, in the case of British North America, banishment.[25] Jails played a minor role in the system – as detention centres for persons awaiting trial, execution, or exile, and places for short-term punishment, often in combination with fines, whipping, the pillory and/or burning in the hand. They were also used to detain insolvent debtors, the dangerously or homeless insane and, where there was no correctional workhouse, beggars and vagabonds. As in Britain, the Lower Canadian prisons (a former barracks in Quebec and a former monastery in Montreal) were schools for crime, unhealthy, far from escape-proof, and invariably overcrowded. Indeed, a statute of 1799 declared that the jails at Quebec and Montreal could be used as Houses of Correction but that, given the chronic space problem, neither could lodge more than ten of these 'vagabonds or incorrigible rogues' at any one time. Not surprisingly then, sentences were extremely short when compared with the post-penitentiary modern era. During the 1790s and 1800s in Lower Canada jail terms of more than a year for any offence were very rare. The first longer term I have been able to locate – two years for non-capital larceny in a dwelling house – dates from 1805.[26] The standard heavy sentences were six months or a year.

The rioters' sentences were close to the norm for the time. Nevertheless, political offenders were treated somewhat less harshly than petty thieves and other minor criminals of the period. About 25 per cent of the political offenders convicted in the 1790s received sentences of six months or more, while fully 60 per cent of ordinary convicted criminals received such terms.[27] The Lower Canadian sentences were also modest by contemporary and analogous British standards, where jail terms of one year, eighteen months, and two years for sedition were common. Three or even four-year sentences were not unknown.[28]

I can offer no direct proof to explain such leniency in 1794–5, but remembering Dorchester's caution and that of many of his advisers, and the punitive temperaments of chief justices Monk and Osgoode (where political offenders were concerned) it seems almost certain to have been political, reflecting fear at the Château and on the Bench that several prison sentences of a year or more might provoke renewed rioting.

By the late winter of 1794–5 the crisis was over. The Jacobins had ignored Canada and the province was tranquil. Lord Dorchester had returned to his initial opinion that the new subjects were not disloyal. On his orders political prisoners were gradually released from prison and the sections of the Alien Act (renewed for one year) suspending habeas corpus and expanding the concept of sedition were allowed to lapse.

LEGISLATION AND ASSIZES, 1796–1797

By the early months of 1797 government officials were aware of the high stakes for which the French Directory was playing in North America. Intelligence reports indicated that French agents were at work, not only in Lower Canada, but among the Kentucky frontiersmen and Indian tribes in Upper Canada, particularly the Mississauga and Joseph Brant's Iroquois.[29] France and Spain, assisted by Kentucky adventurers, southern Indians, and perhaps some Upper Canadian tribes as well, seemed about to mount an invasion via the Mississippi.[30] And Richery's fleet was expected in the spring or summer. In these circumstances government officials demanded the power of incarcerating suspected political subversives at will. But given the results of the recent election, how was that to be done?

Richardson and Sewell early in 1797 worked out the strategy to outwit the 'democrats' in the Assembly. Three Montrealers who the previous September had attended the meeting with Adet's agents, Louisineau and Ducalvet, would be arrested and indicted for high treason. The revelations from the resultant evidence would destroy any contention that there was no need to repeat Monk's inquisition of 1794. As Richardson put it in a letter to Sewell,

proof of intended invasion and insurrection, would do away [with] every argument the evil disposed in the Assembly might urge, against ... Clauses suspensive of the Habeas Corpus ... The Democratic Members might affect to treat a general communication as unfounded, but the circumstances that must necessarily come to light ... would confound them – If still refractory, I should not hesitate ... to treat them in Debate as Traitors abetting the Invasion.

After the Provencales were arrested in early February, Richardson wondered what the response had been: 'Pray how does Papineault [sic] look since these discoveries – the Democrates here since the Arrests, wear faces almost a yard long – Guilty consciences perhaps tell them their turn may not be far off.' Various documents, including depositions by paid informers on the activities of suspected agents and the voluntary examination of Louisineau, who agreed to turn king's evidence, were sent to the attorney general with a caution to withhold papers disclosing names of informers from the Assembly. True, a secret committee could be struck, but it was likely that 'some who wish success to the Plot may get upon it.' The new house was not like the Commons, where the ministry had influence enough to insure the safe composition of any special committee.[31]

Armed with Richardson's documents and copies of the treason indictments, Sewell, in late March, sought the Assembly's assent to reviving the provisions in the first Alien Act which had suspended habeas corpus and extended the definition of sedition. He had little immediate success. Far from agreeing to the amendment introduced by Judge De Bonne and William Grant, Papineau talked of liberalizing the statute as it then stood. Confronted with this opposition Sewell made a tactical retreat, giving up the restoration of the detention powers and the definition of seditious offences in the original Alien Act. On 3 April Sewell introduced a separate bill dealing exclusively with the suspension of habeas corpus. This bill would become the annually renewed 'Act for the Better Preservation of His Majesty's Government as by law happily established in this Province' and it was largely copied from a British statute of 1794.

Adopting this device enabled Sewell to cite the imperial Parliament – that bastion of constitutional liberty – as a model. And since, according to Richardson, Sewell's tactical change was designed to make the suspension more palatable to the Assembly majority than reviving the 1794 Alien Act *in toto*,[32] the attorney general must have stressed contrasts to argue that his proposed statute was more liberal than that of Monk. Under the Better Preservation bill a warrant signed by three Executive councillors – normally including at least one of the chief justices – would be required, whereas under the former clause any one justice of the peace had been able to order the internment.[33] Richardson approved Sewell's gambit, but was very pessimistic about the response of 'Citizen P. & suite': 'I really did not think he [Papineau] had impudence enough, after what has happened, to venture openly to oppose the Alien Act – If the Habeas Corpus bill contemplated by you should fall through, it will evince not only the extent of our danger, but that the imperious majority in the Assembly, are determined under cover of their Legislative liberty of action, to deliver us over ... bound hand & foot to the Sans Culottes.' If Sewell failed, Prescott should take 'upon himself the Measure of proclaiming Martial Law, and trusting to Parliament for an indemnity.'[34]

Richardson needn't have worried, for Papineau soon changed course. There can be no doubt that the Road Act riots, particularly the talk of starving Montreal, had unnerved the Roman Catholic clergy and, in the words of John Fleming, had 'so much alarmed all men of capital and large landholders within the Province' that there was a strong current of public opinion, Canadien as well as English, for severe measures to preserve social order. Fleming also noted that the change in attitude on the part of the Canadien MPPs was in no small part due to the 'alarming information ... communicated to the House of Assembly, by the Crown Lawyers,' suggesting that the Richardson-Sewell strategy had succeeded. It may well be, too, that Prescott's assiduous social courtship of Papineau had had an effect.[35] Whatever the explanation, the co-leader of the *parti canadien* not only ceased opposing the suspension of habeas corpus, he became a supporter of the bill, even seconding the attorney general's motion to have it engrossed.[36] It passed third reading without any significant opposition and in a show of unity, which must have caused mirthful delight at the Château, the Assembly nominated the Montreal tribune of the people and the attorney general to communicate the bill to the Legislative Council.[37] Papineau and his colleagues should have been more careful, for Sewell, relying on the inexperience of the Canadien members in matters of constitutional law, had been very clever indeed.

Like the British statute of 1794, the Better Preservation Act suspended habeas corpus when the prisoner had been charged with high treason or imprisoned on suspicion thereof. But it added the case of persons charged with the misdemeanour misprision (or concealment) of high treason, which had never been an internable category in post-1688 Britain. Sewell's act also left it arguably open to intern on mere *suspicion* of treasonable practices (itself undefined), and not on a charge for that crime as was required in Britain.

There was also something more fundamental. The British statute of 1794, like all its antecedents back to 1689, had prudently protected members of Parliament from arbitrary arrest:

III. Provided always, and be it enacted, That nothing in this act shall be construed to extend to invalidate the ancient rights and privileges of parliament, or to the imprisonment or detaining of any member of either house of parliament during the sitting of such parliament, until the matter of which he stands suspected is first communicated to the house of which he is a member, *and the consent of the said house obtained for his commitment or detaining* (emphasis added).

The comparable section in the Better Preservation Act did not make the consent of the Assembly or Legislative Council an essential condition to the internment of one of their members. Instead the section contained the vague proviso 'that nothing in this Act shall extend or be construed to invalidate or restrain the lawful rights and privileges of either Branch of the Provincial Parliament in this Province.'

What, if anything, did the Lower Canadian proviso mean? With regard to 'freedom from arrest' (arrest meaning imprisonment), the privileges vested in the members of the House of Assembly were identical to those enjoyed in Britain by members of Parliament. There, the general rule was phrased to admit the privilege (exercisable only during sessions and for short periods before and after) in all cases except treason, felony, or 'breach of the peace.' Since misprision of treason and treasonable practices were misdemeanours (non-capital offences) rather than felonies (capital crimes) and did not necessarily entail *actual* breach of the peace, it might be thought that Sewell's proviso had considerable protective scope.[38] This was not the case.

By the late eighteenth century, breach of the peace encompassed all misdemeanours, whether they involved actual breach of the peace or not. The rationale was that misdemeanours, as indictable offences, were *by definition* breaches of the king's peace.[39] In the celebrated case of John Wilkes in 1763, for example, both houses of Parliament proceeded on this basis, when by joint resolution they reversed a decision of Chief Justice Pratte in the Court of Common Pleas and declared that freedom from arrest could not be claimed by a member of either house imprisoned on a charge of seditious libel, which of course did not necessarily involve disturbance. As of 1797, then, the privilege was clearly claimable only in cases of imprisonment for civil debt, contempt of court in a civil case, and following summary conviction for a petty offence as regulated by statute (for example, failure to perform militia duty).

It seems quite obvious what Sewell was doing when he departed from his British statutory model. Reference to 'lawful rights and privileges' – which the local judiciary was likely to hold did not exist in any criminal cases – was camouflage designed to hoodwink the Canadien majority in the Assembly, while leaving the way clear to intern Papineau, Panet, and their parliamentary supporters if that should appear necessary. The perceived necessity for doing so did not materialize in 1797, but would in 1810.

Throughout its life (1797–1802 and 1803–12) the Better Preservation Act was never used for the mass imprisonment Monk had exploited through the Alien Act. During 1797, for example, only a handful of prisoners were affected by the suspension of habeas corpus. But the act in its early months undoubtedly made its contribution to a growing atmosphere of tension. In late 1796 and early 1797 anti-revolutionary informers abounded. Those seeking any favour from the government or the magistrates stressed their loyalty, and relations between the nationalities had deteriorated sharply. Something of the act's contribution is suggested by one case, where loose conversation at a café in the capital had created suspicion that a young Canadien law student was a democrat. The man who had made the offensive remarks realized the danger to his friend and hastened to apologize publicly by writing to the *Quebec Gazette*.[40]

Assizes: Trials and Punishments in the Montreal District, 1797

Colonel Nairne knew how to rule the Canadiens. 'There is a mixture,' he wrote in February 1797, 'of Ignorance ingratitude and folly ingrained in these people which reminds me of what I heard General Bourgainville say in 1760 at Genl: Murray's table ... that they were ... a brave and Submissive people, but that he could venture to foretell that our method of governing them would soon spoil them, it has since often appeared as if we had been fostering them to mischief, and when a wrong System is long persisted in it must come to some violent explosion at last.' As Prescott had recently done, the British must give them a 'Specimen of their ... [previous] Government ... as they themselves declare that they cannot Comprehend ... any other.'[41] Nairne and the many who thought like him would be frustrated by the results of the assizes, but encouraged by the authoritarian sentiments emanating from the Bench.

Early in the March assizes of 1797 in Montreal, events took a dramatic turn when Sewell spotted an imprudent Jean-Baptiste Bizette among the spectators packed into the gallery[42] and called for his committal. The court assented and Bizette was led away to join the two Provencales in jail. Neither his doubts on the legality of the arrest nor the many long faces among the Canadien spectators could dampen lawyer David Ross's enthusiastic endorsement of this coup against the Ducalvet junta: 'I hope the cat will now come out of the Bag and that all those vile Traiterous rascles [sic] may be discovered and that their ungrateful, Democratical Rebellious conduct, may meet with that punishment that it deserves.' These sentiments are remarkable in view of Ross's normal clear-sightedness and his credentials as energetic counsel for political offenders, dating back to the defence of Leveillé. Indeed he would defend all but one of the Canadiens tried at the Montreal assizes for Road Act offences and with some striking success. The man responsible for hiring Ross to act for many of these prisoners was none other than Joseph Papineau! Bizette, the Provencales, and the absent Ducalvet were indicted for high treason on two counts: compassing the death of the king and adhering to the king's enemies. Their trial was postponed in order to comply with the statutes of William III and Anne.

During the March term eleven Canadiens were tried for misdemeanours arising out of the Road Act riots. Nine were convicted and two acquitted. The most celebrated accused was Luc Berthelot, supposedly the instigator of the disturbances, who was tried with his wife Scholastique Mathieu and one Guillaume Fontaine on two counts: aggravated assault on Constable Marston and common assault. Ross thought the wife thoroughly guilty but Berthelot and Fontaine probably innocent. The trial lasted an entire day with defence counsel addressing the jury for nearly an hour in English and French, provoking alternate fits of laughing and crying from Berthelot. Scholastique Mathieu was convicted on both counts. The other two were found guilty of common assault only, thus reducing their 'mountain of an offence to a mole-hill.' Mathieu was sentenced in September to a mere fine of £15; Fontaine was fined £20 and Berthelot £10.[43]

Berthelot was also convicted of assisting in his own rescue, given a three-month jail sentence, and an additional fine of £5. Three of the rescuers were likewise sentenced to three months, two being fined as well. Two men were convicted of conspiracy to withhold food supplies from the city, fined and sentenced to three months each. Amable Constant, one of the couriers, who had forced the militia captain at the parish of St Roch de l'Assomption to bring his company to Montreal for the purpose of joining the agitation, was given three months and fined £20. The most severe sentence of one year was imposed on Charles-François Ferrière of Ste Rose for seditious conversation and libelling the House of Assembly – which then or very soon after was widely known among the working people as the 'maudit chambre.'[44]

Assizes: Trials and Punishments in the Quebec District, 1796–1797

Four Canadiens involved in the August incident were tried at the September 1796 term in Quebec[45] for riotously opposing the execution of the Road Act. They were defended by counsel described by Osgoode, who presided, as a 'virulent Patriot who is revered as an Oracle.' These expressions probably refer to Jean-Antoine Panet, whom the chief justice had earlier taken to calling the 'Arch patriot,' no doubt to distinguish him from Joseph Papineau who was the 'Arch demagogue of Montreal' in Osgoode's lexicon. During the trial 'Panet' adopted a tricky but ultimately unsuccessful stratagem: to convince the jury that the indictments were so broadly framed that the court would be able to execute the prisoners as in cases of high treason. The accused were convicted, fined, and sentenced to two or three months in jail (two cases each).

At the March 1797 assizes six months later, twenty-three individuals, all Canadien, faced trial for various misdemeanours related to the Road Act riots, including four who were charged with two distinct offences.[46] Three groups of Pointe Lévi farmers – twelve accused in all – were convicted of assaulting and imprisoning overseers of the roads. At least seven and perhaps as many as eleven of the prisoners pleaded guilty.[47] The punishments were one shilling and six weeks (six cases), £1 and two months (two cases), £1 and three months (four cases). One Antoine Dionne, Sr, farmer of St Roch, convicted of seditious conversation and libelling the House of Assembly, received six months, a fine of £10, and £200 security. Dionne, his son and one other man were convicted of assaulting a magistrate in St Roch. They were fined £5 each, sentenced to three months, and required to post £100 security. The numerically biggest trial, *Rex* v. *Pierre Huard et al.*, involved eleven Pointe-Lévi farmers charged with assaulting deputies of the sheriff and effecting the rescue of three Road Act rioters then being escorted to jail in Quebec. The prisoners offered no defence and eight were convicted. Five were sentenced to £1 and six months, while two were fined £1 and ordered to prison for nine months. The heaviest sentence meted out to any of the Quebec District rioters was imposed on Huard as leader of the rescue gang. He was fined £1 and sent to jail for a year.

One curious feature about the trials of Dionne et al. and of Huard et al. is that the petit juries in each included at least nine and perhaps ten English residents. Since duplicates of the general jurors lists were not required to be publicly deposited until 1832, there was no simple way for the prisoner to make certain the crown-appointed sheriff had not selected the panel unfairly in any given case.[48] The possibility of undetected manipulation in the political trials of the 1790s certainly existed.

Prescott did not share Dorchester's general views about governing the Canadiens and was prepared to use military force to suppress rioting where his predecessor had not been. But his penal policy seems similar. No Road Act rioter, in either Montreal or Quebec, was indicted for treason, and the sentences imposed were modest. The Provençales, Bizette, and the absent Ducalvet were successfully prosecuted before the grand jury for compassing the death of the king and adhering to the king's enemies, it is true, but as this manoeuvre was part of the Richard-son-Sewell strategy to obtain a suspension of habeas corpus, the prosecution was pushed energetically by the attorney general.[49] When tried in September they were acquitted. Unfortunately no records of the trial have been found except for terse reports in the *Gazettes*. We therefore cannot be sure that the crown prosecuted forcefully, much less attempted to manipulate the jury panel.

The Ideological Use of the Assizes

As in the case of the Bench of England in the 1790s, the judges of Lower Canada often made use of the criminal assizes (addresses to the convicted accused, charges to the trial jury, and so on) for political propaganda. This was particularly so when internal security was in issue, since judicial remarks on those matters were published in the newspapers. Themes included the awfulness of political crimes and the virtues of Britain's 'mild' constitution, including the criminal law. Judges stressed the need for vigilance, especially as French agents had caused the riots and the ignorant Canadien people, while not innately depraved, were prey to designing men who falsely taught them they had grievances. Contrasts were sometimes drawn to New France and more often to modern France, painted of course in the most sanguinary colours.[50]

A lengthy harangue delivered by Judge De Bonne at the end of the March assizes of 1797 and published in the Quebec Gazette on 6 April covered most of these bases. After praising Osgoode for his leniency in sentencing, De Bonne agreed with the chief justice that the principal cause of the late riots lay in the ignorance of the Canadien masses. A moment's reflection, he said, would convince anyone of the inestimable benefits of the British constitution, including liberty of the person and religious freedom as guaranteed to Roman Catholics by the Quebec Act of 1774. Thirty-seven years experience should convince all that the Canadiens were infinitely better off than they had been in New France. Unfortunately, foreign emissaries and some misguided, France-loving Canadiens had recently used the Road Act as a stalking horse by distorting its provisions with 'frivolous, absurd and ridiculous' arguments. Had the riots not been put down with vigour, the government would have been overthrown and replaced by French republicanism. What that bloody system involved was clear to all. It therefore behooved Canadians to exhibit exemplary obedience to the laws and the utmost loyalty to the British Empire.

One wonders if the farmers, artisans, and labourers at the Bar were made to feel significant or were suitably mortified by De Bonne's diatribe. Perhaps most were merely puzzled.

Royalist Interpretations of Security Law

During the 1790s the two chief justices interpreted security law in a royalist or authoritarian manner that would not necessarily have been accepted by contemporary judges in England. A court presided over by Osgoode had indicted five Charlesbourg rioters for high treason, although he seems to have had private doubts whether resistance to the enforcement of a statute in the existing circumstances was sufficient to warrant such a charge.[51] There are many examples of Monk's royalism.[52] The best is his address to the grand jury in March 1797 wherein he explained the concept of levying war found in Edward III's Statute of Treasons and applied it to the Road Act riots.[53]

Edward's act restricted judicial abuses which had greatly increased the number of forfeitures of land under the feudal system. In particular the Bench in the previous decade had classified as traitorous the act of 'accroaching' on royal power, which could mean almost anything: murdering the king's messenger, holding persons to ransom, interfering with the course of justice, or even highway robbery.[54] The statute limited treason to seven cases, including one phrased as follows: 'if a man doe levie warre against our lord the king in his realme.' As with the other main treasons in the statute, levying war became extended in meaning by the courts over the years. By the late eighteenth century these 'constructive treasons' as Henry Hallam, the constitutional historian, remarked, were often 'repugnant to the general understanding of mankind' and even that of 'most lawyers.' They were indeed widely condemned outside of ministerial circles in the 1780s and 1790s. Even such a robust Tory as Samuel Johnson found them repulsive.[55]

For almost a century after 1352, levying was interpreted as applying strictly to formal war – with organized and properly equipped armies, unfurling of banners etc. – waged by magnates against the king. Thus the indictments arising out of Wat Tyler's Peasants' Revolt of 1381 only rarely and obliquely referred to levying. But in the aftermath of Jack Cade's rebellion in the mid-fifteenth century, it was permanently established that popular insurrections aimed at overthrowing the government were to be classed as levying. This first important constructive treason was but a prelude to far less justifiable extensions by the judiciary. In a series or cases dating from 1595 to 1710, it was laid down that risings, which would otherwise be mere riots, were levyings if the insurgents (although not in rebellion; indeed, even if open partisans of the monarch) held some *general* objective, such as to destroy all dissenting chapels within reach or to force the king to alter his ministers, his policies, or the law. If the insurgents' aim was local and particular – for example, to release specified prisoners from jail – the offence amounted only to the misdemeanour of riot. By the 1790s, then, the two main types of levying were rebelling to usurp political power, and rioting to pursue some generalized political aim falling short of revolution. I shall refer to the latter as 'treasonable rioting.' Since the statute required an *actual* levying, mere conspiracy to rebel or to engage in treasonable rioting did not qualify as high treason under this head and the courts never claimed that it did.

After a customary eulogy of the British constitution, Monk explained the law of high treason. After defining constructive levying, he pointed our that resistance to law enforcement was included in the concept, stating that the guilt of treason 'attaches upon all those who rise in tumultuous assemblies and openly by force, oppose the execution of the Laws.' As thus enunciated the rule was without exception and was not justified by explanation or citation of authority.

There was no reported case on point.[56] In *Dammaree* (1710), the leading precedent on constructive levying, the court had held that the mob's actions in tearing down Presbyterian meeting houses amounted to an attempt to render the Toleration Act totally ineffectual and for that reason among others constituted high treason. The case, though, did not deal with riotous obstruction to officials trying to execute statutory law. In Lord George Gordon's trial (1781) the judges unanimously held that a direct attempt by rioters to intimidate Parliament into repealing an act was levying war, but nothing was said in the judgment about resistance to statutory law enforcement.[57] Although the pre-1800 jurists classified as constructive levying insurrections to alter the established law, none treated the question at hand. Nor did a 1793 pamphlet on treason, written by 'A Barrister at Law.'[58]

In 1797, then, the question was an open one and required for its resolution application of the basic test whether the aims of the putative insurgents were 'general' or 'particular.' If the former, resistance to law enforcement could be said to be levying war; if the latter, it had to be classified as a riot only. 'Particular' seems to have meant geographically isolated or involving the self-interest of the insurgents. The early eighteenth-century jurist William Hawkins, for example, wrote that 'where a Number of Men rise to remove a Grievance to their private Interest, as to pull down a particular Inclosure intrenching upon their Common etc. they are only Rioters.' The mid-eighteenth century treason specialist and judge, Sir Michael Foster, summarized constructive levying as insurrections 'for the reformation of real or imaginary evils *of a public nature and in which the insurgents have no Special Interest'* (emphasis added).

It is doubtful if any Road Act rioters had levied war on the basis of these tests, vague as they are. In the Quebec District violence or tumultuous assembly had occurred in three different confined places at three separate times: the capital in late August, St Roch in October, and Pointe-Lévi in January 1797. In the Montreal area there had been attempts at a more collective resistance – the Longueuil starvation plot and the planned mass meeting of 11 October – but neither scheme resulted in the use of force. The mysterious nightly meetings and peripatetic couriers probably coordinated non-compliance with the act over a number of parishes, but the crown found no evidence they had stimulated violence. Joseph Papineau had promised repeal of the Road Act but intended to proceed by the ordinary legislative process rather than using crowds (as Lord George Gordon had done) to coerce the legislature. Finally virtually all of the rioters could have claimed a 'special interest' – in Foster's usage – in that their resistance was designed to avoid having personally to work on the roads.

On the available authorities, then, Monk's statement of the law was not self-evidently correct. But it must be admitted that it was not necessarily wrong since the general/particular distinction might arguably lie in the nature of the statute itself. Sir Edward Hyde East, in his *Pleas of the Crown*, first published in 1803, asserted that it was treason 'to obstruct the execution of some general law [as opposed to a private turnpike or enclosure Act] by armed force.' He was able to cite in support obscure manuscript judgments showing that some of the Yorkshire and Northumberland militia rioters were executed in 1757 and after had been convicted of treason.[59] Monk was construing the law in a grey area, and while not clearly distorting it, he did opt for a royalist solution which was not inevitable.

Besides the unqualified holding on resistance to law enforcement, Monk explained to the grand jury that it did not matter a bit whether a participant in the resistance was aware of the treasonable design or not. The chief justice was thereby closing the door on pleas of ignorance based, for example, on the supposed illegality of the Road Act. In so doing he accepted without question the leading, but unconvincing, decision in the case of *Purchase* (1710) where it was held that 'if a man knowingly join with others in breaking the peace, and ... if in that breach of the peace they were rebels, he is so too, whether he knew them to be so or not.[60] In rebellions it was common that 'few are let into the real design, but yet all that join in it are guilty of the rebellion.' The eighteenth-century judge did not usually consider himself bound by a single precedent and particularly one such as this. In the first place, three of the judges rendering opinions had dissented. Nor did the decision commend itself to the jurists. Although not referring to the case, Hawkins wrote a few years later that persons aiding rebels, though unaware of the traitorous design could 'perhaps' be found guilty of high treason. Foster agreed. The *Purchase* decision was also vulnerable in that it did not square with the notion of high treason as conscious betrayal and the almost universal practice in treason indictments of using the word 'traitorously' to characterize the accused's behaviour. Some years later this was clearly understood by Chief Justice Jonathan Sewell. In his charge to the Quebec grand jury opening the war assizes of September 1812, Sewell drew a careful distinction between obstructing law enforcement with traitorous intent and without it. The first constituted high treason; the second amounted only to misdemeanour or riot.[61] Monk obviously did not wish to restrict the government's options by rejecting *Purchase*. Here again he was being more royalist than the British legal authorities necessitated. Although rigorous by any standards, such was the atmosphere that Monk's address drew praise from even a moderate like David Ross: 'our Ch.[ief] charged the Grand Jury in a very long speech, it seemed to give satisfaction pretty generally, and I cannot say otherwise than that I was pleased with it myself.'[62]

The sense of imminent peril among English-speakers in Lower Canada generated an elastic definition of treason. This hard attitude, fed by alarm, was particularly evident during the trial of David McLane.

7

The Trial of David McLane, 1797

Close to midnight on 10 May 1797 the governor's civil secretary, accompanied by a party of soldiers, knocked at the Quebec City house of shipbuilder John Black, a recently elected member of the Legislative Assembly. Almost three years before, Black had been imprisoned without trial as a suspected agent of revolutionary France. As he bitterly remembered, his prosperous business had been nearly ruined and he had become, in his own words, 'the scoff and reproach of the times.'

Things would be different now. Black knew he was not the object of the search. The quarry was an American then asleep in Black's bed. The French 'General,' David McLane,[1] was awakened, arrested, and placed in prison on suspicion of high treason. McLane had the misfortune to be apprehended at a time when government officials believed the long-feared invasion, uprising, and massacre were imminent. The government, too, had evidence that the prisoner had attempted to recruit a 'fifth column' to seize the Quebec garrison.[2]

MCLANE, HIS ESPIONAGE AND CAPTURE

Opinion in Lower Canada on the danger McLane's conspiracy might have posed to the colony was divided. Chief Justice Osgoode estimated that the subject was 'well qualified for the undertaking,' while John Richardson believed that 'McLanes plan about surprising Quebec appears so wild as to leave one at a loss to determine whether his folly or villainy predominate.' The receiver general and seigneur, Henry Caldwell, re-ferred to McLane as having 'formed a wild scheme of possessing himself of this Country.'[3] Historians, likewise, are not unanimous, although the greater number have shared Richardson's view and therefore questioned the harsh treatment meted out by the government. A modern student of the McLane affair, Claude Galarneau, was of the view that 'the scheme attributed to McLane involved many improbabilities' and hence the dominant historical consensus was correct in treating McLane as 'an unlucky fool rather than a conspirator.' Among the few dissenters were Christie's contemporary chronicler, Joseph-François Perrault, the archivist Douglas Brymner and William Kingsford, all of whom tended to believe even the more exaggerated, contemporary interpretations of the security danger.[4]

McLane certainly was involved in a serious conspiracy. France did intend to mount an invasion of the colony and material in Citizen Adet's account book leaves no doubt that McLane was Adet's agent charged with undercover missions to Canada. Had the conspiracy been brought even to partial fruition in coordination with the naval invasion, the confusion entailed might well have contributed to make the latter a success. McLane's charisma and ability to play the confidence trickster should not be underestimated, and he was determined and brave enough – perhaps due to psychological desperation – to have carried off the coup. But he was not sufficiently trained, patient, or discreet to have prepared the groundwork effectively by himself.

Who then was David McLane? Although almost nothing certain is known of his antecedents prior to 1796, sources drawn from archival holdings in Rhode Island or published there can be used to create a reasonably clear picture for the years 1790–5. When arrested McLane was probably in his thirties. He had likely been born in or near Boston to a Massachusetts family named Lane, with roots in Scotland and possibly the north of Ireland as well. By 1790 McLane, having added the prefix for business reasons, was established as a merchant in Providence, Rhode Island.[5] For a while he prospered. Trading ventures to the southern states were successful and his growing status was recognized when he was nominated by the General Assembly, in 1792, 1793, and 1794, as a militia major in the Providence Independent Light Dragoons. By 1794 he was describing himself in real estate deeds as a gentleman, rather than a mere merchant as formerly. McLane married Joanna De Eckhoot in July 1794.

In the early 1790s McLane achieved local renown as a pioneering architect-builder in partnership with one Paul Draper. Their most notable achievement was to design, build, and operate a commodious, three-storey Exchange Coffee House on Market Square, Providence. The coffee house functioned as a tavern, gossip centre, gourmet restaurant, billiards hall, and gaming establishment. But it was in advance of customer demand and even a lottery granted the smooth-talking McLane by the state legislature failed to save the enterprise. In August 1793 the partnership was dissolved and the coffee house and a general store were sold. In the spring of 1796 McLane left Providence to escape from his creditors – including prize lottery ticket-holders and, above all, Draper. After his execution in 1797 Joanna discovered her husband's estate consisted of one military uniform and a multitude of financial obligations.

McLane seems to have been cursed with a foolhardy temperament and an overwhelming desire for approval. The local historian, Walter R. Danforth, described him as tall, robust, handsome, decisive, and possessed of 'a restless spirit of enterprise and adventure.' As his business prospects grew bleaker, according to Danforth, McLane was heard to declare to his fellow townsmen that he would become a highwayman and 'collect such duties from travellers as his wants might require.'

Instead of pursuing this career, McLane offered his services to France. Adet's account book records four payments totalling $345 to 'Major Macklay' ordered by the minister and four receipts signed by McLane. The payment orders were dated 13 and 16 October, 27 December 1796, and 31 January 1797. In the entry for 27 December 1796 the minister noted that McLane 'has been employed by me to obtain intelligence about Canada – he has made a trip into that country.' That for 31 January 1797 authorized a mission entrusted to 'major M'Klay.' Adet was doubtless attracted by McLane's financial plight and recklessness.[6]

McLane quickly adapted to his new function in life. Curiously blending a very personalized Christianity with the new gospels of 1789, he discovered righteousness, self-esteem, and excitement in becoming an emissary charged with perilous missions to the backward British colony to the north: a place, he now learned, sadly lacking in the Rights of Man and careers open to talent. McLane revelled in his undercover role, but he was incompetent. Despite a widespread belief in official circles that he and Ira Allen were working in tandem, there is no convincing evidence that McLane coordinated his efforts with those Vermonters favourable to Allen, or with Allen himself, who was then in Europe.[7] Indeed, one of Ira's friends claimed that Allen had never heard of the spy until after his execution.[8] McLane, moreover, divulged his secrets to the wrong people.

McLane first came to the attention of the Lower Canada government in mid-November 1796 through information supplied by Montreal tavern-keeper Elmer Cushing, a native of Massachusetts who had settled in the colony four years before. Encouraged by the promise of custom from the 'moneyed interest' of Montreal, Cushing invested heavily in his American Coffee House only to see it fail because the merchants insisted on bargains or took their custom elsewhere. The tavern-keeper had known McLane slightly in the United States and the latter had frequently stayed at Cushing's inn during his many visits to the city dating back to February. In a pamphlet published thirty years later, Cushing claimed that in a long conversation with McLane on 5 November 1796, the spy had tried to convert him by inveighing against the divine right of kings and giving instruction in Rousseau's social contract.[9] The spirit of royal divinity, McLane purportedly asserted, poisoned Lower Canada's entire system of government. The 'mutual compact' between ruler and ruled had been broken and the Canadiens stood released from their allegiance to George III. McLane – and hopefully Cushing – could offer them a chance to escape from ignorance and the small material pleasures allowed by the British. Details of the plot were soon forthcoming and Cushing, binding himself with 'most sacred & horrid oaths,' promised to keep the plans confidential. The tavern-keeper was not one, however, to guard a secret when profit could be made. A few days later he visited his lawyer, Stephen Sewell, on business.

During the conversation Sewell expressed the opinion that the Road Act disturbances were at an end and that the English now had it in their power to make the Canadiens obedient subjects. Cushing contradicted him, then admitted contact with an unnamed agent of France who had told Cushing that French plans to invade the colony had been finalized. Fearing for his life, he would say nothing further, except that 'if what I do know now is not divulged I would not be in this Country in July next for anything and I am settling my affairs here as fast as I can, and will in all human possibility leave the Country in the Spring.' Sewell immediately offered to go to Quebec with the information and before releasing Cushing's name would attempt to get some promise of reward.

The next night Sewell visited the American Coffee House. Cushing had by then decided to embellish his story to suit the lawyer's paranoia. As Sewell reported it to his brother in a letter recommending a reward and protection for his as yet unnamed informant, Cushing intimated 'there had been a man in this Town about a fortnight ago [that is at the height of the Road Act riots], not a Canadian, nor American, nor Englishman who had communicated to him a plan for the extirpation of the English in this Country.' Cushing then gave him an American almanac and 'told me to read half a sheet. I should find the mans name. I did & the only name I saw was Citizen Adet.'[10]

Sewell hurried Cushing down to Quebec to talk to his brother. A letter written by the attorney general in 1799 records the transaction then worked out.[11] The government as represented by Jonathan Sewell, Ryland, and Prescott, agreed that the information received from Cushing was so significant that he could be granted his desire: the cession to him and his associates of an entire township. The government also promised protection for the informant's family, and compensation in case he was assassinated. Prescott refused to finalize the arrangement until his principal adviser, Osgoode, approved. In Sewell's words, 'Mr. Ryland accordingly accompanied me and we had a long conference with the Chief Justice ... [with the] result ... that we were all of opinion that the expected information appeared of sufficient importance to justify an absolute promise of the Township of Shipton to Mr. Cushing.' Cushing's friend William Barnard, to whom McLane had also talked, was promised the Township of Brompton. Both informants deposed against McLane and both were ultimately rewarded.

Cushing swore in his deposition, before Chief Justice Osgoode,[12] that he had conversed with McLane at the American Coffee House on 5 November 1796, having known the man for about ten years. McLane, his clothes covered with burrs, told him he had just finished examining every part of Mount Royal which he had found to be a place of great command over Montreal in case of war. When Cushing hinted that the Canadiens were disaffected, the spy stated he was employed by Adet to help the invasion's success, then hastened to prove it: '[he then] went to his saddle-bags and took out an old pair of shoes, one of which had a hole near the toe from which he drew out a paper in the English language signed "Adet".' The paper, which dealt with family affairs, McLane explained, was a disguised letter of credence. The attack, he went on, would concentrate on Montreal and Quebec. At Quebec collaborators would spike the cannon and excite disturbances when the French fleet approached. Bodies of volunteers were being raised in the United States. They would be armed by Adet and invade Montreal, where McLane himself would command. The primary aim there was to secure money and valuables for a war fund. Those favourable to the French cause would be protected, but it would 'fare hard' with those who opposed it. When Cushing refused to join, McLane asked him, as he had asked several others, to at least keep the Canadiens from rioting during the winter, since 'all opposition against the present Government at this moment would be highly detrimental to the Cause' and threatened execution if the shopkeeper informed on him. Cushing wisely did not risk his credibility, or a charge of misprision, by swearing before Osgoode that he had seen Adet in Montreal.

In Montreal, before Richardson, William Barnard swore that in Alburg, Vermont, on 26 July 1797, McLane had blurted out that he was 'bringing about a Revolution in Lower Canada' and needed Barnard's assistance.[13] Barnard refused. On 7 November when the two met in Montreal, McLane complained that the Road Act disturbances were against the cause he represented, asserting rather vaguely that the French army was to be sent to Canada in the spring. If Barnard joined in, his fortune would be made. In the meantime the shopkeeper 'should discover what money the Seminary [of St Sulpice] and all the principal Persons in Town had and where it lay [and] who would probably be their friends and who their enemies.' The immediate object of the invaders, according to McLane, 'would be to seize all the money and confine the leading characters but that it was not their intention to take away any Lives.'

McLane eluded capture in November 1796. In late January or early February he received new instructions from Adet in Philadelphia, a meeting duly reported by Liston to Prescott. About the middle of March of 1797, in company with his brother Daniel, he proceeded to New York and thence to the Vermont–Lower Canada frontier, meeting with a confederate, Thomas Butterfield, a sawmill owner in Swanton. Butterfield then went to St Jean to bring back habitant Charles Frichette whom McLane had failed to recruit the previous summer. This time he was more successful. Frichette agreed to guide McLane through the province. McLane would assume the name Jacob Felt and would pose as a timber speculator and purchaser of horses.[14]

On the last day of the month the two conspirators crossed the frontier clandestinely near St Jean, proceeding in a leisurely manner to St Nicolas, where Frichette's brother and relatives lived. They reached the outskirts of the colonial capital on 10 May. McLane sent Frichette into town to have John Black brought to him – on the disastrous assumption that Black longed to serve revolutionary France. According to Black's deposition,[15] Frichette first asked if he wished to buy oak timbers, but soon let out the true object of the visit, telling Black that the French minister to the United States knew he had suffered gravely at the hands of the British government and that he enjoyed much influence over the common people. The minister had sent a general into the province to aid Black 'and other Friends to the French Republic,' and he was now awaiting Black some little way outside the city. Seeing a perfect opportunity to complete his social rehabilitation, the shipbuilder accompanied Frichette to a coppice near the Plains of Abraham, where he and McLane discussed plans for another conquest of Canada. McLane lost no time in informing Black that 'his object was to thrust the British Government out of America.' He came in the cause of 'Humanity and he would spill no Blood but where there was Resistance, his sole Motive was to give Liberty to Canada and free ... the People from the Tyranny of the British Government.' As an initial step, McLane hoped to surprise the garrison at Quebec. He had fifteen thousand in the States ready to march on the province the moment the garrison was attacked. Mr Adet, whom he had left on 7 April, was proceeding to Europe to raise an additional force. The minister did not, however, intend to turn Canada into a French colony. His sole aim was to make the 'Canadians Free and Independent.' McLane needed ten men who like Black had influence over the common people. They would recruit as many volunteers as possible who would come together at the appropriate time. After that it would be quite a simple matter to make the soldiers of the garrison drunk or drugged with laudanum.

If credence be given to Black's deposition, McLane now seems to have contemplated attacking Quebec before the French fleet arrived. The scheme made sense if coordinated with a naval invasion, but as recounted by Black it was hare-brained. McLane had no access to arms, no saboteurs recruited, and no knowledge of the city's defences. And if after the capture of the *Olive Branch*, and in Allen's absence, McLane had fifty men – let alone fifteen thousand – in the States truly prepared to march on the colony, it would have been astonishing. Black, of course, may have misconstrued the conversation or have dramatized and distorted the truth for self-interested reasons.[16] He also deposed that McLane had asked him about the political sentiments of Joseph Papineau and the Dorion brothers, inquired of the value of British property, in goods and specie, and informed his new associate that he personally had quelled the riots in Montreal in the autumn because 'the People were not ripe to go sufficient Lengths.'

After convincing McLane to come to Quebec that evening and promising him safe quarters, Black hastened to John Young, his patron. He informed Young of the meeting and swore out the deposition. McLane was arrested later that night. He was found to have $140 in his possession and signed a receipt in the name of Jacob Felt, whom McLane claimed at the trial was his brother-in-law and partner in a Providence store.

Frichette, who had conducted McLane to Black's house, was apprehended in the city shortly after. He signed a voluntary examination in which he conceded little of damage to McLane. But the next day, being 'convinced that for the Benefit of his soul he ought to speak the Truth,' he signed a new statement. In it he admitted guiding McLane through the province and corroborated in detail Black's account of the meeting near the Plains of Abraham. About a week after Frichette's examination, Butterfield and Daniel McLane were arrested together at St Jean and then brought to Montreal, where they signed voluntary examinations before Richardson (22 May), confirming much of the other evidence against McLane which the government had gathered.[17] Butterfield, who claimed he had come to St Jean to sell lumber and purchase salt, stated he had heard McLane admit he was employed by France and say that 'the Canadians were to be assisted by the French some time this Summer, and that they were expected to come to Quebec in a Fleet.' Daniel McLane, who claimed he had entered the province solely to ascertain the fate of his brother, incriminated the latter in several ways, particularly by conceding that David had told him he had had dealings with Adet. Both were interned on suspicion of treason under the Better Preservation Act.

The crown's case was virtually complete and the government had already begun to spread abroad its version of the facts. On 29 May a resident of Fredericton, New Brunswick, described the plot in a letter, which was later published in some of the London newspapers. The writer, obviously deriving his information from opinion in Quebec, claimed that McLane had operated under a commission from the Directory, had carried French army commissions with him in the hope of raising a battalion or two of Canadien rebels, and had been the intended second-in-command of a projected invasion of Lower Canada. This American adventurer's primary purpose, the writer continued, had been 'to get as many of the soldiers as possible stupified by rum drugged with opium, and, then, by surprize, to seize and massacre the officers civil and military.' A month later Vermont merchant Samuel Willard, then visiting the Lower Canadian capital, noticed the same pessimistic consensus on McLane's bloodthirsty intentions: 'There has been a conspiracy formed against the Government and one of the Blackest kind – from what has been discovered the plan was to have commenced with murdering the Governor, Chief Justice, Attorney General and all the principal Officers of Government & then to have urged the people to Arms & to have taken the Garrison of Quebec in the name of the French Republic.'[18]

Although unsubstantiated by evidence, this belief in massacre, should the French prevail, expressed in many near-contemporary letters written within Lower Canadian government circles, would be exploited by the prosecution at McLane's trial and remain the accepted version of events among the English élite long after the accused was in his grave.[19]

THE TRIAL

Prescott had hesitated to proceed quickly against the Provencales and Bizette. They had been arrested in February and early March and the ordinary course of justice had been followed, meaning that they could not be tried at the March sessions, given the ten day notice of indictment required in treason cases. In April Ryland informed Monk that he had absolutely no intention of issuing a special commission to try the prisoners in advance of the regular assizes in September. After the capture of McLane, this outlook changed, with Prescott writing that 'the spirit of the Times [required] ... an immediate Example' to teach a lesson to would-be spies, 'democratic' politicians, and disloyal habitants alike. Accepting Osgoode's advice, the governor issued a special commission of oyer and terminer on 24 May.[20]

Historians have tended to ignore the trial of David McLane. On the basis of the trial report, Mr Justice Riddell concluded during the First World War that the case provided yet another monument to British impartiality, which had always prevailed, even in time of war and threatened insurrection. Earlier, in 1869, Théophile-Pierre Bédard saw it quite differently. The witnesses, many of whom received lands for their testimony, had exaggerated the supposed plot out of all proportion. A more intelligent jury or one less imbued with English prejudice would have judged the accused, with his extravagant schemes, to be 'a fool rather than a conspirator and have consigned him to an asylum.' While not entering into archival detail or exploring questions of law, Claude Galarneau also made a number of comments suggesting manipulation.[21] He alluded, in particular, to the composition of the jury, the weakness of the crown's case, and the suspicion to be attached to witnesses who were promised rewards as well as those who were accomplices.

Bédard and Galarneau were essentially correct, although the crown's factual case was not particularly weak. An understanding of contemporary law and an examination of relevant primary sources should convince anyone that there was a gross manipulation of justice, despite the fact that McLane had done substantially what the crown said he did. Indeed, the trial provides a case study of what has happened more than once to the administration of justice during a perceived security crisis in Canadian history. It also reveals a great deal about Lower Canada's security situation during the period and in particular demonstrates the garrison mentality of the governing élite. In the apt words of Galarneau, the affair is a telling example of 'what happens in wartime when the effects of fear and psychological propaganda lead to exaggeration so that some lose their heads and others become informers for profit.'

Preliminary Proceedings

The judges named in the commission of oyer and terminer comprised the members of the Executive Council, with the sole exception of the Anglican bishop, Jacob Mountain.[22] They included presiding Justice Osgoode, merchant John Young, and Justice De Bonne. Each thought Adet had orchestrated the Road Act riots which had brought the colony to the verge of rebellion. Although a former French party supporter, Justice Thomas Dunn had come to believe, in the early years of the war, that the colony faced a potentially serious security danger. In the summer of 1794 he had served as provincial president of the Loyal Association campaign and at a more private level had instructed his Eastern Townships land agent to make absolutely certain the loyalty of settlers was beyond question.[23] Antoine Juchereau Duchesnay, François Baby, and Joseph de Longueuil were seigneurs highly favoured by government patronage. Hugh Finlay had long worried about demagogues exploiting the ignorance of the habitants. Lastly, the chief justice of Montreal, James Monk, attorney general during the witch-hunt of 1794, had made a successful recent career of alarmist loyalism.

Only three years before the trial, Thomas Hardy, Horne Tooke, and other supposed British 'Jacobins' – agitators for parliamentary reform – had been acquitted by juries for high treason. To Attorney General Sewell, Chief Justice Osgoode, and doubtless many other government officials, the verdicts were disgraceful and they determined there would be no slip-ups in the McLane case. The crown observed the outward forms of law. The special rights guaranteed to the accused under the statutes of William III and Anne, for example, were fully complied with and Osgoode enunciated the reasonable doubt principle. But at almost every point where discretion was available to the prosecution or the Bench, it was exercised, often crudely, for the purpose of foreclosing any chance McLane might have had.

The grand jury was a prosecutor's ideal. Among its twenty-two members were two men with a special incentive to demonstrate loyalty: merchants George Allsopp and Peter Stuart. Allsopp's son Carleton, a firm believer in French republicanism, had embarrassed him by going to France in 1793. Stuart's domestic servant, Jean-Baptiste Lévesque, had helped provoke a riot at a tense militia parade in Quebec in 1794 by shouting 'vive les français.' Others included officials such as jury foreman François Le Maistre, lieutenant-governor of Gaspé and adjutant general of British militia; John Coffin, loyalist lawyer, inspector of police in Quebec, and surveyor general of woods; John Craigie, commissary general; and merchant Georges-Hypolite Lecompte Dupré, justice of the peace, colonel of militia, and inspector of police in Montreal, whose outstanding quality according to the *Quebec Gazette* was 'that of knowing and rendering the justice due to his Britannic Majesty's government, which he considered as the most solid basis of the welfare of his countrymen.'[24] Three of Papineau's supporters in the House of Assembly, including notary Dumas, were safely isolated among their betters, but gave the appearance of impartiality.

The Law of High Treason

In order to assess Osgoode's interpretation of treason law in his addresses to the grand and petit juries, it is necessary to have in mind its basic principles in the late eighteenth century. I have already outlined the evolution of levying war. The other major treasons under Edward III's statute were 'adhering' and 'compassing.'

The adhering clause read: '... or be adherent to the kings [sic] enemies in [or out of] his realme, giving them aid and comfort in the realme or elsewhere.' Enemies came to mean nations at war (whether declared or not) with the king and filibustering raiders from countries at peace with Britain. It did not include rebels, who as subjects could not be called enemies. A literal construction of the adhering clause suggests there had to be actual assistance rendered (rather than a simple intention or attempt to give it), such as selling arms, joining the enemy's armed forces, treacherously surrendering a fortified position or successfully transmitting useful military intelligence. The 1708 extra-judicial opinion of the judges of England asserted that sending military intelligence to the enemy was adhering, even if the intelligence were intercepted by the British authorities. This construction was applied in a number of eighteenth-century cases and was accepted as authority by Foster, Blackstone, and East. In 1797 then, proof of attempted adhering was sufficient for conviction, although it was far from clear whether this was so in all cases. Nor was it clear whether the attempt had to have reached the final stage, so that the accused had had nothing left to do but put the enemy in possession of the aid he or she was tendering.

Compassing the death of the king ('... when a man doth compasse or imagine the death of our lord the king, or our lady his queene, or of their eldest sonne and heire') meant such things as wishing it, trying to bring it about, or conspiring for that purpose. It did not mean murder. The regicides of Charles I were found guilty of the incipient offence of compassing, with the actual beheading being considered proof of same. The word 'death' in the statute obviously referred to physical, not political death, since the compassing head protected the queen consort and the eldest son as well as the reigning king. Compassing had to be proved by 'open deed' or 'overt act', such as conspiratorial conversations, the writing of some insurrection plan, or a publication advocating the replacement of the monarch. Mere spoken words, however hostile to the king, did not qualify unless uttered to incite others to regicide or to forward measures aimed at rebellion.

From the late sixteenth century judges magnified compassing well beyond the original intent. Decisions bringing plots to imprison or depose the king under this head reflected Machiavelli's dictum that 'between the prisons and graves of princes the distance is very small.' Inviting foreigners to invade the realm was classed as compassing, as was the actual levying of war by rebels, since the king's life was thereby imperilled. This latter proposition enabled the courts to hold that a mere conspiracy to rebel – which was not levying – amounted to high treason under this head, which referred to simple intention.

The precise scope of this last rule is important to understand. The context in which it had been laid down invariably involved plots concocted in the British Isles and aimed at genuine political rebellion there, whereas McLane plotted to aid a foreign invasion of a colony in which the king was absent. There was no juristic or judicial authority extending the doctrine to conspiracies hatched in an overseas colony aimed at overturning British sovereignty over the colony. This would be Canada's contribution to treason law in 1797. In the second place, down to the 1790s neither the courts, the jurists, nor prosecuting law officers suggested that conspiracy to bring about treasonable rioting – which did not usually endanger the king's life – amounted to compassing. Just the opposite. Referring to insurrections to redress public grievances, where the insurgents had no 'direct Design' against the king's person, Hawkins stated: '... it is certain, That a bare Conspiracy to levy such a War can not amount to Treason ... [although] a Conspiracy to levy War against the King's person may be alledged as an Overt Act of compassing his Death.' The same clear distinction had been drawn in 1696 by Chief Justice Holt in *Freind's Case*:

There may be a war levied without any design upon the king's person ... which if actually levied, is high treason; but a bare designing to levy war, without more, will not be treason. As for example; if persons do assemble themselves, and act with force in opposition to ... [statutory] law ... and hope thereby to get it repealed; this is levying a war and treason, though purposing and designing it is not so.

In *Lord George Gordon's* case of 1781,[25] arising out of the riots in London, which had been designed physically to intimidate Parliament into repealing the Toleration Act of 1778, the accused was charged with levying but not compassing the king's death. At the trial, which resulted in an acquittal, the judges held that using a mob to coerce Parliament was the high treason of levying war, even though the rioting, while a levying, was directed at the king's political office rather than his person. The distinct implications of the judges' holding and Lord Mansfield's description of it in his instructions to the jury, were that treasonable rioting did not amount to compassing and *a fortiori* conspiracy to so riot could not be either.

The 1794 trials of the English Jacobins, who had planned to convoke a national convention to press for parliamentary reform, spawned a vigorous debate on the justice of constructive treason. In the short run defence counsel Thomas Erskine won the debate by attacking the concept in several lengthy addresses to the jury and by obtaining acquittals for all the accused. The specific question of law relevant here was whether a conspiracy to promote treasonable rioting constituted compassing the death of the king. If the convention had been designed to replace Parliament by force of arms, the plot was clearly treasonable. If on the other hand, juries accepted Erskine's contention that the reform societies were merely exercising the birthright of Englishmen to freedom of speech, assembly, and association and had hoped the convention would bring the pressure of public opinion to bear on Parliament, acquittal was certain. But there was a third position, which would come into play if a case were made that the purpose of the convention movement was to intimidate Parliament by a show of force into changing the electoral law.

Would such a conspiracy, which had not led to rioting, amount to treason?

In addressing the grand jury, Chief Justice Sir James Eyre admitted the answer was very doubtful, but suggested that if factual grounds existed the jurors should indict on this basis so that the matter could be decided at trial. The first accused tried, Thomas Hardy, was indicted in such a way as to leave the question open. At trial Attorney General Scott (later Lord Eldon) argued that plotting to intimidate the Houses of Parliament into passing a bill was the same as conspiring to physically coerce the king into assenting to it and was 'unquestionably an overt act of treason in deposing him, and in compassing his death.' Sir John Mitford, the solicitor general, contended that 'the life of the prince being so interwoven with the constitution of the state ... an attempt to destroy the one, is justly held a rebellious conspiracy against the other.' These arguments implied that 'death' in the Statute of Treasons included political as well as natural death, which if accepted would have reintroduced the unconfinable notion of 'accroaching.' The doubts of Chief Justice Eyre, however, had deepened. He refrained from seconding the crown's arguments on this point and ignored the legal ramifications of the third position.[26] Eyre had left the law where it was, namely that conspiracy to engage in treasonable rioting did not constitute high treason. It could not be levying, since there was by definition no actual resort to force and it could not be compassing as the king's life would not thereby normally be endangered. One year later Parliament, in the throes of reaction, made conspiracy to promote treasonable rioting, including that aimed at overawing Parliament, the equivalent of levying war. But, as we have seen, the Treason Act of 1795 did not form part of the criminal law of Lower Canada.

High treason could be committed only by persons under the king's protection and hence with a reciprocal duty of allegiance. Because protection was absent, there was no allegiance owed to a *de jure* king while a *de facto* king (or probably by the late eighteenth century any kind of *de facto* government) exercised power.[27] Similarly, it is likely that invaders, even from a nation at peace with Great Britain, could not (as enemy invaders certainly could not) be tried for treason. A person born in His Majesty's dominions owed allegiance for life (as did his or her children and grandchildren), a duty which could not be dispensed with by becoming naturalized in a foreign country. According to British court decisions in the 1820s and 1830s, persons born in the American colonies, who remained there as permanent residents after Britain's acknowledgment of

United States independence in 1783, were not deemed to come under this rule.[28] Earlier, the question had been one of great doubt as Paul Romney has shown conclusively. This, however, is irrelevant in the present case since in the indictment, the attorney general and the chief justice assumed that McLane was not a subject of the crown. Foreigners who enjoyed protection – resident aliens and tourists, for example – owed a 'local allegiance' for the duration of their stay and could commit treason within British territory.

Osgoode's Address

In his address the chief justice stifled in advance any doubts the jury might harbour on points of law. The local allegiance owed by aliens was explained but without mentioning that 'treasonable' acts committed by them outside British territory were not crimes or distinguishing the duties of alien friends (amys) and alien enemies, a critical omission, as will be shown. Osgoode asserted that any and all unsuccessful attempts to aid the enemy amounted to adhering and offered an extremely broad interpretation of compassing the king's death. In his opinion it was an established inference of law that he who attempted to aid the enemy, however unsuccessfully, for whatever purposes and wherever he may be located, supported 'a warfare, by which the king's personal safety is endangered.' This doctrine was ideally designed to undeceive any juror who might persist in thinking, contrary to Osgoode's direction, that adhering required giving actual aid to the enemy and who wondered at an indictment for compassing when McLane had operated three thousand miles from the king's residence.

The chief justice also reminded the jury that the colony was facing grave danger, as evidenced by the passage of the Better Preservation Act. Until recently, he claimed, the Canadiens had been suitably docile and grateful subjects. The trouble had begun with 'the sanguinary revolution in France, since which time emissaries have been sent forth, as well native as proselytes ... to disturb the quiet of all settled governments.' Since then symptoms of disobedience and marked disaffection had appeared in Lower Canada. The jury would discover a plot 'some time since on foot, which, if carried into successful execution, would ... endanger the life, liberty, and property of all his majesty's faithful subjects in this province.' The court was adjourned to 14 June when the grand jury presented a bill of indictment against McLane for high treason which they had unanimously found a true bill. Three days later Sewell personally delivered to McLane a copy of the indictment, a list of the jurors summoned, and a list of crown witnesses.[29]

The crown took no chances with its witnesses. A 'confidential person' rounded up those living outside Quebec City, escorting them to the capital, and Prescott even provided a guard for John Black to protect against assassination attempts.[30] Five of the seven who took the stand had a special incentive to make a damning case against McLane. One Francis [François?] Chandonet, who would testify to a conversation held with McLane near the Lower Canadian frontier in the summer of 1796, was an expatriate Canadien who had accompanied the retreating Americans in 1776 and been banished from the colony as an undesirable alien in the winter of 1796–7. It came out during the trial that Chandonet had later corresponded with Richardson, hoping to obtain official permission to settle in Upper Canada. Butterfield and Frichette were accomplices. Both were in prison. Butterfield had been promised his freedom, if he would turn king's evidence. What promises, if any, were made to Frichette are not known, but it is noteworthy he was never put on trial for treason, despite the overwhelming evidence against him. His self-serving testimony was much relied upon by the attorney general in his address to the jury, but largely discounted by Osgoode. In the spring of 1798 Frichette was convicted of misprision of high treason. According to Robert Christie, Frichette, given the mandatory sentence of life imprisonment peculiar to this misdemeanour, was released shortly after his conviction.[31] Barnard and Cushing had been promised a township apiece and as the trial approached the latter was growing desperate to acquire the land and was viewed as unreliable.[32] Civil Secretary Ryland, in a letter to Cushing's lawyer, dated 17 April 1797, admitted that the governor would likely take a liberal view of Cushing's land claim but warned that 'by his indiscretion (to give it no worse name) he has recently prevented one of the principal Agents in the Plot ... from being brought to Justice' [Ducalvet?]. In another letter, dated 18 May 1797, Ryland pointed out that the 'approaching Trial of Mr. McLane will probably afford Mr. Cushing an opportunity to clear up his own Conduct ... and evince how far he is deserving of the attention and favor of the Government.'[33] Black, of course, needed no special incentive to make his testimony as dramatic and convincing as possible. As a suspected traitor he had tasted social ostracism. He would now reap the benefits of active loyalty, continuing the rehabilitation he had begun when he supported the government candidate for Speaker of the Assembly and voted against consideration of amendments to the Road Act. In 1798 and later years he would use his part in the McLane affair as the basis of an ongoing campaign for government patronage, which except for the grant of part of a township, proved fruitless, despite his reputation in government circles, as the witness principally responsible for McLane's conviction.[34]

Immediately following his indictment on 14 June, the prisoner requested the assistance of counsel. The court appointed two lawyers, George Pyke and George Germaine Francklin, to act for him. Both were just beginning their careers. Pyke, then twenty-two years old, had studied under the Tory solicitor general of Nova Scotia, Richard John Uniacke, and been admitted to practice in Lower Canada only seven months before. His biography suggests that at about the time of admission he had been taken into the patronage of another former Nova Scotian, Chief Justice James Monk. Shortly after the trial Pyke would begin a very successful career of office-holder and office-seeker. Francklin, admitted the previous January, had, incredibly, articled for five years in the office of Attorney General Sewell and was actually living in his house.[35] The appointment of Francklin becomes even more astounding in view of the fact that in April 1797 he had written to Ryland in the capacity of 'Agent for Mr. Elmer Cushing' to request that his client be given immediate possession of the promised township and that the government survey the land in order to avoid settlements on portions to be set aside as crown or clergy reserves. No final disposition of Cushing's claim had been made by the time of the McLane trial, although Ryland, through Cushing's lawyer, had warned him that his performance at the trial would 'evince how far he is deserving of the ... favor of Government.' Considering Francklin's intimate links to the attorney general and to one of the crown's leading witnesses, it is not surprising that the young lawyer later informed the trial jury and spectators that he had not undertaken the defence of the accused voluntarily. Defence counsel made a feeble effort and one wonders what might have happened had a courageous, intelligent advocate such as Jean-Antoine Panet, Berthelot d'Artigny, or David Ross been nominated as one of McLane's lawyers.

About 22 June, with everything apparently taken care of, Ira Allen's brother Levi arrived in the capital with two horses.[36] Reflecting the government's alarm, Ryland instructed Levi to leave the colony forthwith. Allen did leave town the next day but made no effort to quit the colony, later claiming a lack of funds. The government decided on firm measures, establishing a special standing committee of the whole Executive Council to enforce the Better Preservation Act. With Osgoode presiding and Justice Dunn a member, it met on 29 June to consider Allen's mysterious comings and goings in the Quebec City area.[37] Ryland informed the committee members that the suspect could 'give no satisfactory account of himself.' Nathaniel Taylor added that Allen had recently been seen several times at a farm outside Quebec City rented by one Hugh Hogan, a suspicious character. The agent for the farm owner gave information that Hogan had not bothered to cultivate the land and his house had become a place of resort for strangers and suspected persons. A letter from Richardson to Sewell was produced in which the former related the rumour that a certain group of American republicans was planning to rescue McLane from jail. Such had been the purpose, Richardson continued, of Daniel McLane and Butterfield entering the province. On the basis of this rather flimsy evidence the committee resolved to issue warrants against Allen and Hogan on suspicion of high treason, which was accordingly done. Hogan's fate is not clear but Allen remained in detention until September when he was released for want of any further proof of treason.

With the 'rescue' plot squelched, the trial could proceed. And none too soon. Prescott ordered a concentration of available troops in Quebec City and fretted about the ruinous state of the fort at St Jean, the insufficient number of regulars, and the shortage of bomb-proof powder magazines in the capital. A heavily armed and manned French fleet, he thought, was probably now at sea with orders from the Directory to invade Lower Canada. Even if no immediate attack was planned, the situation appeared increasingly critical, as Lower Canadian officials learned with horror that defeated Austria had made its peace with the Directory and France was apparently poised to invade the British Isles.

Trial Proceedings

In the early morning of Friday, 7 July 1797, the Quebec court house was alive with activity and anticipation. The day promised to be a hot one – and indeed the temperature would rise to more than 32° Celsius. Heedless of discomfort, spectators quickly filled the galleries, anxious to learn what fate the French revolutionaries had planned for them and their small city. They would become the largest audience ever to attend a trial in Quebec to that time. Seven judges led by Chief Justices Osgoode and Monk filed in and took their places. The prisoner was brought into court; the jurors impanelled by the sheriff were called over. The first trial for high treason held in British Quebec/Lower Canada after the introduction of civil government and the first one of significance in what is now Canada had begun.

A copy of the panel of jurors summoned to try the case has been preserved in the King's Bench records at the Archives nationales du Quebec.[38] Of the eighty-six names on the list, thirty-three to thirty-five appear to be French. Thus, even if defence counsel exercised all thirty-five peremptory challenges, the crown was in a position to keep Canadiens off the jury – an important consideration in view of the unanimity rule and the common opinion among officials that most Canadiens were disloyal.[39] The order in which the names were called is striking. The first fourteen were English, as were all but four of the next eighteen, and several of these twenty-eight English names belonged to persons in the higher ranks of society: merchant-seigneur William Grant; leading import-export trader and supplier of the British Navy at Quebec, James Tod; and prominent merchant-magistrate John Blackwood, to name only three. This arrangement made it easy for the crown to ensure selection of a safe English jury, especially as the inexperienced defence counsel were unlikely to challenge the city's merchantile élite. Eight jurors were selected from the first fourteen names listed and three others from names fifteen through thirty-two.

The fact that several of the mercantile élite appeared on the panel is itself peculiar, since they were rarely called for jury duty in the 1790s, except to serve on the grand jury. Petit juries were almost invariably dominated by clerks, artisans, and shopkeepers. The English majority and the order of names on the list also contrast with the prevailing practice in the years 1795 to 1797. The usual panel listed names alternatively: English, French, English, French and so on to the end of the list. This, for example, was the case with respect to four 1797 trials in the Quebec District.[40] Clearly this divergence might have afforded grounds for a challenge to the panel as a whole. Defence counsel made no such challenge. Nor did they challenge peremptorily or for cause the first eight jurors called, seven of whom were leading Quebec merchants. Altogether the defence issued twenty-four challenges, the crown eleven. The end result could hardly have been better for the prosecution. Exactly half the persons selected had sat on the accusing grand jury in March and therefore had detailed knowledge of Sewell's French plot interpretation of the Road Act disturbances.[41] Eight jurors were well-established import-export merchants: Blackwood, John Crawford, Henry Cull, Robert Morrogh, David Monro, John Mure, George Symes, and John Painter. Of the political orientation of these men, Cull believed the Papineau-Panet faction to be republicans, and Painter had long distrusted the loyalty of Canadien politicians. As justice of the peace, Painter had also been involved in helping to prepare the prosecution's case against the Pointe-Lévi Road Act rioters and Blackwood, in his capacity as magistrate, had helped gather evidence against McLane, including information of a rumoured plot so extensive that Prescott had transmitted it to the Secretary of State. The four remaining jurors were all dependent on the economic élite of the city. John Jones was an auctioneer-broker, James Orkney a watchmaker, and James Irvine a successful ship's chandler and storekeeper who would soon move into transatlantic commerce and become a magistrate. James Mason Goddard operated the brewery of St Roch, a principal owner of which was John Young, one of McLane's judges.

After the jury was sworn, the indictment was read. McLane was charged with two counts of treason: compassing the king's death in that he intended to dethrone him, and adhering to the king's enemies. Fourteen overt acts were alleged in support of both counts. These can be summarized as follows: that he conspired with various persons to solicit enemies of the king to invade the province and did so solicit himself; that he conspired with, solicited, and incited various persons, subjects and aliens, to raise rebellion and assist the enemy in a hostile invasion; that he conspired with various persons to convey arms and ammunition into the province; that he collected intelligence as to the political sentiments of Lower Canada residents and the best means of attacking Montreal, with intent to communicate such intelligence to the enemy; that he conspired with various persons to seize Quebec City and slaughter His Majesty's subjects, and himself entered the city with that intent; and that he entered Quebec secretly under the name of Jacob Felt. The indictment did not make a distinction between overt acts performed within and without the province. Nor did it allege that the enemies of the king had received the intelligence gathered by McLane or in any other way had received aid and comfort from the accused's activities.

Alexis Caron, a Canadien barrister acting as Sewell's junior, opened for the crown by summarizing the indictment. The attorney general followed with a lengthy address. He contended that while a philosopher might find greater turpitude in treason committed by a subject than by an alien, the law made no such distinction, because the evil consequences to the public were the same. What those evil consequences would have been had McLane succeeded in his endeavour he made graphically clear:

our properties, our lives, and, what is still more valuable than either, the happy constitution of our country, all that man can value in civil society, all that attaches us to existence, ourselves ... our government, our religion, our rational liberty, which we boast as British subjects, all must have been laid at the mercy of the French republic. – What that mercy is ... there indelibly recorded for the horror and execration of posterity, in the blood of their lawful sovereign, in the blood of their nobility, in the blood of their clergy, in the blood of thousands of the best and most innocent of their citizens.

Well blooded, the jury prepared to hear the prosecution's case.

Barnard, Cushing, and Black repeated what they had sworn to earlier, with Black supplying additional details to make the story more impressive. One point in Black's story – missing from his deposition – was guaranteed to arrest attention. McLane, he testified, intended to arm his followers 'with pikes of eight feet in length, headed with iron, and hardened in the fire, which he considered to be eighteen inches longer than the British musket and bayonet.' Frichette's testimony repeated what he had admitted in his second voluntary statement, with two major exceptions. He now revealed that when the accused had asked if the Canadiens were prepared to revolt, he had answered, 'No, they were not very warlike, nor desirous of a war.' And according to this new account, after Black had ultimately convinced McLane that his scheme was hopeless, the latter 'then told Black that he would go away as soon as the tide served.' Probably these attempts to mitigate his own guilt provoked Osgoode to describe Frichette's testimony as disgraceful and worthy only of credit when confirmed by others or where it added detail to evident facts.

Butterfield admitted his part of the plot, swearing that in mid-November at Swanton the accused 'told me he was employed by the French minister ... "Adet"' and that the people of Montreal 'were disposed to lend a hand in a revolution ... if they had anybody to lead them.' Ryland testified that, accompanied by a party of soldiers, he had arrested McLane in bed at Black's house on 10 May between 11.00 p.m. and midnight. The accused called himself Jacob Felt and signed a receipt in that name for the money found in his possession.

The defence lawyers' cross-examination revealed little more than the fact that McLane was an American citizen. There were, however, two interesting exchanges between Pyke and Barnard and Cushing. Counsel asked Barnard if he had received any promise or reward from government for having informed against the accused. The witness answered 'None.' Chief Justice Osgoode, one of the officials who had agreed in

November 1796 to giving Barnard and Cushing a township each, interjected that the 'question has been allowed; but I think it was an improper one.' Sewell said nothing. Cushing responded to a similar question evasively and mendaciously: 'I have a promise of a township, but not as a reward for any information which I ever gave against the prisoner.' Pyke did not pursue the point. Francklin, Cushing's lawyer, remained silent at this outright lie. Nor did counsel call any witnesses for the defence. The court gave McLane permission to make a personal address and have his lawyers follow with argument.

Apologizing for his ignorance of legal form, McLane proceeded to argue for his life in a lengthy speech which revealed little in the way of well thought out strategy, but rather a confidence trickster plying his facile trade in an unsuitable forum. He admitted virtually the whole of the crown's case except the compromising statements attributed to him. The store which he ran in Providence with his brother-in-law Jacob Felt had been on the verge of failing. McLane had heard from customers that there was money to be made in Lower Canada and decided to investigate business prospects there. The witnesses against him might be all honest men, but they were gravely mistaken as to his views 'which were only views of trade, and not at all political.' He had, for example, asked Barnard and Frichette about the temper of the Canadiens, for if renewed disturbances were likely he would have to consider locating his business elsewhere. He had spent some hours examining Montreal mountain in November but only because several American acquaintances had recommended it as a tourist attraction 'well worthy of curiosity.' It was also the case that he had shown Cushing a certificate signed by a French official, an admission which seems to have been particularly damaging. The accused tried valiantly to explain this circumstance away. His wife had recently inherited property in France and he had hoped to obtain a certificate that the French minister in the United States was interested in his family concerns. This was the document – signed not by Adet but by a clerk in the French embassy – which had become lodged in the shoe merely through accident! In April he had learned he might obtain timber on credit in northern Vermont which he could exchange for horses in Lower Canada. Frichette agreed to take him to see the best horses for sale in the province and they entered the colony for that purpose. Since he had information that his American creditors would pursue him even across the frontier, he asked Frichette to call him by the name of Felt. They found few horses to his liking, but McLane did purchase one. In Quebec he hoped to sell Black some timber. They had talked about a variety of subjects of obvious interest to a tourist, including the strength of Quebec and whether it could easily be taken by an enemy.

McLane's defence must have raised many damaging questions in the minds of the jurymen. If he was so pressed for money, why had he not gone to France immediately? Why had he conducted virtually no business in Lower Canada? Where did he get the $140? Why if his creditors were such a threat had he chosen his partner's name for an alias? Why especially had he risked returning to the United States in July and November? Perhaps the only assertion the jury was prepared to accept was the statement with which McLane began his story: 'It is true to say, my life has been a day of sorrow.' McLane ended his defence with a fervent prayer for God to pour wisdom into the hearts of his judges and touch the lips of his lawyers with eloquence.

Pyke followed McLane. He devoted a third of his speech to praising the British judicial system and another third to summarizing the accused's defence. McLane's curiosity about Lower Canadian security was natural, he argued. The jury would remember that when Admiral Richery appeared on the verge of ascending the St Lawrence, 'all ranks and descriptions of people here endeavoured to obtain information of the disposition and sentiments of the Canadians in the distant parishes.' Pyke also made two legal points. The first was to argue that the idea of compassing the king's death in such a distant dominion was absurd. Even if Lower Canada were to be separated from the crown of Great Britain, the king's personal safety would not be endangered. As for the count of adhering, it required that the prisoner physically *attempt* to aid and comfort the enemy. In the case of letters of military intelligence, for example, they must at least be sent, even if they were not received. The evidence against the prisoner – various conversations with the witnesses – even if taken in the manner preferred by the prosecution, related only to intention. Pyke did not cite authorities and did not raise the question of alienage.

Francklin also spoke in McLane's defence. He too expressed belief in the accused's explanatory statement, suggested Butterfield and Barnard were lying and argued that much of the crown's case was based on the evidence of accomplices. Francklin supported Pyke's argument on compassing, citing Foster to show that the rationale for characterizing plots against the government in Britain as compassing was grounded in Machiavelli's aphorism on the short distance between the dethronement and the grave of princes. It would be monstrous to apply that rationale to plots against a distant colony 'when even a revolution, which severed thirteen colonies from the British empire did not in the least affect his [the king's] sacred person.' Francklin did not deal with the legal aspect of adhering and did not raise a defence of alienage. He did, however, refer to McLane's status as an alien from a neighbouring friendly country, and pointed out that the jury was presented with the opportunity 'to exhibit to them [the American public] an instance of the liberality and impartiality' of the British system of justice. In asking for an acquittal Francklin recalled 'how scrupulously juries in England have in modern times weighed the proof in trials of the present nature, particularly in the late state prosecutions' of 1794.

Sewell's reply for the prosecution exposed the glaring holes in McLane's story, exploited his admissions, and emphasized the consistency of the crown's witnesses. Despite evidence that McLane had hoped to minimize bloodshed, the attorney general hinted that the accused had planned to massacre ordinary citizens. The eight-foot pikes were 'not to be opposed to the musket or bayonet, but appropriated, I fear, for the more dreadful purpose of assassination.' Sewell repeated his arguments that *political* death was envisaged by the Statute of Treasons and that adhering was a crime of intention. He also made the unqualified and misleading statement 'that you cannot acquit a foreigner on evidence that would convict a native.' To contain any possible sympathy for McLane's plight, Sewell ended by quoting Edmund Burke's opinion of the 1794 state trials which resulted in the acquittal of Hardy, Tooke, and others: 'that public prosecutions are become but little better than schools for treason, of no use but to improve the dexterity of criminals in the mystery of evasion, or to show with what impunity men may conspire against the government and constitution of their country.'

The Verdict

Chief Justice Osgoode summed up, directing the jury that their only task was to satisfy themselves that the crown witnesses were worthy of belief. If so, the prosecution's case was solid. The accused had conspired with Adet and others to foment rebellion and invade the province, and entered Quebec for the purpose of seizing it, had collected military and political intelligence in Lower Canada for revolutionary France, and so on. The prisoner's story was not to be credited except where by admission he corroborated the prosecution. Barnard, he noted, had testified he had not received any promise of reward while the court thought 'it a matter of justice due to Mr. Black ... that ... he has behaved like a zealous and faithful subject,' conducting himself with great 'propriety and discretion.' Aside from Frichette and Butterfield, the crown had produced 'five disinterested persons, whose characters are beyond reproach.' Some of them were indeed known to the jury.

The chief justice referred to the 'very slender topics' advanced by defence counsel and could not understand why they had repeatedly asked witnesses whether McLane was an American citizen. It was established that the accused 'was a sojourner in the province' and therefore owed local allegiance in return for the protection to life and property afforded him by the king. Osgoode did not distinguish between acts committed by McLane in Lower Canada and those committed in the United States. The chief justice repeated his view that the overt acts amounted to compassing the king's death, despite the distance from England and the absence of judicial decisions or jurists' statements on point. Osgoode did admit that the jury might find some difficulty with this artificial doctrine. If so, they could find the prisoner guilty on the count of adhering alone, under which the overt acts charged 'seem to range themselves most naturally.' The question whether adhering was a crime of completion, virtual completion, or merely of intention obviously assumed vital importance in Osgoode's mind. Leaving nothing to chance, he adopted the unusual course of explaining past decisions so that the jury would not be left with the slightest doubt 'the doctrine I advance has long since been declared, acted upon, and confirmed by the most respectable characters that have administered the English law.'

Osgoode defined adhering in the widest possible way: 'every attempt to subject this province ... to the king's enemies, is high treason, and every step taken in furtherance of such attempt is an overt act of high treason.' This interpretation was in Osgoode's view but an example of the proper approach to *all* forms of high treason, which was the crime of intention par excellence: 'So in the case of treason, if a traitorous intention is disclosed by words or writings, and they are followed up by any *acts* tending to execute such design, although it be not complete, it is sufficient to ground a charge of treason.' This statement distinctly implied that mere conspiracy to engage in treasonable rioting, manifested by overt act, was high treason. Thus persons *conspiring* to resist the enforcement of a provincial statute in order to force its repeal, could be found guilty of high treason, even though no rioting (that is, an actual levying) occurred. Such a doctrine went well beyond anything found in the jurists or English cases. The jury after retiring for about twenty minutes brought in a verdict of guilty.

Upon Sewell's motion for the death sentence, defence counsel moved in arrest of judgment, arguing two points of law: that the Statute of Treasons was a domestic statute confined to England; and that the indictment had not alleged that McLane was a temporary subject. The second point was purely technical; it did not raise the issue of principle. As the attorney general easily showed, it was not supported by the authorities. The first argument was also weak in that the statute was one of very general application and readily transferrable to the colonies. As such it became part of the law of Quebec at the time of the British Conquest and was confirmed in force by the Quebec Act. The fact that it often referred to the 'realm' was as Pyke and Francklin argued, irrelevant. Almost all of the British criminal law statutes in force in Lower Canada had been enacted without the colonies in mind; indeed, many had been passed before England had possessed any overseas colonies at all. The motion in arrest of judgment was denied.

SENTENCE AND EXECUTION

Shortly before 9.00 p.m. the crier called for silence. Chief Justice Osgoode addressed the prisoner. Wearing the traditional black hood, he pronounced the sentence:

That you, David Maclane, be taken to the place from whence you came, and from thence you are to be drawn to the place of execution, where you must be hanged by the neck, but not till you are dead; for, you must be cut down alive and your bowels taken out and burnt before your face; then your head must be severed from your body, which must be divided into four parts, and your head and quarters be at the king's disposal; and the Lord have mercy on your soul.

Although the treason sentence was not statutorily altered until 1814 (for the British Isles, not for the Canadas), when it was restricted to drawing, fatal hanging, beheading and quartering, the enlightenment of the eighteenth century had long since moved the judges and especially the hangmen to mitigate it in practice. Prisoners were usually hanged from ten to thirty minutes to ensure death by strangulation before disembowelling commenced. Acting under the prerogative of mercy, the king could commute the sentence in any way he saw fit, provided the result was less punitive. By the end of the eighteenth century it was not uncommon for the king to prescribe that the hanging be fatal and that the disembowelling and quartering be dispensed with.[42]

If Prescott pondered the possibility of 'unofficial' commutation – to fatal hanging, symbolic disembowelling, and symbolic beheading – his resolve to have the sentence carried out as dramatically as permitted by current practice must have been strengthened by the military context and the advice he received. The mother country's first line of defence, the Channel fleet, had mutinied at Spithead and the Nore. Indeed, at home things were so gloomy the best the government could hope for militarily, or so one MP claimed, was a 'day without disaster.' As for the advice, Osgoode was adamantly opposed to mercy, as were two influential sources. Liston, on learning of McLane's capture, urged 'the infliction of exemplary Punishment ... in order to render the Visits of daring adventurers of the same stamp less frequent in the Province.' The Duke of Kent wrote John Young from Halifax about McLane, noting that 'an example in such an affair, cannot be too quick, or too striking.'[43] No commutation was suggested. No reprieve was extended.

For many days it appeared that no one would accept the job of executioner, although Stephen Sewell sent in an eager-beaver report that 'rather than McL. should want a hangman' the officers of the Royal Canadian Volunteers stationed at Montreal 'would go down themselves and execute him.' Finally on 20 July, the eve of the day scheduled, a mercenary and mysterious fellow extorted $600 cash from Sheriff James Shepherd to undertake the task.[44] The next morning McLane dressed in white and outwardly composed was placed on a sledge, which according to the trial report 'moved in slow solemnity towards the place of execution,' conveniently located on top of a slope just outside the St Jean gate which led to the working-class suburb of the same name. McLane was attended by the 'sheriff and peace officers of the district, a military guard of fifty men and a great multitude of spectators.'[45] Among them was the ten-year-old Philippe Aubert de Gaspé, who many decades later vividly recalled scores of lamenting women who, struck by McLane's considerable size and handsome features, cried out that someone should marry the prisoner to save him from the gallows. After prayers, McLane ascended the ladder. He then warned the assembled military that they too must die 'in a short time, some of you perhaps in a few days; let this be a warning to you to prepare for your own deaths,' and added: 'you, with arms in your hands, you are not secure here, even with your arms, I am going where I shall be secure without them.' McLane drew the cap over his face, exclaimed 'Oh God receive my soul! I long to be with my Jesus' and dropped his handkerchief as a signal to the hangman, who 'instantly turned him off.' McLane died quickly, without a struggle. After twenty-five minutes the body was cut down and the hangman, claiming he was no butcher and was finished for the day, extorted another $300 from the harassed sheriff before he would complete the sentence.

JUSTICE?

The day after the execution Osgoode wrote John King, permanent under-secretary of state, expressing the opinion that McLane 'was well qualified for the undertaking had he had suitable materials to work withal.' The execution demonstrated the superiority of his court compared to those which had tried Hardy and his friends: 'It is hoped that his majesty's Courts of Justice in his Province of Quebec will not be found obnoxious to the Censure cast on them in other quarters.'[46] One supposes Edmund Burke agreed.

In his biographical sketch of Osgoode written in 1888, David B. Read of the Ontario Bar cited the trial report at various points to support his judgment that the proceedings against McLane had been 'conducted with the utmost fairness, before eminent Judges and an impartial jury.' Judge W.R. Riddell, basing himself solely on legal materials, concluded from his research on the McLane trial that its conduct merited the highest praise. There was no reason to think any miscarriage of justice had occurred. Indeed 'a perusal of the shorthand notes of the trial will prove to the lawyer that the proceedings were conducted with the utmost fairness and decorum, and that no other verdict was possible.'[47] These assessments, which lack primary historical research, cannot be accepted.

In the first place, the presiding judge could not possibly have been impartial. Perspective here is provided by the behaviour of contemporary English judges in security cases. The empirical approach to constitutional development has the great virtue of flexibility to meet changing conditions. Its great defect – lack of clarity – has never been more apparent than in the practice, which lasted into the 1790s, of having state prisoners examined by the cabinet in the presence of judges who were to sit on their trials. Despite the growing acceptance of the judiciary's independence of the executive, this curious mixture of functions had a solid pedigree in the eighteenth century. In the 1790s both chief justices – Eyre and Kenyon – presided at the trials of state prisoners they had helped examine prior to committal. When the constitutional issue first emerged politically in 1806, leading spokesmen for the opposition and the government and political independents such as Lord Eldon agreed that the practice was improper. But up to that time there had been no hint of impropriety.

It is difficult to describe the examining role of the judges in the 1790s with great precision, but some generalizations can be offered.[48] Their prime function was to advise on what if any charges could be laid. They did not consider themselves bound by the procedure and certainly did not involve themselves in building a case for the prosecution. The clearest near-contemporary definition of the pre-1806 judicial function in security cases considered by cabinet is found in a passage in Lord Castlereagh's speech to the British House of Commons on the Ellenborough appointment. Chief Justice Eyre, he claimed, 'was summoned to the privy council ... to hear evidence against the prisoners, to decide whether it was sufficient to warrant a committal, and for what crime.' If Eyre had gone beyond these tasks and 'consulted in Cabinet on the political expediency of bringing those persons to trial, if he had engaged in all the councils of government ... it would be monstrous to contend ... he would with propriety have been sent to sit in judgment upon the parties accused.' The examining role of the judge in England, then, was conceived of as magisterial, not prosecutorial.[49]

Osgoode went far beyond the British norm and beyond local precedent as well.[50] As 'prime minister' he acted as the political head of security in Lower Canada and in so doing absorbed a great deal of extra-judicial evidence and numerous impressions of the dangers involved and how those were perceived by the Montreal magistrates, the attorney general, the Executive Council, and the governor. Osgoode advised on the Montreal fortifications issue; he chaired the Council's security committee which investigated the doings of Levi Allen; he (with Prescott) gave approval to Louisineau turning king's evidence in the Ducalvet affair.[51] Osgoode also helped build the prosecution case against McLane by taking the deposition of Cushing and making the bargain that benefited Cushing and Barnard. The chief justice was the major influence behind Prescott's decision that McLane would be tried immediately for high treason (instead of being detained as a prisoner-of-war or executed as a spy), and by a commission which was expressly limited to the Quebec District.

In the second place, the crown and Bench appear to have exercised their discretion not for the purpose of ensuring a fair trial but to guarantee in advance a verdict of guilty. The lawyers chosen by the court to represent McLane, for example, were hardly such from whom a vigorous, persuasive defence could be expected. Why did they not attempt to divide the jury or elicit from it a recommendation of mercy by portraying McLane as a weak-minded dupe of Adet and by pointing out that he had done the colony no harm, and owed no moral allegiance to George III?

Why did they not engage in a frontal attack on constructive adhering, as they had on constructive compassing? Why, especially, did they not raise the substantive issue of alienage?

The obvious first line of defence was that McLane should be accorded the status of temporary alien enemy, who in the circumstances of the case owed no allegiance. It was clearly established in the writings of the jurists that an alien subject of a foreign prince at war with Great Britain could not commit treason by invading the realm or assisting British rebels to levy war against the king. It was also generally accepted that alien enemies residing in British territory owed a local allegiance in return for protection and could be guilty of treason. Only one of the authorities addressed the question of allegiance (if any) of an alien enemy sent by his government to Britain as a spy. Sir Mathew Hale, however, was explicit on this. After stating that an enemy alien invading the realm could not be indicted for treason, since no allegiance was owed, he added that 'the like may be said of such as are sent over merely as spies by a forein [sic] prince in hostility.'[52] Thus what authority there was supports the proposition that had Adet sent a French national into Lower Canada to do what McLane had done, the Frenchman could not have been charged with treason. And since treason is a crime grounded in allegiance, surely one could argue that the duties of enemy aliens were to be restrictively interpreted.

But could McLane have claimed the status of an enemy alien? According to the judgment in *Vaughan's* case (1696) he could have. Vaughan had accepted a French commission as a sea captain. It came out in evidence that some of his crew were Hollanders. The court laid down that such alien friends become temporary alien enemies: 'Now the prisoner having this commission to be commander of this vessel, though they who served under his were not native Frenchmen, but other foreigners, yet their subjecting themselves to him, acting by virtue or colour of that commission, makes them to be the French king's subjects, during their continuance in that service.'[53]

In a civil case, heard just a few months after the McLane trial, the right of a German captured while serving on a French ship to sue in the courts was questioned. The issue depended on whether or not the German was an alien enemy at the time of the suit, for alien enemies had no access to the courts. Chief Justice Eyre, approving the *dictum* in *Vaughan*, held that a neutral serving in the military forces of the enemy was certainly to be treated as an enemy alien, but only for so long as he was engaged in hostilities.[54]

Obviously McLane operated under instructions from the French minister to the United States. Was he employed in a military capacity? If evidence of the accused's conversations with the crown witnesses was used to prove his supposed treason, it should have been available, too, for use in his defence. That McLane had claimed to be acting as a military officer for Adet came out in the testimony of Cushing, Frichette, and Black and by implication in that of Barnard, Butterfield, and Chandonet as well. Frichette, for example, swore that in June 1796 McLane said he was an officer in the French army. And the evidence of McLane's status presented at the trial was sufficient to convince, among others, the editors of the *Annual Register* for 1797 that the prisoner 'had received a military commission from Adet.'

Was counsel's failure to raise the issue of alienage due to incompetence? If so it was of the grossest kind. This seems unlikely, especially in the case of Pyke, who later established himself as an able legal scholar.[55] Francklin, who articled with Sewell during the militia and Road Act riots, must have been well versed on the laws of treason. One strongly suspects that counsel's reticence was due to fear for professional advancement at the outset of their careers. In any event, McLane had a strong, substantive defence which was not made by this counsel and was not noticed by the chief justice despite his familiarity with the *Vaughan* case.

Public Reactions

McLane's trial, conviction, and execution created ripples of interest outside the colony. In Kingston, merchant and Upper Canadian legislative councillor Richard Cartwright expressed relief that the lower province, so recently 'bordering on revolt,' was now safe: 'The execution of a Mr. McLean, one of Mons. Adet's emissaries, and other vigorous measures of General Prescott have ... effectually checked every seditious symptom for the present.' Among New Brunswick lawyers of the loyalist élite, Sewell became something of a hero for his 'masterly epitome of the law upon High Treason.' Several London papers, basing themselves on accounts in the *Quebec Gazette*, gave the trial and execution laudatory coverage of a paragraph or two with some, in addition, emphasizing the assassination plot. The *Annual Register* for 1797 concluded that by means of the hangman's rope 'a stop was put to the machinations of the republicans against the peace and happiness of the Canadas.' Secretary of State Portland noted that 'The Trial of McLane appears to have been conducted throughout in a manner which reflects the highest Credit on the Administration of Justice within the Province.'[56]

In New England, New York, New Jersey, and Pennsylvania the case generated much recrimination against both informers and accomplices, debate on the cruelty of the sentence, and Federalist-Republican controversy over French policy towards the Canadas.[57] Adet's successor in the American capital sent Talleyrand a copy of Neilson's short report of the trial, remarking he had never seen this so-called criminal and that such was the way the English trifled with human lives.[58]

In Lower Canada itself the immediate reaction was striking. McLane's conviction and execution were everything the English élite desired. The famed mildness of His Majesty's British rule and the renowned leniency of the criminal law now wore a different aspect. According to the later recollection of Joseph-François Perrault, a member of the House of Assembly in 1797, McLane's gruesome dispatch to eternity made a terrifying impression on the common folk and 'there was no more talk of emissaries to make the people rise.'[59] Stephen Sewell basked in his brother's glory for having saved the province. He noticed that the Canadiens of the Montreal District had changed their ways: 'they are more observant of the laws than can be expected of the best subjects ... and the roads are universally good in consequence.' For Colonel Nairne the truly heroic Prescott had intimidated the Canadiens who now 'compare him to Genl: [Sir James] Murray, whom they very much feared, [and] therefore keep themselves vastly Submissive of late.'[60]

At long last the government had convinced the Canadiens that the pliable Dorchester no longer ruled at the Chateau. In the words of Joseph Chew, the new governor would 'not trifle with them.' The whole McLane episode, even if the victim was not one of the conquered people, confirmed the English élite in its view that the Canadiens had to be treated with toughness. Saboteurs, collaborators, and conspirators would not be tolerated.

8

War's End and Ethnic Breakdown

Ira Allen's Civil Society Plot

As the century of Enlightenment came to an end, the unspeakable 'wickedness' secretly driving the French Revolution, was unmasked by 'scholars.' Abbé Barruel, citing McLane's Intrigues, included Lower Canada in his exhaustive geographical review of Weishaupt's shadowy but lethal tentacles. The first edition of Professor Robison's *Proofs of a Conspiracy* (London, 1797) sold out almost immediately and the book went through four editions before the turn of the century, while Barruel's *Mémoires* was published in two British versions prior to 1800. These works strongly influenced parliamentarians. The report of a Commons' committee dated 15 March 1799 exploited their ideas as obvious truths to justify its recommendation of a statute outlawing secret societies. This, the Combination Act, 1799, was duly enacted later that session.[1]

Barruel and Robison soon became authorities in Lower Canada as well. Bishop Mountain, for instance, praised their scholarly achievements in his thanksgiving sermon on 10 January 1799 to celebrate Nelson's victory of the Nile. These brilliant writers had laid bare the 'the *Conspiracy* directed with remorseless treachery, with envenomed malice, and with unwearied perseverance, not only against all established forms of *Christian Worship*, but against the Religion of *Jesus Christ itself*. The progress which they have made, in this diabolical warfare,' he concluded, 'is recorded in the characters of blood!'² At the urging of his congregation, which included many prominent officials, Mountain published the sermon.³ It would soon appear to these men that the 'conspiracy' had returned to the colony.

In July–August 1801 the government received information from Colonel John A. Graham, an erstwhile friend of Ira Allen (who had betrayed the latter early in 1797 by revealing the *Olive Branch* plot) that the adventurer had organized secret societies in Vermont to manipulate 'Jacobins in Upper and Lower Canada'⁴ with the aim of subverting and plundering the two colonies. A dependent society, Graham claimed, had been established at Montreal under the leadership of an American schoolteacher named Rogers. The Montreal magistrates investigated and discovered that indeed Rogers was running a secret association. They were proceeding discreetly in an attempt to compile conclusive evidence of high treason, when rumours of the conspiracy surfaced in September and the public panicked. The magistrates arrested six of the leaders, although the main quarry, Rogers, escaped. On 21 September the Executive Council's permanent committee on security examined the magistrates' evidence, including the prisoners' statements. On the basis of its report, warrants were issued under the Better Preservation Act to confine the six in the Montreal jail.

Readers who have made complex textual arguments before the courts will know that the placing of a comma can make or break an argument, a case, a client. Such was the situation in 1801 when the placement of a comma proved very convenient to the government. The warrants ordered committal on the grounds that the persons to be detained were *suspected* of the undefined crime of 'treasonable practices,' presumably because Sewell could not amass sufficient evidence to support charges. Such warrants would almost certainly have been illegal in Britain, since the 1794 act, which the attorney general had used as a model, specified that internment could take place only 'for high treason, suspicion of high treason, or treasonable practices.' This would seem to have required the warrant (aside from high treason cases) to specify suspicion of treason or to charge the accused with treasonable practices. Sewell's 1797 act was subtly different, requiring warrants 'for High treason, misprision of High Treason, suspicion of High Treason or Treasonable Practices.' By omitting the comma before the connective 'or' the Better Preservation Act could be read as requiring a 'warrant for high treason or a warrant for suspicion of either high treason or treasonable practices.' That Sewell dropped the comma purposefully cannot be proved, but it seems likely given his unrelenting attention to detail, his acute, experienced legal mind, and the prevailing fear of insurrection in 1797. He had certainly shown finesse on the question of parliamentary privilege. In any case, the interpretation adopted in 1801 – the first time the situation arose – could be justified by literal construction.

The committee likely based its political decision largely on a report of the same day drafted by the attorney general.[5] The Civil Society, he wrote, had sixty-one members – all English-speaking and mostly American. Similar groups had been formed or were in the process of formation in Quebec, Trois-Rivières, Carillon, Cornwall, and York. Although Rogers intended to reveal his subversive aim only to an inner circle of cronies, the mass of an expanding membership was to be controlled by midnight meetings, 'Ceremonies and mummery,' and Rogers's Delphic utterances that hunting for treasure – the society's ostensible purpose – involved 'a greater work than any of you think.' It was clear to Sewell that the 'most effective Engine employed by France in subverting so many of the Governments of Europe' had made its diabolical appearance in the colony. The 'principle of Illuminism and of the Irish and British Political Societies is distinctly visible.' It had been the 'regular connection from the primary Societies of Ireland in regular succession to the Executive Directory in France tho' unknown to the mass of members, that gave exertion, consistency, solidity and force to the late Rebellion in that Kingdom.'

A month later Sewell submitted a second report to Milnes giving further findings of detail.[6] The plan of the Civil Society, as formulated by Ira Allen, had been to blow up the powder magazine and seize the city of Montreal. At this signal well-armed Vermonters would join the local conspirators. Although Rogers and associates had no confidence in the Canadiens, French emissaries had recently begun to corrupt them 'with offers of money and direct assurances that the plan would be carried on [continued] under the auspices of the Government of France.' The possibility of France infiltrating small groups of soldiers into the colony had to be taken seriously, as it had been contemplated by the French in 1796–7 and was perfectly feasible. Pillage had been the immediate object of the conspirators and had that started, massacre of the residents would have inevitably ensued.

Was Sewell correct in assuming, first, French involvement and, secondly, Ira Allen's leadership? Historians have failed to find evidence of the former. Sewell's only ground was a deposition by Terrebonne shopkeeper and *parti canadien* supporter Charles-Baptiste Bouc claiming that an agent from France had informed him that French troops would be infiltrated into the colony in small groups.[7] Bouc, a former MPP, had been expelled from the Assembly in 1798 upon conviction for conspiracy to extort money. This circumstance gave Bouc the appearance of being disaffected and hence, in Sewell's mind, a likely recruiting target of enemy agents. But after a lengthy investigation into the case, Richardson satisfied himself that the story was a fabrication.[8]

As for Allen's leadership, there is no evidence of it in the two collections of the Allen Family Papers held by the University of Vermont and the Vermont State Archives. There are over 190 items in the former, dating from 1 July 1800 to 30 June 1802 but not a mention of Rogers, the Civil Society, or Vermont secret societies. Only one prisoner clearly implicated Allen, claiming the plot had been initiated the previous winter. Sewell accepted this assertion. Allen, however, did not return to Vermont from Europe (via Philadelphia and Washington) until May 1801! Nor is the evidence of John Graham, a paid informer, very persuasive. Indeed, Allen's biographer, J.B. Wilbur, may have it correct in claiming that Graham himself organized the secret society to establish his credibility, which was none too strong with the Lower Canadian authorities until Rogers's group was detected. Allen's involvement then is not proven.[9]

Like Sewell, Milnes took the danger very seriously. In particular he thought it likely that Allen was orchestrating the plot and was 'supported and employed by the emissaries of France.' The lieutenant-governor accordingly ordered the militia of the Montreal area to hold one-eighth of their men in a state of alert. An armed volunteer association was organized by the Montreal magistrates and patrols of the city began on 2 November. By the end of the month the readiness of Montrealers to defend their city and intelligence from Vermont on Allen's waning influence there because of his financial problems suggested the crisis was over. On 17 December warrants were issued to release the five remaining suspects (one had been bailed for health reasons) on giving satisfactory security for their good behaviour until the war ended.[10]

The Le Couteulx case

French-born René Le Couteulx, a naturalized American citizen and Albany merchant, connected to a prominent Parisian banking family, had lived in the United States for many years.[11] In 1798 Liston, Portland, and Prescott had concluded that he was assisting Directory agents to enter the colony and army deserters leave it.[12] In October 1800, while proceeding to Detroit on business, Le Couteulx decided to visit Niagara Falls. He was arrested by the commandant at Fort George and sent under armed guard to Quebec, arriving on 4 November. Le Couteulx had been imprudent enough to carry with him copies in his own hand of compromising letters he had written during the year 1797 – a fact Liston wisely marked as indicating that the prisoner had *not* entered the Canadas to engage in espionage or subversion. As extracted and translated by the Lower Canadian authorities, the letters lack proof of Le Couteulx's plotting but portray him as an extreme francophile, aching to liberate the Canadiens, 'whom the English make *Beasts of Burthen*' and who 'wish *to a man*, to return under the French Government and to be free like their brothers.'[13] As had occurred with Ducalvet, McLane, Aubins, and others, government officials had their version of Canadien disloyalty corroborated by an enemy agent or supposed enemy agent.

Le Couteulx's arrival in Quebec posed a serious dilemma for Major General Hunter, commander-in-chief of the troops in British North America. He wished to keep the prisoner incarcerated for the remainder of the war, but this could not be done under the Lower Canadian Alien Act and there was no evidence to suggest that Le Couteulx could be tried for treasonable, seditious or other criminal acts committed in the Canadas. Within a day or two Sewell provided Hunter with a hastily drafted solution.[14]

Sewell took refuge in the British and international doctrines of indefeasible allegiance: 'Mr. Le Couteulx being born a Frenchman must remain such, and being the subject of ... [an Enemy] Power ... he is liable to be detained as a Prisoner of War.' Naturalization made no difference whatever. The prisoner was to be considered an American citizen only so long as he remained within the territory of his adopting country; outside its boundaries he was a Frenchman. Sewell was correct in his analysis of permanent allegiance – if that question be narrowly defined – both as it applied in British law and the laws of other nations. Until 1870 a native-born British subject continued to owe allegiance to his monarch despite naturalization or abjuration and the rule applied regardless of how ridiculous it seemed in any given circumstances.

Most European nations at the turn of the nineteenth century had a similar rule which denied that a subject could shed allegiance at will.[15] This was true also of the United States despite inalienable rights, vested in the individual, to liberty and the pursuit of happiness. For many decades after the Declaration of Independence the common law doctrine prevailed in this matter, as in several others. It was not until the pressure of European immigration became overwhelming in the 1850s and 1860s that the American government adopted the view that naturalization cut all ties with the country of origin.

The weakness in Sewell's opinion on expatriation flows from an unwarranted extension of the inalienable allegiance concept to nations *other* than the state of origin and the state of naturalization. While paying lip service to the law of nations he was essentially claiming that the domestic law of Great Britain on allegiance should be applied where Britain was a third-party state. The proper source of the rule to be applied to Le Couteulx, as Sewell himself indicated, was the law of nations, the customary branch of which had become part of the common law by at least the second third of the eighteenth century. Had Sewell examined state practice, he would have discovered precedents suggesting that expatriation was a question solely between the two nations most immediately involved – in this case France and the United States. Even by focusing exclusively on British law and British diplomatic practice, the same conclusion would have been inevitable. Clearly Sewell should have concluded that Le Couteulx, born in France but naturalized by the United States in 1787 – well before the Anglo-French war[16] – was to be considered an American citizen and entitled to the American government's protection when within the Canadas, territory belonging to Great Britain, a third-party state.

Hunter and Portland were satisfied by the pretext provided by Sewell, although the British law officers gave only lukewarm approval. The minister to Washington, Edward Thornton, found the opinion quite unconvincing. In a letter to American secretary of state, James Madison, he justified the incarceration, not by Sewell's reasoning, but on the 'common principles of self-preservation.' Despite the legal weakness of the Lower Canadian position, several diplomatic interventions by the United States' government and an official protest by Madison, Le Couteulx remained in jail for almost two years – without trial and apparently without legal counsel – until after the peace treaty of Amiens. He was freed in August 1802 and escorted across the border.

The whole episode conveys the extraordinary stock the Lower Canadian authorities put in the machinations of supposed French agents, even when they operated from the United States. It also demonstrates that on security issues those same authorities, including the attorney general, could easily lose sight of that very rule of law for which they proclaimed Britain was fighting. Le Couteulx's fate, after all, was decided by those penal laws which, as Sewell himself many times claimed, were to be interpreted in favour of the prisoner in case of doubt. The policy of treating suspect enemy aliens as prisoners of war continued down to the end of the period.

ANGLICIZATION POLICIES, 1793–1801

Desire to assimilate the Canadiens grew in response to fears of the French revolutionaries. The first attempt in the colony's history to make English the sole official language (1793) was justified in the name of fostering loyalty and came at a time when the English élite's insecurity would rapidly develop into the garrison mentality. The English merchants had not advocated the abolition of the seigneurial system in the 1780s, but by 1795 they pressed the issue in the Assembly, pointing to the French Revolution in support. Individuals' viewpoints also changed. Once a political moderate who in 1787 had favoured increasing the scope of the French civil law, lawyer Thomas Walker had become a thorough-going anglicizer by the early 1800s.[17] Judge Thomas Dunn, formerly of the French party, was concerned both publicly and privately for the security of the colony during the war and by the century's end favoured anglicization through the schools. Civil Secretary Ryland had arrived in Lower Canada in 1793 as a firm believer in the French party's stand on cultural autonomy, but the militia riots of 1794 converted him to an enemy of Canadien identity.[18] The cases of Dunn and Ryland point to another significant development. With France, rather than the United States, having become the more serious external threat, the loyalist ideal of cultural homogeneity gained relevance, while Mabane's concept of Canadienism as a barrier to American penetration lost credibility. The English wing of the French party did not, in fact, long survive the doctor's death in early 1792 and was entirely gone from politics by the early months of the war. Mabane's belief in aristocratic values did not of course disappear. But the main political proponent of this ideology, Chief Justice Osgoode, had become an assimilator in the interests of security soon after his arrival in the colony. Writing to a friend in 1795 on the dangers posed by the democrats' agitation against the seigneurs, he complained that although the British had possessed Quebec/Lower Canada for more than thirty years, 'the Body of the people are not anglicised at all. The Ruling Policy has been unaccountable ... If the superior class of Canadians had any Influence over the people this Policy might be justifiable but the Contrary is the fact ... [as] the Seigneurs are universally unpopular throughout the Country.'[19] The election of 1796 and the Road Act riots confirmed Osgoode in his condemnation of the ruling policy, and he was certainly not alone. By the late 1790s and the early 1800s English government officials concluded that the ideas behind the Quebec Act – to grant the Canadiens cultural autonomy in return for loyalty and to rule through the seigneurs and an autonomous clergy – were nothing short of absurd. Anglicization became the new ruling policy in Quebec City if not in London, and Lord Dorchester as the architect of the Quebec Act began, in retrospect, to look like a fool.[20]

Between 1799 and 1801 Lieutenant-Governor Milnes and his advisers worked out a series of interrelated policies designed to reproduce aristocratic England in the St Lawrence valley by establishing a system of public schools under state control, providing the legal impetus for abolishing seigneurial tenure and enforcing the royal supremacy in religion. These policies would have many medium-term security advantages and eventually would realize the total assimilation of the conquered subjects. This alone, it appeared, would guarantee the safety of the English minority and ensure that Lower Canada remained within the British Empire.

It has often been suggested that the Education Act of 1801 was framed by Bishop Mountain to provide a means of proselytizing Canadien schoolchildren[21] and, again, that the act was not greatly influenced by assimilationist ideas but was simply an attempt to promote the economic development of the province by reducing illiteracy.[22] Neither of these interpretations is supported by the evidence, which indicates that the Education Act was primarily a product of the garrison mentality. Bishop Mountain did hope to use the schools, as he had put it some years earlier, to induce the 'Inhabitants to embrace by degrees the Protestant Religion.' It was Mountain who initiated the idea of publicly financed elementary and secondary schools, with the government appointed teachers obliged to give instruction on the English language free of charge. These principles, embodied in a plan Mountain submitted to Milnes in 1799 and approved of by him and by a committee of the Executive Council, were ultimately incorporated in the act of 1801.[23] But Bishop Mountain was not the government. His plan had to be acceptable to the Executive Council committee and the lieutenant-governor and as well to the latter's advisers not on the Council, such as Judge Isaac Ogden of the Montreal King's Bench, whom Milnes consulted on educational matters, and above all Jonathan Sewell. In these early years of Milnes's governorship, the attorney general dominated thinking at the Chateau on all security matters. In particular, the evidence indicates he was the main architect of the Education Act of 1801.[24]

Mountain succeeded not because the bureaucracy supported his program of ecclesiastical empire-building at the expense of the Roman Catholic rival but principally because of the government's concern for Canadien disloyalty. The members of the Council committee which approved the plan – Osgoode, Dunn, Young – and Sewell had long assumed that one root of the security problem lay in habitant illiteracy which, as the attorney general had put it in 1796, rendered the lower orders 'liable to be imposed upon by the grossest assertions.'[25] Sewell and Milnes particularly recognized that any direct assault on the Roman Catholic religion would jeopardize the entire project and Mountain's hope that English Protestant teachers be appointed even in Canadien areas was never seriously considered by them.[26] Their idea seems to have been to make use of pro-British schoolteachers of the Labadie type like François Malherbe, schoolmaster at Rivière Ouelle, whose indoctrination of his pupils on Britain's magnificent ordered liberty brought praise from the *Quebec Gazette*, and ultimately reward from the government.[27] As for fostering economic growth, one is hard put to find proof of this motive, although it doubtless had some minor effect.[28]

Milnes and his advisers anticipated that once the school system was operative the security problem would be on the way to solution. In the medium term, the spread of English would reduce tensions between the nationalities, while increasing literacy would by itself reduce danger. For Sewell the lessons drawn from the riots of the 1790s and the habitants' resistance to counter-revolutionary propaganda were strongly reinforced by Adam Smith's views on popular education. In the *Wealth of Nations* Smith had contended that the safety of 'free countries' depended upon educating the lower orders, so that they became deferential to their sociopolitical superiors and less prone to capricious condemnation of the government.[29] One way to achieve this goal directly was to teach children the contrast between anarchistic democracy and the *non pareil* balanced constitution. It was urgent, Milnes wrote the colonial secretary in 1800, to foster a 'Spirit of Zeal and Loyalty for monarchical Government' among the Canadiens and to inoculate them against the encroaching 'spirit of democracy.' Sewell's preoccupation with public education arose largely from a conviction, which he claimed was widely shared, that the 'security of the Government of Canada under the New Constitution ... depends much upon the discernment of its Excellency.'[30] It was, of course, commonplace at the time that once a man was able to understand even a little about the superb British system of government, he could be nothing but actively loyal.

In the longer term, framers of the government's education policy expected that as Canadiens became more and more capable of using the English language, they would gradually assimilate in other areas as well. Bishop Mountain was of the opinion that English-language instruction in the schools was a vitally important means whereby the government could confirm the 'loyalty of the people by the gradual introduction of english acquirements, english habits & English sentiments.' Judge Ogden had long held a similar view, while Osgoode believed it essential in the interests of security to 'introduce our Language by the Establishment of schools and thus by degrees to accustom the people to the Notions Habits and Attachments of British subjects.'[31]

Land Tenure

To reinforce the effects of its education policy, the government looked to the gradual disappearance of the seigneurial system. The militia and Road Act riots proved that French agents could exploit habitant resentment against the Canadien seigneurs and that the latter could not restrain the habitants' lingering affection for France or their propensity to disobey unpopular laws. The election of 1796 confirmed that the seigneurs could not control their *censitaires*. Citing common English opinion, Milnes informed the colonial secretary in 1800 that because of their disinclination to engage in trade and the equalizing law of succession, the 'Canadian Gentry have nearly become extinct.' Many lacked the means to live more affluently than their habitant tenants, who therefore felt 'themselves ... as independent as the Seigneur himself.' Unless the government acted quickly to promote a much greater aristocratic inequality of property there was every chance of rebellion at some future time, for the 'Canadian habitants ... are from their want of Education and extreme simplicity, liable to be misled by designing and artful Men.'

It was well understood in government circles that a frontal attack on the seigneurial regime had to be avoided.[32] Milnes and Sewell would conceal their ultimate purpose by exploiting the crown's longstanding failure to collect mutation fines – the *lods et ventes* – in the royal seigneuries, located mainly in the cities of Quebec and Trois-Rivières.[33] A government bill was introduced in the house in 1801 empowering commissioners to reach equitable monetary compromises with those *roture* owners who owed mutation fines arising from past transactions. It passed easily in the Assembly and, despite Osgoode's protest that the aristocratic house must protect the royal prerogative, in the Legislative Council as well.[34]

This signal that the crown's rights, past and future, would be enforced was intended by Milnes and Sewell as 'a material step towards abolishing ... Feudal Tenure.'[35] The crown's immediate tenants, many of them English merchants, would now become 'clamorous for ... a conversion ... into free and common soccage.' The government Church would accede to such requests and regrant the lands in freehold. Once this example was set in the royal seigneuries, conversion would be demanded in all parts of the province. From Sewell's Notebook it is apparent the government envisaged a subsequent statute which would enable seigneurs to commute (into fixed rents) with the crown for the quint and with their *censitaires* for the *lods et ventes*. Thereupon the seigneurs would become absolute owners of the unconceded lands, which they could sell or lease. When conversion became widespread, 'English Gentlemen resident in Canada,' Sewell wrote, would become purchasers of large tracts and an 'English Yeomanry and peasantry' would begin to settle in the region of the seigneuries, an area they had long avoided. The lieutenant-governor foresaw that this would eventually result in a mixed aristocracy of English and Canadiens whose influence over the smallholders would rival that of the county families in England. The attorney general also saw manifold security advantages flowing from conversion: 'where the Canadians are disaffected [the government would] have the benefit of information and intelligence as to their conduct ... and of that restraint which a body of resident English would impose upon them.' Ultimately the Canadiens residing in the countryside would be assimilated by an 'intermixture of the English and Canadians throughout the different Seigniories of the Province, the introduction of reciprocal confidence, of the English Language, of the English System of Agriculture, and an assimilation of manners and pursuits.' Then and only then would the government 'reap the solid advantages of a numerous and well affected militia in the heart of the Country.'[36]

The framers of the Lods et Ventes Act of 1801, in summary, designed it as a tool with which to undermine the seigneurial system. The overriding aim behind the long-range policy was to guarantee the internal security of the colony. This objective clearly took precedence over the short-term pecuniary interests of those English merchants who were direct tenants of the king.

The Royal Supremacy

The policy of permitting the Roman Catholic Church internal self-government, which dated back to Carleton and 1775, also came under attack. Officials were anxious to impose dependence on the clergy, because, uncontrolled, they might well encourage anti-English prejudice, fail to support the governor at election time, and work against the implementation of the education policy, in order to keep the people ignorant.[37] On all these accounts they might well undermine the whole anglification program, essential for the colony's long-range security. Suitably under state control, they could not do such things and, in times of popular disturbance, would be even more united and active in the interest of loyalty than they had been in the 1790s. Milnes urged upon the colonial secretary that the royal supremacy be enforced in order to 'secure the Province from any interior Commotion or Disaffection.' Given the go-ahead by Portland, Milnes lost little time in setting Sewell to work on the question.[38]

Sewell's secret report, dated 29 May 1801,[39] stressed the need to counter the 'general system of the Church of Rome' which was 'an Imperium in Imperio' creating a distinct ecclesiastical power 'between Prince & the people.' The answer was to emulate the mother country, where control of preferment gave ministers of the crown great political influence over the Anglican clergy, from the Bishops' Bench in the House of Lords to the lowliest curate, an influence which could be exploited effectively at election time. Therefore Sewell proposed that Milnes procure an imperial statute, which would recognize the offices of the Roman Catholic bishop and his coadjutor, but otherwise merely state what the law was: by declaring that bishoprics were within 'the absolute appointment of the Crown' and that the king (represented by the governor) should consent to all future postings, with the incumbents to hold office during pleasure. To ensure the hierarchy's satisfaction with the new arrangements, their worldly status should be significantly improved. The bishop and his second-in-command should be forced to live in the capital, where the government could keep an 'immediate eye' on them. Generous compensation for the extra expense involved and for the loss of patronage should be paid. Both Catholic bishops should be appointed to the Executive and Legislative Councils and treated as the heads of a government department, much like the Archbishop of Canterbury was in England.

Sewell took delight in contemplating the many advantages of his system. The dependency of the bishops would 'insure their support in all government measures.' Their internal ecclesiastical influence would be greatly reinforced by the government's power over preferment, with the curés, for example, being 'in expectation of promotion to better livings should they merit them by good behaviour.' The result, given the 'profound ignorance and superstition of the country,' would 'enable every parish priest to govern and lead his flock as he is directed.' And if the worst happened, with Lower Canada again plunged into chaos similar to 1794 and 1796–7, the Canadien clergy could be expected to react with even more spirited support of British rule than they had already shown.

In neither Milnes's dispatches of 1800–1 nor Sewell's report is there any clear implication that the government intended to use the royal supremacy to foster religious conversion by promoting liberally minded, malleable clerics, indifferent on matters of liturgy and theology.[40] Ryland in 1804 certainly looked on the supremacy as the high road by which the country would become Protestant, and Mountain agreed.[41] These statements were made some years later and by persons highly motivated by religious animus – unlike Sewell and Milnes, who thought of anglicization in political terms almost exclusively. It seems unlikely, though, that the policy framers of 1801 ruled out conversion in the long run. Sewell conceived the weakening of the hierarchy's moral authority in the eyes of the laity (and hence their ability to act independently of the government) to be vital: 'To make them political characters, and to hold them up to observation and criticism, as men of the world, is to sap the very foundation of their influence.'

Failure of Implementation

None of the three assimilation policies had any success. The *parti canadien*, led by Pierre-Stanislas Bédard and Panet, was able to amend the Education bill to require that before the governor could establish a school in any parish, a majority of the local landowners must petition for it. This effectively undermined the royal school system in the countryside. For reasons which remain obscure, the Lods et Ventes Acts did not lead to a clamour for soccage tenure. Sewell's attempt in 1804 to appear in cases to oppose two seigneurs' claims to the gristmill monopoly – and thus if successful devalue French tenure – was thwarted by Milnes.[42] After the session of 1801 the lieutenant-governor had come under the influence, successively, of Judge Pierre-Louis Panet and Thomas A. Coffin, the inspector general of public accounts. Panet was a worrier about Canadien disloyalty, which aggressive anglicization could easily reinforce, while Coffin was a former protégé of Lord Dorchester who had perfected the art of governing the Canadiens with circumspection. Milnes began to see himself not as the great anglifier but as an impartial referee between the political parties and concerned himself with the details of administration.[43]

The most sensitive question involved the royal supremacy. Milnes did not even send home a copy of the attorney general's report and by the summer of 1803 the lieutenant-governor had washed his hands of the whole business, on the ground that his predecessors back to the Quebec Act had done nothing. The new colonial secretary, Lord Hobart, applauded such prudence.[44]

In 1804 Sewell agreed to appear in a trial (*Bertrand* v. *Lavergne*) challenging the Roman Catholic bishop's power to create parishes, on the basis of the royal supremacy. The attorney general was ordered to desist by Milnes and the case was lost. Due to the intervention of the latter's successor, Administrator Thomas Dunn – as cautious as Milnes – the Executive Council on appeal declined to decide the merits. With *Bertrand* v *Lavergne* pending, the attorney general, with Milnes's consent, had been able to convince Bishop Denaut to draft an ambiguous petition to the king (1805), asking for a regularization of the Roman Catholic clergy's status in law. Milnes sent the petition home, where it became a casualty to officialdom's indifference and its wartime reluctance to rock the ecclesiastical boat.

Such then was the immediate fate of the three anglicizing initiatives. Despite failure, they are significant to the student of early Canadian history in showing how the garrison mentality had undermined tolerance of the Quebec Act policy and demonstrating that attempts at cultural assimilation preceded the Gaols Act dispute of 1805. The initiatives were taken by government officials and the near-absence of local political coverage in the newspapers of the day makes it impossible to say how widespread support was outside government circles, except that leading merchants such as McGill and Richardson[45] were highly favourable. There can be no doubt, however, that during the war against Napoleonic France, anglicization in the interest of security, if it was not already generally accepted by the English élite, came to be so. Indeed, Canadien resistance to assimilation, passive or active, became a leitmotif of the garrison mentality, as it continued to poison relations between the nationalities.

THE DEMISE OF THE BOURGEOIS ALLIANCE AND THE CONSTITUTION

During his visit to Lower Canada in 1804 Lord Selkirk learned that the Legislative Assembly was divided into a 'French party' and an 'English party.' The former had emerged in the years of the French Revolution and its members, Selkirk claimed, had emulated the revolutionaries even to the point of seeking political independence. The English party had naturally evolved to thwart these nefarious aims, and the two factions remained ever after locked in combat.[46] Selkirk was repeating the English élite's interpretation of recent political history, one salient feature of which (in reality as well as perception) had been the demise of the bourgeois alliance in the years 1793–7. No doubt several other factors were at play, such as the weakness of the Canadien seigneurs as an electoral force, the ultra-conservative, often anglophobic, mentality of the habitant electors, and the lesser need for cooperation felt by ex-Canadien reformers once the constitution began to operate. But one of the most important causes of breakdown was the garrison mentality, shared in as much by ex-reformers as by other segments of the English élite. English party leader John Richardson had characterized Papineau and Panet in 1793 as being 'infected with the detestable principles now prevalent in France.' By 1797 Papineau and many of his Montreal supporters had become, to him, out-and-out traitors. These judgments precluded continuing cooperation. The demise of the bourgeois alliance, due in significant part to the garrison mentality, had important repercussions on the evolution of the constitution.

While the successors to the Canadien reformers continued to press for constitutional liberalization during the war against revolutionary France, the English reformers, now allied with English officials, quickly became arch-conservatives in matters constitutional. Their votes helped doom the *parti canadien*'s 1794–5 attempts to realize such earlier ideals as a politically independent judiciary, restrictions on the suspension of habeas corpus, an extension of jury trials to all civil cases involving the crown, and an Assembly role in the appropriation of public monies. The constitutional divorce between the factions continued to the end of the war against revolutionary France. English party votes, for example, ultimately negated democraticizing notions that MPPs be paid put forward by Papineau in 1799 and Berthelot d'Artigny in 1802. In the end McGill managed to give it the hoist in a thinly attended House.[47]

The gyrations of William Grant illustrate this transformation. Grant, it will be remembered, had been a leader of the English reformers on and off the Council. In Old Quebec he had gained renown for his successful effort to have Council enact a habeas corpus ordinance and his unsuccessful one to write into law a libertarian rule of interpretation. Unlike many of his former colleagues, Grant remained a radical for some months after the war. In 1794 he was the only English member to vote for the *parti canadien's* initiatives on judicial tenure and jury trials in crown cases. In April of that year, seconded by de Rocheblave, he proposed his libertarian idea once again. Supported by Papineau and other *parti canadien* members, Grant's motion was nevertheless defeated by sixteen to nine, with nine English members (including ex-reformer activists Richardson and McGill) voting for the majority. A few weeks later the militia riots broke out and we find a suddenly sobered Grant proposing that the legislature empower the governor-in-council to suspend habeas corpus at will and 'to proclaim ... the law martial, whenever the Province in ... their judgment and discretion,' faces imminent 'invasion, rebellion or insurrection.'[48] In 1797, with De Bonne and Sewell, Grant took the lead in having habeas corpus again suspended. The stifling effect of the garrison mentality, and hence the French Revolution, on Grant's constitutional thinking is obvious.

PARTY POLITICS, 1803–1811

Conflicts over the Civil Law

Besides continuing to attack uncertainties in the administration of civil justice, despite the professionalization of the Bench, – the English élite regularly complained of the anti-commercial features of the Canadien law: absence of land registry offices; seigneurial tenure in general; its particularly feudal characteristics; customary dower; inadequate bankruptcy rules and much more.[49] In 1809 the lawyer and MPP Ross Cuthbert mounted a root and branch assault on the 'outdated' *Coutume* which most of the English merchants and officials likely applauded. He likened it to an edifice built 'by the gloomy and wayward architects of the dark ages' who had 'most majestically, accommodated [it] with ingeniously contrived trap doors ... and with numberless latent back stairs, and subterranean alleys' in which rights and wrongs played 'hide and seek.'

No legislative changes occurred. The demise of the bourgeois alliance in the early years of the war against revolutionary France had resulted in the *parti canadien* being far less interested in commercializing the law and much more prone to protect traditional Canadien customs and laws.[50] This was obvious as early as 1795–6 when the party opposed the Road and Engagés bills and the elimination of the feudal aspects of seigneurial tenure. The divorce in mentality, though, is best captured by the attempt, in February 1805, of Ross Cuthbert to abolish the *retrait lignager*, which allowed a blood relative of the vendor to repossess sold real estate within a year and a day by paying the price and certain expenses to the buyer. Only some of these expenses were collectable – those incurred to make the acquisition (such as the notary's fee) and necessary repairs to preserve the property being the most important. The buyer's expenditures on improvement could not be recaptured.[51] The exceedingly complex *retrait lignager* did not protect vulnerable family members and did not financially benefit habitant vendors or purchasers of *roture* lands. The drawbacks of the *retrait* had been obvious even to French party judge John Fraser and to prosperous country merchants Bonaventure Panet and Pierre-Guillaume Guerout, who had moved for its abolition in the first session of the legislature.[52] It did not, then, uphold vital Canadien values (comparable to, say, customary dower).[53]

To support his motion, Cuthbert argued that if a person bought a lot for a few pounds, then 'expended on it £5000 in building a wharf or manufactory' he or she could be dispossessed, perhaps by 'a cousin of the fiftieth degree, on condition of reimbursing the few pounds paid for the lot.' Lawyer Berthelot d'Artigny and notary Louis Bourdages of the *parti canadien* maintained in opposition that 'what had been long practised should be touched with caution; that the *Retrait Lignager* was a part of the law of the land, and that it had the good tendency of preserving in families the property they had long possessed.' Cuthbert's motion that the bill be engrossed was defeated by thirty-one to six, the *parti canadien* clearly opting to uphold extreme feudal values as against commercial ones.

This issue reveals that by the very beginning of 1805 the *parti canadien* had become rigid in protecting the traditional laws, which would very soon be referred to as a well-constructed 'édifice' articulating the wisdom of the forefathers and to be kept almost entirely intact.[54] This defensive posture, visible in many areas, was a natural, perfectly human response to attacks on the culture. Those attacks in the first years of the nineteenth century derived primarily from security concerns. The debate on the *retrait lignager*, significantly, occurred before the famous Gaols Act dispute and the outpouring of assimilation demands based on economic arguments.

The breakdown of the bourgeois alliance under the stress of the French Revolution obviously contributed to the paralysis of the movement to commercialize the civil law. This paralysis was obvious in the period and after, and the conflict it engendered played a significant role in the descent to rebellion.

Political Groupings

Division along ethnic lines was somewhat blurred by the existence of a third party or grouping: the Canadien *ministérielistes* who looked to De Bonne for leadership. These men included, at various times, such office-holders and would-be office-holders as Justice Panet, Solicitor General (later provincial judge) Foucher, Joseph-François Perrault, prothonotary of the King's Bench (Quebec), notary Jean-Marie Mondelet, and merchant Claude Dénéchaud, later to become a seigneur and grand voyer of the province. They also included, from time to time, some of the few seigneurs still able to get elected, such as Antoine-Louis-Juchereau Duchesnay and Philippe de Rocheblave Jr. The Canadien ministerial faction usually supported the government's interest in the house, except where questions of anglification arose. Until 1810 the combined forces of the English members, the *ministérielistes*, and 'loose fish' detached from the opposition, were sometimes able to defeat the *parti canadien* on a vote. This was particularly so late in the session when attendance was poor and also where radical-seeming constitutional proposals were in issue. Outside the house De Bonne was supported by a number of fellow seigneurs and some of the well-to-do bourgeoisie: the Scottish-educated Dr Jacques Labrie, law student Joseph-Rémi Vallières de St Réal, and lawyer-litterateur Louis Plamandon, to name a few. With Labrie as principal editor, De Bonne founded a newspaper, *Le Courier de Québec* in 1806. The paper argued in favour of a conservative interpretation of the balanced constitution but fought anglification proposals, which were a regular feature of the English party's newspaper, the *Quebec Mercury*, founded in 1805. The owner-editor of this journal, Thomas Cary, united in his person both the mercantile and the bureaucratic strains in the party, being himself a merchant and a former secretary to Governor Prescott.

Ideology of the Parti Canadien

Despite Selkirk's view, it would be hard to find any positive legacy of the French Revolution in the *parti canadien* after 1800. Indeed, one of its leading polemicists, MPP Denis-Benjamin Viger, devoted a large portion of a widely read 1809 pamphlet to attacking the Revolution and all its works, citing such evidence as Burke's analysis of abstract reasoning versus gradual, organic change, the immorality of eighteenth-century France, and the questioning of traditional authority.[55] More specifically, the ideal of social equality – which the Canadien reformers of 1789–91 accepted – had resulted in the political emancipation of French Jews early in the Revolution. When that issue arose in Lower Canada in the Ezekiel Hart affair the result was quite different. Moreover, anti-clericalism of the kind prevalent in the 1780s and early 1790s – seems not to have influenced Bédard and his followers during the 1800s.[56] Lawyers and notaries occasionally battled the priests on matters of practical importance to them, such as the church's prohibition of lending money at interest, and some quietly harboured general attitudes hostile to clerical influence. But such disputes and attitudes hardly ever surfaced in the political arena. Just the reverse. The *parti canadien* strove to protect the interests of the church in such areas as elementary schools (1801), higher education (1809), and the enforcement of the Royal Supremacy (1804, 1806). In sharp contrast to Mesplet's *Montreal Gazette*, the *parti canadien*'s paper, *Le Canadien*, founded in 1806, was almost entirely free of Voltairean attacks on the clergy and Thomas Paine's deistical account of the Bible in his *Age of Reason* was condemned out of hand.[57]

A hostile response to the Revolution can also be detected in the party's approach to the constitution, particularly in the ideas of Quebec lawyer Pierre Bédard, a brilliant scholar, main leader of the party from 1801, and principal writer on political issues in *Le Canadien*. Bédard and his associates, utterly rejecting the theories of Rousseau and Jefferson, drew no inspiration from the various constitutions of revolutionary France or the United States.[58] They looked instead to the British system of government as revealed in history by specific precedent and in the eulogistic writings of such respectable jurists as Montesquieu, Blackstone, and De Lolme. This anglophile stance had the virtue of allowing the party to advocate change in loyal dress, but it went well beyond political self-interest. Bédard and his lieutenants sincerely believed that American and French notions of liberty fostered instability. The tripartite balance of powers, which prevented anarchy as well as oligarchy and tyranny and had reached perfection in England, need only be genuinely transferred to the colony for the Canadiens to be content. To achieve this, the empirical British approach – arguing from and creating precedents – seemed far safer and more practical than enunciating constitutional first principles and was as satisfying to lawyerly minds trained in the common law as to those in the more definitional civil law. There was in consequence a great deal of attention paid in *Le Canadien* to precedents as found in Hatsell, Blackstone, and the proceedings of other colonial legislatures. There was no sympathy shown to radical parliamentary reformers such as William Cobbett and hardly any abstract theorizing on the social contract and the rights of man. A recent study of Canadien political language in the period 1805–1810 detected almost no usage of words such as 'liberté', 'citoyen', 'egalité' in the senses meant by the makers of the French Revolution.[59]

The Gaols Act, 1805

In spite of Selkirk's impression, the English party was not always united, at least prior to the critical years 1810–11. The best example of the occasional division between office-holders and merchants is the famous Gaols Act dispute of 1805 over the means of raising taxes to pay for public improvements. This pivotal struggle pitted commerce and the merits of land taxation, represented by the English merchants, against agriculture and the virtues of import duties, represented principally by the *parti canadien* but supported by English and Canadien seigneurs.[60] Some English officials in the Assembly sided with Bédard, while the Legislative Council passed the bill, complete with import duties, unanimously. Milnes, advised by Sewell, assented to it and successfully recommended against imperial disallowance, despite vociferous protests from the mercantile interest. The lieutenant-governor realized that supporting property rates would mean no statute at all and that, given the deplorable state of the prisons, failure to act could be disastrous. As he warned the colonial secretary, Lower Canada might well in future experience a crisis similar to 1794, 1796–7, and 1801. In such a case, spacious and escape-proof jails would be essential for the 'protection and safety of the Government itself.'[61]

Almost the entire commercial community was roused to fury by the Gaols Act issue. At a banquet held in Montreal near the end of March, merchant diners toasted their representatives for opposing a tax on commerce as unconstitutional and contrary to the sound practice of the mother country; belittled their Canadien opponents; and, in a slap at Milnes, hoped that, in future, the 'Commercial Interest of this Province' would enjoy 'its due influence in the administration of its Government.' The Assembly majority responded in 1806 by ordering the arrest for contempt of the fur trader Isaac Todd who had chaired the banquet and Edward Edwards whose *Montreal Gazette* had reported the proceedings in detail. This unprecedented use of a legally doubtful privilege failed when the sergeant-at-arms was unable to locate the culprits.

The Gaols Act dispute came at a time when the structure of the colonial economy was undergoing profound adjustments, as the fur trade lost its primacy to the export of agricultural produce and especially timber in response to British demand. At the same time the bi-ethnic cooperation of the fur trading era receded, there appeared to the capitalistic mind an urgent need to modernize, in order to foster resource production and transport, to facilitate commercial contracts, credit, and the free circulation of land in order to outcompete New York. Thus, as Donald Creighton has argued, the commercial empire of the St Lawrence would be fully exploited and become a thriving export route for goods from both Canadas and the American Middle West as well. Not surprisingly, the English now began to characterize the *parti canadien* as a major barrier to economic progress. 'Scevola's' letter to the *Quebec Mercury* in 1809 was typical of this sentiment. The French-speaking members of the legislature, he wrote, were 'as much fitted to direct the measures of a commercial and enterprizing people, as a church beadle is to be Chancellor of the exchequer.'[62]

On the hustings, in the Assembly, in *Le Canadien*, in pamphlets and elsewhere, Bédard and his lieutenants reacted to the continuous attacks on Canadien culture by defending the prevalence of the French language as a bulwark of loyalty, the civil laws for their clarity, the religion against charges of superstition, and the seigneurial regime for its fairness to the farmers. Although there had been signs of nationalist sentiment before, the opening decade of the century saw the emergence of the first self-conscious articulation of French-Canadian nationalism. Preservation of the traditional way of life – 'la survivance' in later terminology – should be a Canadien's highest secular goal. The concept of 'vendu' or sell-out was emerging, although the word then used was 'chouayen' which meant traitor or prostitute. Judge De Bonne, assimilator in educational matters, proponent of enforcing the royal supremacy, and staunch, sometimes highly effective, ally of the English party, naturally became 'le Grand Chouayen.'[63]

In the pages of *Le Canadien* the agrarian destiny of French Canada as a kind of rural Arcadia took its place in the defence of 'la nation.'[64] The peaceful, moral, and simple ways of the rural folk were contrasted to the commercial life, given over to wallowing in luxury, avarice, debauchery, and the periodic ruin of families through bankruptcy. The English merchants were little better than 'Yankees' who would sacrifice loved ones for any chance to make money. Indeed, the disloyal merchants were trying to defrenchify the colony by inviting into it a swarm of real Yankees, republican anarchists, and semi-savages, reminiscent of the Goths and Vandals. The Montreal gold-seekers and their friends were out to establish a mercantile aristocracy, 'the most abominable, the most pernicious of all orders, equally detrimental to the authority of the Crown, the interests of landed proprietors and the liberties of the people.'[65]

There can be no denying the importance of the now traditional use of commerce versus agriculture as a major interpretative tool of the political history of Lower Canada from 1805 on. Relations between the nationalities were exacerbated and political divisions envenomed on this basis. Pressure to anglicize for economic gain was added to anglification demands resulting from the perceived security situation. Yet, despite the common tendency to date Lower Canada's political troubles from the *Gaols Act* dispute, the damage had already been done by 1805. Anglicization and 'survivance' were already in conflict, while the previous dozen years had never been the period of political peace portrayed by Fernand Ouellet, still less an era in which 'peasants ... shared in the glorification of Imperial soliditary.'

9

The Shadow of Napoleon in Lower Canada, 1803–1811

As war again loomed in 1803, intelligence reports forecast the infiltration of the colony by a plague of agents preparing for Napoleon's invasion. Merchant Alexander Auldjo, for example, had learned from informants in London and Paris that 'whether theres [*sic*] a war or peace Buonaparte will be at work in this Country [Lower Canada] by his Emissaries – that they will come in all shapes & under all pretexts.' According to Auldjo, the Canadian-born artillery captain François-Joseph Chaussegros de Léry, son of the late seigneur of Gentilly who had been an executive and legislative councillor in the 1790s, would command the projected attack. To judge from his later career, de Léry would have been highly competent for the task. He commanded a French division at Austerlitz, the engineering corps in Spain in 1813, and would become a member of the Legion of Honour as well as Baron of the Empire.

Lieutenant-Governor Milnes immediately formed seven voluntary militia companies to assist the regulars in an emergency, which seemed to many to have arrived when, in June and again in August, Montreal was devastated by fires and some residents fled in panic.[1] Although no attack materialized during 1803, Milnes remained apprehensive, especially after being informed by Thomas Barclay, the British consul general at New York, that Jerôme Bonaparte, Napoleon's brother, then visiting the United States, was proceeding to Albany in order to communicate with Canadien subversives. Milnes ordered his counter-intelligence chief to recruit Jacques Rousse as a double agent. At a February meeting in

Montreal, Rousse accepted Richardson's offer. Posing as a still-faithful francophile revolutionary always ready to assist French officials in the United States to liberate the Canadiens, he performed his tasks competently and in good faith, in a marked contrast to most of Richardson's people.'[2]

His immediate job was to find out from the French consul at New York if an attack was in the offing. On the way to New York Rousse stopped in to see Citizen Genêt, then a gentleman farmer near Albany. In the guise of a fellow francophile he sought the former minister's advice. Genêt suggested the consul would not be entrusted with much authority in political-military matters and that Rousse should proceed directly to Washington and speak to Citizen Pichon, the French chargé d'affaires. Rousse did this and in May reported the results to an impressed and satisfied Richardson. Pichon had confided that there had been 'an idea of attempting the Invasion of Canada by some of the Embarkations intended for St Domingo, on the breaking out of the War but that the idea was dropt from various causes.' The projected attack 'certainly could not be executed this year, as England was too powerfull yet at sea, and matters of greater importance were in contemplation.' The chargé d'affaires urged Rousse that 'the Friends of France in Canada' should 'remain quiet and avoid every thing which could make them suspected.' They would be given notice of invasion in due time. He also learned that Jerôme Bonaparte 'had no political mission or confidence reposed in him by the Brother.'[3]

In November 1804 General Louis-Marie Turreau presented his credentials as minister plenipotentiary to the United States and Richardson, acting on Milnes's instructions, sent Rousse to probe the latest developments in France's Canadian policy. Turreau was interested and completely taken in by the former agent of Genêt, confiding that although his superiors had given some thought to the question, the decision to invade Lower Canada depended on the circumstances of the war in Europe. A French fleet would be used but, to minimize risk, it would sail away immediately upon landing troops. While awaiting the time of liberation, Rousse should help keep the Canadiens quiet; but nevertheless, if events approached the point of revolution, he was to keep the minister informed.[4]

In late 1809 Turreau was visited by one Chevalier Le Blond de Saint-Hilaire, who came recommended by his cousin, a general in Napoleon's army. Saint-Hilaire suggested that since he had friends and in-laws living in Lower Canada, he should be sent there on an extended mission to organize rebellion. The ambassador, a decided proponent of Canadien conquest, agreed and instructed his new agent 'to prepare everything for insurrection, but not to bring it about until the Government of France has taken a decision to support it.' Saint-Hilaire accordingly visited the colony, returning to the United States in March. In December of 1810 he gave Turreau a roseate account of the political sentiments of the Canadiens. Conquest would 'be ... a mere taking of possession' as all 'the hearts and arms, not only of the residents of Canada, but also the savages on its frontiers, are devoted to the Emperor. The English are so convinced of this predilection that if the French fleet were to appear in the Gulf of St. Lawrence, the widely scattered troops would instantly retreat to Quebec and Halifax.'[5] The authorities in Lower Canada never identified Saint-Hilaire, but were well aware by late 1809 or early 1810 that an important French spy had been sent into the country.[6]

Turreau's superiors in Paris took little interest in the Canadas. The ambassador complained that he had had to cancel a fact-finding trip to the Canadian border in 1805 because not a sou had been set aside for such secret service expenses.[7] Napoleon's indifference to Lower Canada changed somewhat in 1810. He was master of continental Europe (except Spain), looking for new fields of conquest, and rebuilding the French navy. In March the former vice-president of the United States, Aaron Burr – now, after his fatal duel with Alexander Hamilton, a desperate soldier of fortune – turned up in Paris. On Napoleon's express order, Talleyrand's successor, the Duc de Cadore, put Burr to work drafting a strategy for the French invasion of the Canadas.[8] With the deterioration of the French position in Spain during the later months of 1810, the emperor abandoned his designs to 'liberate' the Canadiens, but it should be borne in mind that at the exact time of the crisis known to Quebec historians as the 'reign of terror,' Bonaparte was in fact contemplating the attack for so long feared by the English élite.

Reaction of the Canadien Élite to Napoleon

Canadien reaction to Napoleon was almost uniformly hostile. Napoleon's 'organic articles' of 1802, which subjugated the French church to state control and fostered a catechism wherein it was difficult to discern how Bonaparte differed from the Deity, outraged the Canadien clergy, as did the public humiliation of Pius VII when Napoleon crowned himself emperor in 1804. The incorporation of the Papal States into the Kingdom of Italy in 1808 and the imprisonment of Pius VII in 1809 eliminated any last straws of toleration.[9] Quite likely the emperor was seen by the Canadien clergy as the anti-Christ foretold in the Book of Revelation, which was readily interpreted to refer to nepotism with crown and sceptre, the tribulations of the pope, and even the continental system. The seigneurs of course understood that their self-interest did not lie in a Napoleonic Lower Canada. They generally looked upon the emperor as a usurper and the empire as a vile dictatorship, which revealed the shallowness of the modern French character and the benefits of Britain's mild rule.[10]

Similar attitudes surfaced among middle-class *ministérielistes*. Readers of the *Courier* were regularly instructed in the balanced beauties of the British constitution and taught that Napoleon's merest whim was law in Europe, enforced by his armies who spread ubiquitous terror and unleashed rivers of blood.[11] There can be no doubt of the fundamental loyalty, either, of the vast majority of the *parti canadien* activists. Britain, which they referred to as the mother country, gave them protection against the United States, religious freedom, their own civil laws, a supposedly sane criminal law, and above all the 'rare treasure' of an enlightened constitution. This constitution had raised the human dignity of Canadiens far beyond what it had been under French rule when the Bourbon governor was a despot before whom no one dared raise his head. There were, it is true, fanatical English in the colony who wished to deprive Canadiens of their constitutional rights, but the English of the mother country were thought of as noble-minded gentlemen who would resist these plots, as they had at the times of the Quebec, Constitutional, and Gaols acts.[12]

Britain thus exercised a positive appeal to the men of the *parti canadien*. Socially conservative and hostile to the French Revolution but convinced believers in such basic liberal concepts as representative government, free elections, and liberty of the press, they could find no inspiration in modern France. Indeed, the leaders detested Napoleon the usurper-dictator who browbeat their church and posed as a continuator of the events of 1789. He aimed to export his civil code of 1804, which elevated abstract reasoning over customary law and individual ownership of land over seigneurial tenure, while seeming to sanction the break-up of the family (civil marriage, divorce for cause). In September 1808 *Le Canadien* noted in alarm that the British navy was 'now the only bulwark against the crushing tyranny and usurpations of the lawless head of France.' In an Assembly address of 1810, Bonaparte was described as the common enemy of the civilized world.[13]

In March 1809 at Montreal, Denis-Benjamin Viger of the *parti canadien* anonymously published the first scholarly justification of 'la survivance.' *Le Canadien* raved about its profundity, the writer's style, and the overwhelming proof offered in rebuttal of English party calumnies. It was the duty of every compatriot to study this work entirely dedicated to the defence of the Canadiens.[14] Viger had indeed justified the Canadiens' way of life: retention of their native language, the unfairly maligned educational system, their devotion to the Roman Catholic religion and to the French civil law. The main thrust of the pamphlet, though, was geopolitical. The English party's plan to submerge the Canadiens with Yankee rebels peopling the frontier townships, Viger argued, was extremely dangerous. It was in Britain's interest to help the Canadiens remain culturally distinct and as demographically strong as they were. In that way sympathy for the enemy would be minimized in case of an American invasion. The dictates of Roman Catholicism and the desire not to be absorbed by the United States would, as always, make the Canadiens the most reliable of subjects in such an event. Viger was also at pains to demonstrate that maintenance of the culture in no way jeopardized security with regard to Napoleon – that 'too illustrious tyrant' who had reduced Europe to slavery. If only the assimilators would realize the truth that modern Frenchmen and modern Canadiens were two different people:

We [Canadiens] are relegated to an isolated corner of the world ... because of our geographical position we are destined to become a people entirely different from Frenchmen ... The nature of our soil, the enormous difference in our needs and our agriculture, must necessarily create a marked difference in our manners and customs and those of other peoples ... Some years before the conquest, when a greater number of Frenchmen came to this country than was usual, there had already formed two peoples and this was mutually recognized. These distinguishing characteristics have by now multiplied so much [because of geography and, as well, differences in education, laws and historical experiences] that although their separation dates back only half a century, the common origin of Frenchmen and Canadiens is difficult to detect, save for a similarity in language.[15]

The loyalty of the *parti canadien* was amply demonstrated, too, in its willing support of security legislation. At the special war session of August 1803, the Assembly sanctified the Alien and Better Preservation acts for having helped ensure 'tranquility [*sic*] and happiness' during the recent war. These acts were accordingly revived with the approval of all parties in the house,[16] a tripartisan approach to security needs manifest in every session to 1809 inclusive. The acts were continued annually, with Pierre Bédard or one of his followers usually found among the movers or seconders.[17] Bédard's group also joined in adding security provisions to the statute book. The 1804 act to authorize money payments for residents who apprehended deserters from the regular forces was drafted by Richardson and presented by McGill. Despite its auspices, the bill had smooth sailing through the House.[18] In 1808 the Assembly agreed with alacrity to the administration's proposed amendments increasing the rigour of the Alien Act. These classed as an alien anyone who voluntarily entered French territory and empowered the governor to intern aliens where it was deemed too dangerous to transport them out of the province.[19]

In these and later years the Canadien élite exhibited one characteristic which mitigated their hostility to Bonaparte. While thoroughly rejecting the idea of a Napoleonic Lower Canada, there were times when they could not restrain their admiration for the military achievements of a man who was leading Frenchmen to victory after victory. Le Canadien often reported the military news without distorting comment, thus making Napoleon appear to be the strategic genius he was. The English newspapers, by contrast, commonly portrayed Bonaparte as a mere soldier of fortune of no particular brilliance. The allied defeat at Ulm, for example, was attributed to the physical disability of the Austrian General Mack, who was so fat he had to be carried around the battlefield in a litter, or to his having accepted a French bribe. The seigneur de Gaspé was forthright in praise of Bonaparte as a magnificent commander. On the eve of Ulm and Austerlitz he expressed the opinion that 'Alexander and his Cossacks are no match for Napoleon ... [who] with only thirty thousand men in the first Italian campaign ... [had] successfully defeated four Austrian armies twice the size.' Abbé de Calonne ascribed Bonaparte's inaction in Spain (1809), not to military difficulties, but saw it as a plan to dampen the enthusiasm of the guerillas and divide the Spanish citizenry. At the right time Bonaparte would respond with effect, for 'his inactivity always ends in a decisive stroke.' To one Canadien, at least, Napoleon was simply unbeatable. After subjugating Europe, he would carve out an empire in North and South America and ultimately rule the entire world.[20]

In some cases the attitude described merely reflected a greater detachment from the war than the emotionally involved English were able to muster. De Gaspé Sr., for example, could distinguish Napoleon the general from Napoleon the parvenu tyrant whom he detested and certainly hoped would be defeated. In many cases, if we are to believe English party publicist John Henry and the historian J.-Edmond Roy, there was an emotional response to French success. In other words, the rejection of a Napoleonic Lower Canada, for some, was a matter of the head not the heart. Significantly, the formal celebrations of Nelson's great victory at Trafalgar attracted few Canadiens except the *ministérielistes*. And according to Elizabeth Frances Hale (John's wife), many a Canadien(ne) of Quebec who illuminated his or her windows did so 'de bien mauvais coeur.'[21] Late in the war, when news reached the colony that Bonaparte had been exiled to Elba, Civil Secretary Andrew Cochran discovered a curiously muted reaction:

The sensation created here has been great; but I confess to you [his mother] I doubt whether joy has had much share in the sensations of the Canadians; – they may perhaps rejoice in it ... but I have heard many say that they have so much of French feeling left as to lament what they consider a diminution of French glory ... I have never heard one Canadian testify the smallest satisfaction at the extraordinary occurrences in France, although I have talked to many about them.[22]

Somewhere, perhaps below the level of consciousness, and among those hurt by the constant ridicule of things French, the collective soul of poet Octave Crémazie's 'vieux soldat Canadien,' awaiting the return of mother France, stirred ever so gently in the valley of the St Lawrence.

Canadien detachment did not sit well with English residents. Speaking favourably of Bonaparte's military talents indicated that, deep down, the speaker hoped that France would win the war. De Gaspé and de Calonne, for example, were accused of precisely that. Britain was fighting for her very existence and the slightest inclination away from utter condemnation of the enemy implied treason. As one English resident told the painter William Berczy, 'to have the right [even] to aspire to the title of a Christian or British subject,' it was essential to want to 'massacre those who harboured any sentiments or compassion for a Frenchman.'[23]

Reaction of the Habitants

The source of the security problem, if such there was, lay in the Canadien countryside. It is difficult to be precise about habitant attitudes to Napoleonic France. There was no widespread rioting connected with possible French invasion and few visits by French emissaries to the colony –

incidents which might have prompted government investigations and bequeathed to the historian some evidence about the Canadien farmers and their feelings towards France. One thing seems clear: the habitants in general would have resisted enrolment in the active militia to fight against Bonapartist troops. This was the opinion of several well-qualified observers[24] and it was held even as late as the War of 1812. In December of that year Chief Justice Monk was able to quote frequent remarks by Canadiens that '"happily the French have not joined the Americans to debauch our habitants."'[25] On the other hand there is no persuasive evidence suggesting popular sentiment favoured the conquering Napoleon. Galarneau's study of parish records reveals that almost no one in Lower Canada was baptized with the name Napoléon during the war and, more telling, for fifteen years after. Probably most habitants knew very little about the emperor. In one case a number of farmers dutifully handed their seigneur a 'pamphlet' they thought subversive as it attacked the English and appeared to be of French origin, for it had clearly been signed by the present ruler of France. The 'pamphlet' was an issue of Le Canadien, bearing the name of its printer: Charles Roi.[26]

Quite likely habitant enthusiasm for the idea of French reconquest was gradually diminishing in this period as a result of cumulative propaganda and the changing age composition of the population. Year by year from 1792 the number of adults effectively propagandized by the Canadiens élite grew, as le Comte de Maulevrier observed in 1798, although he thought that as yet only a minority of habitants believed the atrocity stories they were told.[27] Moreover, children successfully indoctrinated in 1792 or 1793 by the few teachers in the rural areas or by the curés would have little effect on habitant opinion in the 1790s but a great deal more in the latter years of our period when many would be in their twenties or thirties. In 1808 British traveller Hugh Gray noticed that the habitants referred to Frenchmen as 'nos pauvres gens,' rather than 'nos bons gens,' a common expression in the 1790s.[28]

Year by year the number of those who could remember the French regime in Quebec from personal experience diminished rapidly. In the mid-1790s about one in four habitants had lived ten or more years under French rule; by 1808 the proportion had dropped to about one in ten.[29] Stephen Sewell learned from Canadien informers in 1801 and again in 1810 that the oldest captains of militia in the countryside were by far the most disloyal of the habitants.[30]

In May 1805 the seigneur of Vaudreuil, Michel Chartier de Lotbinière, gave Jonathan Sewell an assessment of the likely habitant reaction if the

French succeeded in mounting an invasion. He had long experience in gauging opinion among the farmers and as usual presented carefully thought-out conclusions. De Lotbinière was inclined to be optimistic, particularly should the invaders commit atrocities: 'If the French pillage or burn two habitants' houses, the whole country will be against them and they will be quickly chased away.' Otherwise the farmers would remain determinedly neutral in action and quite indifferent in sentiment. But there was a proviso: the government must avoid annoying them with 'novelties' such as the land taxes recently proposed by some merchants in the Assembly.[31]

While the neutrality anticipated by de Lotbinière was probably close to the truth, a great deal depended on circumstances. If a Canadien-born officer, say Chaussegros de Léry, commanded the attacking force, as rumours suggested,[32] would the momentary emotion of old memories be strong enough to overcome the growing effectiveness of propaganda? If the attack came in the aftermath of a poor harvest would tales of some impending oppression by the British and of Bonaparte's benevolent intention towards the habitants have spread through the countryside? One cannot be sure. Much, too, would have depended on the relative strength at the outset of the French and British forces. If the invaders appeared to be much stronger, the prospective change of government might well have inspired a prudent enthusiasm and at least non-military assistance from the habitants. The response depended also on the policy adopted by the colonial government; if it attempted to call out the militia there would almost certainly have been serious riots, perhaps armed rebellion.

Suggestive of what might have happened in these circumstances was an incident during the maritime rights conflict, known as the *Chesapeake* crisis, which brought Britain and the United States to the brink of war in 1807. In the great majority of rural parishes habitants understood it was the Americans who might invade and were willing to defend the province. But at Yamaska, near William Henry, rumours circulated that the men might have to fight against French soldiers. Colonel J.-M. de Tannancour informed the administrator that the farmers' determined resistance to active service in the militia was grounded in their stated belief that 'the Americans are supported by the French and maybe they'll come together.' The habitants were also saying that 'the English took us, if they find us useful they'll keep us, we don't ask for more, we will help them so long as it's not necessary to fight, if they want to abandon us we don't see what we have to lose.' They preferred 'to stay and farm their lands than to get killed in a quarrel where they have nothing to gain and if anyone forces them to take up arms they will turn them round against those who are doing the forcing.'[33] The garrison mentality, even in the Napoleonic period, was not founded entirely on myth.

THE GARRISON MENTALITY ENDURES

The External Threat

Many among the English élite, during these years, thought a French invasion likely or at least quite conceivable. Such opinions were often justified by pointing to Bonaparte's insatiable ambition for conquest and to Canadien disloyalty – by now an article of faith. Stephen Sewell, for one, was certain that 'Buonaparte will make every possible Exertion to land troops in the Province at the risk of the loss of his ships.' The 'country is represented to B. as the Garden of Eden of America and that the people wait anxiously for the arrival of his troops and in fact in the extensive views which his mind embraces this must be the [most?] desirable Conquest.' Sewell warned his brother, 'Depend on it the Canadians will join them in numbers ... I think we stand on the brink of convulsion here, but God grant I may be mistaken.'[34]

An exaggerated sense of their colony's importance led the English to ascribe any number of specific motives reinforcing Napoleon's ambition: the possession of a convenient base from which to coerce or even conquer the United States, the exploitation of a new source of provisions and manpower for the Grand Armée, the re-establishment of a colonial empire for commercial reasons, and so on. After 1807, with the perfection of the emperor's continental system and the closure of Baltic trading, the British fleet became vitally dependent upon timber exported from New Brunswick and Lower Canada. Here was an obvious and convincing reason for believing Napoleon would not neglect France's former colony. As General Isaac Brock, in a letter written at Quebec to his brother on New Year's Eve 1809, put it:

You can scarcely conceive the quantities of timber and spars of all kinds which are lying on the beach, ready for shipment to England in the spring ... Whence can England be supplied with these essential articles, but from the Canadas? Bonaparte, it is known, has expressed a strong desire to be in possession of the colonies formerly belonging to France, and now that they are become so valuable to England, his anxiety to wrest them from us will naturally increase.[35]

How Napoleon's army would get to the colony was the subject of much speculation. Some thought he might sacrifice his ships by attempting a 'coup de main,' meaning a surprise naval assault landing a few thousand troops to establish a beachhead and then leading the Canadien insurrection. Estimates of the numbers necessary to do this varied from four to twelve thousand.[36] In 1808 British officials in Washington and Quebec heard rumours that the enemy's fleet would land at or near Spanish Florida, in order to minimize the risk of its loss. A French force proceeding up the Mississippi valley would work to detach the Indian nations of the Ohio country from their tacit alliance with Britain and then launch a joint invasion, beginning on the almost defenceless frontier of Upper Canada. This story was believed. Governor Sir James Craig ordered the Indian Department to redouble its efforts south of the Great Lakes, by increasing presents, contacting the more distant tribes, and making discreet promises to protect native lands from the constant American onslaught. It was also thought conceivable that France would not have to risk its fleet at all. French officers and men could be gradually infiltrated into New York City and then, joined by Vermont adventurers, attack Lower Canada in the Richelieu–Lake Champlain area.[37]

From the renewal of war in Europe in 1803 through 1811 significant segments of the English élite gave credence to almost constant rumours that the United States would either join Bonaparte in attacking the Canadas or that Washington would look the other way. These beliefs reflected a tendency to exaggerate French influence on American policy, a tendency dating back to the generosity of the Louisiana cession of 1803.

The key figure in the plot was General Victor Moreau, famed for his success against the Austrians in the campaign of 1800. Implicated in a royalist conspiracy to assassinate Napoleon in 1803 Moreau was exiled to the United States. The *Quebec Mercury* assured its readers in 1807 of the credibility of a current rumour that:

BONAPARTE & MOREAU ARE *RECONCILED*

If *Moreau* can persuade America to break with England, ten thousand french troops are, in conjunction with the Americans, to drive the English from the continent. – Canada and Nova Scotia are to be erected into a *Monarchy*; and *Moreau* to be crowned *King* of *Acadie* and *Both the Canadas*. America is to have the Floridas as well as Louisiana; and the Island of Porto Rico, or some other valuable West India Island.

General Brock, for one, found the story perfectly believable and likely John Richardson also.[38] This astonishing flight of fancy reflected anxious times. With the United States caught in the ever-tightening vice of British maritime supremacy and Napoleon's continental system, it seemed the republic would have to align itself militarily with one side or the other. The American Embargo Act of 1808 implied a willingness to do so. Britain was causing more of the damage: impressment of American citizens from their own nation's ships; seizure of alleged deserters, often on flimsy evidence; violent enforcement on the high seas of an expanding definition of contraband, and so on. It was conceivable that the United States might cast its military lot with Britain; but it appeared far more probable that Jefferson or Madison, both pro-French presidents, would not hesitate a moment in choosing Napoleon.

Even if the American government did not actively join France in an expedition against the Canadas, Richardson advised, it would likely connive at a French attack originating on its territory. It might also be helpless to prevent the organization of a mixed force of French soldiers and American volunteers. In April 1807 one R. Mathews, in a letter to the office of the British commander-in-chief, quoted the views of a Lower Canadian whom he described as 'a well informed, observing man, an old Resident ... and well acquainted with the People.' His correspondent had written as follows:

It had been reported that on board every Vessell from France to the United States, from twelve to twenty soldiers arrive, and that New York is at this moment full of French Officers ... I should ... not be surprized to hear of a second Miranda, or Burr[39] starting up at the head of these Fellows, and of Their marching towards Canada – They will find enough of the Vermonters to join Them, even for the sake of Plunder, for it would appear that the American Government has not sufficient energy to prevent its Citizens forming similar Expeditions, and why not against a British Colony ... as well as a Spanish one.

Mathews went on to say that Lower Canadian merchants visiting Britain that winter 'all declare the evident, growing defection and insolence of the Canadians. – In Vermont (the green mountain Boys) 10,000 men, hardy Vagabonds, may be got together in three Days.'[40]

The English could find any number of reasons to believe that a few thousand French troops would be sufficient to effect the conquest. The division of military and civil authority until late 1807 suggested divided leadership in time of crisis was therefore likely and in any case the

Canadiens, a simple people of authoritarian heritage, could be governed only by a tough-minded, fully fledged governor and general à la Prescott of 1796–7.[41] The fortifications at Quebec were in ruins and the colony was inadequately garrisoned. At the outset of war only about a thousand regular troops garrisoned the colony – not enough, General Hunter thought, even for peacetime duties. Reinforcements were modest for several years with total troop strength in both Canadas rising gradually to approximately five thousand in early 1809 and seven thousand at the end of 1811, far from sufficient in the view of senior military officers.[42] The continued high rate of desertion suggested that these troops were unreliable and no trust whatever could be placed on the Canadien militia, particularly as they would fight as distinct French-speaking units.[43]

Publication of Le Canadien and the Courier

The launching of Le Canadien and Le Courier de Québec, the first exclusively French-language newspapers in the colony since 1779, created a furore among the English. Upon reading the prospectus of Le Courier, 'Akritomuthos' (writing to the Mercury) pondered long over the 'secret machinations of our truly formidable adversary, Napoleon.' If, as was probable, he hoped to conquer the United States, Lower Canada would be 'a very promising door for the introduction of his designs,' and a 'Gallicizing' paper in the French language would be an obvious first step.

In January 1807 an unidentified resident of Quebec, reflecting an opinion common among the merchants of the colony, thought it evident that 'steps are taking to animate the minds of the Canadians from Their Fellow subjects – two newspapers, wholly in French, which have a strong tendency that way, have lately started up – The Editors are those firebrands of society (Lawyers) who make Themselves so conspicuous in all Civil Commotions, which frequently end in subverting the Government.' According to the writer, it was well known that Turreau had made a fruitless attempt to start up a French paper in New York, 'but it is strongly suspected He has been more successful here, as the Types from one, if not both these papers, were sent from the States.' From another source it appears that the rumour had an agent, sent by the promoters of Le Canadien, meeting with Jefferson and Turreau (or their subordinates). The agent was furnished by them with types of a French manufacture which were smuggled into the province in barrels of black lead.[44]

The stereotyping of the parti canadien under Bédard's leadership as pro-Napoleon was commonplace in the years 1806 to 1811. That these politicians were 'using every endeavour to pave the way for a change of Dominion, and a Return under that Government [France],' Governor Craig wrote in 1810, 'is the general opinion of all ranks with whom it is possible to converse on the Subject.' Since the leaders were self-seeking petty attorneys with 'no property of any sort' they had 'everything to gain, and nothing to lose by ... any state of Confusion into which they may throw the Province.' Edmund Burke could not have expressed his thesis any better.[45]

The liberalizing constitutional positions taken by Bédard and his colleagues were invariably interpreted by the administration and the *Quebec Mercury*, not merely as regrettable and legally dubious stands expected of a party in control of the elected house, but carefully calculated preparations for Bonapartist insurrection. During the Gaols Act dispute, the Assembly used the controversial privilege to imprison critics for contempt by (unsuccessfully) ordering the arrest of merchant Isaac Todd and Edward Edwards whose *Montreal Gazette* had published the proceedings of the merchants' protest meeting. In the *Mercury* Thomas Cary speculated that Napoleon might be behind the move and in any case 'nothing could be more gratifying to our arch-enemy ... than a prohibition on our presses.' Cary was thereupon arrested and forced to apologize to the house. A worried Ryland complained that if the Assembly's encroachments were not firmly resisted, 'the Means will gradually be prepared whenever a crisis should happen, for the overthrow of His Majesty's Government in this Province.' It was for that reason Bédard et al. had revealed such an 'eager desire to exercise the high and dangerous Power of Arrest, Fine and Imprisonment.' If each new demand for power not be countered with vigour, it would be impossible 'for any Governor to draw forth the Energies of the Country with effect, either to repress internal Commotion or to repel external attack.'[46]

That the Assembly had apparently become, as Ryland put it in 1808, 'the centre of sedition, and a receptacle for the most desperate demagogues in the Province,' came as no surprise to those English who had some acquaintance with the operation of the British constitution. What could one expect, asked English party activist John Henry in an 1810 pamphlet, from a house which resembled a common stagecoach, filled with 'notaries, attornies ... clerks, country clowns, dram sellers and bankrupts' and was elected by 'ignorant, wooden-shoed peasants'? The Canadien seigneurs exercised little electoral influence (a common lament) and the patronage resources of the governor were negligible. Only a minute proportion of the population in Britain had the vote or 'any thing to do with the laws but obey them.' In addition, of the 'representatives of these five hundred thousand in the House of Commons, at least six tenths are under the *immediate influence* of the crown and of illustrious families.' The remaining members owned sufficient property to be 'deeply interested in the safety, tranquility [*sic*] and glory of the nation.' Had the 'quacks' of parliamentary reform succeeded in placing 'the democratic branch as completely in the hands of the great mass of the population *as it is now in Canada*, Old England might now be sought for only amidst the *rubbish of revolution.*' Many agreed with Henry's assessment.[47]

The English élite, peering through the blinkers of the conspiracy theory of history, could not see the *parti canadien's* fundamental loyalty. Not only were the leaders ambitious lawyers with little property and *Le Canadien* insufficiently condemning of Napoleon, but the constitutional ante kept rising as Bonaparte went from success to success. Professing loyalty of course meant nothing. In the English perspective, conspirators always masked the real transaction by publicly avowing the opposite. Weishaupt had undermined Christianity in Europe by pretending to preach the purest version. Until the Declaration of Independence the Adams brothers, Franklin, Jefferson and the rest had allegedly plotted revolution while insisting on unimpeachable loyalty. The regicides in France had started off in 1789 as declared monarchists. John Henry was merely repeating this tortured faith when he compared the self-styled loyalists of the *parti canadien* – friends of the poor who taxed the wealthy – to the 'men who meditated the massacres and confiscations in France.' Those people, early on, had been 'in their outward behaviour the mildest, gentlest, tamest creatures in the world ... YET WE HAVE ALL SEEN WHAT HAPPENED.'[48]

The Cultural Distinctiveness of the Canadiens

The preservation of cultural differences between conquerors and conquered was thought to result in dangerous mutual antipathies which nurtured francophilia amongst the Canadiens. Since it appeared obvious that had the situation been reversed, a conquered English majority would have rallied in arms to support the British fleet, why wouldn't the Canadiens act in a like manner? In May 1803 John Hale informed his brother-in-law, Lord Amherst, that the 'Inhabitants of Canada are just as much French as the Generation we found here, & to a man they will join a French army whenever it lands.'[49] Early the next year Lord Selkirk recorded that:

There is but one opinion as to the universal disaffection of the French Canadians to the British Government ... The English at Quebec & Montreal cry out in the true John Bull style against their obstinate aversion to institutions which they have never taken any pains to make them understand – & are surprized at the natural & universally experienced dislike of a conquered people to their conquerors & to every thing which puts them in mind of their subjection – In these ideas some individuals of great good sense & liberality (among others Bishop Mountain & Ch Justice Elmsley) join to a surprizing degree.[50]

The quintessential position of the English élite was expressed by Chief Justice Sewell in an analysis which anticipated Lord Durham and the Rebellions of 1837–8 and has yet to be disproved:

The great links of connection between a Government and its subjects are religious [religion], Laws, and Language, & when Conquerors possess the same religion, and use the same Laws and the same Language as the Conquered, the incorporation of both into one political body is easily effected: But when they are at variance on these points, experience seems to have demonstrated in Canada, that it cannot at all be effected while this variance subsists. Obedience may be rendered by conquered subjects under such circumstances, but it is the obedience of a Foreigner to a Government which in his estimation is not his own, and as he views it as an alien power, there is no attachment, no affection in his mind towards it, and consequently no disposition to unite with those who constitute the Government or its natural subjects ... the People of Canada at the Conquest were Frenchmen, and Roman Catholics, They spoke the French Language, and no other, they were attached to French Laws, & fostered in their minds a National antipathy against Englishmen ... They are still Frenchmen, their habits ... are still the habits of Frenchmen, and so much in opposition to the habits of our own people.

If the French predilections of His Majesty's Canadien subjects were not undermined or rendered harmless, they would 'augment until by some crisis, force will be required and the future state and condition of Canada will then be decided by a recourse to arms.'[51]

Sewell had a certain sophistication, but most expressions of this sort revealed a simple-minded prejudice. Lawyer Ross Cuthbert explained Canadien disloyalty as the inevitable outcropping of a countryside, aggressively French in everything from language, song, architecture, and dress to lowly soap. 'On surveying,' he went on, 'the typical *"chambre de compagnie"*, among many other saints he [a visitor] would see the portrait of Napoleon!' The representation of 'that fiend, may be found in many country houses ... It cannot be supposed these portraits are procured as a mere historical memento.' Quebec timber merchant Samuel Bridge, likewise, required little proof of Canadien disloyalty. Having heard that the crafty habitants put stones in the butter and maple sugar they sold by weight at the town market, Bridge recorded this conclusion in his diary: 'they are terrible imposing Rascals (I mean the Habitans or French Canadians) *who are Frenchified* looking *Fellows* & half of them I believe would prove Rebels should the French send a Force here.'[52]

A new element in the period was a rapidly waning confidence in the loyalty of the Roman Catholic clergy. This first appeared at the turn of the century in response to the moderation of religious persecution in the later years of the Directory and the negotiations between Rome and Paris, begun in June 1800, which would lead to the Concordat of 1801. Pius VII's sanction of Bonaparte's imperial crown in 1804 and his expressed hope that the French church had entered a new era were interpreted by Ryland as presaging a popish plot in the valley of the St Lawrence. The danger to Lower Canada was obvious, since 'the patronage of the Romish Church in this Colony' vested in Bishop Plessis is 'completely derived from the same holy Personnage who crowned the pious Emperor of the French!' Ryland's sentiments were echoed by John Black in his 'Observations' of 1806 and by many others.[53] The imprisonment of Pius in 1809 only increased the unpleasant possibilities and the next year it was rumoured in Montreal that Bonaparte had somehow brought the Lower Canada hierarchy under the authority of the pliable French bishops (who had among other things agreed to the divorce from Josephine), with Plessis becoming a 'suffragan of a Metropolitan in France.' As for the lower clergy, the English government officials in 1810 generally thought their attachment to France and Napoleon as the restorer of the French church since the Concordat was 'undoubted.' All this was of course paranoia, not factual analysis, but it was by no means confined to the Chateau.[54]

From the beginning of the century the official element among the English élite had also worried that the Roman Catholic clergy would become active co-conspirators with the *parti canadien*; after all, both were of the lower orders. This attitude had originally emerged in response to two highly exceptional incidents in 1800. At Terrebonne the parish curé successfully campaigned for the election of a popular Canadien candidate rather than the solicitor general, and another priest at St Laurent opposed the establishment of an English-owned tavern near the church, a project which, he announced, sufficiently bespoke the moral standards of the Anglo-Saxon.[55] Since both offending clerics operated in close proximity to each other, north of Montreal, in Joseph Papineau's political territory, it was obvious to Stephen Sewell what was happening. Just to make sure, he had a Canadien informer investigate the scandal at St Laurent and hurried off a summary of the resulting report to his brother in the capital:

... this opens such a scene of villainy practiced by the priest at St. Laurent (and he says there are many of the same class) which made me shudder ... This he said, that the priest[s] in the parishes back of Montreal were devoted to P[apineau] ... My man concluded with saying if God does not punish and put a stop to the iniquity of these villains in less than five years the English must feel the Effects of it for no opportunity is lost to excite the people to a revolt. P[apineau] is determined to be Buonparte in the province.[56]

Additional cause for concern was that many of the priests were, as Governor Craig put it, 'under ties of family connexion with the Lawyers.' Two of Pierre Bédard's brothers were clerics, while Coadjutor Bishop Bernard Panet was Speaker Jean-Antoine Panet's brother. In 1810 Craig sent to the Colonial Office a pessimistic assessment of the hierarchy's loyalty. Bishop Plessis could obviously not be trusted, since he was the son of a blacksmith. Panet held higher social rank, but still came from a 'new family which has risen in the law.' He was 'the Brother of the leading Demagogue of the Democratic Party,' a perfect example of the 'wonderful connection' between the church and the politicians.[57]

The ecclesiastical problem was gravely compounded in the minds of the English by the presence of about thirty-five emigré priests who since 1793 had settled in the colony.[58] These men – victims of the Revolution though they might be – were thought to represent a potential fifth column, a possibility which had been anticipated in the late 1790s. The Concordat and the repatriation to France of at least three of them during the Peace of Amiens acted to sustain and strengthen these earlier apprehensions. One problem Milnes foresaw in 1803 was that the emigré priests who had returned might attempt to subvert the colony through the local clergy. In particular the leader of the emigré group, Abbé and Dr P.-J.-L. Desjardins, former vicar-general of Quebec and brother of Abbé Louis-Joseph Desjardins, a protégé of Bishop Plessis, had made his peace with Napoleon and, rumour had it, was given an important clerical post in Talleyrand's former diocese of Autun. Ryland warned Richardson in December that if 'any attempt is actually in contemplation for the disturbance of this Government ... Mr. Desjardins, and those persons with whom he was most intimately connected here, may be engaged as Parties in the Business.' A few years later Elizabeth Frances Hale wrote of 'intelligent people' in the capital being worried that if the French fleet managed to reach the Gulf of St Lawrence, Desjardins would be on board to guide it up the river and act as informant. She herself was sure that if it landed 'the Canadians wd. immediately join them.'[59]

If Desjardins or any other resident of France was plotting with the emigré clergy remaining in Lower Canada, the possible damage was incalculable. As educated Europeans holding many of the most important clerical offices[60] they exercised considerable influence over the Canadien clergy and laity. Approximately one-third of the emigré priests were members of the Sulpician Order, which held vast seigneuries on the island of Montreal and in the area north of the island and monopolized higher education for the district. Mgr Jean-Henri-Auguste Roux, the superior general, bursar Alexis Molin, two directors, and the three leading professors at the college were all emigrés. While no refugees seem to have taught at the Quebec Seminary between 1803 and 1811, the theologian Desjardins was warmly remembered by his ex-colleagues, particularly by his correspondent friend Abbé Antoine-Bernadin Robert, the superior from 1802 to 1805 and 1809 to 1815.

Not surprisingly then, government officials continued to discourage the immigration of refugee priests.[61] Jonathan Sewell, no religious bigot, described the seminaries in 1810 as 'foster parents of french Predilictions, and of a Natural Antipathy against England and her heretical Government.'[62] During the last years of the period, paranoid rumours circulated at the Chateau that the Sulpicians were sending intelligence and money to General Turreau![63] Such attitudes – pure garrison mentality – had no basis in fact. Indeed, clerical refugees like Abbé Jacques de Calonne, chaplain to the Ursulines at Trois-Rivières, and Roux loathed what the 'tyrant' Napoleon, perpetuator of the French Revolution, stood for.[64] As for Abbé Desjardins back in France, this fervent monarchist did not engage in pro-Napoleon intrigues with the church in Lower Canada. He remained profoundly grateful to the British authorities for having treated him and his fellow exiles so generously. Desjardins became a state prisoner of Napoleon from 1810 to 1814.[65]

The Strength of the Garrison Mentality

English opinion on the disloyalty of the Canadiens in the Napoleonic era was not unanimous. Merchant John Fleming thought that the danger was not sufficiently serious to deprive them of the civilizing benefits of representative government, as many in the English party then advocated. Lawyer Ross Cuthbert believed that while the security threat was indeed serious at the moment, it would in the future fade as inevitable assimilation took place.[66] A minority view held that, whatever their other faults, the Roman Catholic clergy did not add to the security problem. And the opinion expressed by British traveller John Lambert on religious differences may well have been inspired by some of the more clear sighted among the English: 'if the Roman Catholics were really such a desperate body of people as they are represented to be, I am really astonished that the Canadians have not long ago cleared the colony of every English heretic that had set foot in it.'[67] According to their retrospective accounts, dating from 1818, the owner-printers of the *Quebec* and *Montreal Gazettes*, John Neilson and James Brown, had thought the fear of disloyalty ridiculous,[68] as did the occasional correspondent to Brown's paper. It is significant, though, that so few such letters got published (they were vastly outnumbered by letters arguing the opposite, even in Brown's *Gazette*). I have been able to find only four or five clear examples – arguing the Mabane case against assimilation – from the many dozens of letters on security published by the *Quebec Mercury* to the end of 1811. Most of the English élite were perfectly confident that with few exceptions the Canadiens would rally to the defence of the colony in case of an American attack, provided it was uncomplicated by any French presence.[69] The real danger was not American but French invasion.[70] The former would be a military contest, pure and simple; the latter would involve an armed uprising. That the very large majority of the English élite partook of the garrison mentality in this period (some with qualifications) is also supported by the assessments of such contemporaries as the travellers Selkirk and Gray, the historian Christie (who from 1805 resided in the colony), the bureaucrat Ryland, Governor Craig, the *parti canadien* leader Pierre Bédard, and the party's noted intellectual, Denis-Benjamin Viger.[71]

10

The Garrison Finds Its Leader: Security and the Governorship of Sir James Craig, 1807–1811

It was almost as if fate had taken a hand. Sir James Craig's credentials for the role the English party wished him to play were impeccable, right back to his birth in 1748 and his early years as the son of a Scottish judge in the civil and military courts of Gibraltar, a garrison colony par excellence. The son had joined the regular army at fifteen and in a few years proved himself a decisive, brilliant commander. His distinguished record during the American Revolutionary War included command of the advance guard which forced the rebels out of Quebec in 1776. Some nineteen years later, a senior officer responsible for wresting the Cape (South Africa) from the Dutch, Craig governed that garrison colony until 1797. Following service in India, Sir James, now a lieutenant-general, acted as the commander of England's Eastern District from 1801 to 1804. The next year he was appointed to lead an expeditionary force to link with the Russian army in Italy but Ulm and Austerlitz frustrated the scheme. Fearing war with the United States, the imperial government offered Craig the appointment of governor-in-chief of British North America. His prime task would be to make the colony as secure as possible and, in particular, to hold the fortress of Quebec at all costs, should the Americans invade. He accepted, despite his age and despite suffering from chronic dropsy, which often resulted in nearly intolerable pain. It was from a sick bed on the frigate *Horatio* that Craig dealt with his first matters of state relating to Lower Canada, convincing a hovering Ryland that a new age was dawning, with the 'weaknesses' of a Dorchester, Milnes, or Dunn banished forever.[1]

Sir James Craig was a man of uncomplicated Tory opinions, simple loyalties, and above all, an authoritarian personality. He insisted that subordinates, civil and military, toe the line absolutely. Craig threatened Bishop Plessis with summary deportation on board ship should he persist in opposition to the royal supremacy and dismissed Solicitor General James Stuart in 1809 for voting against the government in the Assembly.[2] The journal of timber merchant Samuel Bridge provides a vivid description of Craig's method of handling deserters:

the Poor fellows attended by a Sergeant's Guard marching very slow were placed behind their coffins ... they proceeded to the place of execution at ½ mile out of Port Louis Gate in the following order – a party of Soldiers, the Two Coffins carried by 4 men each & follow'd by the criminals entirely drest in white ... at a short distance behind the full Band of the 98th playing a Solemn Tune then 2 pieces of Cannon. The Regt. of Artillery & the remr. of the ... military in Divisions. They were executed at ½ pt. 10 & Buried immediately in a grave prepared near the spot. It was thought by many they would have been pardon'd but desertion is so frequent here the Govt. conceived it absolutely necessary to make a severe example but notwithstanding 4 men deserted yesterday & this Day.[3]

Sir James carried this punitive tendency over into the political sphere. Throughout his governorship he knew he was dying at his post, which stoically he would not consider leaving if he could be of any use. His main aim in life was to do his duty whether to His Majesty, his subordinates, his relatives and friends – who were equitably provided for in an ever-changing will – and even his favourite horse Alfred whom he bequeathed to Brock 'to secure to his old favorite a kind and careful master.'[4] He did his duty in distressing circumstances and he simply could not understand the failure of others to do so, including the 'disloyal' majority in the Assembly.

Craig's stern sense of duty was tempered by a number of redeeming qualities. Canadiens and English alike respected his selflessness, his many donations to charitable causes, and his generosity to indigent individuals. Travelling from Quebec to Montreal in June 1809, Chartier de Lotbinière discovered that even the farmers and villagers, who would not normally vote for his candidates, held the governor in high regard, 'praising his fairness, his talents, his splendour and above all his great charity ... They say ... [of] our general that here is a man!... the Governor ... wishes only that everyone do his duty.'[5] In his letters to friends Craig's ironic sense of humour could not be repressed and he there reveals himself as a sorely tried but confident Gulliver, alternating between genuine consternation and tolerant amusement at the antics of the Lilliputians of the *parti canadien*. But he was far from vindictive: all would be forgiven a dismissed subordinate or an imprisoned MPP if he confessed his political sins and promised to do better in the future. Although detesting the political opinions of a Joseph Borgia (one of Bédard's lieutenants), Craig, a literate man with an intelligent grasp of legal questions, could praise Borgia for his rare understanding of Roman law.[6] He was in fact a curious, but not uncommon, combination of a rigid disciplinarian and kindly patriarch. The best short description of Craig was that of his quartermaster general in the Mediterranean theatre, Colonel Henry Bunbury:

Sir James Craig was a man who had made his way by varied and meritorious services to a high position in our army. He had improved a naturally quick and clear understanding by study, and he had a practical and intimate acquaintance with every branch of his profession. In person he was very short, broad, and muscular, a pocket Hercules, but with sharp neat features as if chiselled in ivory. Not popular, for he was hot, peremptory, and pompous: yet extremely beloved by those whom he allowed to live in intimacy with him; clever, generous to a fault, and a warm and unflinching friend to those he liked ... [The adjutant general and I] were both entire strangers to Craig, and his manner to us at first was not engaging or conciliatory; but when he came to find we were disposed to do our duties actively and carefully, he warmed to us by degrees; and in the latter and more difficult times of his command I found Sir James Craig one of the kindest men I have ever had to transact business with, and one on whose just and honourable feelings I could always place an entire reliance.[7]

In his influential economic interpretation of pre-Confederation Canadian history, Donald Creighton describes Craig as one who 'cherished the nineteenth-century middle-class ideals of education, respectability and material progress.'[8] In this version Sir James comes out an earnest Victorian somewhat like Cobden, Bright, or Gladstone, with the governor acting as the political arm of the English merchants, leading them into battle against the agrarian minded *parti canadien*. The governor did indeed look to the merchants as needed political allies, but Sir James was an eighteenth-century military aristocrat. Almost everything he wrote while in Lower Canada reflected his view that loyalty, intelligent service to the crown, birth, and gentlemanly behaviour, not business acumen or success, were the main determinants of a man's worth.[9] Craig's aristocratic instincts emerged clearly in his regal bearing and his love of display, characteristics which had earned him the nickname 'little king Craig' in England and which impressed even the hard-headed Richardson. The annual *fête champêtre*, held at the governor's country residence at Powell Place on the road to Cap-Rouge, a village just west of Quebec, and featuring senior military officers and the episcopacy in full regalia, open-air dancing and sumptuous banqueting, was the high point of the summer season at Quebec.[10] Such a man might wish to further the economic development of the colony but it was nothing like a high priority. Maintaining the proper social graces was probably more important to him, while his duty as governor and commanding general to preserve the colony's existence was the overriding concern. In 1808, for example, Craig's dispatches began to take on an alarmist tone but did not discuss Richardson's legislative proposal to establish Lower Canada's first bank. The priority Craig gave to security over serving the financial interests of the merchants would come out clearly during his so-called reign of terror in 1810.

THE LEGISLATIVE SESSION OF 1808

Although it has been suggested that Craig came to the colony already biased against the Canadiens from his experiences during the American Revolutionary War, this was not so.[11] Moderation would survive Craig's first legislative session. Two questions proved controversial. Neither ruffled Craig's calm, but they require some comment in view of their later importance as constitutional and security issues.

Ezekiel Hart's Expulsion from the Assembly

Hart's legal position was strong. The Constitutional Act of 1791 contained a number of express disqualifications but did not refer to Jewry. In the United Kingdom until 1858 conscientious Jews were excluded from Parliament, since one of the required oaths – that abjuring the Stuart pretenders – had to be taken 'upon the true faith of a Christian.' By contrast, section 29 of the Constitutional Act simply required a prospective member of the Lower Canadian Assembly take an oath of allegiance. The imperial Naturalization Act of 1740 provided that foreigners naturalized after seven years' residence in a colony were to 'be deemed ... to be his Majesty's natural born subjects of this kingdom.' A clarifying statute of 1773 stated that persons naturalized under the 1740 act were capable of holding *'any* office or place of trust, either civil or military' *outside* the realm (emphasis added). And the Constitutional Act itself qualified for the Assembly all persons naturalized by any statute of Parliament. If foreign Jews naturalized by seven years' residence in a colony could sit in the Lower Canada Assembly, *a fortiori* natural-born subjects of the Jewish religion (of which Hart was one) enjoyed that right. It could not be denied by insisting Hart take the qualifying oath on the Christian scripture, since the Constitutional Act did not require this form and in the Lower Canadian courts Jews were sworn (with their heads covered) on the five Books of Moses.

On the Hart issue the Assembly divided into three distinct groupings, each attempting to maintain or increase its numbers.[12] Administrative officials wished to throw the seat to one of their fellow bureaucrats, Thomas A. Coffin, who had run second to Hart in the polls. They did not explore the question of legal eligibility but insisted, rather unconvincingly, that British law required all oaths to be taken on the New Testament. The merchants of the English party, led by Richardson and Quebec shipping magnate John Mure, looked upon Hart as a welcome addition to the representatives of the commercial interest in the house and presented a simplified version of the legal arguments outlined in the previous paragraph. Leaders of the *parti canadien* were concerned with consolidating their majority position, which was often undermined by absenteeism and/or an alliance of the English party, Canadien *ministérie-listes*, and 'loose fish.' Bédard contended that the statute of 1773 did not apply to *elective* office since it could not be presumed that Parliament would think Jews fit persons to make laws for Christians, even in the colonies. Jews after all were transients owing allegiance to nothing but the awaited Messiah and, he implied, making money. The act of 1740, Bédard argued, conferred on naturalized Jews the rights of natural-born Jews in England, not the rights of natural-born subjects in general. Although these contentions reflected anti-semitic nationalism and political expediency more than objective legal analysis, they carried the day. The Assembly resolved in the end that Hart 'professing the Jewish Religion, cannot take a seat, nor sit, nor vote in this House.'

Intense as it was at times, the Hart debate did not generate a confrontation between the *parti canadien* and Craig. The Assembly majority had made no claim that the house could exercise the extreme privilege of expelling and/or disqualifying Hart simply because he was, as a Jew, deemed an unfit person to be elected. Had this been attempted, a first-rate constitutional crisis would inevitably have ensued. The final resolution, however, proceeded on the basis that the house was enforcing a disqualification that already existed in law. Enforcing such a legal disqualification was an undoubted privilege. In any case Governor Craig remained, as yet, indifferent about the Hart affair.

Exclusion of Judges

On the exclusion of judges from the Assembly, the *parti canadien* – particularly Bédard, Panet, and notary Joseph Planté – argued the case for insulating the judiciary from partisan politics, as was done in England with regard to the twelve common law judges.[13] This modernistic view of exclusion was not shared by the English party – with the notable exceptions of John Mure and John Blackwood – or the Canadien *ministérielistes*. Richardson and De Bonne, for example, took refuge in the archaic point that the twelve judges were excluded from the House of Commons solely because they were called to be assistants to the House of Lords. Government spokesmen also stressed the need for respectable men in the house. Sewell frankly stated that making judges ineligible would reduce the already small number of enlightened members prepared to support the 'just rights' of the crown. The bill passed easily but was unanimously given the hoist in the Legislative Council on the principal ground that it unduly interfered with the royal prerogative, which the aristocratic branch must protect against democratic usurpation. Throughout these debates, Craig seems to have accepted developments with equanimity and probably recognized that even majority opinion in the English party was not adamantly opposed to the basic principle of the legislation.[14] Had the Legislative Council not interposed its veto this issue, which would soon grow to burning intensity, might have found a quick and painless solution.

THE GENERAL ELECTION OF 1808

The general election of May 1808 was the most strenuously and bitterly fought for a dozen years past.[15] The tone of the campaign was struck in Quebec's Upper Town where the Speaker Jean-Antoine Panet was unexpectedly defeated by *ministérieliste* Claude Dénéchaud. Punch-ups and pitched verbal battles accompanied the voting, with Dénéchaud's men – orchestrated by Sewell and Ryland – ironically yelling 'Vive les bonnets rouges, vive les sans culottes' when Panet left the poll.[16] Not to be outdone, the *parti canadien* portrayed *ministérieliste* leader De Bonne as a vindictive, political judge; a willing tool of the Chateau's low purposes; a traitor to his heritage, but loyal to his emoluments; a free thinker who merely pretended to be a Roman Catholic; a callous adulterer; and much else.

This election was the first in which opposition politicians mounted a coherent attack on the system of government, denouncing, for example, the policy of facilitating grants of crown land in the Eastern Townships to the alien 'Yankées,' an obvious plot directed against the true possessors of the country. The major target, however, was the rapidly swelling and wasteful civil list, with its multiple office-holders (Ryland's name appeared five times), high official salaries, and unnecessary pensions paid to retired bureaucrats or their widows. When Sewell had referred to the need for more MPPs to maintain the just rights of the crown, he must have been thinking of the £3,500 plus he had drawn from the civil list in the most recent fiscal year or Judge De Bonne's annual remuneration exceeding £900.[17] The governor had a direct interest in having the next Assembly dominated by these pliant 'gens en place' (placemen), a species of humanity that, in the view of Blackstone and De Lolme, threatened the autonomy of the House of Commons. Unless the governor were defeated here, he would multiply lucrative offices without limit. Land taxation to pay for them would inevitably follow and a small *anglais-canadien* oligarchy would reduce the people to a state of slavery. Therefore the voters must elect Canadien representatives who were entirely independent of the government (or the Legislative Council) and incorruptible by patronage. After all, the British Parliament had intended the Constitutional Act to enable the Canadiens 'to conserve their laws and their jurisprudence, to uphold their civil and religious status by giving them a majority in the Legislature.'[18]

The results were not entirely favourable to the *parti canadien*. John Hare's careful statistics on Assembly voting indicate that in the fourth legislature (1805–8) those members supporting government positions 70 per cent or more of the time numbered fifteen, while the *parti canadien* counted on twenty-eight. The comparable figures for the fifth legislature (1809) were about eighteen and twenty.[19] Given this ambiguous result, one can understand why the exclusion of the re-elected Hart and of judges from the House was to assume such explosive proportions in the ensuing session. By then, however, Craig's complacency towards Assembly proceedings had ended. He no longer thought, as he had in early 1808, that all parties exhibited loyalty and dedication to the public good.[20]

Not surprisingly, the *parti canadien*'s attacks on the constitutional status quo and the scurrilous rhetoric it employed against De Bonne were interpreted by many opponents as masking a francophile Jacobinism. Perhaps the most revealing document to emerge from the election was a letter written by Montreal lawyer David Ross to Judge Isaac Ogden, describing the vote in Leinster.[21] The candidates for the two seats were Ross's brother John, a Quebec attorney (and Ogden's nominee), Joseph-Edouard Faribault, and Joseph Turgeon. Both the Canadiens were notaries, justices of the peace, militia officers, and political independents if not *ministérielistes*.[22] Faribault was elected by acclamation. At that point he stood on the hustings stating, 'that altho he had been Elected he would not attend the Provincial Parliament ... if they did not Elect a Canadian with him.' Emboldened by this Turgeon declared, 'Mes amies, on vous forge des feres, Je vous en dit pas plus long, mai m'effiez vous!!!'[23] At this point 'a general wonder & movement took place – and ... a cry, here and there amongst the people, of *point d'Anglais, point d'Anglais*!! [No more English] In a short time the dye seemed to be cast and the Inhabitants were apparently soon united, as if in the defence against a common Enemy.' The governor informed the colonial secretary of the incident, thinking it peculiarly illustrative of a threatening security situation.[24]

CRAIG'S ANALYSIS OF THE SECURITY DANGER, 1808

Craig had tolerated *Le Canadien* as long as it confined its role to the defence of the culture against the jibes of the *Mercury*. But when its attacks on the government became increasingly virulent during the election, the governor perceived a dangerous plot. He found that the paper was run by the leaders of the *parti canadien* and that the utmost efforts were made to circulate its message of disaffection (often free) throughout the province. The consequence was a new language springing from the people, in which the words 'Revolution' and 'Reform' were prominent. Craig saw no option but to act decisively. In mid-June Panet, Bédard, Borgia, Dr François Blanchet, and Jean-Thomas Taschereau, were dismissed as militia officers on the grounds of their suspected ownership of a publication, 'calculated to vilify his Majesty's government, and to create ... discontent among his subjects, as well as ... animosity between the two parts of which they are composed.' Taschereau was also relieved of his position as deputy grand voyer for the Quebec District. Joseph Planté was dismissed from two minor offices, but a contrite plea for mercy and a promise to disavow *Le Canadien* brought restoration.[25] Needless to say, English party men and Canadien *ministérielistes* applauded Craig's martial response to insubordination, but none seems to have pressed the question why the governor had not also instructed Sewell to institute a prosecution for seditious libel. The answer, presumably, is that officials had no confidence that a trial jury would convict, despite the absence of legal provisions equivalent to Fox's Libel Act.

Craig's about-face on the loyalty question from April to June obviously reflected his pessimistic interpretation of the election campaign. It is equally obvious that he had come under the influence of such advisers as Sewell, Mountain, Richardson, and Ryland. It would be wrong, however, to view Craig as captive to a small self-interested coterie of officials; he was too intelligent, honourable, and strong-willed for that. But he did find the security danger analysis of his executive advisers widely shared by the English élite in general and by a number of Canadiens as well. Indeed, he often supported his own judgment by referring to 'public opinion': to the 'english [sic] part of the Inhabitants,' to 'all ranks with whom it is possible to converse on the Subject' and so on.[26] Craig in other words reflected the garrison mentality.

Craig's view of the security problem was largely set by the late spring and summer of 1808.[27] Although the chances of war with the United States had receded in the governor's opinion, its possibility must be kept constantly in view. The more immediate and serious danger came from the ambitious Bonaparte seeking to revive the French empire in America. This was not as far-fetched a judgment as it might seem. In the three previous years Napoleon had subjugated almost all of Europe, most recently by forcing Russia to support the Continental System of embargoing Britain. With the emperor looking for new areas of conquest, what was more natural than to suppose British North America would be a prime target? Britain's commerce and shipping would be severely damaged, the United States appeared likely to remain neutral, while Spain, then a puppet state of Napoleon, would not oppose a French invasion through West Florida or Spanish territory in what is now southeastern Texas.[28] Rumours of just such a scheme had been circulating in Washington for some months.[29] Craig took these stories seriously.

The Governor's calm assessment of the internal security danger as of mid-May – Bonaparte would perhaps find 'not an unfriendly population' – had undergone drastic change by early August, when he composed two lengthy dispatches to the colonel secretary, Lord Castlereagh. One dealt with the militia in general; the other explained why the governor had withdrawn the commissions of Bédard and his political colleagues. The root of the security problem, Craig advised, lay in the replacement of the seigneurs as the political spokesmen for the Canadiens by a faction of lawyers:

If the Noblesse and Seigneurs of the Country possessed the influence which they had in former days ... it would be exerted for the restoration of that spirit of subordination on which ... the Militia System ultimately rests; but from a variety of Causes that influence has been totally annihilated and it is now in the hands of a new order of Men who have of late sprung into notice and who were formerly of little consequence; these are the Lawyers and Notaries, and with these has sprung up at the same time a spirit of insubordination among the People that is intirely [sic] adverse to the ancient system of the Country.

Since few seigneurs had been able to secure election to the new house, that body was sure to be controlled by the legal faction who caucused together on all occasions and were able to manipulate the many Canadien MPPs from the lower orders. The latter 'from their extreme ignorance and incapacity of judging of themselves are almost intirely [sic] led by those who they hear talk the most.' The lawyers had adopted opposition as a tactic to force themselves into office, but it seemed likely many of them had even more nefarious aims and were capable of extending these to the most dangerous lengths.

Craig's harsh judgment of the *parti canadien* was conditioned by the conventional wisdom deriving from Burke that artful, grasping, low-born attorneys, with everything to gain and nothing to lose, had made the French Revolution. This supposed truth and its relevance for the colony can be detected in many a contemporary document emanating from the English élite. And it comes out clearly in Craig's character sketches of those he had dismissed from the militia. Planté was 'a Man of some abilities, extremely poor and not supposed likely to hesitate at any Means by which he could better his Condition.' Borgia would not 'scruple at any means by which he could better his fortune.' Panet was 'discontented at his own folly in having ... resigned the Bench [in 1794] ... sour'd at the additional mortification he felt when the Salary of the Judges was encreased.' Bédard possessed the best abilities of the lot and this son of a baker was 'by far the most dangerous ... Those who know him best ... give it as their opinion that there are no lengths to which he is not capable of going.'

As to the military situation, Craig readily admitted the Canadien

militia was in sad shape, both because the martial spirit had long disappeared and because loyalty was uncertain. Castlereagh must understand
that the question had to be examined with two scenarios in mind: an
American invasion, and a French invasion. In the former case, the governor believed, disaffection or sentiment favouring the enemy would not
be a problem and 'we would have little against us but the natural disposition of the People, which is certainly not such as will render them
forward in military Duty.' Yet some useful military support for the
regulars would be given. In the case of a French attack though, prospects
were bleak:

I am persuaded We must not expect the slightest assistance from the Province,
on the Contrary I should in such a case be extremely sorry that the People should
be found with arms in their possession. They are in their hearts french yet and
whatever attachment they may affect to feel for a Government, under which it is
impossible for them to deny the benefits they enjoy, yet there would not ... be
Fifty dissentient voices to a Proposition that should be made tomorrow, for their
reannexation to ... France, even in its present form; with respect to that Form,
however ... such is the total want of Information among the People, that they
have not the slightest notion of its true state.

The attachment of the Canadien lower orders to their old country was so
strong and obvious that 'the general opinion among the english part of
the Inhabitants is, that they would even join an [attacking] American
Force, if that force were commanded by a french officer.'

THE CONSTITUTIONAL IDEAS OF PIERRE BÉDARD, 1807–1811

In his dispatch on the dismissals, Craig advised Castlereagh that the
leaders of the *parti canadien* 'either believe, or affect to believe that there
exists a ministry here and that, in imitation of the Constitution of Britain
that Ministry is responsible to them for the Conduct of Government.' It
was unnecessary, the governor added, 'that I should point out to your
Lordship the steps to which such an Idea may lead them.'[30] It is true that
the party leaders, Pierre Bédard especially, insisted there was a ministry
already existing in the colony and that its members were accountable to
the house.[31]

This concept did not anticipate the responsible cabinet government of
the 1830s and 1840s but derived from Blackstone's dictum that the executive power was checked by the two houses, through the 'privilege they

have of inquiring into, impeaching, and punishing the conduct ... not indeed of the king, which would destroy his constitutional independence; but ... of his evil and pernicious counsellors.'[32] Impeachment was a political trial before the High Court of Parliament, with the Commons acting as accuser and the Lords sitting in judgment. One principal purpose was to rid the nation of 'wicked' ministers, who were too powerful to be removed and punished in any other way. By 1807 impeachment in England was already obsolescent but this would have been concealed from contemporaries, since what was to prove to be the last instance had occurred only two years before.

In the pages of Le Canadien and in the house, Bédard argued there had to be a local ministry of advisers, individually accountable to the Assembly. His opponents, he insisted, were quite wrong to say that because the governor operated on instructions from the Colonial Office, he could not be advised by ministers. The constitution of Lower Canada was a replica of Great Britain's and in practice the transient representatives of the king were forced to rely on the advice of Executive Councillors and other residents. If his opponents, such as Sewell, De Bonne, and seigneur James Cuthbert Jr, were correct and the governor did all, constitutionally speaking, the 'monstrous' and dangerous result would be that the Assembly either must make the governor himself personally accountable to it or it must abdicate its responsibilities to legislate intelligently against abuses in administration and to preserve its independence from constitutional encroachments by the executive. To accept, as the English party and Canadien ministérielistes did, that the governor, like the king, could do no wrong but deny he had ministers on whom responsibility could be pinned, would almost inevitably lead to revolution or despotism.

The means which Bédard envisaged for enforcing accountability remain obscure. While the idea of a ministry contributed to the nervousness of the English élite, it remained a hypothetical construct during the Craig years. No 'minister' was censured, let alone impeached, for having advised the governor to act in an abusive way. It is in fact doubtful whether Bédard ever had a majority of the Assembly in favour of this notion, a radical one in substance even if presented in the conservative dress of Blackstone. Bédard's understanding of the privileges enjoyed by the house had more concrete effects.

In 1792 Jean-Antoine Panet's attempt to claim for the Assembly the privileges of the Commons had been rebuffed by Lieutenant-Governor Clarke, who consented only to the 'enjoyment of all just Rights and Lawful Privileges.'[33] These privileges were never defined authoritatively during the period. Since the Assembly, unlike the Commons, could not appeal to the law and custom of Parliament going back centuries, its privileges were not those of the elected house in England. Because the Constitutional Act made no reference to the subject, it follows that the Assembly enjoyed only those privileges necessary for it to function as a legislative body. Pierre Bédard and Jonathan Sewell would probably have agreed on that general proposition, but would have differed greatly on the meaning of 'necessary,' the former interpreting it as 'useful to' the preservation of the independence of the Assembly, and the latter insisting privileges had to be 'absolutely essential' (for example, freedom of speech and freedom from arrest but not the power to exclude members or to arrest for seditious libel) to the small tasks performed by the democratic branch. Later, in 1815, Sewell successfully pressed his view on the British law officers.[34] And in the end, the insistence on obvious necessity prevailed in law.[35]

Bédard and his associates did not claim the privileges of the house were identical to those of the Commons. The precedents relating to the latter body were guides, not a straitjacket, with each case decided on its own merits. This very British empiricism was somewhat tempered in that the *parti canadien* does appear to have had a definitional test in mind: whatever contributed to protect the autonomy of the house.[36] Sanction for breach – besides formal protest – was presumably impeachment or other proceedings against the 'ministers' responsible. By 1808, if not earlier, the *parti canadien* also claimed the right for the Assembly to cleanse itself, by mere resolution, of placemen. The exercise of this supposed privilege would precipitate the 1810 crisis.

Craig viewed Bédard's constitutional arguments through the same alarmist filter commonly at work among the English élite. He believed, for example, that the notion of executive accountability assumed the right to put the governor himself on trial at the bar of the house[37] and interpreted the Assembly's claim to expel members as part of a Turreau-financed plot.[38] More generally, he thoroughly agreed with the conventional English wisdom that the *parti canadien*, as Ryland put it in 1811, wanted to convince 'the mass of the people that the House of Assembly was superior to, and independent of the other branches of the Legislature.'[39] This position emerges regularly in documents emanating from the English party in these years. When in 1809, for example, *Le Canadien* referred carelessly to the Assembly's right to pass laws rather than bills, the *Mercury* editorialized that the 'trick' was intentional: 'Its object is to confirm the ignorant multitude in the belief that the house is every thing, possessing all power. Who ever hears from the mouth of Canadians, when speaking of our legislature, a word of any branch but the *Chambre!*'[40] Such fear of the Assembly taking over becomes understandable when it is remembered that in the years leading up to the American Revolution many of the elected colonial houses had reduced the influence of the governors and councils to virtually nil. In the early years of the French Revolution the Third Estate had swallowed up the two upper houses and then the king.

THE SESSION AND ELECTION OF 1809

The session of 1809 requires little comment. For the most part the *parti canadien* was frustrated in its constitutional aims. An attempt by notary Louis Bourdages, a founder of *Le Canadien*, and Bédard to establish that a ministry existed in Lower Canada was defeated by more than a two to one majority. Bourdages failed to induce the house to exclude judges by simple resolution but did succeed in having a special committee appointed, which blackened the reputation of De Bonne and recommended exclusion of judges from the Assembly. A bill to so exclude easily passed through second reading but died when Craig brought the session to an abrupt and fiery end after only five weeks by singling out the English party and *ministérielistes* for praise, while condemning their opponents as shallow-minded, factious incompetents.[41]

During the session the Assembly had again expelled Ezekiel Hart by resolution, despite the fact that Hart, this time, had taken the oath on the Christian Bible. Craig asked the Executive Council for legal advice on this matter and on the exclusion of judges by simple resolution of the house. A Council Committee of the Whole reported on 9 May that the Assembly had no power of expulsion where the member was legally qualified, as in the case of judges and of Jews who took the oath on the Christian Bible. The report amounted to an extra-judicial opinion by judges on legally controversial matters which might easily have come before the courts. The committee was chaired by Chief Justice Sewell, and the other six members, included judges De Bonne and Jenkin Williams of the King's Bench, Quebec District. No hint appeared in the opinion of any possible impropriety should these questions arise in litigation.[42]

The election of 1809 need only be touched upon. Although Craig began with very good prospects,[43] for unknown reasons the vote was delayed until October, by which time the *parti canadien's* propaganda had taken hold in the countryside. During the long and bitter campaign, English party men and *ministérielistes* rang the changes on the 'sans culottes' theme, while the governor made an unprecedented electoral progress through the province in June. *Le Canadien* featured suggestive articles comparing Craig to the Stuarts. In particular, extracts from the Bill of Rights, 1689 complaining of James II's unjust interference with free elections were printed on the masthead and on 16 September an article instructed readers on John Locke's right of revolution.[44] The results were disastrous for the governor, with his supporters among elected candidates being outnumbered by *parti canadien* adherents about eleven to twenty-five.[45]

The Canadien people had disobeyed their governor's orders and their leaders would soon pay the price.

11

Craig's 'Reign of Terror,' 1810–1811

As 1809 turned into 1810, British-American relations reached an explosive point. In November President Madison informed the hawkish United Kingdom ambassador, Francis James Jackson, that 'no further communications will be received from you.' While bellicose words filled the American press and Congress, Jackson and his staff moved to New York where for some months they functioned like a hostile government in exile. The ambassador warned Craig on 17 November to prepare for the worst.[1]

Thus in late 1809 and early 1810 war with the United States seemed imminent. Two silver linings enlivened this dark cloud: the American military forces were ill prepared, and it seemed highly probable that New York and New England would bitterly oppose the war as disastrous to their vital shipping industry and trade with the old mother country. Any careful reader of the American newspapers might have concluded this, but the government at Quebec also had the reports of its spy, John Henry, who had been sent by Craig on an undercover mission in early 1809 to Vermont and Massachusetts. Henry, who gathered his information from newspapers, coffee-house chatter, and dinner parties, uncovered no plot of secession, but confidently concluded that in the event of war the Federalist 'Junto of Boston' would, as a preliminary to separation and an alliance, make 'application to the Governor General of British America for aid ... which would protect the seaport towns.'[2] Whatever Craig believed about detaching New England, he was impressed by Henry's reports. At the Chateau, conventional wisdom maintained that the northeastern states would not, in substance, participate in a war although a joint French-American invasion in the near future had become a distinct possibility.

With intelligence sources indicating that Turreau had sent an important spy into Lower Canada,[3] the international situation, as perceived by Craig and his advisers in the days leading up to the opening of the legislative session in January 1810, appeared threatening. Confrontation seemed inevitable in the domestic front. In his New Year's letter to his brother, Brock summarized Lower Canadian politics as entirely governed by Napoleon's successes and almost out of control:

The idea prevails generally among them [the Canadiens], that Napoleon must succeed, and ultimately get possession of these provinces. The bold and violent [of the *parti canadien*] are becoming every day more audacious; and the timid [seigneurs], with that impression, think it better and more prudent to withdraw altogether from the society of the English, rather than run the chance of being accused hereafter of partiality to them ... More troops will be required in this country ... The governor will ... have a difficult card to play next month with the assembly, which is really getting too daring and arrogant. Every victory which Napoleon has gained for the last nine years, has made the disposition here to resist more manifest.

Le Canadien did not improve matters by boasting that the people as supreme judge had ratified the *parti canadien*'s constitutional position.[4] Governor Craig was more and more prone to define the issues in stark terms. The question, in his mind at least, had come down to this: who was going to govern the colony – Great Britain by right of conquest and inherent virtue, or the illiterate *Canadien* people manipulated by a pro-Bonaparte faction of self-seeking lawyers?

Shortly before the legislative session Craig received a letter from the secretary of state, Lord Castlereagh, authorizing him to assent to a statute disqualifying judges from membership in the Assembly and stating that the exclusion of Hart had been justified. The colonial secretary apparently assumed that the situation in Lower Canada as to eligibility was the same as in England – and that the Assembly had satisfied itself that Hart had not converted to Christianity in good faith when he took the oath on the Gospels. Neither assumption was warranted by the facts, but Castlereagh had defined what would be the legal position of Jewish candidates until the Lower Canada emancipation statute of 1831, which granted Jews the same rights and privileges as other subjects in the province. In 1810 the issue was academic, since Hart had withdrawn his candidacy during the October 1809 election.[5]

Castlereagh's overall message was conciliatory. Craig's behaviour, while keeping within the letter of his instructions, was the opposite and provides a classic demonstration of the autonomy enjoyed by a strong-willed and wily governor under the colonial system of the second British Empire.

THE SESSION AND ELECTION OF 1810

Virtually all attention was devoted to constitutional questions.[6] A bill to appoint an agent of the Assembly in London made its way to Committee of the Whole, where it eventually died. The idea of the framers (Borgia and Taschereau) was defensive: to protect against expected English party attacks on representative government (elimination or gerrymandering), while Craig assumed the object was a 'firebrand' in England to push the parti canadien's most extreme constitutional demands.[7] The house also passed a sanctionless resolution condemning attempts by other branches to censure proceedings in the Assembly. This vote demonstrated the ever-increasing polarization of politics, with moderates L.-J. Papineau and Viger, both of whom had opposed the ministry resolution in 1809, voting for and Quebec auctioneer John Jones, previously a political independent, voting against. A bill was passed excluding judges from the Assembly, designed for immediate effect rather than after the next general election, as required by Craig in his speech from the throne. The Council amended the bill to conform with the governor's wishes.

Resolutions proposed by Bédard, and bitterly fought by the English party and ministérielistes, indirectly asserted for the Assembly the rights and privileges of the House of Commons in the appropriation of public monies. It was resolved that the province (in view of greatly increasing import duty revenue) now pay all civil expenses of government; that the house would vote (not the legislature enact) all the necessary sums for the year, and that His Majesty and Parliament be addressed in that sense. By not specifying that the ultimate form of appropriation would be by statute (with the Council able to veto, although not initiate or amend) preceded, as invariably in England, by a message from the crown recommending the expenditure, Bédard left the initiative open to interpretation. To Craig it was clear the Assembly majority was trying to take over the executive government entirely by controlling salaries, all of which he thought they intended to allocate on an annual basis by mere vote of the house.[8] That Bédard thought in terms of proceeding by vote rather than Appropriation Act is doubtful. This would be going well beyond his model and no government in Westminster would seriously contemplate it. In the result, Craig agreed to transmit the address to His Majesty, while lecturing the house on the constitutional proprieties: that any initiation of public money grants must be preceded by a royal recommendation and have the concurrence of the upper house. The address was sent home, soon followed by a gloom-and-doom scenario if it should be acted upon – which it was not.

Barely three weeks into the session Craig poured out his frustrations in a long letter to his friend, Colonel Bunbury, complaining of all the unconstitutional initiatives of his opponents and speculating what might happen in the judges issue. If, as was probable, the Assembly refused to accept the Legislative Council's amendments and proceeded to exclude De Bonne by resolution, which Craig had probably planned all along, he would have to make a stand, since that would amount to amending an imperial statute. If the *parti canadien* were to achieve their goal on this question, Craig continued, one could expect them to exclude, not merely office holders in general,[9] but to 'vote that no Englishman could be eligible' for seats in the house. Craig would have to dissolve again if they persisted. The *parti canadien* was starting to succeed in convincing the masses that 'it is the House of Assembly that is to govern the Province.' The leaders 'have hitherto been making [only] gradual advances to their Object, but as was the Case in Charles the First's Reign the time of the Explosion is now come.'

Prophetic words. On the very day Craig wrote his letter Bourdages succeeded in having the Assembly postpone consideration of the Alien Act Renewal Bill until 20 March.[10] This obvious attempt (a long-matured scheme) to avoid a second, precipitate dissolution, would not deter Craig.[11] On 23 February the Assembly voted to search British precedents with regard to Craig's answer to the financial resolutions – in effect, to sit in judgment on the governor. On the following day two motions by Bourdages were passed by nineteen to sixteen. The first declared that 'P.A. DeBonne, being one of the Judges of the Court of King's Bench, cannot sit nor vote in this House'; the second stated that De Bonne's seat for the County of Quebec was vacant. The governor now reacted to what the *Mercury*, in anticipation, had characterized as a rebellion against the sovereignty of the imperial Parliament.

On the 25th, after taking the advice of the Executive Council (unanimous), Craig appeared in the legislature to announce immediate prorogation and the forthcoming dissolution, which occurred three days later. He repeated all the constitutional objections to exclusion by resolution. The governor could not be party to a violation of the Constitutional Act by disenfranchising a class of His Majesty's subjects. The people, he was sure, would understand.

The election campaign that followed reached new depths of vitriol and hysteria. The *parti canadien* spread rumours that Craig was going to impose conscription and viciously attacked the placemen.[12] These public thieves, parasites living off the people's toil, and their colleagues had forced the dissolution in order to avoid the Assembly gaining any supervision over the civil list. The placemen wanted to multiply posts and expenditures as they saw fit and if they succeeded in controlling the new house, huge land taxes were inevitable. De Bonne's recently established Quebec newspaper, *Le Vraie-Canadien*, and other *ministérieliste* literature replied in kind.[13] Bédard's offer to assume responsibility for public finance would mean £50,000 per year in new land taxes and £150,000 to pay for the military, which would plunge the colony into misery. *Le Vraie-Canadien* claimed its opponents even intended to tax the clergy, the latter being warned to remember 'the unfortunate experience of 1789' and stop this plot against religion in its tracks. De Bonne's paper also accused the *parti canadien* of secretly aiming to reduce the governor's authority to nil and to eliminate the veto of the Legislative Council. What was this if not revolution?

The 'sans culottes' theme flowed from the lips and pens of government supporters. An electoral song, printed by the *Montreal Gazette* on 5 March, for example, likened Bédard to Robespierre. Numerous addresses to the Governor were prepared defending the prerogative as essential to peace and stability. Typical of the more extreme among such polemics was one, dated 5 March 1810, prepared by the 'Magistrates & principal Inhabitants of Terrebonne & its Environs' and signed by some of the best-known names associated with the fur trade: Roderick McKenzie, builder of Fort Chipewyan on Lake Athabaska, former Nor'wester Simon Fraser (not the explorer) who had been in charge at Grand Portage in the late 1790s, and Peter Pangman, one of the pioneers who had opened the Saskatchewan trade in the 1770s. After noting that the 'pernicious maxims, which have deluged Empires with the blood of the Inhabitants' had taken root in Lower Canada, the address expressed horror that the *parti canadien* was attempting to 'stir up ... National Prejudices, Fears, Alarms & discontents ... insult the throne ... subvert the Constitution; [and] sacrifice the Interest and Tranquillity of the public to their own private views & animosities.'

A letter, composed by John Henry as 'Camillus' and published in the *Quebec Mercury* on 19 March, compared Bédard and his associates to Wat Tyler and Jack Cade in their attempts to provoke peasant uprising. In 1792–3, 'Camillus' observed, Paine's subversive writings had been distributed at reduced prices in England, but 'it was left to the infamous Duke of Orleans and the popular leaders of Lower Canada alone, to mature their revolutionary plans, by libellous publications printed and distributed *gratis.*' The Canadien revolutionaries held secret meetings at each other's houses and at a mass gathering in the Quebec City market had burned pro-government literature 'amidst shouts of *"Vive la Nation"*. ' Everything pointed to the conclusion that 'this faction have in view to [re-en]act now the same enormities which were committed' during the French Revolution.

Rumours had the *parti canadien* leaders in sympathetic contact with the enemy. Ryland expected French emissaries would be sent in to exploit the situation and warned the magistrates accordingly. One story had it that damning correspondence from Turreau had been intercepted by British agents in the United States. But most of the tales involved financial aid from France. The historian Christie recalled rumours that 'the french minister in America had supplied large sums in gold, to promote the views of the seditious in Canada,' while the scholarly artist-historian George Heriot was convinced that 'French Money, as well as influence have for some time past found their way into this province.' Craig and Ryland were among the believers.[14] In this garrison mentality atmosphere *Le Canadien*, feigning ignorance and horror, published an electoral ditty which suggested the people hunt down the 'scum' (*canaille*) whom the governor hoped to reward from land taxes.

Craig struck, placing the military on alert status.

THE CRISIS

The next priority was to gather evidence of high treason or treasonable practices. On 16 March two English tavern-keepers were sent to the printing office of *Le Canadien* to become subscribers. Their depositions (sworn to before Sewell) identifying Charles Le François as the printer, and the three last numbers of the paper were examined by the full Executive Council the next day.[15] After discussion the Council agreed with Craig that the printer should be apprehended; but to preserve appearances, the governor, Sewell, and Bishop Mountain withdrew while the formal decision to issue a warrant was taken in Committee of the Whole.

The warrant charged Le François with 'treasonable practices' and according to Christie was executed with flourish: 'a party of soldiers headed by a magistrate and two constables, proceeded to the *Canadien* printing office ... where ... [they] forcibly seized the press, with the whole of the papers of every description found in the house.'[16] By order of the full Council the press and printing materials were deposited in the vaults of the courthouse. The raid produced no treasonable correspondence or subversive draft articles, although the raiders did seize an inflammatory electoral broadsheet in the press which recited Canadien grievances back to the Conquest.

On 19 March the Council examined this document and depositions sworn to by Le François, three of his assistants, and a medical student of Dr Blanchet. The depositions revealed that among the owners of *Le Canadien* were Bourdages, Blanchet, Bédard, Taschereau and Borgia; that during the election Blanchet and Taschereau had been the active managers of the paper; that the notorious 'Chanson' referring to Craig's advisers as scum had originally been printed at the *Le Canadien* office; and that Bédard was the author of the party's main electoral address of 1810. These were hardly startling revelations and amounted to no more than a basis for charges of seditious libel. One statement by Le François, however, probably banished any lingering doubts that there might not be a deeply laid plot. Dr Blanchet, it appears, had given orders to the printers that all original articles be returned to the editors or else burned, to prevent identification of the authors' handwriting. A committal warrant signed by Dunn, Baby, and Young and charging Bédard, Blanchet, and Taschereau with the unknown crime of 'treasonable practices' was immediately executed. Unlike the case in 1801, the prisoners were actually detained on charges, not merely on suspicion. This minimized the chances of successfully invoking parliamentary privilege. A similar warrant to commit three *parti canadien* activists from the District of Montreal was executed and warrants against other Montrealers such as Viger were signed but execution suspended.

The capital was agog with excitement, talk of plots and narrowly averted civil war. On 21 March Craig issued a proclamation explaining the purity of his motives, implying that the *parti canadien* leaders were in the pay of the French, and instructing the captains of militia and magistrates to arrest anyone spreading 'false news in any way derogatory to His Majesty's Government.'[17] *Le Vraie-Canadien* and the *Quebec Mercury* naturally applauded the governor's warlike stand. Not to be outdone, Bishop Mountain devoted his Sunday sermon to portraying Craig as the saviour of the province. Mountain's sentiments were shared by General Brock:

We have been in a bustle and on the alert for the last ten days ... The spirit of insubordination and revolt was advancing so rapidly among the Canadian population of the province that it became absolutely necessary for the peace to put a check to it, and fortunately a person was found at the head of Government of sufficient energy to meet and crush at once the monster who strived to draw the people ... to all the horrors of civil commotion ... I hope ... terror will prove effective ... the bubble [of conciliation] set up by Lord Dorchester and Sir. R.S. Milnes, has completely burst never to rise again.[18]

The news as it spread from Quebec lost little in the telling. Letters written by Louis-Joseph Papineau and John Henry describe a frenzied ecstasy among English Montrealers over the arrests and many loud pronouncements about Bédard being in league with the enemy. Readers of the *Halifax Gazette*, *The Times* of London and *Le Moniteur* in Paris learned of a treasonable alliance between the Canadien MPPs and General Turreau. Turreau himself was pleased that he might have unknown collaborators in Canada, but worried lest a rebellion break out before he could convince his superiors in Paris to mount an invasion. In far-off Hyderabad, India, Major François-Louis de Salaberry, Louis's son and an officer in the British army, read in one newspaper that 'there was a conspiracy discovered which was to murder all the English inhabitants.'[19]

Although confident he had succeeded in thwarting rebellion, Craig left nothing to chance. The mails from Quebec to Montreal were briefly detained, in order, it was said, 'to get hold of the threads of the insurrectionary web ... before the news of the vigorous dash ... could reach their outlying fellow-conspirators.' To make sure that the democrats did not seize them, the governor had the adjutant general of the Canadien militia mount a guard over several dozen muskets used for training purposes. Until the last days of the month special military patrols marched up and down the streets of the capital – in perfect peace of course. As late as July Brock found it impossible to obtain leave to visit England. The governor, still worried about insurrection, wished to retain as many experienced officers as possible in the colony.[20] The fact that no hard evidence of a French plot was uncovered did not in the least affect the governor or his advisers and Bédard long remained a proven traitor in their eyes.

In Montreal, Chief Justice Monk, James McGill, and other Executive councillors examined numerous witnesses to the inflammatory electoral polemics of a François Corbeil, habitant of Ile Jésus, and notary Laforce of Terrebonne. The examiners detained these two hotheads under the act, having proved to their own satisfaction (for example, Laforce had received a letter from France), that they could bring 'all the facts to one single and great point of ultimate design' – that of preparing for general rebellion.[21]

To Louis-Joseph Papineau, the charges against his leaders had been fabricated in order to sway the elections. This idea of cold-blooded opportunism – already commonplace in *parti canadien* circles – has been echoed by historians writing on the 'reign of terror.' In this view, Craig was acting sincerely but under the influence of his advisers, the latter – and indeed the English party in general – being portrayed as knowingly creating a false security scare to maintain their own aims.[22] But the garrison mentality was rooted in genuine fear, although it could easily be exploited for personal, ideological, or partisan advantage. The partisan electoral advantage suggested by Papineau was not the crucial factor in the thinking of the executive. Within five days of the main arrests, Craig, explaining how the rebellion had been nipped in the bud to Lord Liverpool, wrote prophetically, that the 'mischief, with respect to the elections is, I fear, done, and the same set of inveterate democrats will be rechosen before the people can be disabused.' The main point, though, had been to intimidate the leaders. This had been achieved.

In the last eight days of March Craig transmitted home three explanations of the arrests, in one of which he referred to talk among Canadiens of a 'Sicilian Vespers' – a contemporary term meaning massacre of an ethnic minority – as illustrative of the agitated public mind.[23] But it was not until May 1st that he prepared an exhaustive account of the crisis to the colonial secretary.[24] In it he detailed all the elements of the garrison mentality: the disloyalty of the clergy, especially the emigrés; the danger presented by upstart lawyers in the Assembly; the need for anglicization; French intrigues; the demographic vulnerability of the English; and so on. With regard to the working people of Lower Canada, Craig's opinion had not changed since 1808: 'the great Mass of the people are completely infected, they look forward to the event, they whisper it among themselves, an [*sic*] I am assured that they have even a song among them, which points out Napoleon as the person who is to expel the English.' It almost passed belief how much influence the Bédard party had on the masses. The latter publicly declared that no crown officer, Canadien seigneur, or Englishman was to be trusted or elected, and it is now to 'La Chambre ... for they never even mention the Council, that the people look up [to] as the Governors of the Country.' The imperial Parliament should suspend representative government – the solution most desired by the English, Craig claimed – or at least consider unifying the Canadas.

In May Craig's 'prime minister,' Chief Justice Sewell, prepared a set of 'Observations' on the security problem.[25] They recommended *inter alia* thoroughgoing anglicization, massive American immigration, reorganization of the courts, and a union of the Canadas. Craig sent the report to the Colonial Office (where it was ignored) as representing the work of a man whose intelligence and experience with the people of the colony made him highly 'competent to form a true judgment of the State of it' and to recommend 'the most effectual means of obviating the Evils to which it is liable.'[26] Union might contribute to economic progress, but Sewell did not mention the latter, being preoccupied with security.

The next month Craig sent Ryland to England to justify the arrests, press a number of assimilation proposals on the Colonial Office, and lobby for a suspension of representative government or a political union of the Canada.[27] By now the governor was prepared to concede there was no definite evidence of plotting but, along with the entire English community, he claimed that serious danger existed and this had to be impressed upon the imperial authorities: 'such is the state of the People's minds that, sooner or later, Revolution may be looked for, and that perhaps, without any view to an immediate occurrence of such an event, the proceedings of the Party all tend, to facilitate and prepare the way for it. There is every reason to believe however that Turreau is setting Engines to work among us.'[28]

THE LEGAL AFTERMATH, MARCH–APRIL 1810

Sewell on Sedition

On 22 March the chief justice opened the spring assizes with a thoroughly Burkean address to the grand jury.[29] It was obviously designed to justify the arrests and hence was politically inspired. But it also reflected Sewell's genuine concern for internal security and his sincere interpretation of the law. After reading Craig's proclamation, the chief justice launched into an elaborate political and legal explanation of seditious libel. Sewell's understanding of this crime, more royalist than that prevalent in the mother country, revived the elastic concept of the first Alien Act. He did not mention the right to criticize the government: obviously, even temperate criticism was illegal or at best carried a heavy presumption of sedition.

Freedom of the press meant the absence of prior censorship, as established since the Licensing Act lapsed in 1695. The factious in various periods of political effervescence thereafter had spread about the notion that the newspapers could 'offer each and every thought however pernicious.' This was totally false. The function of the press was not to advocate change, but to aid in 'the preservation of all that is valuable to us as Men and as subjects.' Government, not the people at large, had the responsibility 'to promote and secure the happiness of the Individuals who compose it.' Any writing, therefore, which was 'detrimental to the public safety or happiness,' which raised discontents against the ruling authorities, or whose 'effect is prejudicial to the public'[30] could not be tolerated by the government 'without a dereliction of its own fundamental principles.'

It followed that the abuse of the freedom from prior restraint 'in ... the smallest Degree should be the object of legal punishment.' For the government to forego control of the press was dangerous everywhere, particularly after the French Revolution, but especially so in Lower Canada with its simple-minded population: 'In all countries, the ignorant, the credulous and the desperate are to be found, Yet in proportion as the hearts of the Inhabitants of any Country are good and simple, in that proportion they become more readily a prey to the crafty, who in these respects have the Cruelty to deceive them – In no country therefore can attempts so to deceive, be more dangerous, than in that which we inhabit.' The governor's proclamation had taken all this into consideration and the grand jurors should do likewise in their deliberations. Leniency when faced with seditious publications was 'the path that leads to Rebellion and civil War or to the subjugation of the Country by some foreign Power,' as events in Europe demonstrated.

Despite Sewell's obvious invitation, the grand jury (composed mainly of English party supporters and Canadien ministérielistes) indicted no one for seditious libel. Nor did it recommend indictments. It did, however, condemn recent issues of Le Canadien and some of the electoral publications struck off its press as perilous to the security of the colony. Sanctions were left up to the court. The jury also censured the Mercury for exciting jealousies and distrusts among Canadiens.[31]

Although the failure to indict or recommend prosecutions could not have pleased the administration, there were other ways to control the opposition press. Bédard and his editorial colleagues could be kept in prison almost indefinitely. The printing equipment could also remain in the court vault. When in late April a printing press in Montreal was put up for auction, Stephen Sewell (now solicitor general), as directed by Craig, made sure it did not fall 'into the hands of the Canadian gentlemen who were desirous of establishing the opposition paper in this town.' Merchant James Ogilvy attended the auction and outbid representatives of the *parti canadien*. Stephen jubilantly reported to his brother that since a new press would cost about £700, the ardour of the democrats would soon cool. In June 1811 some of the proprietors of *Le Canadien* instituted a damages action against the magistrate who had effected the seizure, but the suit was dismissed on a technical point of procedure.[32]

Bédard's Application for Habeas Corpus

On 16 April Bédard gave notice of motion to Attorney General Norman F. Uniacke that he would apply to the King's Bench for a writ of habeas corpus.[33] Craig decided Uniacke, a British-trained barrister, would lead for the crown and told him through Ryland that the interests of public security demanded an effective opposition to the application.[34] Uniacke was to be assisted by Advocate General Olivier Perrault and Edward Bowen, a Quebec lawyer who had articled with the chief justice when the latter had been attorney general. Bédard's lawyer was twenty-five-year-old Andrew Stuart, James's brother, who had been admitted to the Bar only three years before. His inexperience was evident. To prove Bédard's membership in the dissolved Assembly and in the newly elected one, he filed only indentures between his client and constituency electors, rather than certified copies of the official election returns, and he did not argue the case on general principle, an omission which reduced the prisoner's already remote chance of success. Although De Bonne decided or was instructed not to sit, those who did – Sewell, Jenkin Williams, and James Kerr – were in substance judging their absent colleague's principal political opponent, a man Craig and the chief justice thought was a traitor. With the best will in the world, Sewell particularly could not have been impartial. As attorney general in 1797 he had drafted the Better Preservation Act to enable the government to intern MPPs without being met with valid claims to parliamentary privilege. As a member of the Executive Council, the chief justice had advised Craig to imprison Bédard under the act; he had, therefore, already taken a position in the case that the imprisonment was not subject to privilege – which was of course the central issue of the hearing.

At the hearing Stuart argued for Bédard's release on the ground of his privilege as a member both of the old and new assemblies. The proviso in the Better Preservation Act expressly maintained the lawful privileges of the house and no one could deny it was vested with those essential to its proper functioning, of which freedom from arrest was certainly one. British practice indicated as much and in England Judge Pratte's judgment in *Wilkes* (1763) showed that the privilege was denied only in three cases: treason, felony, and actual breach of the peace. Counsel went into some detail proving the obvious: that treasonable practices, while having some qualities of high treason, did not amount to that crime. Stuart also contended that the privilege existed for forty days after a dissolution.

Seditious libel, Perrault claimed, amounted to an actual breach of the peace, while Bowen argued that the privilege extended only to such reasonable time after dissolution as would allow the member to return home. Considering that Bédard resided in Quebec, this would be one day at most. Bowen cited *Bacon's Abridgment* in an attempt to show that if a member were in prison when elected, the privilege was voided. He also outlined the relevant chronology to demonstrate that the applicant had not been a member either of the old or the new assemblies at the time of his arrest. All three counsel denied authority to Pratte's judgment in *Wilkes* since it had been repudiated by Parliament, with Uniacke and Perrault interpreting the resolution as meaning that the privilege was not available for any indictable offence. Bowen and Uniacke argued the case for denying the Assembly the same privileges as the Commons' enjoyed, and contended that since the security of the colony was at stake, judgment should go against Bédard. Bowen was the more colourful here: 'Should the argument in support of the motion be admitted, the House of Assembly might be composed of fifty traitors, and no remedy be had against them.'

Three separate concurring judgments were rendered dismissing the application. Kerr confined himself to the technical point that there was no valid proof before the court that Bédard had been a member of the dissolved house or was a member of the present one. Williams and Sewell agreed on this, which therefore constituted the *per curiam* ratio of the case. Williams in a short note concurred with everything said by the chief justice who delivered the most elaborate judgment. After disposing of the case because of the evidentiary defect, he proceeded in *obiter* (non-binding comments) to address the question in a wide-ranging hypothetical fashion. His explicit purpose was to avoid future litigation on the issue.

Sewell conceded that freedom from arrest had the same scope in Lower Canada as in Britain. He therefore set out to demonstrate that in England no such privilege existed in serious criminal cases. Before treating the substance, the chief justice made two technical points. Citing respectable authority, he concluded that while the privilege lasted for forty days after prorogation, it extended only to a reasonable time after dissolution. He also accepted Bowen's argument that being in jail at the time of the election voided the privilege, the electorate having no right to be represented by such a man. Under this doctrine Bédard and his fellow political prisoners could not claim privilege so long as they remained in jail. Potentially it would allow the crown to control the composition of any house where bail and the right to a speedy trial were not available, simply by arresting leading opponents before the vote was completed and detaining them as long as possible.

On matters of substance, Sewell demonstrated that, even if Pratte were correct and authoritative, his judgment would not help in this case. Of the two crimes, seditious libel and treasonable practices, the former was the minor one. The *Wilkes* case, therefore, 'if admitted to be law, proves that the privilege ... extends thus far, that is, to *seditious acts*, but affords no proof whatever that it extends beyond them to *treasonable practices*.' But the *Wilkes* decision was not law, the chief justice went on, since it had been 'solemnly disclaimed by both Houses of the British Parliament.' Sewell interpreted the resolution as properly construing breach of the peace to include all major criminal offences: 'All indictable crimes (and all treasonable practices must be indictable) are held in law to be *contra pacem domini regis*; and upon this ground, in England, it is now understood that the claim of privilege does not comprehend the case of any indictable crime.'

Assessment of Sewell's Judgment

One cannot seriously quibble with the evidentiary argument, except to suggest that a court sympathetic to the applicant might have got round it.[35] Nor can one argue with the conclusion that the applicant's privilege (if any) as a member of the old house had ceased by the time of his arrest, eighteen days after dissolution. One can, however, seriously question the point that because Bédard was in jail at the time of his election to the new house, he was not entitled to privilege (assuming it otherwise existed). To say that the electors had only themselves to blame is not convincing, since the privilege of freedom from arrest, like all privileges, existed for the benefit of one or other house of the legislature, rather than the public at large, the electors, or any segment of the electors. Sewell's use of authorities was also highly selective. He cited two precedents in support of this holding. One dated from the Tudor period, when Parliament was essentially an adjunct of royal power. The other was *Sir Richard Temple's* case (King's Bench, 1661), which if anything proved the opposite of Sewell's contention,[36] proceeding, as it did, on the assumption that incarceration at the time of election did not void the privilege. This was manifested in an 1807 precedent, which Sewell chose to ignore or was unknown to him. A Mr Mills, under arrest on mesne process, was elected to Parliament. The Commons resolved that Mills was privileged and ordered him released from custody.

One further question calls for answer: was Bédard entitled to his freedom on the basis of general principle, that is, the central purpose of parliamentary privileges?

The argument from general principle asks whether a member of Parliament could be imprisoned, without the consent of the House of Commons, on a criminal charge where the accused had no right to a speedy trial by ordinary course of law – that is, where habeas corpus had been suspended in relation to the criminal charge in issue. A negative answer involves a restrictive interpretation of the exceptions ('treason, felony or breach of the peace') to privilege, confining them to ordinary criminal cases where internment was impossible, an approach consistent with the general rule of construing exceptions restrictively and which could draw support from the rationale expressed by the parliamentary resolution in the Wilkes affair that privilege not 'obstruct the ordinary Course of the Laws, in the speedy and effectual Prosecution of so heinous and dangerous an Offence.' Thus the rationale of the two houses of Parliament in giving breach of peace its widest possible interpretation was non-interference with speedy trials according to the common law. That rationale did not apply where the crown was able to take advantage of and had in fact taken advantage of a suspension of habeas corpus. Bédard had no way of forcing a court to order his trial, which in the ordinary course of justice should have occurred at the March assizes of 1810. But he had not then even been indicted. Nor had the governor issued a special commission. To deny a privilege in such cases was to give the crown obvious power to coerce the Commons in England or the Assembly in Lower Canada.

No clear supportive British precedent was on point, simply because the situation was invariably provided for in the statutes suspending habeas corpus: imprisonment of MPs and peers was prohibited without the consent of the appropriate house. But there was no negative precedent either. The provisos in the suspending acts did not deny pre-existing privilege. Nor did the mere fact that protection of parliamentarians took statutory form imply there was no privilege in common law: the long-established freedom of debate, for example, had been reiterated in the Bill of Rights, 1689. The provisos, then, could reasonably be interpreted as reassertions of existing privileges, included *ex abundanti cautelâ* (from an excess of caution). Had the draftsmen in England ever omitted the proviso, it is inconceivable that the Commons or Lords would fail to protest the crown's prolonged internment of one or more members without consent. If the question had arisen in litigation, the courts of necessity would have had recourse to the central purpose of parliamentary privilege. This had been unambiguously stated by Blackstone: 'Privilege of parliament was principally established, in order to protect its members, not only from being molested by their fellow-subjects, but also *more especially from being oppressed by the power of the crown.*'[37]

Lord Ellenborough's *dictum* in the case of *Burdett* v. *Abbot* (1811) is to the same effect: 'The privileges which belong to them seem at all times to have been, and necessarily must be, inherent in them, *independent of any precedent*: it was necessary that they should have the most complete personal security, to enable them freely to meet for the purposes of discharging their important functions, and also that they should have the right of self-protection.'[38]

As defined by Blackstone and Ellenborough, the central purpose of privilege was to guarantee the autonomous functioning of each house of Parliament. When applied to the Bédard incident, this concept suggests that the Assembly was wrongly prejudiced by Sewell's denial of privilege in cases of treasonable practices under the Better Preservation Act.[39] The analysis can be pressed further to suggest that the arrests were not justified in the first place.

In his anxiety to demonstrate that treasonable practices were more heinous than sedition and required an actual plotting against the government, Sewell inadvertently admitted that the arrests had been unjustified. There had been no evidence whatever of rebellious design before the Executive Council. This was immediately perceived by the British attorney general, Sir Vicary Gibbs, when in 1810 he examined the proceedings of the Council and the documents (including copies of *Le Canadien*) on which it had based its decisions.[40] In his report to Lord Liverpool, Gibbs allowed that the political situation in Lower Canada had probably been such as to excuse a stretching of the law. But stretched it certainly had been:

I cannot say that the paper published in 'Le Canadien,' and upon which the proceedings of the Council were founded are such as fix upon the publishers the charge of treasonable practices, and therefore it may be difficult strictly to justify the steps which have been taken against them; but the passages which are adverted to were certainly calculated to do much mischief in the Province; they might, I think, be prosecuted as seditious libels, and with the apprehensions which were entertained of the effect of this paper, it may have been excusable to resort to means not strictly justifiable in law for suppressing it.

Liverpool enclosed a copy of Gibbs's report in a dispatch, dated 12 September 1810, to Craig, but did not call him or the chief justice to account or issue instructions to release any remaining prisoners.[41]

During the months of July and August 1810 all the prisoners except Bédard were released on bail. Some such as Blanchet and Taschereau made full confessions of wrongdoing. Others were liberated because of the danger to health. In one case discharge apparently came too late. Within weeks of his leaving the damp cells of the Montreal jail, François Corbeil died, from a disease contracted in prison according to his family.[42] Bédard, who refused to confess any impropriety and demanded a trial, remained in prison for over a year. Opinion at the Chateau was divided as to the advisability of trying the suspects for treasonable practices or seditious libel and in the end none was prosecuted. After the legislative session of 1810–11 in which the leaderless, intimidated *parti canadien* floundered, little was heard of radical constitutional change, and an amended Better Preservation Act was passed for the last time as it turned out.[43] Craig deemed himself in control of the colony. Bédard could be released without the people believing the Assembly was responsible. He left prison in early April 1811.

CRAIG'S DEPARTURE AND HIS POLITICAL ROLE IN LOWER CANADA

Although the session could hardly have gone more smoothly for the English party, security fears were not of course entirely abated. The *Canadian Courant* in late July, for example, offered another exhortation in favour of increasing American immigration and anglicizing the Canadiens. Strangers were to be watched very carefully, as a number, acting under French influence, had been sent into the province for the 'sole purpose of sowing the seeds of discord among us, and if in their power, to subvert our Government.'[44]

Some weeks before this Craig had left the colony to return home to die. Naturally the men of the *parti canadien* were glad to see him go. In the English community, the governor's departure generated an out-pouring of regretful good wishes, in marked contrast to Milnes's leaving in 1805, which had been unlamented and largely unnoticed. Delegates from the centres of English concentration carried emotional, laudatory addresses to Quebec. The Montreal merchants, for example, nominated James Dunlop, a prominent trader with Scotland, for such a mission. Although apolitical,[45] facing urgent business demands and making the trip solely to present the address, Dunlop was happy to comply as 'too much respect cannot be shown to our worthy Governor in Chief whose departure is most highly regretted by [every?] description of People.' The English living in the capital were particularly demonstrative according to Christie, attending 'his excellency on his departure, from the castle of St. Lewis for embarkation, taking from his carriage the horses, in the castle yard, the multitude conveying it thence to the king's wharf, where he embarked, under every mark of affection and respect it was in their power to shew him.' According to the *Mercury*, Craig's administration had been 'marked throughout by pure intentions and successful results.' This noble, generous human being, whose 'reigning passion was to perform his duty completely and conscientiously' had already 'taken his seat in history' where his fame would ever increase.[46]

Craig's political role in Lower Canada was not that of a politically naive and sick old soldier manipulated by his senior advisers, as a tradi-tional viewpoint has it. Far from it. He, more than anyone else in those years, ran the English party and did so with Machiavellian skill. Nor did he function as a gubernatorial battler for the commercial empire of the St Lawrence. Although sympathetic to the aims of the merchants,[47] these were not his priority. A.L. Burt recognized that while Craig, in 1808, understood his Indian policy would advance the interests of the Montreal fur trade south of the Great Lakes, he placed much greater importance on its contribution to defence.[48] The same priorities are found in those documents in which the governor reviewed the political state of Lower Canada. Almost every line of his famous dispatch of 1 May 1810, which runs to more than seven thousand words in Doughty and McArthur, dealt with the colony's safety. Fewer than three hundred and fifty words referred specifically to economic progress.[49] Of Craig's twelve points in summary, one related to population, one to furthering prosperity, and ten, directly or indirectly, to security. The most exhaustive analysis Craig wrote on the politics of Lower Canada, then, was *not* a brief for 'commerce' in its struggles with 'agriculture.'

It is significant, too, that Craig was inclined to doubt the wisdom of political union with Upper Canada, which was one of the favourite constitutional reforms desired by the merchants and those publicists making the case for economic progress.[50] Craig much preferred suspending the Assembly. His hesitancy about union was conditioned by security concerns. As he explained to the colonial secretary: 'I am more inclined to keep the Province of Upper Canada as a foreign, and [politically] distinct population, which may be produced as a resource against that of this Country in case of necessity. It must always be interested in opposing revolution of every sort here.'[51] These words were strangely prophetic. In the rebellion of 1838 the Glengarry Volunteers from Upper Canada wreaked impressive havoc in the Beauharnois area of Lower Canada.

Craig's administration is best explained as an acting out of the garrison mentality. The governor quickly absorbed what by 1808 had become the established view of colonial Britons to security and he gave the English party an aggressive posture in meeting supposed Canadien disloyalty for the first time, except briefly, since 1793. On Craig's departure, the English 'garrison' understood it was losing a leader able to intimidate the 'disloyal, dangerous and still French' conquered subjects by whom they were surrounded. The sense of loss was real, but there was hope Craig's precedent meant conciliation was dead forever. This was not to be – as the detested Sir George Prevost during the War of 1812 and the unpopular Lord Gosford in 1835–7 were to prove. The English élite would not find a Sir James again until Lord Dalhousie in the 1820s and above all, that 'old Firebrand' Sir John Colborne in the wake of the 1838 Rebellion.

Conclusions

The French Revolution moulded the development of Lower Canadian law in manifold ways. The impotence of the royal court at Versailles in the years 1789 to 1791, for instance, encouraged the imperial government to embark on a complex overhaul of the Quebec constitution, including the potentially risky grant of elected assemblies. I have discussed the crucial importance of timing and refuted the recurrent thesis of representative government resulting from fear of the French Revolution in chapter 3. The riots against the enforcement of militia laws and the Road Act of 1796 owed more to specific grievances (real and apprehended) entertained by the working people than to the activities of foreign agents and local sympathizers. And senior French officials in the United States probably had nothing to do with them, despite common English élite opinion. But these riots were strong stimuli to the garrison mentality and remain important to historians as striking illustrations of a long-standing tradition of 'rebellion à justice.'

One of the 'legacies of fear' is the impact of the Revolution on the civil law. The revulsion against the French Revolution and the state it had spawned remained strong among the Canadien élite after 1811. With the defeat of the liberal, anti-clerical *patriotes* in 1837–8 it again became the orthodoxy which lasted into the middle decades of the twentieth century. It falls beyond the scope of my book to describe this ideology, except to emphasize that nothing like a cultural divorce developed between Lower Canada/Quebec and post-revolutionary France. There were, rather, patterns of selective borrowing orchestrated by the francophone élite, particularly the clergy, which for a century after 1850 enjoyed almost hegemonic ideological authority. Right-wing individuals and concepts were welcomed, including, for example, the emigré clergy in the 1790s and the proto-fascist ideas of Maurice Barrès and Charles Maurras, popular between the two world wars. Mainstream and radical France were filtered out.[1] In 1950 the archbishop of Montreal, to give one example, formally forbade the Roman Catholic population of the diocese to celebrate the death centennial of the novelist Honoré Balzac![2]

In the cultural area a similar selectivity seems to have operated. I suggest that a useful approach is to assume that for a century from about 1840 French Canada borrowed 'form' from France but tended to eschew substance. I believe this dichotomy might illuminate such cultural endeavours as novel writing and (with obvious qualifications) painting, among others. The form/substance distinction certainly applies to the codification of Lower Canadian civil law in the years 1857–66. The process provides an almost ideal case study since the codifiers (one English, two Canadien jurists) had their minds directed to the Code Napoléon which had incorporated many of the legal reforms spawned by the Revolution. They were, moreover, permitted to suggest modernizations to the existing law and final passage was dependent upon the votes of francophone MPPs. The key politician pressing for codification was George-Etienne Cartier, who is quoted by his biographer as praising the British Conquest for having 'saved us from the misery and the shame of the French Revolution.'[3]

During the codification period *rouge* (advanced liberal) lawyer Gonzalve Doutre correctly complained in 1864 that the 'advocates of French-Canadian nationality are unwilling to accept modern France, but rather the France of the time of the Conquest. If you ask them to accept the laws ... of present-day France, they shout blasphemy and infamy.'[4] One of the men Doutre undoubtedly had in mind was young attorney and would-be jurist, Joseph-Edouard Lefebvre de Bellefeuille, who published scathing but well-received articles claiming that the codifiers – particularly with regard to marriage – had become intellectual slaves to the modernizing Code Napoléon, an atheistic product made for 'a people emerging from anarchy – an expression and consequence of ... the Revolution.'[5] De Bellefeuille was ridiculously wide of the mark. True, the codifiers largely followed the 1804 work with regard to matters of form. But modernity was firmly opposed in the substantive law where values diverged.[6]

Let us illustrate this important point by example.[7] The disjunction between the modernity of 1804 and the traditionalism of 1866 is most apparent in the area of family law. For instance, illegitimate children could not inherit except by will and tutors (guardians) in Lower Canada were to be appointed only by the courts on the advice of a family council (as opposed, for instance, to nomination in a will: article 249). While the 1804 work, for reasons related to the medical health of the population, raised the minimum ages of marriage to eighteen for males and fifteen for females, the Lower Canadian codifiers retained the canon and customary law rule of fourteen and twelve years (article 115). By contrast to the Code Napoléon, there were no provisions for civil marriage (article 128, 129) or for adoption which in devout Roman Catholic circles was thought to encourage illegitimacy and discourage propagation. Article 185 declared marriages indissoluble except by death, whereas the French code had originally allowed divorce. The sanctity of the marital tie was such that the codifiers unhesitatingly rejected a Louisiana innovation permitting the husband or wife to remarry after the partner had been absent for ten years or more. The codifiers did permit separation from bed and board, but only for cause (for example, 'ill-usage'), not by mutual consent as in France (article 186). Finally, articles 187 and 188 enunciated what became the notorious double standard whereby the husband could obtain a separation for his wife's adultery, while the wife had no legal cause for complaint unless the husband had his concubine living in the common residence. This had its roots in the *Coutume* (there was no similar provision in the Napoleonic Code), the notion that women could and should be sexually purer than men and Pothier's aphorism that it 'does not behove the wife who is an inferior to inspect the conduct of her husband who is her superior.'[8]

Thus with regard to morality, the rights of the Roman Catholic clergy and above all family law,[9] the Lower Canadian civil law codified in 1866 was pre-Revolutionary and not Napoleonic in inspiration. This would be the case until the 1960s.

THE GARRISON MENTALITY

Most legacies of fear were of course generated by the garrison mentality: the enactment of security legislation more draconian than British law; its enforcement; sentencing of the 1790s rioters; the manipulation of justice in the *McLane*, Le Couteulx, and *Bédard* cases; much of the constitutional warfare in the Craig era; the emergence of strong anglicization sentiment; and the Baconian stances taken by the judiciary. Some of these legacies had their prime or sole impact during the period, but, as I will show, many had an impact in the future as well. I shall concentrate here on those. Where imprecise or speculative my conclusions can be looked upon as questions arising from the study, questions which will, hopefully, receive better answers as research proceeds.

McLane and Craig Remembered in French Canada

The fate of David McLane remained in the popular consciousness as long as witnesses to the execution lived. The dominant perceptions seem to have been that McLane had suffered martyrdom as a convenient substitute for a Canadien and that his treatment revealed the true visage of conquest.

Both Black and Cushing, to the end of their days, were reviled in francophone Lower Canada. In 1826 Cushing complained that for almost three decades 'Treachery and perjury have been floated upon a thousand babbling tongues against me.' The *patriote* Amury Girod remarked in 1835 that 'public opinion hounded him [Cushing] as a Judas.'[10] A generation later *Les Soirées canadiennes*, the monthly journal of the *nationaliste* Quebec Literary School, recalled that Black had 'never escaped the contempt inspired by his double dealing as an informer' and that he had 'died in profound misery, hardly helped by the cold pity of the public.'[11]

Nationalistes used the McLane incident to illustrate British misrule. Girod and Garneau, for example, published damning accounts of the trial with this purpose in 1835 and 1852–9 respectively, as did *Les Soirées canadiennes* in 1862.[12] In 1871 former *patriote* rebels Edmund B. O'Callaghan and Louis-Joseph Papineau pressed John R. Bartlett, custodian of the John Carter Brown Library in Providence, to publish an exposé of the gross manipulations of justice which had doomed McLane. As O'Callaghan, repeating Papineau's assessment, put it in a letter:

The government party in Canada knowing the [hard-line] policy of the Ministry in England, and being desirous to commend themselves by their zeal to the possessors of patronage, laid hands on McLean; connected him by perjury and inferences with the French propagandists, and brought about his condemnation and barbarous execution in order to recommend themselves to the favor of the British Ministry, who were laboring to hang somebody and couldn't, so McLean's head was served up to them on a trencher.

Several 'most respectable lawyers' in the province, O'Callaghan claimed, had 'represented to me that it was a case of pure judicial murder.' Bartlett ultimately obliged by having a report of the trial and execution published (1873) in the Providence *Evening Bulletin*. In this commentary Bartlett reprinted several damning assessments of the trial and concluded that McLane's ordeal had 'justly been styled a political necessity, his condemnation a tory triumph, his execution a judicial murder.'[13]

With regard to Craig, his regime embittered Canadien politicians and hence made it more difficult to avoid an ultimate resort to violence. As early as 1812 the Assembly censured his conduct and in 1814 attempted to impeach Chief Justice Sewell for, *inter alia*, advising Craig to indulge wholesale in arbitrary and unconstitutional acts directed against a free press and a free political system.[14] In 1814, too, an anonymous French language pamphlet described Craig as exceedingly vain and having governed like an arrogant and rash grand seigneur or court favourite.[15] Three year later the death of François Corbeil – allegedly as a result of his totally unjustified imprisonment in 1810 by Craig, Chief Justice Monk, and others – was the subject of acrimonious debate in the house. A careful examination of the newspapers would likely produce many more examples of grievances related to the Craig era, which soon became known to Canadiens as the 'reign of terror,' a term remaining current at least until the 1850s.

In the long run Craig entered into Canadien mythology. In 1832 a Montreal *patriote* meeting toasted the 'memory of those who were imprisoned in 1810 for the liberty of the country,'[16] while at one of the mass protests held on the eve of the first Rebellion, Louis-Joseph Papineau pointed to 'le tyran Craig' as one of the governors who symbolized the true meaning of British sovereignty.[17] From Garneau on, francophone historians often devoted considerable space to the governor and his advisory entourage as the first major threat to 'la survivance.' The *nationalistes* among them – for example, Garneau, Lionel Groulx, and Wallot – assumed or stated that the period reflects the tragic consequences of the Conquest for French Canada.[18] And it is interesting that the plaque on Jonathan Sewell's Quebec City residence laconically characterizes the chief justice as leader of the Chateau Clique and 'adviser to Governor Craig.'

The Civil Laws

It seems that the breakdown of the bourgeois alliance in the mid- 1790s – due in large part to the garrison mentality – guaranteed that the civil laws would not be commercialized so long as the Canadiens controlled the Assembly. Even had the alliance continued, of course, there would likely have been serious differences of opinion whenever the needs of commerce as perceived by the English merchants came into conflict with familial values imbedded in Canadien law – as had in fact occurred in 1787–88. A move to abolish customary dower, for example, would likely have split the alliance and even moderate adjustment might have proved impossible.[19] But there were many, more neutral areas where one can imagine change taking place: elimination of the *retrait lignager*, the *lods et ventes* and/or the *banalité*; increasing the negotiability of promissory notes/bills of exchange; extending the right to a jury trial in commercial conflicts where the defendant was not a merchant; enacting a pro-creditor bankruptcy law; lengthening prescriptions; even establishing land registry offices and so on.[20]

Instead, there was paralysis and constant conflict on this front. The evidence makes clear that mutual recrimination over the civil law was a major cause of the Rebellions of 1837–8. The *patriotes* of the 1830s, for example, complained bitterly of ignorant and/or anglifying judges.[21] This thesis is greatly strengthened if we accept, as Lord Durham and the historian Gérard Filteau did and the facts indicate, that the first uprising was precipitated by an aggressive English minority frustrated by the failure to abolish seigneurial tenure and establish land registry offices.[22]

The Security Laws

The judges of Lower Canada gave both the law of sedition and the law of treason very wide interpretations, going beyond British precedent. Virtually any criticism of government was deemed seditious or at least gave rise to a strong presumption of criminality. One case in 1795 suggests that the principle of Fox's Libel Act was not accepted as part of the law of the colony. No equivalent act was passed by the Lower Canada legislature during our period. Indeed, the principle of jury control in seditious libel cases was not enacted for Lower Canada/Quebec until 1874.[23] There are hints in the sources that until 1840 sedition was very widely interpreted by government officials and judges and that the Erskine-Mansfield debate on jury powers had at least the occasional echo in the colony.[24]

As for the various holdings of Osgoode in *McLane*, they had little impact in the United Kingdom or the empire outside the two Canadas. The decision became an authority for the logical proposition that alien travellers as well as residents owed local allegiance and, with many others, for the completely uncontroversial proposition that sending intelligence to the enemy amounted to adhering, even though it were intercepted. One author has suggested that the crown lawyers might have used *McLane* to effect in the trial of Sir Roger Casement, where a major question was whether adhering could take place outside the realm (Germany in Casement's instance).[25] But they overlooked the case, perhaps due to its obscurity as a colonial decision although it had been printed by Howell in his *State Trials*, 1819.[26]

Osgoode's most extreme doctrine – that conspiracy or attempting to foment rebellion in an overseas colony during war amounted to compassing – was largely irrelevant in the United Kingdom and the empire. The Treason Act of 1795, as amended by the Treason Felony Act of 1848[27] covered the situation of colonial conspiracies, if the accused were to be tried in the United Kingdom. And most colonial rebels, from the Irish 'croppie' rising in New South Wales in 1804 to the Boer War, were tried by military tribunals. In any case, the basic nineteenth-century texts such as the many editions of *Russell on Crime* and James Fitzjames Stephen's *Digest of the Criminal Law* (first published in 1877) make no mention of it.[28] In the twentieth century, *Russell on Crime*, C.S. Kenny's influential *Outlines of Criminal Law*, and the occasional journal article include brief, damning reference to *McLane* as an outstanding example of the dangers inherent in judge-made constructive treasons. In the Canadas during the Rebellion period of 1837–9, four judges (Sewell, Chief Justice Robinson, Archibald McLean, and Justice James Macaulay) extended the *McLane* doctrine to peacetime situations, with Macaulay explicitly citing Osgoode's judgment as authority.[29]

Thus two legacies of fear spawned by the garrison mentality were elastic, royalist interpretations of sedition and high treason.

Anglicization

The garrison mentality undermined tolerance for the Quebec Act policy of granting cultural autonomy to the Canadiens. By the end of the eighteenth century the local government had adopted anglicization as a policy. There were no longer any significant voices to argue the old French party's case that Canadien distinctiveness might provide a useful barrier against American designs on the colony. This development was not surprising as France after 1792 had supplanted the United States as the greater external danger in the minds of the English élite. Even the anti-American aristocratically inclined Osgoode,[30] who would normally have embraced Carleton's policy of ruling through the upper clergy and seigneurs as fervently as Mabane, did not do so. Osgoode found the ruling policy of cultural toleration utterly incomprehensible, given the dangers emanating from France and the manifest political weaknesses of the clergy and Canadien seigneurs.

In contrast to the period 1789–92, assimilation sentiment was sufficiently strong by 1801 to provoke a defensive reaction among Canadiens. They developed a nationalist ideology of survival, which had already emerged by the time the Gaols Act issue was fought out. In other words, it was the garrison mentality, rather than the needs of commerce in its battles with agriculture, which was the prime generator of government sponsored anglicization and its natural response of defensive cultural survival. The conflicts over the economic destiny of the colony added to the intensity of the debate over the culture future, but did not create that debate, as is often assumed.

In his Laurentian interpretation of the period, Donald Creighton expressed doubts on the strength of anglicization sentiment: '... despite the protestations of the French Canadians, then and since, it is questionable if many of these elements of their culture were seriously in question. Canada, and North America in general, have proved curiously tolerant of peoples of different races, languages and religions, so long as the peoples so distinguished have been ready to accept and uphold the somewhat materialistic variant of West-European culture.' This distinctly implies that the English élite wanted only economic assimilation, in order to better exploit the potentially grand commercial empire of the St Lawrence: elimination of seigneurial tenure and other anti-commercial laws, trimming the number of holy days, providing a more secular higher education, encouragement of 'scientific' farming, and so on. The Creighton thesis would be highly persuasive if the only thrust for anglicization were based on the pocketbook. But it was based also on the garrison mentality. Life and death appeared to be the stakes – at least the future stakes – not just money. Hence it is not surprising that many assimilators wanted total or near total anglicization. This was the position of Milnes and Sewell in 1801, Chief Justice Elmsley and Bishop Mountain in 1804, the *Quebec Mercury*, 1805–11, and Sewell, Ryland, and Craig in 1810–11. Other suggestive examples have been given in the text, particularly in relation to maintaining the French language, a feature of the Canadien way of life which does not, in itself, seem to have militated greatly, if at all, against commercial development.[31]

After 1811 internal security concerns eased, particularly those emanating from France, and the United States again became the prime external danger. A few among the English élite responded dramatically. Jonathan Sewell, for example, began to see that security against Lower Canada's southern neighbour depended on assuring the Canadiens that their laws, language, and religion (but not their political power) would be protected in the British Empire. Sewell, however, was exceptional in the English party. There were those who pressed vocally and insistently for economic assimilation (change in tenure, a bankruptcy statute, land registry offices, commercialization of the civil law, and so on.) But the idea of total anglicization, spawned in significant part by the garrison mentality, remained strong. This is hardly surprising, since thorough assimilation and security had been firmly linked in the minds of the English élite for over a decade prior to the War of 1812 and internal security fears, although eased and changed in nature after 1811, did not disappear.

Many supporters of the imperial government's abortive Union Bill of 1822 saw in it the means to eliminate most if not all of the Canadien way of life. The bill itself suggested as much, and Louis-Joseph Papineau complained bitterly to the Colonial Office that the proponents of union aimed at general assimilation – that is, at taking away the Canadiens' 'birth rights.' This object, he went on, was justified by the 'preposterous calumny against the Canadians of French origin, as to their supposed attachment to France.'[32] Papineau had some warrant for these statements. In 1822 John Richardson was dean of the colony's business community and principal leader, with Sewell, of the English party and pro-union activist in the Legislative Council. At a public meeting of unionists held in Montreal, Richardson delivered a lengthy speech in which he referred to amalgamation with Upper Canada as a way of outflanking the Canadien majority in the Assembly, notorious for their being 'anti-commercial in habits.' But he went much further. The fundamental issue, Richardson urged, was whether the Canadiens and their posterity would remain 'foreigners in a British land' or, preferably become British, which would be in everyone's interest.[33]

The precise extent to which this extreme strain of anglicization sentiment poisoned politics and helped to bring about eventual rebellion cannot now be determined. It does seem reasonable, though, to include it as a powerful, if elusive, legacy of fear. And so does the breakdown of any chance to liberalize the constitution, on which little further need be said.

The Constitution

By 1812 it had become clear that a French attack on the colony, while conceivable, was not likely. The garrison mentality in its characteristic appearance as defined in this book, then, virtually ceased to exist after that date. But it continued down to the Rebellions of 1837–8 and beyond in an attenuated form, as an exaggerated perception of French-Canadian disloyalty. This was manifest most often in the constitutional area. In 1822 John Richardson, for instance, accused the secret accounts committee of the Assembly of perhaps being 'a committee of public safety' meeting to replace the governor and of which there was 'no example in England, except in the time of Charles the first,' while in the intense political year of 1832 many among the English élite in Montreal worried about rebellion.[34] The precise impact of continuing security fears lies beyond the scope of this work, but they certainly contributed to the recurrent attempts by the English party to reduce the powers of the Assembly or increase those of the Legislative Council – in the areas of appropriation, election of the Assembly Speaker, and parliamentary privileges, for example – or to submerge the Lower House by union with Upper Canada. All these manoeuvres of course contributed to the strains under which the constitution finally broke down.

The Baconian Judiciary of Lower Canada

A clear test of the degree to which any judiciary is really independent of the executive occurs during state trials of persons dissenting from the mainstream political and constitutional consensus. By this test England of the late eighteenth and early nineteenth centuries had a mixed record. Most of the judges, of course, tended to sympathize with the administration of the day, in its periodic offensives against perceived treason and sedition. The contemporary development of constructive treason and Lord Mansfield's authoritarian interpretations of the law of seditious libel in the 1760s and in the Dean of St. Asaph's Case are well known. In the 1790s Lord Kenyon went further than Mansfield had on sedition and with less justification in view of Fox's Libel Act of 1792, which Kenyon continually distorted.[35] Kenyon in fact seems to have conceived of his role in terms reminiscent of Bacon: adjusting the law to suit the crown, hastening to do his duty by providing the king with a private extra-judicial opinion on Roman Catholic emancipation in Ireland, and on at least one occasion, sending the attorney general copies of opposition newspapers he thought seditious. But Kenyon's Bacon-like stance seems to have been exceptional in his day among the judges of England. There are a sufficient number of striking examples of judicial impartiality in the face of minatory government to indicate that independence was far from a mere shibboleth.

In Lower Canada, it seems to me, all judicial decisions and reasonings on security matters from 1794 to 1810 – the light sentences meted out to the rioters, the royalist interpretations of treason law by Monk and Osgoode in 1797, Sewell's lecture on sedition and his judgment in *Bédard* in 1810 for example – were highly favourable to the crown. As has been shown, the legal interpretations would not necessarily have found favour on the English Bench. Other contrasts with England stand out: the involvement of judges in electoral politics, the rendering of extra-judicial opinions, involvement in executive politics and in security prosecutions. The last two practices may have been, arguably, within the limits of proper judicial behaviour in the 1790s and early 1800s, but certainly were not after the parliamentary debate on Ellenborough's appointment to the cabinet in 1806. Finally, leading judges themselves, in Lower Canada, conceived of their role as Baconian. Osgoode's letter of self-praise to the Colonial Office following McLane's execution has already been cited. In 1810 Sewell sent Craig a copy of an opinion on the reorganization of the courts, which he had prepared five years before. One of the many advantages to the Crown, as Sewell saw it, was that the justices of the new, single King's Bench ('being free from the bias of Local prejudices') would by means of their holding assizes on circuit in every judicial district, 'become twice in every year the best Informants to His Majesty's Representative of the True State of his Whole Province [and] of the dispositions of his people[,] their inclinations, intentions and motives.'[36] The judges, in other words, would act as political spies.

Baconianism as a dominant judicial attitude in Quebec/Lower Canada seems to have emerged only during the wars against revolutionary and Napoleonic France. The evidence suggests that it was only in 1796 and after that the practice developed of having the judges help prepare the prosecution in security cases. There was also a change in the nature of extra-judicial opinions. In the earlier period such advice certainly occurred. But with the exception of Mabane's counselling the governor on legal strategy prior to *Haldimand* v. *Cochrane* – a complex case in 1784 regarding Haldimand's personal liability for public debts[37] – these opinions do not appear to have been given where the matters in issue were likely to arise in litigation. Indeed, extra-judicial advice in such situations was clearly regarded as improper by Lord Dorchester in 1788.[38] By contrast, Monk gave Craig an opinion in 1810 on the law governing the erection of Roman Catholic parishes, at a time when a court case raising questions similar to those in *Bertrand* v *Lavergne* seemed quite possible.[39] In the same year Sewell advised the governor on the legal implications of the royal supremacy and the weaknesses in the Sulpicians' title to their landed estates.[40]

It is true that in the Old Province of Quebec the French party judges often acted in an ultra-loyal manner. But even a superficial review of the behaviour of the chief justices shows that the Baconian urge was far from uniform in the early years. William Hey (1766–76) publicly denied that the crown alone could legislate for Quebec as a conquered/ceded colony, which helped frustrate the imperial government's plans to sort out Quebec's legal tangle by prerogative legislation and helped undermine the colonial government's attempts in court to collect import duties which had been imposed in New France.[41] Hey also opposed Carleton's policy of restoring the Canadien civil law in general, and after the passage of the Quebec Act contended for the reintroduction of English commercial law and civil jury trials.[42] Chief Justice Smith persisted in his *Gray* v. *Grant* interpretation of the Quebec Act despite disapproval from Lord Dorchester and the British Law Officers.[43]

Chief Justice Peter Livius provides a particularly instructive example of willingness to put judicial conviction before the political needs or desires of the executive, even in cases where internal security was directly in issue. In the late summer and autumn of 1777, Livius protested against Lieutenant-Governor Hector Cramahé's internment of a married couple for supposedly babbling sedition.[44] Some years later the chief justice again took up the subject. In a note prepared for the Colonial Office he requested that Governor Haldimand be brought to task for his military internments. Otherwise, when he, Livius, returned to Quebec (he never did) there would be serious conflict between the military and civil powers. As chief justice he would have to rule that these were clear 'cases of illegal imprisonment,' the detentions having been made 'without the warrant of any civil Magistrate.'[45] In other words, Livius was prepared to challenge from the Bench the executive's main internal security policy, which Haldimand thought vital, and do so in wartime, when it was known that French and American propagandists had been and perhaps still were at work in the colony.

There was no equivalent of Livius in Lower Canada during the period under review.

Was Baconianism Inevitable?

There can be no doubt that colonial judges in Lower Canada and throughout the empire were predisposed to take an authoritarian approach in
security cases. In part this attitude arose out of London's ultimate control
of their career prospects. The overwhelming majority of them, moreover,
emotionally and intellectually identified with the interests of the mother
country, including its need to keep its dependencies dependent. Smith,
Osgoode, Elmsley, Sewell, Monk, and Ogden are examples. This imperialism provides one obvious way to explain the predisposition, especially
when certain common assumptions are examined.

Imperialism, then, worked to predispose colonial judges to Baconianism, but it was not inevitable. It required historical experience – in our
case the development of a garrison mentality – to make Baconianism the
clearly dominant approach. Judges, after all, took oaths to administer
justice impartially and were well aware of the mother country's ideal of
independence from the executive. And there were a great many situations
in which the colonial Bench behaved in a Cokean fashion. Examples may
be drawn from Old Quebec; Ireland (here considered a colony),[46] 1798–99;
India, 1830,[47] and Upper Canada, 1805–38.[48]

With some few exceptions but hardly any among English Judges,
Baconianism characterized the Lower Canada Bench down to at least
1839. The King's Bench (Quebec) was even prepared in one security case
in 1814 to have the imperial government, taking into account its political
interests, dictate interpretation of the law to be followed in Lower Canada.[49] In 1832 the same court decided that the Legislative Council had
the power to imprison newspaper editors who wrote unfavourably of it,
despite the English party's long-standing refusal to admit the Assembly
had such a privilege and despite the fact that Chief Justice Sewell had
obtained an opinion from the British law officers which pointed to the
very opposite conclusion.[50] The action of the Legislative Council (acting
as a court presided over by Sewell), followed by the decision, left several
political legacies. The Upper House became the main target of the
patriotes. Resolutions calling for its election passed the Assembly in the
session of 1832–33, putting the majority on a collision course with the
Whig government in London.[51] Many *patriotes* saw the incident as absolute proof of the political partiality prevailing on the Bench, a truly major
grievance in the 1830's.[52] Finally, the incident for the first time provoked
serious talk among *patriotes* about the need for political independence
and even full-scale rebellion.[53]

During the Rebellion period the Baconian legacy of the past generation or so was dramatically illustrated by the Montreal King's Bench. In November 1838 all the judges but one, plus Chief Justice James Stuart, rendered an unpersuasive extra-judicial opinion condemning two Quebec Canadien colleagues who had held void the appointed Special Council's suspension of habeas corpus.[54] Only Stuart – and he belatedly – realized the gross breach of British constitutional norms such advice entailed.[55] A few months later the court upheld the legality of the general court martial established to try accused rebels from the second Rebellion. It went further and gave the Special Council *carte blanche* by holding, without warrant, that the *vires* of ordinances could not be tested in the courts but only by Parliament which had enacted the Council's constitutional act.

FINAL REFLECTIONS

The tendencies during perceived political crises to drastically curtail civil liberties, by legislation going beyond the British model and by adopting Baconian positions from the Bench, have been recurrent ones in Canadian history down to recent times[56] and may still have potency. Assessing that potency and accounting for these aspects of Canadians' well-known deference to governmental authority must await further research. I suspect that the long-lived hostile reaction of the francophone élite in Quebec to the French Revolution and the garrison mentality of the English minority will play prominent roles in the explanation.

Looking back on the operation of law during the period of study, two general points seem to emerge. The first is that the law did afford some protection to Canadien and other dissidents. After all, only two people died as a result of governmental repression: McLane and Corbeil. The crown had to proceed through the courts or by means of legislatively authorized internment. Using the courts involved using juries, which meant some accused were acquitted and prosecutions for seditious libel were virtually unknown. The existence of an Assembly, which had to renew suspension of habeas corpus annually, undoubtedly worked to limit internments, except during Monk's witch-hunt of 1794. When the next major use of internment occurred in 1810–11, the Assembly responded by protecting members and then by refusing to renew. And the existence of the Assembly ensured that major anglicizing initiatives by way of local legislation failed. Of course, much protection derived from the long-standing tendency of Canadiens to excuse political crime (for example, unmanipulated juries could not be counted on to convict for seditious libel) and from the habitants' propensity to riot (such as the lenient sentences meted out to rioters in the 1790s). The second point is that when the government was determined to make examples, the law was easily manipulated to achieve the desired result, as in the cases of McLane, Le Couteulx, and Bédard. The ease with which that was done should give pause, for it teaches, I think, that Bench, Bar, academics, journalists, and concerned citizens should be particularly vigilant that the administration of justice operate fairly during perceived security crises, the drastic regulations issued during the October Crisis of 1970 being a recent reminder. Otherwise, there will be further legacies of fear degrading to Themis.

Abbreviations

AAQ	Archives de l'archevêché de Québec, Quebec City
AHAR	American Historial Society, *Annual Report*
AHR	*American Historical Review*
ANQ	Archives nationales du Québec, Quebec City
AO	Archives of Ontario
BRH	*Bulletion des recherches historiques*
CHAR	Canadian Historical Association, *Annual Report*
CHR	*Canadian Historial Review*
CO	Colonial Office, Great Britain
Const. Docs.	*Documents Relating to the Constitutional History of Canada: 1759–1791*, ed. Adam Shortt and A.G. Doughty, 2nd ed. (Ottawa: King's Printer 1918); *1791–1818*, ed. A.G. Doughty and D.A. McArthur (1915); *1819–1828*, ed. A.G. Doughty and Norah Story (1935)
DCB	*Dictionary of Canadian Biography*
FO	Foreign Office (Great Britain)
JHALC	*Journals of the House of Assembly of Lower Canada*
LOC	Library of Congress, Washington, DC
LQR	*Law Quarterly Review*
NAC	National Archives of Canada, Ottawa
Parl. Deb.	*Cobbett's Parliamentary Debates* (London: T.C. Hansard et al. 1804–1818), 22 vols

Parl. Hist.	*The Parliamentary History of England from the Earliest Period to the Year 1803* (London: T.C. Hansard et al. 1806–1820), 36 vols.
PRO	Public Record Office, London
PTRSC	Royal Society of Canada, *Proceedings and Transactions*
QDA	Quebec Diocesan Archives
RANQ	Archives nationales du Québec, *Rapport*
RHAF	*Revue d'histoire de l'Amérique française*
RNAC	National Archives of Canada, *Report*
SLC	Statutes of Lower Canada
SOQ	Statutes of the Old Province of Quebec, 1775–1791
SUC	Statutes of Upper Canada

Notes

AUTHOR'S NOTE

1 See particularly Briggs, 'The Language of "Class" in Early Nineteenth Century England'

2 As in England there were vertical economic divisions into, e.g., 'Landed Interest,' supposedly comprising all involved in agriculture, and 'Commercial Interest.' One can also find, before 1789, the occasional use by a Canadien of the concept of three estates deriving from pre-revolutionary France.

3 Craig to Liverpool, 1 May 1810, Q series, vol. 112

4 The principal sources used for calculating population are Dorchester to Sydney, 8 Nov. 1788, *Const. Docs., 1759–1791*, 958; Plessis, 'Les dénombrements de Québec'; Gray, *Letters from Canada*, 55–6, 146, 165; Craig to Liverpool, 1 May 1810, *Const. Docs., 1791–1818*, 387–8; census of 1789–90, printed in vol. 4 of the *Census of Canada, 1871* (Ottawa: Queen's Printer 1876); Ouellet, *Economic and Social History*, 659; Dechêne, 'La croissance de Montréal au XVIIIe siècle'; Hare, 'La population de la ville de Québec, 1795–1805.'

5 Greer, *Peasant, Lord, and Merchant*, 196. In 1791, L'Assomption, north-east of Montreal in the County of Leinster, had eighty-two heads of household, of whom seventeen were artisans, six were professionals and fifteen were merchants: St Georges, 'Pratiques de la communauté marchande du bourg de l'Assomption,' 325.

6 Greenwood, 'Development of a Garrison Mentality,' 287–8; Roy, *Histoire*

de la seigneurie de Lauzon, 342–4; Greer, 'Pattern of Literacy in Quebec,'
299

7 Estimates are based on Colonel John Nairne to James Kerr, 15 Aug. 1797,
Nairne Papers, vol. 3; the *Quebec Gazette*, 1791–5; La Rochefoucauld-Liancourt, *Voyage*, II: 202, 208–9; Ouellet, *Economic and Social History*, 663–5.

INTRODUCTION

1 *R* v. *Maclane* [*sic*] (1797) 26 St. Tr. 721, at 828
2 Creighton, *The Empire*, 153, 162
3 *Economic and Social History*, 172–4, ch. 7; Ouellet, *Lower Canada*, 47–51, 77–93
4 Wallot, 'La crise sous Craig'; Wallot 'La pensée révolutionnaire et réformiste dans le Bas-Canada'
5 Wallot, 'La crise sous Craig,' 163, n41

1 JUSTICE AND ORDER

1 Neatby, *Administration of Justice*, 144–5; Neatby, *Quebec: The Revolutionary
Age*, 217
2 In 1787 the judges with their occupational backgrounds were: Quebec District, Dr Adam Mabane, army surgeon; Thomas Dunn, merchant; Pierre-
Meru Panet, government official; Montreal District, Edward Southouse,
government official; John Fraser, army officer; René-Ovide Hertel de Rouville, government official. As in the case of all judges in the years
1789–1811, these men and the chief justice held their offices at pleasure.
3 14 Geo. III, c. 83. This section is based principally on the following sources:
Monk, *State of Present Form of Government*, Appendices 14–16 (evidence
from the 1787 inquiry into the courts); *Quebec Herald*, 23 Feb. 1789–3 Mar.
1791, particularly the many letters of 'Junius'; Neatby, *Administration of
Justice, passim.*; Upton, *Loyal Whig*, 171–92; Kolish, 'Impact of the Change in
Legal Metropolis.'
4 Robertson, *Diary of Mrs John Graves Simcoe*, 30 Nov. 1791, 56
5 Appeals could be taken from the Common Pleas Courts where the amount
in issue exceeded £10 or future rights (e.g., yearly seigneurial rents) were in
issue. In those cases and where the amount exceeded £500 further appeal
lay to the Plantations Committee of the Privy Council in London. Although
the only professionally trained judge in the colony, the chief justice was
restricted to presiding over appeals; he did not sit on either Court of Common Pleas.
6 See Neatby, *Administration of Justice*, 15–17, 155–60; Jean-Gabriel Castel, *The*

Civil Law System of the Province of Quebec (Toronto: Butterworths 1962), 15–20.

7 SOQ 1777, c. 2, ss. 1, 7, 22; SOQ 1785, c.2, s. 9
8 On this latter subject, see Kolish, 'Imprisonment for Debt,' 604–9.
9 Neatby, *Quebec: The Revolutionary Age*, 217. For a slightly different example (or a slightly different version of the same one), see *Quebec Herald*, 20 Apr. 1789 (letter of 'Junius').
10 Evidence of William Dummer Powell (corroborated by several witnesses to the inquiry of 1787); Neatby, *Administration of Justice*, 121
11 My understanding of the law relating to seigneurial tenure is based on the works of de Ferrière, Pothier, Cugnet, Munro, Harris. The centrality of preserving the link between families and their lands was stressed by de Ferrière (II: 561).
12 Harris, *Seigneurial System*, 69–70, 213
13 These two laws, dated 6 July 1711, are printed in Munro, *Documents relating to Seigniorial Tenure*, 91–4.
14 Cession from François de Beauharnois to Jean-Baptiste Joubert, 6 July 1757, *JHALC*, 1832, App. N.n. This deed also required two days private corvée.
15 On rents and the intendant's role in controlling them, see Harris, *Seigneurial System*, 64–9; Louise Dechêne, 'L'évolution du régime seigneurial au Canada: le cas de Montréal au XVIIᵉ et XVIIIᵉ siècles,' *Recherches Sociographiques* 12 (1971), 151.
16 Solicitor General Jonathan Sewell to Dorchester, 27 Feb. 1794, Q series, vol. 67; Attorney General James Monk to Dundas, 6 June 1794, CO42; Osgoode to Burland, 27 Oct. 1795, CO42, vol. 22
17 That the early purchases were usually made on this understanding is suggested by an advertisement for the sale of the Neuville seigneury which appeared in the *Quebec Gazette* on 14 Feb. 1765. It pointed out that many of the *censitaires* had no concession deeds and could be forced to take them, all to the profit of the purchaser: 'the future Lord, in giving such Deeds of Grant, may undoubtedly substitute reasonable Rents, instead of the too moderate Rents which those Lands pay at present' as quoted in Françoise Noël's thesis, 'Gabriel Christie's Seigneuries,' 109.
18 See, for example, *Journals of the Legislative Assembly of the Province of Canada*, 1843, Appendix to vol. 3, no. F; Ouellet, *Economic and Social History*, 362; La Rochefoucauld-Liancourt, *Voyage*, 206.
19 For evidence there was such a minority, see Baillargeon, 'À propos de l'abolition du régime seigneurial,' 379–81. See also MG8, F80, NAC (seigneury of St Ours).
20 Greer, *Peasant, Lord, and Merchant*, 137. A portion of some of these

exactions, of course, represented payment for services rendered. Just what proportion of the milling charge can be attributed to the seigneurs' monopoly position and that to giving fair value probably cannot now be determined. Similar but even more complex problems arise with regard to the tithe, pew rentals, and church building assessments.

21 Weld, *Travels*, I: 400–1

22 Ouellet, *Economic and Social History*, 157–63

23 *Montreal Gazette*, 22 Aug. 1793 (notice dated 9 July 1793). According to Solicitor General Sewell, writing to Dorchester, *c.* 24 Feb. 1794 (Q series, vol. 67: 86), Cuthbert had recently succeeded in a suit taken 'for the purpose of reuniting the land of his Tenant to his Domaine for default of Cultivation': Galarneau, *L'opinion canadienne*, 234–5.

24 – Mar. 1793, Q series, vol. 67: 79–81

25 Sewell to Dorchester, *c.* 24 Feb. 1794, ibid., 82–7

26 See Kolish, 'Some Aspects of Civil Litigation in Lower Canada,' 364. In 1785 Simon Sanguinet took fifty-four of his *censitaires* to court (Montreal) for non-settlement.

27 See, in general, Trudel, 'La servitude de l'Église.'

28 Briand to a French Bishop, 10 Mar. 1775, printed in John S. Moir, ed., *Church and State in Canada 1627–1867* (Toronto: McClelland & Stewart 1967), 104

29 Haldimand to Briand, 13 June 1780, quoted in Trudel, 'La servitude de l'Église' 43

30 This latter practice became statutory duty in 1803 when priests and ministers were required to read such official instruments as the governor saw fit, outside the church after divine service: SLC 1803 (2nd sess.), c. 4, s. 1. The curés and ministers were also to receive copies of all future acts and preserve them in an archive (s. 2).

31 Hay, 'Meanings of the Criminal Law in Quebec,' 192–6

32 *Ex parte Isaac Rousse* (1828) *Stuart's Reports* 321 (per Sewell, CJLC)

33 (Eng.) 25 Ed. III, st. 5, c. 2. The quotation in the text is taken from Coke's translation from the law French in his *Third Part of the Institutes of the Laws of England*, 1–2.

34 36 Geo. III (1795), c. 7

35 *The King* v *David MacLane* [sic] (1797) 26 St. Tr. 721; CHARGE OF CHIEF JUSTICE *[John Beverley]* ROBINSON, *to the Grand Jury of the Home District; April, 1833* (York, UC: Robert Stanton 1833); Robinson's charge to same in Mar. 1838 (*Toronto Patriot*, 13 Mar. 1838); *Report of the State Trials Before a General Court Martial held at Montreal in 1838–9*, 2 vols. (Montreal: Armour & Ramsay 1839)

36 SOQ 1777, c. 5; SOQ 1787, c. 6; SLC 1794, c. 6; 'Court of Quarter Sessions, 1764–1784,' MG8, C9, NAC; Borthwick, *History of the Montreal Prison*, 238–55
37 *R. v. Poiré*, reported in the *Quebec Gazette*, 2 Apr. 1801
38 7 & 8 Wm. III, c. 8
39 Until the 1830s potential jurors in the Quebec and Montreal districts were summoned almost exclusively from among residents of the cities and suburbs. This practice had made it very difficult in the 1780s to find adequate numbers of male persons who met the common law qualification of holding real estate under a freehold tenure, even though in the Quebec/Lower Canada context that included lands held upon the seigneurial regime. The problem was addressed by an 1787 ordinance (c.1) which qualified householders who paid at least £15 annual rent, a qualification only slightly higher than that which entitled a person to vote.
40 SOQ 1787, c. 1
41 See particularly Jonathan Sewell to Ward Chipman, 16 Apr. 1791, Chipman Papers, vol. 3, (copies); Lower Canadian Law Officers to Cochran, 4 Apr. 1818, S series, vol. 621 Fecteau, *Un nouvel ordre des choses*, 110–11.
42 During the first two decades of Lower Canada, in the District of Quebec, the rate of conviction for persons tried on capital charges was approximately 28 per cent overall and under 25 per cent for property crimes. By way of comparison the conviction rate for non-capital crimes, in the same district and period, was just over 60 per cent. These figures are based on material found in 'Records of Offences, 1765–1827,' vol. 11; Pardons, vols 1, 2; Records of the King's Bench, ANQ; 'Prison returns'; and the reports of assizes appearing in the *Quebec Gazette*, *Montreal Gazette*, the *Times-Du Cours du Tems*, the *British American Register*, *Quebec Mercury*, *Le Canadien*, *Le Courier de Québec*, and *Le Vraie-Canadien*.
43 Hay, 'Meanings of the Criminal Law,' 91; Lambert, *Travels*, I: 179
44 See, for example, de Gaspé, *Mémoires*, 252.
45 Smith's charge to the grand jury (Quebec), opening the November 1792 assizes: *Montreal Gazette*, 15 Nov. 1792; Petitions of Jean-Baptiste Caron, 7 Nov. 1792 and 20 June 1795; Smith to Alured Clarke, 8 Nov. 1792; draft pardons, n.d. and 23 June 1795, the whole contained in Pardons, vol. 1; *Quebec Gazette*, 17 May 1792; Osgoode to ——, Niagara, 25 Sept. 1793, Osgoode Collection, AO; material on convict Ephraim Whitesides in Pardons, vol. 2, 567–91; de Gaspé, *Mémoires*, 249–52; DCB, vol. 7, 785.
46 Francis Maseres, 'A Draught of an Intended Report ... Concerning the State of the Laws' (*c.* 27 Feb. 1769), in Kennedy and Lanctot, eds., *Reports on the Laws of Quebec*, 40; Sir Guy Carleton and William Hey, 'Report upon the Laws and Courts of Judicature in the Province of Quebec,' 15 Sept. 1769,

ibid., 68–9, 72; Solicitor General Alexander Wedderburn's report in the laws of Quebec, 6 Dec. 1772, *Const. Docs., 1759–1791*, 431; William Knox, *The Justice and Policy of the Late Act of Parliament for Making More Effectual Provision for the Government of the Province of Quebec* (London: J. Wilkie 1774), 62–5; Haldimand to North, 6 Nov. 1783, *Const. Docs., 1759–1791*, 738. See also Ward Chipman (Solicitor General of New Brunswick) to Jonathan Sewell Jr, 2 May 1790, Sewell Papers, vol. 3.

47 In 1838–9 during the political-legal crisis over the suspension of habeas corpus differing opinions were expressed on that question: see the judgments of Justices Bédard and Panet (1838) in Q series, vol. 245; *Ex parte John Teed*, reported in the *Quebec Mercury* (16 Feb. 1839); *Judicial Decisions on the Writ of Habeas Corpus*. There was, however, a high degree of consensus that the common law right to habeas corpus had been in force from the beginning of civil government.

48 The common law right to the writ was in force in the older colonies, although the act of Charles II was not: A.H. Carpenter, 'Habeas Corpus in the Colonies,' *AHR* 8 (1902–3), 18.

49 17 Geo. III (1777), c. 9

50 The lengths of imprisonment were Mesplet, three years, three months; Du Calvet, two years, seven months; Hay, slightly more than three years.

51 Memorial of Mary Hay to the Secretary of State, 20 Feb. 1782, Haldimand Collection, vol. B205; deposition of Charles Hay, 10 Feb. 1785, ibid.; Haldimand to Germain, 25 Oct. 1780, *Const. Docs., 1759–1791*, 721–2

52 Quoted in W.R. Riddell, 'Pierre du Calvet: A Huguenot Refugee in Early Montreal: His Treason and Fate,' *Ontario History* 22 (1925), 245. The judges obviously characterized all habeas corpus proceedings as having to do with 'Civil Rights,' rather than being divisible into civil law and criminal law matters.

53 SOQ 1784, c. 2. For a useful analysis of the English act in its historical perspective, see Sharpe, *Habeas Corpus*, 1–20.

54 Charles II's act had no such provision. The Bill of Rights is I Wm. & Mary (1689), sess. 2, c. 2. For the right of an accused misdemeanant to be bailed (either by virtue of the common law or the 1679 statute or both), see Blackstone, *Commentaries*, IV: 297; *R. v. Judd* (1788) 2 T.R., 255.

55 See on this Sharpe, *Law of Habeas Corpus*, 133–40.

56 *R. v. Turlington* (1761) 2 Burr. 1115; *Sommersett's* case (1772) 20 St. Tr. 1

57 *Bastille septentrionale* (1791 pamphlet)

58 For the Restoration judiciary in politics, see two articles by Alfred F. Havighurst: 'The Judiciary and Politics in the Reign of Charles II' and 'James II and the Twelve Men in Scarlet.'

59 Blackstone, *Commentaries*, I: 267–9; De Lolme, *Constitution of England*, 316–7; Paley, *Moral and Political Philosophy*, II: 232–3; *Harcourt v. Fox* (1692/93) 1 Show KB, 535; *Dean of St. Asaph's* case (1783–4) 21 St. Tr., 1040

60 Osgoode to Milnes, 6 May 1800, Osgoode Letters, 161–2; Milnes to Portland, 8 July 1800, CO42, vol. 114; *DCB*, vol. 5, 230

61 *DCB*, vol. 4, 484; *Acts of the Privy Council of England, Colonial Series: Volume 5, 1766–1783*, (Hereford: 1912), 463–71 (Mar. 1779). According to the report the charges against Livius did not include anything done 'in his Judicial Character and Capacity.'

62 Three Lower Canadian judges were suspended in late 1838 for decisions denying the Special Council power to suspend habeas corpus but were ultimately restored to office.

63 About Osgoode it may also be noted that with regard at least to the mother country he was aware of the *ideal* of impartially administered justice during a political crisis. In early 1795 he wrote of Pitt's offensive against the English 'Jacobins' as follows: 'This is an eventful period and I am fearful that something irregular must take place against Horne [Tooke] & his Associates and that Justice may be warped by Indignation': to William Dummer Powell, Quebec, 15 Jan. 1795, Sandham Ms. 273, Department of Rare Books and Special Collections, McGill University.

64 *R. v. Robin alias Robert* (1800), La Société historique de Montréal, *Mémoires et documents relatifs à l'histoire du Canada* (Montreal: La Société 1859), 56–63; Robin W. Winks, *The Blacks in Canada: A History* (New Haven: Yale University Press 1971), 100–2

65 Osgoode to ———, n.d. (1798), CO42, vol. 22

66 For the English judiciary in the eighteenth century see the works of Campbell, Foss, Shetreet, Turberville, and Underhill cited in the Select Bibliography.

67 When making comparisons it is essential to realize that the lord chancellor, an immensely important politician, had no common law jurisdiction and only a specialized civil law or equity jurisdiction. Judges of the Lower Canadian King's Bench (and of the King's Bench in Westminster) had full jurisdiction to hear all manner of criminal and civil matters. And unlike the situation in England where juries prevailed, in Lower Canada they were the interpreters of fact in most civil cases.

68 There was no analogous practice in Lower Canada, probably because the Legislative Council was not a court.

69 Report of the Committee appointed to inquire into Judges running for election, 8 May 1809, *JHALC*, 1809, Appendix 23

70 David Ross to Arthur Davidson, 23 July 1801, Arthur Davidson Letters

71 Newcastle to Hardwicke, 23 Aug. 1757, Philip C. Yorke, *The Life and Corre-spondence of Philip C. Yorke, Earl of Hardwicke, Lord High Chancellor of Great Britain*, 3 vols. (Cambridge: Cambridge University Press 1913), III: 31; *Parl. Hist.*, vol. 18 (7 Feb. 1775); *Commentaries*, I: 269; Hay, 'Contempt by Scandalizing the Court,' *passim*, particularly 456

72 Campbell, *Lives of the Chief Justices*, IV: 198–201; *Annual Register* for 1806, 27–33; *Parl. Deb.*, vol. 6 (3 Mar. 1806); *Romilly Memoires*, II: entry for 1 Mar. 1806

73 Monk to Nepean, 8 May 1793, Q series, vol. 66; 'Report of a Conversation between Attorney-General Sewell and Monseigneur Plessis,' 26 Apr. 1805, *Const. Docs., 1791–1818*, 306; Henry Allcock CJLC to Shee, 5 Dec. 1806, Q series, vol. 101; Osgoode to Milnes, 6 May 1800, Osgoode Letters, 162

74 *Le Canadien*, 9 Mar. 1808 (trans.)

75 Monk to Nepean, 8 May 1793, Q series, vol. 66

76 Osgoode to Dorchester, 12 May 1795, Osgoode Letters, 92; same to Simcoe, 23 May 1795, ibid., 93–5; same to Burland, 27 Oct. 1795, CO42, vol. 22; same to ——, n.d. (1796), ibid. Dorchester himself retaliated when leaving the colony for the final time in July 1796, by warning Prescott to watch out that he 'does not fall into the C.J.'s hands': ibid.

77 Milnes to Portland, 26 Mar. 1801, Q series, vol. 86; John Hale to Lord Amherst, 4 June 1801, Hale Family Papers

78 Prescott to Portland, 18 Mar. 1797, Prescott Papers, vol. 3

79 Osgoode to ——, n.d. (1798), CO42, vol. 22. Prescott praised Osgoode 'for his readiness on all occasions to give the whole weight of his Abilities and knowledge towards enabling me to carry on His Majesty's Government in this Province.'

80 John Elmsley (1802–5) and Henry Allcock (1805–8) aspired to be the principal advisers of the governors but personality traits greatly limited their influence. See *DCB*, vol. 5, 17, 303. Powerful as they were, the lord chancellors could never aspire to the role of first or prime minister, the king's most influential adviser. Sitting in the Lords and being professional lawyers, they were excluded from the two main routes to the pinnacle: as achieved by the Pitts through the oratorical/managerial skills vital to controlling the all-important Commons (for supply), or that achieved by the Duke of Newcastle in George II's reign through patronage and the deference of an hierarchical society. The lord chancellors often acted as the king's special representative in the cabinet, reporting to him on the stances taken by the prime minister and others.

81 See E.C.S. Wade, 'Consultation of the Judiciary by the Executive,' *LQR* 46 (1930), 169; Havighurst, 'James II and the Twelve Men in Scarlet,' 530, 533, 538.

82 State Papers Domestic 34, vol. 9, item 61, PRO; *Proceedings against William Gregg* (1708) 14 St. Tr. 1371; unsigned document entitled 'In this vacation vist Decem. 1797' in Solicitor General (1756–62)/Attorney General (1762–3, 1765–6) Charles Yorke's 'papers': 'Legal Precedents 1602–1752,' found in the British Library. This contemporary record of the questions and answers is probably the only one known today, although four others circulated in the eighteenth and early nineteenth centuries. See *Hensey's* case (1758), 19 St. Tr. 341; *Joyce's* case (1946) AC 347 at 367, 375. Brief references to authorities were given in two of the verbal answers to the eight questions posed. More typical was the answer to the sixth question: 'Whether the writing and sending Intelligence to the Enemy be not an Overt Act of Compassing and Imagining the Death of the Queen and also of adhering to her Majestie's Enemies tho such Intelligence be Intercepted before it comes to the Enemy.

R. – Agreed by all that it is.'

I thank my wife Beverley for making the final, very difficult location of this document among Yorke's uncalendared and unorganized papers.

83 Fort. 389 (case reports, 1748). Fortesque had served as solicitor general and would later be appointed to the Court of Common Pleas.

84 3 Mar. 1760, 2 Eden (case reports) 371–3

85 Francis Hargrave, *Coke upon Littleton*, 18th ed. corrected, 2 vols. (London: J. & W.T. Clarke, R. Pheney & S. Brooke 1823), I: 100a, n5 (emphasis in original)

86 For example, J.H. Thomas, ed., *A Systematic Arrangement of Lord Coke's First Institute of the Laws of England*, 3 vols. (London: Henry Butterworth 1818), I: 71, n11; *Reference Case Reference* (1910) 43 SCR 536 at 550–1; (1912) AC 571 at 586

87 Milnes to Hobart, 1 July 1803 (with enclosed opinions), Q series, vol. 92

2 THE STRUGGLE FOR CONSTITUTIONAL REFORM

1 *DCB*, vol. 7, 522

2 An elected Assembly, of course, might prove to be a second political master to them. Scepticism is apparent from the correspondence of, among others, Attorney General Monk, Hugh Finlay, Provincial Secretary George Pownall, and Chief Justice Smith. One of the few (if not the only) officials to sign the petition was merchant-Councillor William Grant, the deputy receiver general.

3 Judge Fraser to Haldimand, 9 Jan. 1785, Haldimand Collection, vol. B205

4 The petition, with the names of English subscribers, is printed in *Const.*

Docs., 1759–1791, 742–52. The names of Canadien subscribers were published by *Le Canadien*, 19 Aug. 1809.

5 Other important sources include the reformers' 'Plan for a House of Assembly,' *Const. Docs., 1759–1791*, 753–4, and *The Paper Read at the Bar of the House of Commons by Mr. Lymburner*, hereafter Lymburner's Paper.

6 While the wording might suggest that the maintenance of other non-commercial portions of the civil law (e.g., with regard to the family) was left an open question, later documents indicate that this was not the intention.

7 Tousignant, 'La Genèse,' 316–24

8 Finlay to Nepean, 10 Jan. 1785 (enclosing the circular letter), CO42, vol. 17; *Const. Docs., 1759–1791*, 758–62, 765–6

9 Mabane to Haldimand, 23 Oct. 1788, Haldimand Collection, vol. B77; Dorchester to Sydney, 8 Nov. 1788, *Const. Docs., 1759–1791*, 958; Abbé H.-F. Gravé (Superior of the Quebec Seminary) to Hody, 25 Oct. 1791, Honorius Provost, ed., *Le séminaire de Québec: documents et biographies* (Québec: Archives du Séminaire de Québec 1965), 288; Charles Stevenson (army officer) to Simcoe, n.d. [1795], Simcoe Papers, Series 3, Book 3 (p. 137). Stevenson, who was in the colony during the general election of 1792, learned from a number of priests that in their view 'the mass of the people felt they had acquired a [new political] power they were likely to abuse.' For an early exception see Tousignant, 'La Genèse,' 310–11

10 Lymburner's mission in London can be studied through his letters to the Quebec English Committee and related documents found in the Allsopp Papers, vol. 1 (150–77); the sketch he prepared and sent to Pitt (24 Jan. 1788), is in Chatham Papers, MG3, A2, vol. 10, 67–73, NAC; a pamphlet he had published in London in 1788, entitled *A Review of the Government and Grievances of the Province of Quebec*; *Parl. Hist.*, vol. 27, 18 May 1788; *Grievances of the Province of Quebe*; *Parl. Hist.*, vol. 49; Lymburner's Paper.

11 28 Feb. 1785, Collection Baby, vol. 9, (trans.)

12 Petition of the Quebec English Committee to Dorchester, 6 Nov. 1788, CO42, vol. 62, pp. 79–80; Quebec Canadien Committee to same, s.d., ibid., 79–80. See also Dorchester to Sydney, 8 Nov. 1788, *Const. Docs., 1759–1791*, 958–9; Finlay to Nepean, 9 Feb. 1789, ibid., 961; Davison to same, 31 Oct. 1789, Q series, vol. 43; Dumas, *Discours*; *Quebec Herald*, 5 Jan. 1789 (letter of 'Sceliger')

13 In addition to the sources given in the following notes, see particularly John Fraser to Haldimand, 9 Jan. 1785, Haldimand Collection, vol. B205; Finlay to Nepean, 15 Mar. 1787, *Const. Docs., 1759–1791*, 845–7; Jean Vienne to Pierre Guy, 23 Oct. 1788, Collection Baby, vol. 10; De Bonne to Panet et al., 2 Nov. 1788, *BRH* 35 (1929), 188–9; Gabriel Christie to Haldimand, 19

Oct. 1789, Haldimand Collection. vol. B77; Alexander Davison to Nepean, 31 Oct. 1789, Q series, vol. 43; Mabane to Haldimand, 9 June 1791, Haldimand Collection, vol. B77; issues of the *Quebec Gazette*, Oct. 1788–Feb. 1789; Lymburner's Paper; Tousignant, 'La Genèse,' 316–24.

14 1 Feb. 1787, Collection Baby, vol. 10 (trans.)

15 'A Citizen of Quebec,' *Observations on a Pamphlet*, 15–16, 22–3. The author, although publishing in English, declared himself to be 'a Canadian' (15).

16 Blake to Sir John Johnson, 8 Feb. 1785, Sir John Johnson Papers, McCord Museum, Montreal; Fraser quoted in Neatby, *Quebec: The Revolutionary Age*, 202.

17 Neatby, *Quebec: The Revolutionary Age*, 241; Wallot, 'Pensée revolutionnaire,' 259–64. See also *Quebec Herald*, 29 Dec. 1788 and 26 Jan. 1789; *Quebec Gazette*, 30 June 1791.

18 Notary Jean Delisle of the Montreal Canadien Committee wrote in January 1785 that the two organizations in his city 'being but one body corresponds constantly with that of our Quebec brothers between whom and among ourselves [here] the happiest harmony reigns. No one has ever seen a more perfect association.' Delisle to J.-B. Adhémar, 15 Jan. 1785, quoted in Tousignant, 'La Genèse,' 310.

19 Quebec merchants' report to the Council, 5 Jan, 1787, *Const. Docs., 1759–1791*, 902–9

20 Robert Woolsey (a Quebec merchant) to James Morrison, 17 Jan. 1787, Lindsay-Morrison Papers; Joseph-François Cugnet to de Lavaltrie, 1 Feb. 1787, Collection Baby, vol. 10; Finlay to Nepean, 15 Mar. 1787, *Const. Docs., 1759–1791*, 845–7; Duchesnay to Perrault l'ainé, 7 Dec. 1788, Collection Baby, vol. 10; Perrault to same, 18 Oct. 1787, quoted in Kolish, 'Le debat sur le droit privé,' I, ch. 2, 7; same to same, 2 Aug. 1790, Collection Baby, vol. 11

21 Montreal Canadien Committee to Lymburner, 26 Nov. 1787, Collection Baby, vol. 48; Quebec English Committee to same, 8 Nov. 1787, Chatham Papers, vol. 10, 64–6. The latter document also included reference to the Montreal merchants' 1787 report. I have not found the other two sets of instructions, assuming they existed.

22 Quebec English Committee to Lymburner, 23 Oct. 1788, Q series, vol. 43, 757–60; Quebec Canadien Committee to same, 29 Oct. 1788, ibid., 763–9; Monk to Maseres, Quebec, 3 Nov. 1788, Monk Family Papers

23 There is no incontrovertible proof of these points, except in the case of jury trials. But a representative bi-ethnic group of Montreal merchants, including three members of the Canadien Committee, endorsed both a tough bankruptcy law and the establishment of land registry offices in 1787. This

committee's report was ratified at a public meeting of those Montrealers interested in commerce (see *Const. Docs., 1759–1791*, 915–20). Significant Canadien opposition to registration had been manifest in 1785 but we don't know the reaction to the Quebec merchants' 1787 proposal (ibid., 904–5) attempting to meet Canadien objections that registration 'would expose the secrets and Situation of Families,' by suggesting the ordinance should enact that no person would have access to the documents without swearing that he or she had a definite interest therein. Only extracts would have been provided to a reader.

24 The bill is printed in *Const. Docs., 1759–1791*, 767–73.

25 A similar libertarian clause was included in the Powys bill. Had Powys succeeded, the interpreting provision would have been entrenched and one can imagine a host of scenarios more favourable to accused rebels, traitors, and subversives (e.g., the court martial trials after the 1838 rebellion), than they actually received at various periods in our history.

26 Among many examples, see *Quebec Herald*, 10 June; 4, 14 Oct.; 2, 16 Dec. 1790.

27 Imperial taxation was no longer possible since the passage of the Colonial Tax Repeal Act of 1778 – a last-ditch attempt to conciliate the American revolutionaries. This act promised that for the future, Parliament would not tax the American colonies (including Quebec) for revenue purposes. To grant an appointed body such as the Quebec Legislative Council the power of taxation would have been politically unthinkable in the wake of the Revolution.

28 'Discussion of Petitions and counter petitions re change of government in Canada' enclosed in Grenville to Dorchester, 20 Oct. 1789, *Const. Docs., 1759–1791*, 981–2 (hereafter Discussion of Petitions). That the Discussion of Petitions – the best single primary source of the secretary's Canadian constitutional policy – was drafted by or for Grenville, is clear from Grenville to Thurlow, 26 Aug., 12 Sept. 1789, Historical Manuscripts Commission, *The Manuscripts of J.B. Fortesque, Esq., Preserved at Dropmore*, vol. 1 (London: Queen's Printer 1892), 496–7, 506–10.

29 *Commentaries*, I: 153–5, 190, 227–33; *Constitution of England, passim*. See also Paley, *Principles of Moral and Political Philosophy*, II, ch. 7; Edward Gibbon, *The History of the Decline and Fall of the Roman Empire*, vol. 5 [1788], ed. Felipe Fernández-Armesto (London: The Folio Society 1987), 271.

30 He was given the high-sounding but empty title of 'Captain General and Commander in Chief' of Nova Scotia, New Brunswick, and the two Canadas, able to exercise civil authority in the other colonies only when physically present.

31 During the period there were two vetoes, both because of serious drafting errors: Dorchester to Portland, 10 June 1795, Q series, vols. 72–3; Milnes to Camden, 11 June 1805, ibid., vol. 97. A veto on the merits would have been perfectly constitutional. Dorchester had vetoed a French party bill on tutorship in the last session of the old Legislative Council: to Grenville, 14 June 1791 (with enclosures), Q series, vol. 50.

32 Of the twenty-four men appointed during the period, all but four (and none of these was dismissed) held office until death or illness in old age.

33 Merchant John Richardson was offered a seat in 1809 but had declined it. Mercantile appointees (including Richardson) began sitting in the years 1813–7.

34 For example on the quarantine of ships. The bill became SLC 1795, c. 5.

35 Clarke to Dundas, 3 July 1793, Q series, vol. 63; Le Canadien, 2 Apr. 1808

36 The four were Gaspé, Bedford, the Island of Orléans, and William Henry (Sorel). Constituencies were delineated by Lieutenant-Governor Alured Clarke's proclamation of 7 May 1792 and given such British names as Hampshire, Devon, and Kent. The Eastern Townships were not given separate representation until 1829.

37 Since they were not expressly disqualified, women who met the property qualification could and sometimes did vote (until 1834) but were not a serious factor in the elections of this period.

38 At least 738 electors voted or were prepared to vote when the polls closed in Quebec County in 1792 (Quebec Gazette, 5, 12 July 1792). The electorate in the frontier county of Northumberland exceeded 250 (James Fisher to Colonel Nairne, 8 July 1796, Nairne Papers, vol. 3). In rural Huntingdon, south of Montreal, there were well over two thousand qualified voters in 1809: Pierre-Georges Roy, La famille Panet (Lévis: Laflamme 1906), 64.

39 I have taken 11/14 as being 80 per cent. These included the loyalist-military settlement of William Henry (7/7) and the English town of Trois-Rivières (14/14), both with perfect ministerial voting records. William Henry became the preserve of the attorney general from 1796, while a variety of officials sat for Trois-Rivières. Other safe constituencies were Bedford (6/7), which incorporated a part of the settled Eastern Townships; Quebec, Upper Town (11/14) with its concentration of army and government personnel; and Warwick (12/14) where the influence of the respected seigneur Pierre-Paul Margane de Lavaltrie and no doubt the money of James Cuthbert Jr, wealthy seigneur of Berthier, worked to advantage. The main sources used here are JHALC, 1792–1811; DCB, vols. 4–8; Hare, 'L'Assemblée législative du Bas-Canada.'

40 SLC 1794, c. 4; RSC 1985, c. N-5. The maximum of eighty-three sections was found in the Road Act: SLC 1796, c. 9.

41 As late as 1820 the jurist Joseph Chitty thought that the king as head of the executive should not recommend legislation, but should confine his legislative role to the negative one of vetoing encroachments on the prerogative: *A Treatise on the Law of the Prerogative of the Crown* (London: J. Butterworth & Son 1820), 3. See also Blackstone, *Commentaries*, I: 54.

42 There were no disallowances in the period. Only one of the eight bills reserved did not receive royal assent and that was due to the receipt of the assent after the two-year delay had expired: Prescott to Portland, 16 May 1798, Q series, vol. 80.

43 James Walker, made a judge in 1794, was beaten in his riding of Montreal County two years later. De Bonne, also made a judge in 1794, was defeated in Hampshire in 1796 and had to sit for Trois-Rivières. Antoine Juchereau Duchesnay, appointed to the Executive Council in 1794, either did not run again or lost in the second general election, in which feelings hostile to the Canadien seigneurs were manifest in the counties.

44 This was the case with notary Joseph Planté, a highly visible and active member for Hampshire (1796–1808) and Kent (1808–9). Appointed clerk of the land roll in 1802 and inspector general of the royal domain the year following, Planté nevertheless continued his opposition to government measures and indeed became a founder of *Le Canadien* and a leader of the *parti canadien*. Dismissed from his offices (1808) and then reinstated when he publicly disavowed his political colleagues, his electoral career quickly terminated.

45 The Committee of Quebec complained that the province would likely 'reap little or no advantage from the Change in its Constitution but rather be involved in great perplexity and distress than it has ever yet been': extract from a letter to Lymburner, 22 June 1791, enclosed with Lymburner to Dundas, 27 Aug. 1791, Q series, vol. 57, 106. See also Montreal lawyer Arthur Davidson to Whieldon & Butterworth, 7 Dec. 1791, Arthur Davidson Letters.

46 Forsythe, Richardson (handwriting of John Richardson) to John Porteous, 19 Nov. 1791, Porteous Papers; MG23, GIII7, NAC; Jonathan to Stephen Sewell, 1 Jan. 1792, Sewell Papers, vol. 15; Lymburner's notes, submitted to the imperial government, 16 June 1791, Q series, vol. 57

47 *Quebec Gazette*, 26 Jan., 2, 16 Feb., 3 March, 5, 19 April 1792; Dumas, *Discours*

48 *Quebec Gazette*, 17 May 1792. Panet's fellow candidate, merchant Louis Germain fils, joined in this appeal. The absent Lymburner was easily defeated, with merchants Robert Lester and John Young taking the seats.

49 Nine hundred copies of Dumas' *Discours* were printed: Tremaine, *Canadian*

Imprints, no. 768. 'Probus' also warned the voters against electing seigneurs who naturally inclined to despotism over their compatriots.

50 Tousignant, 'La première campagne électorale,' 124, 134–5. The defeated candidates were: (Upper Town) merchant-seigneur George Allsopp and Louis Germain; (Montreal, West Ward) Pierre Foretier, Alexander Auldjo, and James Dunlop.

51 *Montreal Gazette*, 5, 14 July 1792

52 Ibid., 24 May, 14 June

53 One explanation for the success of the seigneurs in the countryside may lie in the fact that it was the first general election. The middle-class Canadiens then had little party organization in the counties, while many traditional-minded habitants probably laboured under the impression they *could not* vote against seigneurial candidates, who as JPs, army officers or both, were so obviously representatives of the king. Many farmers, too, continued to fear the new-fangled Assembly and what was more natural than to vote for its opponents? See, e.g., Dumas, *Discours*; George Allsopp to Thomas Dunn, 12 July 1794, S series, vol. 58.

54 Finlay to Nepean, 9 Feb. 1789, *Const. Docs., 1759–1791*, 961; *Quebec Herald*, 26 Jan. 1788

55 See Neatby, *Quebec, The Revolutionary Age*, chs. 14, 15; Upton, *Loyal Whig*, chs. 13–17.

56 Lymburner's notes, submitted to the imperial government, 16 June 1791, Q series, vol. 57, 48–9

57 See on this, Harlow, *The Founding of the Second British Empire*, II, ch. 10, section 2, *passim*; Nelson, *American Tory*, ch. 9, *passim*.

58 Monk, *State of the Present Form of Government*, 66–7

59 Finlay to Nepean, 15 Jan. 1787, Q series, vol. 28: English residents in general thought that 'Canadiens should enjoy their laws but they wish to have their own suits decided by English law, where the causes are purely English.'

60 This conclusion results from the reading of several documents expressing the merchants' grievances which are printed in *Const. Docs., 1759–1791*; pamphlets published to support the merchants' case for an assembly and various manuscript letters (e.g., John Richardson to John Porteous, 10 Apr. 1787, Richardson Letters; Arthur Davidson to Whieldon & Butterworth, 7 Dec. 1791, Arthur Davidson Letters).

61 There was no dispatch sent home by Lord Dorchester or Lieutenant-Governor Alured Clarke which remotely resembled those advocating cultural assimilation transmitted by Lieutenant-Governor Milnes and Governor Sir James Craig in 1800 and 1810 respectively; Milnes to Portland, 1 Nov. 1800,

Const. Docs., 1791–1818, 249–55; Craig to Liverpool, 1 May 1810, ibid., 387–400.

62 On the diplomatic situation as it related to Quebec/Lower Canada see Trudel, *Louis XVI, le Congrès américain et le Canada*; Burt, *The United States, Great Britain and British North America*, chs. 1–7.

63 For example, Henry Juncken Papers, AP-J-10, Day-Book (p. 275), ANQ. Juncken recorded (Apr. 1789) a rumour among workers on the St Charles River bridge of a joint French-American attack on Quebec having been planned for the summer, with the aim of bringing the province under the government of France.

64 A search of the CO42 series and the newspapers for the years 1788 to mid-1792, *Const. Docs., 1759–1791* for the years 1784 to 1791, and sundry manuscript and printed collections of letters has yielded only one explicit statement by an English resident that the Canadiens should be assimilated in view of a possible war with France: the document authored by Isaac Ogden cited above. Finlay, for example, wrote over a dozen letters to Evan Nepean, under-secretary of state, advocating various assimilating measures, but never once made use of the argument employed by Ogden. See also *Quebec Herald*, 12 Apr. 1790 (letter of 'A Militia Man'). In the absence of French intrigues to stimulate the imagination, some of the English believed that the Canadiens were quickly losing their attachment for the former mother country. See, e.g., William Smith to Dorchester, 5 Feb. 1790, in Upton, *Papers of William Smith*, II: 272.

65 *Const. Docs., 1759–1791*, 881. Finlay to Nepean, 13 Feb. 1787, ibid., 844

66 See Bishop Charles Inglis to the Archbishop of Canterbury, Quebec, 18 June 1789, Inglis Family Papers, vol. 5; La Rochefoucauld-Liancourt, *Voyage*, II: 200; Brunet, *La présence anglaise*, 109.

67 This concept, in embryo, may have been entertained by a few Canadiens, for some referred to themselves as a 'nation distincte': *Montreal Gazette*, 5 Feb. 1789.

68 Brunet, *La présence anglaise*, 89–122

3 FROM PROMISE TO PARANOIA

1 For an enlightening examination of the French columns of the Montreal and Quebec *Gazettes* on this topic, see Galarneau, *L'Opinion canadienne*, 105–39. See also Wallot, 'La pensée revolutionnaire,' 206–4. Very little on the English reaction during the early Revolution has been published.

2 See, for example, *Quebec Herald*, 20 June 1791; *Quebec Gazette*, 22 Mar. 1792.

3 For the British reaction to the early Revolution, see Brown, *The French*

Revolution in English History; Goodwin, *Friends of Liberty*; Dozier, *For King, Constitution, and Country.*

4 *Montreal Gazette*, 9 Dec. 1790 (science to be preferred to religion); *Quebec Gazette*, 14 July 1791 (an attack on Burke); ibid., 20, 27 Jan. 1791: 'DESTRUC-TION of the FEUDAL MONSTER in FRANCE'

5 One must acknowledge that the pro-Revolution message in the letters owed something to the fact that they were selected for publication by the editors.

6 This seems particularly likely given the significant financial dependence of the semi-official *Quebec Gazette* on government advertising and pamphlet publishing.

7 *Quebec Magazine* for Feb. 1793; Richardson to John Porteous, 20 Oct. 1789, Richardson Letters

8 *Quebec Herald*, 25 May 1789, 8 Feb. 1790; Lymburner to Jacques Perrault (in French), 26 Mar. 1790, Collection Baby, vol. 11

9 *Montreal Gazette*, 16 Dec. 1790 (trans.)

10 Mezière, 'Observations sur l'état actuel du Canada et sur les dispositions Politiques de ses habitants,' June 1793, France, Affairs Étrangères, Correspondence Politique, États-Unis, Library of Congress (hereafter LOC/France), vol. 37

11 Mezière to Citizen Dalbarde, 4 Jan. 1794, *BRH* 37 (1931), 195 (trans.). For Mezière, see Mason Wade, 'Quebec and the French Revolution of 1789.'

12 For authorship see Galarneau, *L'Opinion canadienne*, 121–2.

13 Mezière to Dalbarde, 4 Jan. 1794, *BRH* 37 (1931), 197–8 (trans.). See also Amedée Papineau (*c.* 1839), 'Journal d'un fils de la liberté,' Papineau Papers, MG24, B2, vol. 10, NAC; Raoul Roy, *Résistance indépendantiste 1793–1798* (Montreal: éditions québécoises 1973), ch. 1 – a Fanoniste polemic; W.P.M. Kennedy, *The Constitution of Canada* (London: Oxford University Press 1922), 79, 86.

14 Galarneau, *L'Opinion canadienne*, 42, 335, 344 (trans.)

15 Unless otherwise specified, this and the following three paragraphs are based on Grenville's Discussion of Petitions of 1789.

16 Grenville to Dorchester, 20 Oct. 1789, *Const. Docs., 1759–1791*, 969

17 Ibid., 970

18 Had the decision been delayed another year, a grant of representative government might well not have been made, with all that implies with regard to the future history of Canada.

19 Emphasis in the original. As early as November 1790 he had lost any confidence he had had that France – which he then described as being 'in a condition full of terror and apprehension' – would succeed in avoiding

anarchy: Upton, *Papers of William Smith*, II: 263–4; *Quebec Herald*, 9 Nov. 1789; *Quebec Gazette*, 12 Nov. 1789, 4 Nov. 1790.

20 Gravé to Hody, 25 Oct. 1791, Provost, *Le séminaire de Québec*, 288. In November 1789, Grand Vicar Brassier complained about the Montreal laity: 'The European newspapers are really affecting the attitudes of Montrealers: they are everywhere preaching liberty and independence' from the clergy [to Hubert, – Nov. 1789, *RNAQ* (1947–8), 114 (trans.)]. See also, Galarneau, *L'Opinion canadienne*, 133–5.

21 *Quebec Herald*, 30 Nov., 10 Dec. 1789; *Montreal Gazette*, 3, 10 Dec. 1789, 14 Jan. 1790; Galarneau, *L'Opinion canadienne*, 72–9. Until the autumn of 1789, the letters had portrayed the Revolution in flattering terms.

22 Mabane to former Governor Haldimand, 9 June 1791, Haldimand Collection, vol. B77

23 One of the toasts drunk at the Lower Town celebration was: 'Reformation to the laws of Canada in every instance where the good of the British Empire requires it.'

24 Forsyth, Richardson (handwriting of John Richardson) to John Porteous, 19 Nov. 1791, Porteous Papers; *Quebec Gazette*, 29 Dec. 1791

25 Garneau, *History of Canada*, II: 206; *Montreal Gazette*, 19 Jan. 1792 (letter of 'Observator'); *Quebec Gazette*, 29 Dec. 1791, 26 Jan. 1792. Avoidance of this now controversial topic is also evident in the reports of the many sessions held from January to May 1792 by the Montreal Society, the unilingual successor to a 'Society for Free Debate/Société des débats libres.' The Montreal Society took up numerous political topics, such as the virtues of municipal incorporation and the advantages or otherwise of retaining the western posts, but none had the remotest relation to the French Revolution. See the issues of the *Montreal Gazette* from 26 Jan. to 3 May 1792.

26 Galarneau, *L'Opinion canadienne*, 138, n 269

27 Printed in Tousignant, 'La première campagne électorale,' 144–8

28 For a particularly good illustration, see Alexander Davison to Simcoe, 6 Nov. 1792 in Cruikshank, *Correspondence of … Simcoe*, I: 253–4.

29 Romilly to Mons. Dumont, 28 July 1789; same to same, 10 Sept. 1792, *Memoirs*, I: 356–8; II 3–5

30 See Robert de Roquebrune, 'Les Canadiens dans la Révolution française,' *Nova Francia* 6 (1931), 257.

31 24 Jan. 1793, printed in the *Quebec Gazette*, 31 Jan. 1793 (trans.). See also the Legislative Council's reply to the throne speech: ibid., 27 Dec. 1792.

32 De Gaspé, *Mémoires*, 92. See also Smith's address to the grand jury printed in the *Quebec Gazette*, 9 May 1793.

33 Gerrard to ——, 25 Apr. 1793, Collection Baby, vol. 11

34 *JHALC*, 1792–3 (28 Mar., 3, 5 Apr. 1793)
35 Ibid., 1795 (18 Feb.)
36 In the words of a surprised Attorney General Monk: 'Such a law required a pause – The House of Assembly less democratic has rejected the Bill and sent up one that is passed [i.e., was later enacted] granting the powers of appointment to the Governor!', to Nepean, 8 May 1793, CO42, vol. 97; SLC 1793, c. 7.
37 Duke of Kent to Dalrymple, 1 Dec. 1793 [1792], Duke of Kent Letters (typescripts), formerly held by McCord Museum, Montreal
38 See Chapais, *Cours*, II: 47–82; Claude-Armand Sheppard, *The Law of Languages in Canada* (Ottawa: Information Canada 1971), 43–50; F.M. Greenwood, 'Analyse de l'exposé de N.-E. Dionne sur le discours de Pierre Bédard au sujet de la langue officielle, 1793.' *RHAF* 30 (1976–7), 259.
39 Richardson to Porteous, 19 Jan. 1793, Richardson Letters
40 Painter to James Morrison, 24 Jan. 1793, Lindsay-Morrison Papers
41 Dundas to Dorchester, 2 Oct. 1793, CO42, vol. 96
42 See, for example, James Morrison to ——, 28 Jan. 1793, Lindsay-Morrison Papers, and the letter of 'A True Hearted Briton' (*Quebec Gazette*, 4 Apr. 1793)
43 Richardson to Alexander Ellice, 16 Feb. 1793, ed. F.H. Soward *CHR* 4 (1923), 260–3; McGill to John Askin, 20 Jan. 1793, Quaife, *Askin Papers*, I: 459–60
44 *JHALC*, 1792–3 (26 Apr. 1793)
45 See, for example, Hubert to curé Bédard, 13, 14, 19 Aug. 1793, *RANQ* (1930–1), 289.
46 'L'oraison funèbre de Mgr Briand,' *BRH* 11 (1905), 321; *Discours à l'occasion de la victoire remportée par les forces navales de sa majesté britannique dans le Mediterranée le 1 et 2 août 1798 sur la flotte française* (Quebec: John Neilson 1799)
47 Jacques Rousse to Citizen Gênet, 13 Feb. 1794, LOC/France, supp. vol. 28
48 See, for example, Ryland to Charles-Louis-Roch de St Ours, 22 July 1794, St Ours–Dorion Papers, MG23, GIII6, NAC; Pierre-I. Aubert de Gaspé to ——, 7 July 1796, *BRH* 42 (1936), 379; de Gaspé, *Mémoires*, 91.
49 La Rochefoucauld-Liancourt, *Voyage*, II: 209–10
50 Ibid.
51 Galarneau, *L'Opinion canadienne*, 288; *DCB*, vol. 5, 702. See also *Quebec Gazette*, 17 Jan. 1799 ('Poème').
52 Papineau and Panet were normally supported in the Assembly by lawyers Pierre-Stanislas Bédard and Berthelot d'Artigny, merchant Louis Dunière, and de Rocheblave.

53 The Papineau-Panet faction would become the majority in the second legislature (1797–1800) and Bédard's party was a direct descendant (for example, one of his leading supporters was Panet).

54 *JHALC*, 1793–4 (4 Apr., 22 May, 1794)

55 Ibid., 1795 (28 Feb.)

56 Papineau's notes on J.-J. Rousseau's 'Economie politique,' 23 July 1796, Papineau AP-P-5-62, ANQ (trans.)

57 Gerrard to ——, 25 Apr. 1793, Collection Baby, vol. 11

4 THE SECURITY DANGER

1 *AHAR* 2 (1903), 201–11 (trans.). For Genêt's Canadian policy see his correspondence in ibid. and in the Genêt Papers, LOC and the relevant dispatches of George Hammond (British Minister to the United States) in FO5, MG16, vol. 1, NAC. Useful secondary studies in print are Link, *Democratic-Republican Societies*, 141–4; Williamson, *Vermont in Quandary*, ch. 14; De Conde, *Entangling Alliance*, ch. 3; Wade, 'Quebec and the French Revolution of 1789.'

2 'Observations sur l'etat actuel de Canada,' *c.* 12 June 1793, LOC/France, vol. 37. For a full treatment of Mezière's assistance to Genêt, see Wade, 'Quebec and the French Revolution.'

3 Printed in Michel Brunet, 'La Révolution française sur les bords du Saint-Laurent,' *RHAF* 11 (1957–8), 158–62

4 Mezière to Genêt, 20 Sept. 1793, LOC/France, vol. 38. According to Mezière, Jacques Rousse had emigrated to the United States in 1777 and in 1789 had opened an inn on Lake Champlain near the Quebec–New York border (now Rouse's Point). While Mezière spelled his last name 'Rous,' the innkeeper spelled it 'Rousse': Rousse to Genêt, 13 Feb. 1794, ibid., suppl. vol. 28.

5 See Monk to Dorchester, 12 July 1794, with enclosed deposition, CO42, vol. 101; *Quebec Gazette*, 18 Sept. 1794; Monk to Dorchester, 2 Oct. 1794, Q series, vol. 69.

6 This paragraph is based on depositions/voluntary examinations found in CO42, vol. 100, 16–22, 361–5; CO42, vol. 101, 19–26; Records of the King's Bench, 1794

7 9 May 1793, quoted in Christie, *A History*, I: 140–1

8 Richardson to Porteous, 15 Sept. 1793, Richardson Letters. See also same to same, 29 June 1793, 15 Aug. 1793, ibid.; Morrison to ——, 2 May 1793, Lindsay-Morrison Papers; Clarke to Simcoe, 6 June 1793, Cruikshank, *Simcoe Papers*, I: 349; Joseph Chew to Alexander McKee, Montreal, 3 July 1793, ibid., 375.

9 Dorchester to Dundas, 23 Oct. 1793, CO42, vol. 97. See also *Quebec Gazette*, 20 Oct. 1793; Mezière to Genêt, 20 Sept. 1793, LOC/France, vol. 38, pt. 3; 'Jon Charles' to Mezière, 24 Oct. 1793, ibid., supp. vol. 28.

10 *Quebec Gazette* (both languages), 7 Nov. 1793; 26 Nov. 1793, RNAC (1921), 23–4; Nov. 1793, Têtu and Gagnon, *Mandements*, II: 471–3 (trans.)

11 Sheriff Edward Gray to Attorney General James Monk, 9 June 1794, CO42, vol. 100; J. Reid to same, 12 June 1794, ibid.; T.A. Coffin to James McGill, 21 July 1794, 'Civil Secretary's Letter Books, 1788–1829', RG7, G15C, vol. 2, NAC

12 To François Baby, 24 Sept. 1790, Collection Baby, vol. 46

13 'Abstract of the Returns of the Commanding Officers of the Militia of the Province of Lower Canada' (1794), S series, vol. 59, pp. 19,035–47; Campbell, *Travels*, 316; John Richardson to Ryland, 21 Sept. 1801, S series, vol. 74

14 Monk to Dorchester, 29 May 1794, CO42, vol. 100; same to Dundas, 30 May 1794, ibid.; and see also Francis de Maistre to Philip Ruiter, May 1794, Ruiter Family Papers; Militia Returns, 1794, *passim*; James McGill's address to the Montreal Quarter Sessions, *Quebec Gazette*, 24 July 1794; Dorchester to Dundas, 25 May 1794, CO42, vol. 101; Chartier de Lotbinière to Sewell, 25 June 1794, Sewell Papers, vol. 3; deposition of Jean-Baptiste Leclair, 29 May 1794, CO42, vol. 100, 10–11 (re opinion in Charlesbourg and Jeune Lorette, trans.).

15 6 June 1794, CO42, vol. 100; see also Osgoode to Simcoe, 7 Sept. 1794, Simcoe Papers, Series 4, vol. 5.

16 La Rochefoucauld-Liancourt, *Voyage*, II: 183 (trans.). See also Monk to Dundas, 17 June 1794, CO42, vol. 100; Militia Returns 1794, *passim*.; A. Fraser to M. Fraser, 12 Jan. 1794, papiers Fraser. Fifteen Canadien residents from Laprairie, who instructed the French consul at New York (1795) about the colony's defences and offered their military services, claimed the people were saying with a single voice they 'will defend the English against all their enemies except the French, because they will never take arms against their fathers, their brothers or their relations': edited and printed in Brunet, 'Les Canadiens et la France revolutionnaire,' 474–5 (trans.). Internal evidence suggests the letter was written between August and December 1795.

17 Monk to Dorchester, 29, 31 May 1794, CO42, vol. 100; deposition of three Charlesbourg habitants, 29 May 1794, ibid. (pp. 10–15); depositions of habitants Louis Paquet et al., 23 Dec. 1794, S series, vol. 61, pp. 19,519–20

18 Marginal note in Monk's handwriting on a deposition of Jean-Baptiste Leclair, 29 May 1794, CO42, vol. 100 (p. 11). See also Monk's 'State of the Prosecutions in His Majesty's Court of King's Bench. November Term 1794,' CO42, vol. 101.

19 Monk to Dorchester, 29 May 1794, CO42, vol. 100 (p. 5); same to Dundas, 30 May 1794, ibid., (p. 323); deposition of habitant Louis Savard, 29 May 1794, ibid. (pp. 14–15)

20 Gray to Monk, 9 June 1794, CO42, vol. 100 (pp. 355–6); Monk to Dorchester, 18 June 1794, ibid. (paraphrasing Sewell)

21 De Lotbinière to Sewell, 25 June 1794, Sewell Papers, vol. 3 (trans.); Monk to Dorchester, 18 June, CO42, vol. 100, (Monk cited Sewell and Judge James Walker to bolster the case for caution); Dorchester to Dundas, 21 June 1794, CO42, ibid.

22 'Orders of the Committee of Public Safety' (trans.), 15 Nov. 1793, AHAR 2 (1903), 290–3; Robert Liston (British minister to the United States) to Prescott, 28 Nov. 1796, RNAC (1891), 62; De Conde, Entangling Alliance, ch. 12

23 For French sources on the Directory's policy towards North America during this period see its instructions to General Perignon (French negotiator at Madrid), 16 Mar. 1796, AHR (1897), 667–71 and to the proposed minister to the United States, 6 Aug. 1796, AHAR 2 (1903), 938; memorandum by Louis-Pierre Anguetil (official in the Foreign Ministry) to the Directory, 1 Nov. 1796, Corr. Pol. Angleterre, vol. 590 (88–98), Archives des affaires étrangères, Paris, France; George Duruy ed. and Charles E. Roche, trans., Memoirs of Barras, 4 vols. (London: Osgoode, McIlvaine 1895–6), II: 203; the correspondence of Adet and Létombe in AHAR 2 (1903); Consul de Launay (Philadelphia), 'Mémoire: apercus politiques sur les Etats-Unis et la Canada,' 4 May 1796, LOC/France, Mém. et Doc., Ang., vol. 2; Consul J.-A.-B. Rozier (New York), 'Mémoire sur le Canada,' 8 June 1797, 'Mémoires et Documents, Angleterre.' These sources are usefully supplemented by British diplomatic intelligence reports. See, e.g., Liston to Grenville, 18 Nov. 1796, FO5, vol. 14, NAC; same to Prescott, 28 Nov. 1796 RNAC (1891), 62–3.

24 Printed in translation with a covering letter from Talleyrand to the Directory, 30 Aug. 1798, in Wilbur, Ira Allen, II: 191–8

25 A resumé of Allen's proposals, prepared by an official in the French Foreign Ministry, has been printed in translation by Jeanne A. Ojala, 'Ira Allen and the French Directory, 1796: Plans for the Creation of the Republic of United Columbia,' William and Mary Quarterly 36 (1979), 442–8. Copies of Allen's proposals are held in the Allen Family Papers, Box 30, Bailey/Howe Library, University of Vermont, Burlington, Vermont. A useful context is provided by J. Kevin Graffagnino, "Twenty Thousand Muskets!!!': Ira Allen and the Olive Branch Affair, 1796–1800' William and Mary Quarterly 48 (1991), 409. Graffagnino notes that France was in part motivated by a desire to avenge Britain's support for a French royalist invasion at Queberon in the summer of 1791.

26 Unless otherwise specified, the activities of De Millière, Ianson, Louisineau, and Ducalvet are based on the following sources: Sewell to Prescott, 28 Oct. 1796, Sewell Papers, vol. 10; same to Executive Council, 30 Oct. 1796, *RNAC* (1891), 59; William Stanton to Colonel Barnes, 18 Nov. 1796, ibid., 60–1; Richardson to Sewell, 8, 12 Dec. 1796, 19, 23 Jan., 6 Feb. (twice), 13 Feb. 1797, Sewell Papers, vol. 3; Liston to Prescott, 23, 28 Mar., 4 May 1797, Prescott Papers, vol. 11; Sewell's report to Prescott (12 May 1797) on the Road Act riots and his calendar of cases (hereafter Sewell's report and calendar), *RNAC* (1891), 73–8.

27 Trans. A copy of the letter (10 Nov. 1796) may be found in CO42, vol. 108, 128.

28 Minutes of the Executive Council, 26 Aug.–7 Sept. 1795, Lower Canada State Book B; proclamation of 9 Sept. 1795, *RNAC* (1921), 30–1; Osgoode to John King, 3 Aug, 1796, CO42, vol. 22; Ouellet, *Economic and Social History*, 663–5

29 Osgoode to Simcoe, 7 July 1796 Osgoode Letters, 151

30 SLC 1795, c. 8, 9; La Rochefoucauld-Liancourt, *Voyage*, II: 185. The working people often smoked (although most habitants grew their own tobacco), were notorious consumers of rum, and used quantities of brandy on special occasions. Salt, of course, was essential for the preservation of meat.

31 SLC 1796, c. 10. The main mischiefs addressed were canoemen etc. failing to appear for departure or deserting en route. In most cases they would have received money in advance; see also the petition of the Montreal merchants in *JHALC*, 1795–6, 20 Jan. 1796. For the longstanding nature of the problem see *Montreal Gazette*, 24 Dec. 1789.

32 *JHALC*, 1795, 21, 23, Jan., 23 Feb., 5, 23 Mar., 15, 21 Apr.; Osgoode to Simcoe, 30 Jan. 1795, Osgoode Letters, 91; same to Burland, 27 Oct. 1795, CO42, vol. 22; *The Times – Du Cours du Tems*, 9 Feb. 1795 (letter of 'Modestus')

33 *JHALC*, 1795–6, *passim*; Fleming, *Political Annals*, 23–4; SLC 1796, c. 9

34 *Quebec Gazette*, 23 June 1796 (emphasis in the original). Master shipwright John Black, then down on his luck, advertised himself to the voters of Quebec County (the city and surrounding country area) as a reliable fellow who had never 'reposed on the downy couch of luxurious opulence': ibid., 16 June 1796.

35 *DCB*, vol. 5, 83; Osgoode to Simcoe, 7 July 1796, Osgoode Letters, 151; Monk to Dundas, 6 Aug. 1794, CO42, vol. 100. Black was indicted for sedition and Paquet for high treason. Neither was tried. Dorion appears to have been imprisoned on suspicion of high treason. He was not indicted. It is not certain whether Menut had been actually imprisoned: see deposition

of Augustin Lavau, 27 May 1794 and Jean-Baptiste Vocel dit Belhumeur, 29
May 1794, CO42, vol. 100 (16–19 [with a note on Menut in Monk's handwriting [p. 18]).

36 Osgoode to Simcoe, 7 July 1796, Osgoode Letters, 151; Prescott to Portland,
3 Sept. 1796, CO42, vol. 107

37 Five of the English members-elect had run in safe government seats and
another two may have been returned because of manipulation by the gov-
ernment-appointed returning officer: unsuccessful petition from electors of
Buckinghamshire (JHALC, 1797, 18 Feb.) against the election of G.W.
Allsopp and John Craigie. Black had been perceived as an oppositionist by
many Canadien voters in Quebec County (Osgoode to Simcoe, 7 July 1796,
Osgoode Letters, 151; Young to Ryland, 9 June 1798, CO42, vol. 111). The
election of Dr James Fisher in Northumberland was due to peculiar local
circumstances and Fisher's adroit manoeuvring to ostensibly join himself to
Pierre Bédard of the parti canadien as a running mate. Northumberland had
significant numbers of Scottish settlers although they were rapidly becoming Canadienized. Fisher himself was a Scot who enjoyed the support of
Colonel John Nairne. Bédard may have gone along with the ticket so as not
to risk alienating Nairne and losing Scots-Canadien votes. Another factor
helping Fisher was that his five opponents (excluding Bédard) were Canadiens. See Fisher to Nairne, 8 July 1796, Nairne Papers, vol. 3.

38 RG4, B28, vol. 70, NAC; DCB, vol. 5, 276

39 JHALC, 1797, 24 Jan. 15 Feb. 1797

40 Osgoode to John King, 3 Aug. 1796, postscript dated 27 Aug. 1796, CO42,
vol. 22; same to ——, 13 Oct. 1796, ibid.; Sewell to Foucher, 3 Oct. 1796,
Sewell Papers, vol. 9

41 The principal sources relied on for the Road Act riots are references given
in the preceding note and the following: Montreal Magistrates to Prescott,
6, 13 Oct 1796, S series, vol. 64, and CO42, vol. 108; Osgoode to —— King,
14 Nov. 1796, CO42, vol. 22; Isaac Winslow Clarke to William Dummer
Powell, 15 Nov. 1796, W.D. Powell Papers, vol. B30; Attorney General
Sewell to Prescott, 28 Oct. 1796, Sewell Papers, vol. 10; same to Executive
Council, 30 Oct. 1796, RNAC (1891), 58–60; Sewell's report and calendar.

42 Gerald S. Graham, Empire of the North Atlantic (Toronto: University of
Toronto Press 1950), 226–7. The first official indication of the news reaching
Lower Canada appears to be Prescott to Prince Edward, 3 Oct. 1796, Pres-
cott Papers, vol. 25. See also Samuel Willard to Luke Knowlton, 8 Nov.
1796, Knowlton Family Papers; Henry Cull to James Dale, 23 Nov. 1796,
Cull Papers.

43 Prescott to Portland, 28 Oct. 1796, CO42, vol. 108; R. v. David Maclane [sic]

(1796), 26 St. Tr. 721 at 786 (per George Pyke, counsel for the defence)

44 Prescott to Lt.-Col. Brownrigg, 25 Oct. 1796, Prescott Papers, vol. 26; same to Major-General Delaney, 14 Aug. 1797, ibid.; Osgoode to ——, 13 Oct. 1796, CO42, vol. 22

45 Denaut to Plessis, 18 Oct. 1796, AAQ, Cartable, Evéques de Québec, II (trans.). See also Louis Labadie's address to the habitants of Verchères, 15 Nov. 1796, Quebec Gazette, 5 Jan. 1797.

46 SLC 1794, c. 5 as continued/amended by SLC 1795, c. 11 and SLC 1796, c. 8

47 RNAC (1913), 45–6

48 Têtu and Gagnon, Mandements, II: 501–2

49 Address of Judge P.-A. De Bonne to prisoners convicted of Road Act offences, 3 Apr. 1797; Quebec Gazette, 6 Apr. 1797; Jacques Vallée, ed., Tocqueville au Bas-Canada (Montreal: Editions du Jour 1973), 175

50 Gaspard de Lanaudière to his wife, 30 Jan. 1797, Collection Baby, vol. 12; J. George Forth to Peter Russell, 2 Feb. 1797, Russell Papers, AO. Forth was an army officer, then stationed at Montreal.

51 Burt, United States, Great Britain and British North America, 171; Webster, 'Napoleon and Canada,' passim; same, 'Ira Allen in Paris, 1800, Planning a Canadian Revolution,' CHAR (1963), 74. The Olive Branch was an American ship.

52 Talleyrand to the Directory, 30 Aug. 1798, in Wilbur, Ira Allen, II: 191–8; Bryant, Years of Endurance, ch. 9

53 Dorchester to Dundas, 25 Oct. 1793, CO42, vol. 97; 'State of the Troops in North America etc.,' enclosed in same to same, 6 Aug. 1794, CO42, vol. 100; 'State of the Troops in North America,' 8 Nov. 1796, Prescott Papers, vol. 15. According to the last document the total troops in British North America numbered 6,163.

54 See, for example, Monk to Dundas, 30 May 1794, CO42, vol. 100; Osgoode to ——, 13 Oct. 1796, CO42, vol. 22; Prescott to Portland, 22 Aug. 1798, CO42, vol. 111.

55 ——, 'Canadian Letters: description of a tour thro' the provinces of Lower and Upper Canada in the course of the years 1792 and '93,' Canadian Antiquarian and Numismatic Journal 3rd series, 9 (1912), 90; Quebec Gazette, 28 Mar. 1793

56 See La Rochefoucauld-Liancourt, Voyage, II: 152–3; Prescott to Prince Edward, 4 Oct. 1797, Prescott Papers, Series 2; Commander-in-Chief Peter Hunter to the Duke of York, 24 Dec. 1800, C series, vol. 1209.

57 Grant to Simon McTavish, 10 July 1794, Collection Baby, vol. 11; Maulevrier, Voyage, 66; Simcoe to Portland, 11 Dec. 1796, Cruikshank and Hunter, Correspondence of the Honourable Peter Russell, I: 104–5. According to

Maulevrier, Richery could have taken the colony with ease, if he had been able to disembark six thousand troops.

58 Prescott to Portland, 22 Aug. 1798, CO42, vol. 111

59 Ibid.

60 Mezière to Genêt, 20 Sept. 1793, trans. taken from Wade, 'Quebec and the French Revolution of 1789,' 356

61 Depositions of Alexis Monjeon and Richard Corbin, 11 June 1794, CO42, vol. 100

62 James Monk, 'State of Prosecutions in His Majesty's Court of King's Bench. November Term 1794,' CO 42, vol. 101. Of these, seven were indicted (one convicted, two acquitted, four continued and later released).

63 Plessis, 'Les dénombrements de Québec,' RANQ (1948–9), 3. I have treated carters and sailors as semi-skilled workers.

64 Sewell to Prescott, 28 Oct. 1796, Sewell Papers, vol. 10; Monk to Dorchester, 18 June 1794, CO42, vol. 100; Prescott to Liston, 2, 10 Feb. 1797, Prescott Papers, vol. 13; Richardson to Sewell, 13 Feb. 1797, Sewell Papers, vol. 3

65 Pierre-Ignace Aubert de Gaspé Sr. to ——, 7 July 1796, BRH 42 (1936), 379 (trans.); Monk to Dorchester, 25 May 1794, CO42, vol. 101

66 See the depositions of François Le Droit dit Perche, 25 May 1794, CO42, vol. 101 and Jean-Baptiste Leclair, 29 May 1794, CO42, vol. 100.

67 Robert Sellar, The Histories of the County of Huntingdon and of the Seigniories of Chateauguay and Beauharnois (Huntingdon: Canadian Gleaner 1888), 528; Fernand Ouellet, 'Les insurrections de 1837–38; un phénomène social' in his Eléments d'histoire sociale du Bas-Canada (Montréal: Hurtubise HMH, Ltée 1972), 366–7

68 Fraser to M. Fraser, Beauchamp, 12 Jan. 1794, papiers Fraser; Osgoode to John King, 3 Aug. 1796, CO42, vol. 22; same to ——, 13 Oct. 1796, ibid.

69 Greer, Peasant, Lord, and Merchant, 79

70 Quebec Gazette, 24 Mar.–28 Apr. 1791; Tremaine, Imprints, nos. 696, 702, 708; Upton, Loyal Whig, 187–9, 197–8

71 See Quebec Gazette, 18 Dec. 1788, 24 Mar.–7 Apr. 1791.

72 It is noteworthy too that in the three known petitions of complaint emanating from the farmers in the 1790s (Longueuil, 1793; Berthier, 1794; Dorchester 1799 [JHALC, 1799, 29 Apr.]) the relief sought was not tenure change but elimination of seigneurial abuses.

73 See depositions of farmer Jean-Marie Renaud et al. and of farmer Louis Paquet, both 23 Dec. 1794, S series, vol 61; Quebec Gazette, 5 July 1792; Tousignant, 'La première campagne electorale,' 142–3. For evidence of other ethnic appeals see James Morrison to ——, 5 Jan. 1792, Lindsay-Morrison Papers; Dumas, Discours; Monk to Dundas, 30 May 1794, CO42, vol. 100.

74 Galarneau, *L'Opinion canadienne*, 294. For the lack of impact through published propaganda, see *The Times–Du Cours du Tems*, 4 Aug. 1794; Prescott to Liston, 14 May 1798, CO42, vol. 110.

75 De Gaspé, *Mémoires*, 91. See also Galarneau, *L'Opinion canadienne*, 330.

76 Maulevrier, *Voyage*, 66. See also Gerrard to ——, 25 Apr. 1793, Collection Baby, vol. 11; La Rochefoucauld-Liancourt, *Voyage*, II: 209–10; Louis Labadie to John Neilson, 4 May 1797, Neilson Collection, vol. 1; Liston to Grenville, 2 Apr. 1798, FO5, vol. 22.

77 Dorchester to Dundas, 12 July 1794 (with enclosure), CO42, vol. 99; S series, vols. 58–60 (letters from the associations); circular letter of the Quebec Association, CO42, vol. 100, (p. 369); circular letter of the Montreal Association, 5 July 1794, *RANQ* (1948–9), 258–9; James McGill (Montreal President) to Dorchester, 6 Nov. 1794, ibid., 272; *Quebec Gazette*, *Montreal Gazette*, and *The Times–Du Cours du Tems* for July–Aug. 1794; Tremaine, *Imprints*, nos. 892–7

78 The recently passed Militia Act (SLC 1794, c. 4) prohibited service outside the colony, except to assist Upper Canada should it actually be invaded or to undermine an imminent attack on Lower Canada.

79 S series, vols. 58–60, exception in vol. 58, 18917–8

80 Liston to Prescott, 15 Jan. 1797, Prescott Papers, vol. 11

81 Prescott to Portland, 1 Oct. 1798, CO42, vol. 111

5 THE GARRISON MENTALITY

1 Hale to Lord Amherst, 2 Feb. 1803, Hale Family Papers. This attitude belongs principally to the English élite. Elements of the garrison mentality were manifested from time to time by individual educated Canadiens. Such Canadien examples, however, are very rare in the extant primary documents, whereas English ones are common. Expressions of fear by Canadiens, also tended to be less pessimistic about Canadien loyalties than the English. Middle-class Canadiens who supported the *parti canadien* seem not to have worried very much about internal security, while English merchants and lawyers were among the most alarmed residents of the colony.

2 Quoted in Wade, 'Quebec and the French Revolution of 1789,' 364. The brother-in-law's letter was dated 10 Nov. 1793.

3 Nooth to Sir Joseph Banks, 28 Oct. 1793 in Rousseau, 'Lettres du Dr. J.M. Nooth,' 170–1; Richardson to J. Sewell, 23 Jan., 6 Feb. 1797, Sewell Papers, vol. 3. See also, for example, D.A. Grant to McTavish, 10 July 1794, Collection Baby, vol. 11; *Vermont Gazette*, 5 Sept. 1797 (re opinion of English Montrealers as of early August)

4 Dorchester to Dundas, 24 Feb. 1794, Q series, vol. 67

5 SLC 1794, c. 6, s. 8; Monk to Dundas, 7 June 1794, CO42, vol. 100

6 Osgoode to Simcoe, 30 Jan. 1795, Osgoode Letters, 91; same to Burland, 27 Oct. 1795, CO42, vol. 22

7 Fleming, *Political Annals*, 20; Garneau, *History of Canada*, II: 227

8 Dorchester to Dundas, 7 June 1794, CO42, vol. 100. Looking back on the crisis in October, Anglican Bishop Jacob Mountain wrote that the 'detection of the numerous conspiracies which were forming, will I trust fully open the eyes of Englishmen [here] to all the horrors that awaited them': to John King, 4 Oct. 1794, Mountain Papers, vol. 1.

9 Grant to McTavish, 10 July 1794, Collection Baby, vol. 11. See also *JHALC*, 1793–4, 22 May 1794 (William Grant's motion for emergency powers); Monk to Dorchester, 18 June 1794 (paraphrase of a report by Solicitor General Sewell), CO42, vol. 100; James Kerr (a Quebec lawyer) to Thomas Dunn, 19 Oct. 1794, S series, vol. 60 ('public disaffection at its most alarming height'). The Indian Agent at Detroit, R.G. England, informed Simcoe that 'my letters from Quebec and Montreal represent the miserable Canadians in a state little short of rebellion': 22 July 1794 in Cruikshank, *Simcoe Correspondence*, II: 334. To like effect, G.S. Smythe to Jonathan Sewell, Halifax, 22 June 1794, Sewell Papers, vol. 3.

10 Monk to Dundas, 30 May 1794, CO42, vol. 100; same to Nepean, 19 Sept. 1794, ibid.

11 Walker to Osgoode, 15 Sept. 1794, Osgoode Papers. See also 'a Loyalist' to same, Montreal, 13 Sept. 1794, ibid.

12 Stephen to Jonathan Sewell, 18 Sept. 1794, Sewell Papers, vol. 3

13 Richardson to Jonathan Sewell, 13 Feb., 23, 30 Mar. 1797, Sewell Papers, vol. 3. See also Osgoode to Simcoe, 7 July 1796, Osgoode Letters, 151; Prescott to Portland, 3 Sept. 1796, CO42, vol. 107; same to same, 28 Oct. 1796, CO42, vol. 108. 'A Good Citizen' warned that if Papineau and Panet succeeded they would 'establish a System of Equalisation which would at once dissolve the cement of Society: *Quebec Gazette*, 23 June 1796.

14 Fleming, *Political Annals*, 27–8

15 Prescott to Portland, 24, 28 Oct. 1796, 21 Jan. 1797, CO42, vol. 108; same to Liston, 1 Dec. 1796, ibid.; same to Portland, 18 Feb, 1797, Prescott Papers, vol. 13. Prescott nearly had apoplexy in October 1796 when he learned that French prisoners of war, sent from Britain to strengthen the garrison at Quebec(!) had arrived in port. Convinced they would prove unrepentant revolutionaries, who might incite mutiny among the Canadien soldiers in the 60th Regiment and in the Royal Canadian Volunteers, he sent the unwanted recruits packing in the first ship home – much to the relief of 'His

Majesty's loyal subjects and the [pro-government] members of the legislature': to Lt.-Col. Brownrigg, 19, 25 Oct. 1796, Prescott Papers, Series 2, Military Letterbook. The Volunteers consisted of two battalions of regular troops raised in the colony. In 1798 the 424 rank and file of the 1st Battalion were mostly Canadiens: Prescott to Portland, 22 Aug, 1798, CO42, vol. 111.

16 Osgoode to ——, 13 Oct. 1796, CO42, vol. 22; same to King, 14 Nov. 1796, ibid; Sewell to Ryland, 17 Mar. 1797, CO42, vol. 108; Prince Edward to John Young, Halifax, 6 Feb. 1797, Young Papers, vol. 4, (referring to the contents of letters received from Young). A few years after the riots, John Hale told a story of provisions being withheld from the Montreal market so they could be given to the French invading force: Hale to Lord Amherst, 2 Feb. 1803, Hale Family Papers.

17 Clarke to William Dummer Powell, Montreal, 15 Nov. 1796, W.D. Powell Papers, B30. Another loyalist from Boston, Stephen Sewell, wrote his brother about the French plot for the 'extirpation of the English': 14 Nov. 1796, S series, vol. 65. Monk believed Adet was behind the riots: Monk to his brother, 14 Nov. 1796, Monk Family Papers, vol 2. Richardson to Jonathan Sewell, 6 Feb. 1797, Sewell Papers, vol. 3. On martial law, see particularly Charles Townshend, 'Martial Law: Legal and Administrative Problems of Civil Emergency in Britain and the Empire, 1800–1940,' Historical Journal 25 (1982), 167. Lindsay to Sewell, 1 Dec. 1796, Sewell Papers, vol. 3. See also Joseph Chew to Edward Winslow, 17 Dec. 1797, Winslow Papers. As in 1794 letters and reports from the colony conveyed the idea of near-rebellion to outsiders. See, for examples, Edward Winslow to Jonathan Sewell, Kingsclear, New Brunswick, 14 Jan. 1797, Sewell Papers, vol. 3.

18 Neilson to his mother, —— 1797, Neilson Collection; Sewell to Prescott, 28 Oct. 1796, Sewell Papers, vol. 3

19 See Greenwood, 'Development of a Garrison Mentality,' 18–22, for a review of the historiography.

20 Garneau, History of Canada, II: 209, 227; Christie, A History, I: 172–3; Chapais, Cours, II: 113; Groulx, L'enseignement, 75–6; Wallot, Intrigues, 10–11

21 Dorchester to Dundas, 24 May 1794, CO42, vol. 101; Monk's reports, dated 25 May 1794, ibid., and 29, 30 May 1794, CO42, vol. 100

22 25, 30 May, 6 June 1794, ibid.

23 To Dorchester: 18 June 1794, ibid., 12 July 1794, ibid.; 12 July 1794, CO42, vol. 99; 15 Nov. 1794, CO42, vol. 101; to Dundas: 17 June, 5, 31 July, 6 Aug., 18 Nov. 1794, CO42, vol. 100

24 This judgment results from reading dozens of Monk letters in CO 42, the S series, and the Monk Family Papers. His attitude from 1793 to 1812 was

that with tough measures, such as using troops to suppress rioting and suspending habeas corpus, habitant disloyalty and anglophobia could be contained. See, for example, Monk to Nepean, 17 June 1794, CO42, vol. 100; same to Dorchester, 15 Nov. 1794, CO42, vol. 101; same to his brother, 14 Nov. 1796, Monk Family Papers, vol. 2; same to Governor Prevost, 12 Dec. 1812, S series, vol. 126.

25 Monk to Dundas, 30 May 1794, CO42, vol. 100

26 See Bishop Mountain to Dorchester, 17 July 1795, quoted in Audet, *Le système scolaire* , 10–11, nn8, 9.

27 12 May 1797, Osgoode Papers (emphasis in original)

28 *JHALC*, 1798, 11 Apr. It is curious that Lindsay would be in the capital on 12 May if he had already received notice of his appointment.

29 Sewell's report and calendar

30 Osgoode to King, 14 Nov. 1797, CO42, vol. 22; Nairne to Malcolm Fraser, 12 Feb. 1797, Nairne Papers, vol. 3

31 Osgoode to Simcoe, 7 July 1796, Osgoode Letters, 151. Osgoode stated that had been the opinion at the Chateau during the March assizes of 1795.

32 See James Kerr to Dunn, 19 Oct. 1794, S series, vol. 60; Thomas Ainslie to Edward Winslow, 5 Dec. 1794, Winslow Papers, vol. 6; Monk to his brother, 14 Nov. 1796, Monk Family Papers, vol. 2; Clarke to Powell, 15 Nov. 1796, W.D. Powell Papers; Nairne to Fraser, 12 Feb. 1797, Nairne Papers, vol. 3.

33 See, for example, James Morrison to ——, 11 Apr. 1793, Lindsay-Morrison Papers; Samuel Gerrard to ——, 25 Apr. 1793, Collection Baby, vol. 11; John Richardson to John Porteous, 29 June, 15 Sept. 1793, Richardson Letters; Simon Fraser to Nairne, 29 Sept. 1793, papiers Fraser; George Allsopp to Thomas Wiggins, 5 Nov. 1795, Allsopp Papers; same to Jacob Rowe, 1 Feb. 1796, ibid.

34 George to Carleton Allsopp, 24 Nov. 1793, Allsopp Papers

35 Prescott to Portland, 18 Mar. 1797, Prescott Papers, vol. 13

36 Edmund Burke, *Reflections on the Revolution in France* (Dublin: W. Watson 1790), 61–4

37 SOQ 1787, c. 6; Fecteau, *Un nouvel ordre des choses*, 79–80

38 Prescott to Portland, 28 Oct. 1796, CO42, vol. 108

39 Untitled document with the marginal notation 'Tea Notes 1774,' Sewell Papers, vol. 14, pp. 7, 337; L.F.S. Upton, ed., *Revolutionary versus Loyalist: The First American Civil War 1774–1784* (Waltham, Mass.: Blaisdell Publishing 1968), 4–6; Jonathan Sewell Sr to Ward Chipman, n.d. (*c.* 1782), Sewell Papers, vol. 2 (pp. 367–8)

40 Sewell to Foucher, 3 Oct. 1796, Sewell Papers, vol. 9

41 D.A. Grant dated the colony's 'ruin' from the failure to punish the Leveillé rioters (to McTavish, 10 July 1794, Collection Baby, vol. 11), while Nairne thought Prescott's use of troops at Pointe-Lévi had come 'in the nick of time' (To Fraser, 12 Feb. 1797, Nairne Papers, vol. 3).

42 Monk to Dundas, 17 June, 6 Aug. 1794, CO42, vol. 100; same to Dorchester, 18 June 1794, ibid.; same to same, 12 July 1794, Q series, vol. 68

43 Richardson to Sewell, 13 Feb., 6 Apr. 1797, Sewell Papers, vol. 3

44 See Bailyn, *Ideological Origins of the American Revolution*, 119–59; Nelson, *American Tory*, 180–2; Edmund S. and Helen M. Morgan, *The Stamp Act Crisis: Prologue to Revolution* (Chapel Hill, NC: University of North Carolina Press 1953), 289–91.

45 Robison, *Proofs of a Conspiracy*; Augustin Barruel, *Mémoires pour servir à l'histoire du jacobinisme*, 5 vols. (Hamburg: P. Fauché 1798)

46 Ernest Volkman and Blaine Baggett, *Secret Intelligence: The Inside Story of America's Espionage Empire* (New York: Double Day 1989), 46

47 Sewell to Ryland, 17 Mar. 1797, CO42, vol. 108; Sewell's report and calendar

6 THE GARRISON MENTALITY AND THE ADMINISTRATION OF CRIMINAL JUSTICE

1 SLC 1794, c. 5; Monk to Nepean, 17 June 1794, CO42, vol. 100; *JHALC*, 1793–4, 22, 26 May 1794. The Alien Act has largely been ignored by modern historians or interpreted, like Mason Wade did, as consisting of but 'mild repressive measures' ('Quebec and the French Revolution of 1789'; 367). See, for example, Burt, *United States, Great Britain and British North America*, 169; Galarneau, *L'Opinion canadienne* at 230.

2 See Stephen, *Digest of the Criminal Law*, art. 114.

3 *R. v. Lambert and Perry* (1793) 22 St. Tr. 953 at 1017. See also *Tutchin's* case (1704) 14 St. Tr. 1095 at 1128; *William Cobbett's* case (1804) 29 St. Tr. 1 at 49–50; *Sir Francis Burdett's* case (1820) 1 St. Tr. (n.s.) 1 at 129.

4 *Stockdale's* case (1789) 22 St. Tr. 237 at 240; *Thomas Paine's* case (1792) 22 St. Tr. 357 at 374; *Richard Francklin's* case (1731) 17 St. Tr. 625 at 628. 'The word "sedition" in its ordinary natural signification denotes a tumult, an insurrection, a popular commotion, or an uproar, it implies violence or lawlessness in some form': *R. v. Aldred* (1909) 22 Cox CC 1 at 3, per Coleridge J. See also W.E. Conklin, 'The Origins of the Law of Sedition,' 277.

5 *Burdett's* case at 120 (per Best J.; emphasis added)

6 *Cobbett's* case at 53; *R. v. Lambert and Perry* (1810), 31 St. Tr. 335 at 363–7

7 *Stockdale's* case.

8 These cases are reviewed by Campbell, *Lives of the Chief Justices of England*, IV: 54–68 and by May, *Constitutional History of England*, II: 280–300.

9 *Dean of St. Asaph's* case (1783–4), 27 St. Tr. 847 at 950

10 F.K. Prochaska, 'English State Trials in the 1790s: A Case Study,' *Journal of British Studies* 13 (1973), 63; Clive Emsley, 'An Aspect of Pitt's "Terror" Prosecution for Sedition during the 1790s,' *Social History* 6 (1981) 155. The Libel Act is 32 Geo. III, c. 60.

11 The pro-Erskine point of view comes out clearly in the newspapers. See *Quebec Herald*, 10 June, 4, 14 Oct., 2, 16 Dec. 1790.

12 *Quebec Gazette*, 7 Nov. 1793

13 *Statutes of the United States*, 1798, Fifth Congress, Sess. 2, c. 74

14 De Bernière to Captain Green, 27 May 1797, C series, vol. 14

15 Ryland to Fortier, 20 Jan., 1794, Civil Secretary's Letter Books, vol. 2; Dorchester to Portland, 25 July 1795, Q series, vol. 72; Robertson, *Mrs. Simcoe's Diary* (entry for 22 June 1795); Simcoe to Osgoode, 6 July 1795, Simcoe Papers, Series 4, vol. 5; La Rochefoucauld-Liancourt, *Voyage*, II, *passim*; Ryland to Foucher, 28 July 1796, Prescott Papers, vol. 9

16 Black to Neilson, n.d., Neilson Collection, vol. 1 (pp. 113–14). See also Young to Ryland, 9 June 1798, CO42, vol. 111.

17 Stephen Thorn to Citizen Fauchet, 11 Nov. 1794, LOC/France, supp. vol. 28; Monk to Dorchester, 2 Oct. 1794, CO42, vol. 100; Declaration of Neilson, 30 May 1795, Declarations of Aliens

18 La Rochefoucauld-Liancourt, *Voyage*, II: 185; 10 July 1794, Collection Baby, vol. 11

19 'a Loyalist' to Osgoode, 13 Sept. 1794, Osgoode Papers, file 9

20 Treatment of the Quebec Assizes for November 1794 is based principally on the several depositions dating from 24 May to 11 June 1794, by Quebec and Charlesbourg suspects and informers, found in CO42, vol. 100 (pp. 10–21, 361–5); vol. 101, (pp. 13–20) and on the *Quebec Gazette*, 31 July 1794; Monk to Dorchester, 15 Nov. 1794, enclosing a document entitled 'State of Prosecutions in His Majesty's Court of King's Bench, November Term 1794,' CO42, vol. 101. The statutory requirements for treason trials are found in 7 & 8 Wm. III, c. 3; 7 Anne, c. 21.

21 Ryland to Sewell, 25 Feb. 1795, Civil Secretary's Letter Books, vol. 4; *Quebec Gazette*, 26 Mar. 1795

22 Ross to Davidson, 9 Mar. 1795; Arthur Davidson Letters; *The Times–Du Cours du Tems*, 30 Mar. 1795; *Quebec Gazette*, 26 Mar. 1795

23 Quoted in Hay, 'Meanings of the Criminal Law,' 108, n66

24 Documentation for Charlotte Hamelin (1794), Charles Gréham (1794),

André Vagner (1795) and Jean-Baptiste Caron (1795) in Pardons, vol. 1;
Quebec Gazette, 15 May, 19 June 1794, 1 Oct. 1795

25 See particularly Leon Radzinowicz, *History of English Criminal Law*, I; Douglas Hay, 'Property, Authority and the Criminal Law'; Ignatieff, *A Just Measure of Pain*; Emsley, *Crime and Society in England*. For Lower Canada, see Pardons, vol. 1. Banishment was by far the most common commuted sentence in early Lower Canada, although transportation was not unknown.

26 Wallot, 'La querelle des prisons dans le Bas Canada (1805–1807),' in *Un Québec qui bourgeait*; Fecteau, *Un nouvel ordre des choses*, 111–23; SLC 1799, c. 6, s. 2; *Montreal Gazette*, 16 Sept. 1805

27 *Quebec Gazette*, 15 May, 11 Sept. 1794, 26 Mar., 2 Apr., 1 Oct. 1795, 6 Oct. 1796, 6 Apr. 1797, 29 Mar. 1798; *Montreal Gazette*, 14 Sept. 1797, 14 Mar., 12 Sept. 1796, 20 Mar., 11 Sept. 1797, 12 Mar., 24 Sept. 1798. Some criminal terms were not reported and the relevant issues of the *Montreal Gazette* for March 1794, September 1794, and March 1795 are missing.

28 Clive Emsley, 'Pitt's "Terror",' Appendix B: 'Trials for "sedition" in the English provinces 1793–1801,' *Social History* 6 (1981), 155

29 Richardson to Ryland, 6 Feb. 1797, Cruikshank and Hunter, eds., *Correspondence of the Honourable Peter Russell*, I: 140; Liston to Prescott, 8 Apr. 1797, Prescott Papers, vol. 11; Prescott to Russell, 11 May 1797, ibid., vol. 25

30 Although Adet urged an attack via the Mississippi, nothing came of it. The rumours were given a heavy discount in Quebec at the end of July when it was learned that a Spanish mobilization in Louisiana during the autumn of 1796 had been carried out to defend against an anticipated British-American invasion: Prescott to Russell, 31 July 1797 (with enclosure), Prescott Papers, vol. 25. Upper Canada responded to this crisis with a death-threatening statute directed against alien enemies: SUC 1797, c. 1.

31 Richardson to Sewell, 19 Jan., 13 Feb. 1797, Sewell Papers, vol. 3

32 Richardson to Sewell, 23 Mar. 1797, Sewell Papers, vol. 3. See also Gaspard de Lanaudière to Pierre-Paul-Margane de Lavaltrie, 27 Mar. 1797, Collection Baby, vol. 12; 34 Geo. III, c. 54; SLC 1797, c. 6.

33 In fact this was not liberalizing change at all. Under the Alien Act a magistrate's hasty committal could have been overturned by the governor-in-council, while the Better Preservation Bill provided for no check on the initial decision. Warrants would not be issued unless approved of by the governor, while the colonial secretary could not possibly police enforcement.

34 Richardson to Sewell, 30 Mar. 1797, Sewell Papers, vol. 3

35 Fleming, *Political Annals*, 29–31. See also Gaspard de Lanaudière to his wife,

30 Jan. 1797, Collection Baby, vol. 12. Prescott had among other things invited the members of the Assembly to a levée: Ryland to Speaker Jean-Antoine Panet, 27 Jan. 1797, Civil Secretary's Letter Books, vol. 5.

36 Richardson to Sewell, 6 Apr. 1797, Sewell Papers, vol. 3; *JHALC*, 1797 (17 Apr.)

37 Ibid. (19 Apr.). The Legislative Council passed the bill without amendment: ibid. (25 Apr.).

38 Treasonable practices could not have been assumed to be a felony, since neither in the British nor Lower Canadian legislation was the death penalty (or any other) prescribed. Since as Sewell pointed out in *Bédard* (1810, *Stuart's Reports*, 1) the term implied a more serious crime than seditious libel it must have been a misdemeanour, rather than a non-indictable, petty offence.

39 Indictable offences, including misdemeanours, were invariably described in the indictments as breaches of the king's peace. The logic of refusing privilege for all indictable offences had been accepted by the Commons as early as 1641, a position repeated almost word for word by an early post-Revolution authority, George Petyt: '*Priviledge* [*sic*] cannot be pleaded against an *indictment* for any thing done out of Parliament, because all *Indictments* are *contra Pacem Domini Regis*.' *A Treatise of the Law and Custom of the Parliaments of England* (London: Timothy Goodwin 1690; reprinted ed., 1974 by Scholarly Resources Inc. of Wilmington, Delaware), 295 (emphasis in the original). See also Blackstone, *Commentaries*, I: 165: no member of either House could 'be arrested and taken into custody, unless for some indictable offence, without a breach of the privilege of parliament.'

40 22 June 1797 (letter of P. Laforce to Pierre Vezina)

41 Nairne to Malcom Fraser, 12 Feb. 1797, Nairne Papers, vol. 3

42 See Sewell's report and calendar; *Montreal Gazette*, 20 Mar. 1797; and the revealing letter written by defence counsel, David Ross and found in the McCord Museum.

43 Ross to Arthur Davidson, 5 Mar. 1797, Arthur Davidson Letters; *Montreal Gazette*, 11 Sept. 1797; Borthwick, *History of the Montreal Prison*, 244

44 White, *Lord Selkirk's Diary* (10 Feb. 1804)

45 See Osgoode to Burland, 27 Oct. 1795, CO42, vol. 22; same to John King, 3 Aug. (with postscript, 27 Aug.), 14 Nov. 1796, ibid.; same to ——, 13 Oct. 1796, ibid.; *Quebec Gazette*, 6 Oct. 1796.

46 See Sewell's report and calendar; *Quebec Gazette*, 6 Apr. 1797; notes on three trials, bearing date of 28 Mar. 1797 in the Records of the Court of King's Bench. These notes list witnesses, and for two of the trials, jurors, as well as including brief resumés of the proceedings.

47 Endorsement on the indictment of Ignace Lambert et al., Mar. 1797, Records of the Court of King's Bench; *Quebec Gazette*, 6 Apr. 1797
48 SLC 1832, c. 22; Girod, *Notes diverses*, 35
49 *Montreal Gazette*, 11 Sept. 1797; *Quebec Gazette*, 14 Sept. 1797. A search for the record was made by the Quebec Department of Justice in its Montreal archives but proved unavailing.
50 See the following newspaper reports of the assizes: *Quebec Gazette*, 9 May, 7 Nov. 1793 (Smith); ibid., 26 Mar. 1795, 6 Oct. 1796 (Osgoode); ibid., 6 Apr. 1797 (Osgoode and De Bonne); *Montreal Gazette*, 20 Mar. 1797 (Monk); *Quebec Gazette*, 30 Mar. 1797 (Trois-Rivières). See also David Ross to Arthur Davidson, 9 Mar. 1795, 5 Mar. 1797 (re Monk), Arthur Davidson Letters'; 'a Loyalist' to Osgoode, 13 Sept. 1794 (re Osgoode at Montreal), Osgoode Papers, file 9, NAC; *The King* v. *David Maclane* [sic] (1797), 26 St. Tr. 721 at 723, 825–6 (Osgoode).
51 Osgoode to John King, 4 Nov. 1794, CO42, vol. 22
52 Monk objected to the Montreal magistrates granting bail to Road Act rioters, although as accused misdemeanants (not felons or traitors) they almost certainly had an indisputable right to bail if the sureties produced were solvent. The British authorities, in any event, made no exception for cases of sedition. In 1795 when Montreal chief justice he attempted to deny the rights of juries in sedition cases, despite Parliament's arguable 'declaration' of the law in Fox's Libel Act. Two years later his court, by indicting Ducalvet et al. for compassing, sanctioned the dubious doctrine that a conspiracy to foment insurrection amounted to plotting the death of the king three thousand miles away.
53 *Montreal Gazette*, 20 Mar. 1797
54 This sketch of levying war in England is based mainly on dozens of cases reported in Howell's *State Trials*, the writings of the older jurists (Coke, Hale, Hawkins, Foster, Blackstone, and East) and the following scholarly works: Bellamy, *Law of Treason in England in the Later Middle Ages* and *The Tudor Law of Treason*; Hurst, *The Law of Treason in the United States*.
55 *The Constitutional History of England from the Accession of Henry VII to the Death of George II*, [1827] 11th ed., 3 vols. (London: John Murray 1866), III: 158; *Boswell's Life of Johnson* [1791], 2 vols. ed Humphrey Milford (Oxford: Oxford University Press 1922), II: 397: 'He said he was glad Lord George Gordon had escaped rather than a precedent should be established for hanging a man for *constructive treason*; which ... would be a dangerous engine of arbitrary power' (emphasis in the original).
56 Foster stated that the *Dammaree* and *Purchase* decisions of 1710 were 'the

last in print which have come in judgment on the doctrine of constructive levying of war.'

57 (1710), 15 St. Tr. 521 particularly, 608–9; (1781), 21 st. Tr. 485

58 *A Treatise upon the Law and Proceedings in Cases of High Treason*, (London: 1793).

59 See the terse reports of the Yorkshire cases in the *Gentleman's Magazine* for April (p. 191) and May (p. 239) of 1758. It is highly improbable Monk knew of the manuscript judgments mentioned by East, since neither Foster nor 'A Barrister at Law' mentioned them or the trials. I thank Douglas Hay for assistance on this point.

60 *Purchase's* case, 15 St. Tr. 521, particularly at 699–702. The accused there had joined the meeting house riots in mid-stream and seems to have been ignorant that the plan was to destroy all such houses as were within reach.

61 *Quebec Gazette* 24 Sept. 1812

62 Ross to Davidson, 2 Mar. 1797, Arthur Davidson Letters

7 THE TRIAL OF DAVID MCLANE

1 McLane's name was spelled in a bewildering variety of ways. This form is chosen because that is how he signed deeds of sale and how his name appears in the army list and vital records (n. 5 below). He did at times, however, employ the form M'Lane.

2 The most comprehensive and reliable trial report is *The Trial of David McLane for High Treason at the City of Quebec, in the Province of Lower Canada on Friday, the Seventh day of July, A.D. 1797: Taken in Short-hand at the Trial* (Quebec: William Vondenvelden, Law Printer to the Lower Canadian Government 1797). The Vondenvelden report (two copies of which are held by McGill University) was carefully reprinted by Thomas Bayly Howell in 26 St. Tr. 721 (hereafter Howell). For convenience I have used the State Trials version. The *Quebec Gazette* published the highlights of the trial in French and English (13 July–17 Aug. 1797) and printed two short pamphlets (21, 22 pages) from the same types: see Tremaine, *Imprints*, nos. 1054, 1055. An anonymous twelve-page pamphlet entitled *The Trial, Condemnation and Horrid Execution of David M'Lean* was published in Windham, Connecticut (no publisher given) in 1797 (copy held by Harvard University). It contains a number of dramatic descriptions not found elsewhere (hereafter the Windham trial report). Later, polemical editions include Girod, *Notes diverses*, 49–53; *Les Soirées canadiennes* 2 (1862) 353–400; *The Evening Bulletin* of Providence, Rhode Island, Supplement, 26 Apr. 1873

3 Osgoode to John King, 22 July 1797, CO42, vol. 22; Richardson to Jonathan
Sewell, 29 May 1797, Sewell Papers, vol. 3; Caldwell to Simcoe, 18 Nov.
1797, Simcoe Papers, series 1, vol. 6. A Vermont informer, to whom
McLane had explained his strategy in November 1796, had then concluded
that the spy was 'totally insane or very materially deranged in his mind or
very much wanting in common sense': Silas Hathaway to Ryland, 26 Sept.
1797, enclosed with Prescott to Liston, 29 Jan. 1798, Prescott Papers, vol. 12.
4 *DCB*, vol. 4, 501–3. See also Galarneau's *L'Opinion canadienne*, 252–60;
Perrault, *Abrégé*, 70. Perrault (clerk of the peace and a member of the House
of Assembly in 1797) justified the trial and execution on the basis that the
habitants had been excited by French emissaries and incendiary writings.
See also 'War with France 1793,' *RNAC* (1891), 38–56, and Kingsford, *History of Canada*, 10 vols. (Toronto: Rowsell & Hutchinson 1887–98), VII: 365,
385–402, 439–55.
5 The article on McLane in *DCB*, vol. 4 (relying on the Windham trial report)
states that he was about thirty at the time of his execution in July 1797 and
may have been born in Ayrshire, Scotland. Richardson thought that one of
McLane's grandfathers had emigrated to New England from the north of
Ireland (Richardson to Sewell, 8 Dec. 1796, Sewell Papers, vol. 3). The local
historian of Providence, Walter R. Danforth, stated that the McLanes were
originally a Lane family of Attleborough, Massachusetts ('Pictures of Providence in the Past,' 96). In his deposition Elmer Cushing stated McLane was
of Scottish descent. Liston (to Portland, 25 Jan. 1797, Prescott Papers, vol. 8)
learned that McLane was 'said to be of Scotch Descent.' According to Black,
testifying at the trial (Howell, 778) McLane had said that Black might be
surprised that one so young should be a general, which would suggest he
was not older than forty in 1797. Another witness at the trial swore that
McLane had told him he had been born in Boston (ibid., 773). The main
sources for McLane's years in Providence are various deeds of sale and
petitions in the Rhode Island State Archives; inventory of McLane's estate,
20 May 1799 and probate records for 1799, 1800, City Hall, Providence;
Joseph Jencks Smith, ed., *Civil and Military List of Rhode Island, 1647–1799*
(Providence 1900); James N. Arnold. ed., *Vital Records of Rhode Island,
1636–1850. First Series. Births, Marriages and Deaths*, vol. 15 (Providence
1906); *Heads of Families at the First Census of the United States Taken in the
Year 1790. Rhode Island*, (Washington: Government Printing Office 1908);
Providence Gazette and Country Journal, 17 Aug. 1793, 21 Jan. 1797; Danforth,
'Pictures of Providence,' 93–6.
6 LOC/France, vol. 19 (trans.); Howell, 770
7 Liston to Grenville, 25 Jan. 1797, FO5; Prescott to Portland, 6 Sept. 1797,

CO42, vol. 109; Sewell to Milnes, 23 Oct. 1801, CO42, vol. 117; Timothy Pickering (US secretary of state) to Andrew Ellicott, 28 July 1797, quoted in Wilbur, *Ira Allen*, II: 139. The curator of the Bailey/Howe Library, University of Vermont, J. Kevin Graffagnino, an expert on the various Allen Papers, has concluded McLane did not coordinate his plans with Allen (oral communication with the author, 30 July 1990). I could find no link in the Allen Family Papers at the University of Vermont or in the Ira Allen and Levi Allen Papers in the Stevens Collection, Vermont State Archives, Montpelier.

8 Samuel Peters to the editor of the *Morning Post and Fashionable World*, 25 Sept. 1797, Allen Family Papers, Box 18

9 Cushing, *Appeal*. This material does not appear in Cushing's deposition or his evidence at trial, but is consistent with what is known of McLane's character.

10 Stephen to Jonathan Sewell, 14 Nov. 1796, S series, vol. 65

11 Sewell to Samuel Gale, 9 July 1799, S series, vol. 68. See also Ryland to J. Sewell, 17, 20 Nov. 1796, ibid., vol. 65; J. Sewell to Cushing, 21 Nov. 1796, ibid.; same to Ryland, 25 Nov. 1796, ibid.

12 23 Nov. 1796, CO42, vol. 108 (pp. 111–18). The self-dramatizing Cushing did not name McLane in this deposition but later gave the government the information it wanted by responding to the attorney general's specific question as follows: 'I will not tell you that He is the man, But I will not say He is not': Sewell to Ryland, 25 Nov. 1796, S series, vol. 65. In January 1797 Liston provided the home government with a detailed synopsis of the plot, based largely on Cushing's deposition: to Portland, 25 Jan. 1797, enclosed in Portland to Prescott, 15 Mar. 1797, Prescott Papers, vol. 8 (instructing prosecution if McLane were caught).

13 1 Dec. 1796 *RNAC* (1891), 64–5

14 Liston to Prescott, 13 Feb. 1797, Prescott Papers, vol. 11; Adet's account book, LOC/France, vol. 19; voluntary examinations of Frichette, 12 May 1797, *RNAC* (1891), 69–70; Thomas Butterfield, 22 May 1797, ibid., 71; and Daniel McLane, s.d., ibid., 72. For lack of a better source the details of the trip described in the following paragraphs are taken from Frichette's examination.

15 10 May 1797, *RNAC* (1891), 67–9

16 Black's statement on this point was corroborated by Frichette, but the latter may well have been induced to do so to escape the gallows. Black's version was later confirmed by a Vermont informer and possible accomplice, Silas Hathaway. According to the latter, he had conversed in detail with McLane at St Albans in mid-November 1796. McLane had told him he would take Quebec by surprise and when that was accomplished the French fleet

would ascend the river and the land forces from Vermont would enter the province. If all went well McLane would become 'Governor' of the place: Hathaway to Ryland, 26 Sept. 1797, enclosed with Prescott to Liston, 29 Jan. 1798, Prescott Papers, vol. 12. But again it is difficult to be certain that Hathaway was telling the truth. Hathaway was something of an extortionist. See Wilbur, *Ira Allen*, II: 172.

17 *RNAC* (1891), 69–70; Colonel de Bernière to ———, 20 May 1797, C series, vol. 673

18 See, for example, *Star*, 11 Aug. 1797; *General Evening Post*, 12 Aug. 1797; Willard to Luke Knowlton, Quebec, 30 June 1797, Knowlton Family Papers.

19 Stephen to Jonathan Sewell, 14 Nov. 1796, S series, vol. 65; William Lindsay to same, 1 Dec. 1796, Sewell Papers, vol. 3; Richardson to same, 6 Feb. 1797, ibid.; *Adventures and Recollections of Colonel Landmann* (hereafter Landmann, *Recollections*), 2 vols. (London: Colburn & Co. 1852), I: 318–26. In 1798, Landmann, then an officer of the Royal Engineers stationed in Quebec, learned that McLane's conspiracy had had 'for its object the assassination of all the officers at Quebec, both military and civil.'

20 Ryland to Monk, 13 Apr. 1797, Prescott Papers, vol. 9; Prescott to Portland, 27 May 1797, CO42, vol. 109

21 Riddell, 'King v. David McLane'; 335, n18; Bédard, *Cinquante ans*, 33–4; Galarneau, *L'Opinion canadienne*, 252–60. See also his article on McLane in *DCB*, vol. 4, 501.

22 Unless otherwise specified, the details which follow are taken from Howell.

23 Dunn to Philip Ruiter, – July 1794, Ruiter Family Papers

24 George to Carleton Allsopp, 24 Nov. 1793, Allsopp Papers, Letterbook; depositions dating from late May 1794 in CO42, vol. 100 (pp. 17, 365) and vol. 101 (pp. 13–20); *Quebec Gazette* , 7 Dec. 1797

25 13 St. Tr. 1 at 61; (1781) 21 St. Tr. 485.

26 *Thomas Hardy's* case (1794), 24 St. Tr. 199 at 208–10, 233, 267–8, 1182–3, 1293–1384

27 The '*De Facto Act*' (11 Hen. VII [1495], c. 1) likely declared the common law on point. See Greenwood, 'The Chartrand Murder Trial: Rebellion and Repression in Lower Canada, 1837–1839' *Criminal Justice History* 5 (1984), 144–5, 152, 158, for a brief legal analysis. A narrow interpretation of the act as being restricted to 'kingly' usurpers had prevented the regicides and Commonwealth officials from using it effectively in their defence after the Restoration of 1660.

28 See especially *Thomas v. Acklam* (1824) 107 English Reports 572 (UKKB). See also Paul Romney, 'Re-inventing Upper Canada: American Immigrants, Upper Canadian History, English Law, and the Alien Question,' in Roger

Hall et al., eds. *Patterns of the Past: Interpreting Ontario's History* (Toronto: Dundurn Press 1988), 82–7.

29 Affidavit of William Vondenvelden and Hugh Mackay, before Chief Justice Osgoode, 30 June 1797, Records of the Court of King's Bench

30 Ryland to Sewell, 29 May 1797, Prescott Papers, vol. 9; Mann to Black, 6 Oct. 1807, Q series, vol. 106

31 Richardson to Sewell, 29 May 1797, Sewell Papers, vol. 3; Sewell to Ryland, – Apr. 1797, Sewell Papers, vol. 10; Christie, *A History*, I: 185

32 George Germaine Francklin to Ryland, 17 Apr. 1797, Prescott Papers, vol. 9. In 1800 the promises were met, Barnard received the township of Brompton, and Cushing that of Shipton. Black received 5/7ths of the township of Dorset in 1799.

33 To Francklin, Prescott Papers, vol. 9

34 Prescott to Portland, 16 May 1789, ibid., vol. 15; Young to Ryland, 9 June 1789, CO42, vol. 111

35 'General Index to Commissions, Quebec and Lower Canada,' RG6, A10, NAC; Petitions for Notaries and Advocates' Commissions (Jan. 1797); Francklin to Sewell, 22 June 1794, Sewell Papers, vol. 3. According to a letter written by Francklin in August 1798, he had lived in Sewell's house for the past six years. After moving out, he thanked his patron for having treated him as a parent or a brother. He had always enjoyed 'the most perfect and disinterested Friendship, and a Tenderness of Conduct, that I could only expect from a near Relation': Francklin to Sewell, 15 Aug. 1798, ibid. See also Francklin to Ryland, 17 Apr. 1797 and Ryland to Francklin, 18 May 1797, Prescott Papers, vol. 9.

36 The main source for Allen's problems in Quebec during the summer of 1797 is the Allen Family Papers, boxes 17 and 18, particularly Allen to Ryland, 23 June 1797; Ryland to Allen, 23 June 1797 and Allen to Jonathan Sewell, 30 June 1797. A brief account may be found in Cockerham's thesis, 'Levi Allen (1746–1801),' 245–7.

37 Lower Canada State Minute Book B (29 June, 2 Sept. 1797). The committee, with three as quorum, was to meet on the summons of the Council's chairman, Chief Justice Osgoode, and was to report its proceedings to the full Council.

38 I was drawn into error, following Jonathan Sewell and Justice Riddell, in stating that *McLane* was the first treason trial in British America ([1991] 20 *Manitoba Law Journal* 3 at 6). Besides the proceedings in New York under a widely phrased local statute against Nicolas Bayard in 1701 (which Sewell tended to dismiss as a precedent, Howell, 815), there were two successful treason prosecutions (but not executions) following the Cumberland Rebel-

lions in Nova Scotia (1776–7). These proceedings were so obscure Sewell apparently did not know of them. See J.T. Bulmer, 'Trials for Treason in 1776–7'; *Collections of the Nova Scotia Historical Society* 1 (1879), 110. I thank Jim Phillips for educating me in these matters.

39 That many Canadiens were sympathetic to the plight of the accused, before and after his trial, is clear from *Les Soirées canadiennes* 2 (1862), 353–6, and Philippe-Aubert de Gaspé, *Les Anciens Canadiens* [1863] (Quebec: Librairie Beauchemin 1863), 216–18.

40 Records of the Court of King's Bench, file nos. 424, 432, 422, 426 respectively. Examples from 1795–6 can be found in file nos. 385, 386, 393, 394, 396, 398, 405, 409, 410, also Langlois file (1796), no file number. For an exception see file no. 384 (an all-English panel).

41 *Quebec Gazette*, 7 Apr. 1797 (Blackwood, Crawford, Cull, Monro, Painter, and Symes)

42 Conviction for treason also entailed severe property losses for the traitor and his family. Goods and chattels owned by the prisoner passed to the crown as of the date of the verdict, or earlier where there had been collusive alienation. Real estate was forfeited as of the date of the treason. By contrast to cases of felony, where the realty was held by the crown for the lifetime of the felon plus one year, these forfeitures were permanent. In addition, the condemned traitor suffered corruption of the blood upwards and downwards. He could not inherit and, more important, no one could inherit through him. If, for example, a man died intestate after his eldest son's execution for treason, the latter's eldest son could not inherit his grandfather's landed estate.

43 See Bryant, *Years of Endurance*, chs. 8, 9; Liston to Prescott, 20 June 1797, Prescott Papers, vol. 11; 24 June 1797, Young Papers, vol. 4.

44 Stephen to Jonathan Sewell, 17 July 1797, Sewell Papers, vol. 3; Aubert de Gaspé (*Les Anciens Canadiens*, 216–28) claimed the executioner was a well-known local character named Ward, who exhibited much finery after the execution. Landmann had it on good authority in 1798 (*Adventures*, 318–26) that the man's face was not seen by Shepherd on the 20th and of course was covered during the execution. He was suspected of being an American who imitated an Irish accent to conceal his identity.

45 Ryland to Sheriff James Shepherd, 19 July 1797 (two letters), Civil Secretary's Letter Books, vol. 5

46 Labadie as quoted in French in Galarneau, *L'Opinion canadienne*, 259, n 113 (24 July 1797); Chew to Prideux Selby, Montreal, 31 July 1797, Claus Papers, vol. 7, AO; Osgoode to John King, 22 July 1797, CO42, vol. 22

47 *The Lives of the Judges of Upper Canada and Ontario* (Toronto: Rowsell &

Hutchison 1888), 24–6; 'King v. David McLane,' 335, n 18. Not surprisingly, Stephen Sewell found the trial 'perfectly consonant to justice and the laws': to Jonathan, 17 July 1797, Sewell Papers, vol. 3. Prescott informed Liston that McLane had been 'convicted on the fullest evidence' (12 July 1797, Prescott Papers, vol. 12).

48 Lord Eldon's Anecdote Book, ed. Anthony L.J. Lincoln and Robert Lindley McEwen (London: Stevens & Sons 1960), 55–7; Horne Tooke's Diary, 15 May–23 Nov. 1794, printed in Notes and Queries, 8th series, vol. 11, 1897, 21–2, 61–2, 103–4, 162–3; Brown, French Revolution in English History, 120–2

49 Parl. Deb., vol. 6 (3 Mar. 1806). Lord Campbell describes it as such in his Lives of the Lord Chancellors, VIII: 418–19: 'when the [state] prisoners [of 1794] were apprehended and examined before the Privy Council, the judges who were to sit upon their trials were called in to listen to the evidence and join in the commitment.'

50 The local precedent was provided by the tangled case of James Gale and Alexander Thompson (1788–90), who had been brought to Quebec from the Indian country and charged with murder committed outside the boundaries of the province. In an attempt to settle a variety of jurisdictional problems, the case was examined in the 'Privy Council' (executive portion of the Legislative Council), which acted under an instruction from Lord Dorchester to dispense with the services of Chief Justice William Smith, since he was likely to preside at any ensuing trial. Dorchester to Sydney, 9 June 1788 (twice – once enclosing the Minutes of the Privy Council for 20 May 1788), CO42, vol. 59; same to same, 14 Oct. 1788, CO42, vol. 38.

51 Richardson to Sewell, 23 Mar. 1797, Sewell Papers, vol. 3

52 Hale, Pleas of the Crown 94

53 13 St. Tr. 485 at 525.

54 Sparenburgh's (1797) 1 Bos. & Pul. 163 at 167–9

55 He was the editor of the first law reports published in Quebec/Lower Canada (1811) and appointed a judge in 1818.

56 Cartwright to Davidson & Co. (London), 4 Nov. 1797, Conway Edward Cartwright, ed. Life and Letters of the Late Hon. Richard Cartwright (Toronto: Belford Brothers 1876), 75; Ward Chipman to Sewell, 18 Mar. 1798, Sewell Papers, vol. 3; reports published during the last week of August or first week of September 1797 in The Times, the London Chronicle, the White Hall Evening Post, the Star, the General Evening Post and the Morning Herald; Annual Register, 279–80; Portland to Prescott, 4 Nov. 1797, Prescott Papers, vol. 8

57 See Windham trial report; Hathaway to Ryland, 26 Sept. 1797, enclosed with Prescott to Liston, 29 Jan. 1798, Prescott Papers, vol. 12; Cushing Appeal. The newspaper controversy can be conveniently followed in the issues

from 2 to 22 Aug. 1797 of the *Gazette of the United States, and Philadelphia Daily Advertiser*. See also, e.g., the *Vermont Gazette* (published in Bennington), 5 Sept. 1797.

58 Galarneau, *L'Opinion canadienne*, 258–9

59 Perrault, *Abrégé*, III: 70. Perrault was appointed road treasurer for Quebec City and parish by a Special Session of the Peace held in July 1796: *Quebec Gazette*, 28 July 1796.

60 Stephen to Jonathan Sewell, 17 July 1797, Sewell Papers, vol. 3; Nairne to Kerr, 15 Aug. 1797, Nairne Papers, vol. 3

8 WAR'S END AND ETHNIC BREAKDOWN

1 *Parl. Hist.*, vol. 34, 579–656; 39 Geo. III, c. 79

2 CO42, vol. 112 (emphasis in the original)

3 Tremaine, *Imprints*, no. 1135. See also ibid., no. 1103; Ryland to Foucher, 6 Jan. 1800, Collection Baby, vol. 13; Foucher to Ryland, s.d., ibid.

4 Graham to Burton, n.d., *RNAC* (1891), 83–4; Burton to Green, 15 July 1801 and enclosures, C series, vol. 673; Milnes to Portland, 1 Aug. 1801, Q series, vol. 87; same to King, 16 Sept. 1801, ibid.; same to Hobart, 28 Oct. 1801, ibid.; Lower Canada State Minute Book C (21 Sept. 1801). For secondary sources bearing on the issue, see Wilbur, *Ira Allen*, II: 318–33; Stuart Webster, 'Ira Allen in Paris 1800, Planning a Canadian Revolution'; *CHAR* (1963), 74; Wallot, *Intrigues*, 46–90; Graffagnino, ' "Twenty Thousand Muskets!!!" '

5 Sewell to Milnes, 21 Sept. 1801, Sewell Papers, vol. 10

6 Same to same, 23 Oct. 1801, CO42, vol. 117

7 9 Oct. 1801, Q series, vol. 87

8 Wallot, *Intrigues*, 66–73; Richardson to Ryland, 2 Nov. 1801, S series, vol. 75; same to same, 27 June 1803, ibid., vol. 80

9 Sewell to Milnes, 23 Oct. 1801 (and enclosures), Q series, vol. 87. The conclusion here differs from that found in my 'Development of a Garrison Mentality,' 45–8, 153–6, where, following some secondary works and Sewell, I assumed that Allen had been behind the plot.

10 Milnes to Hobart, 28 Oct. 1801, Q series, vol. 87; Wallot, *Intrigues*, 74–90; Lower Canada State Minute Book D (10, 17 Dec. 1801)

11 Aside from the legal analysis and the conclusions, my account of the Le Couteulx case owes a great deal to Jean-Pierre Wallot's carefully documented and thoughtful study (*Intrigues*, 25–35).

12 Portland to Prescott, June 1798, with extract from Liston to Portland, 2 Apr. 1798, cited in Wallot, *Intrigues*, 25, n 20

13 Liston to Hunter, 19 Nov. 1800, C series, vol. 14 emphasis in original. The translated extracts (all written in New York State) were enclosed in Hunter to Portland, 2 Jan. 1801, C series, vol. 1209. Le Couteulx acknowledged the authenticity of these extracts: 17 Aug. 1802, ibid., vol. 14.

14 Sewell had rendered his opinion by 6 November: Hunter to Elmsley, 6 Nov. 1800, ibid., vol. 1209. The undated written version (complete) which is about two pages in the C series, was enclosed with Hunter to Portland, 19 Nov. 1800, ibid.

15 This and the following two paragraphs are based principally on correspondence found in the C series, vols. 1209–10 and Diplomatic and Secret Reports; three eighteenth-century British law officers' opinions found in McNair, *International Law Opinions* (pp. 11–12) and Moore's *Digest* (p. 553); Moore, 'Doctrine of Expatriation'; Richard W. Flournoy, 'Naturalization and Expatriation,' *Yale Law Journal* 31 (1921–2), 701–11. The law as I have described was accepted as obvious by Advocate General Sir Robert Phillimore (an international law expert) in 1866: Phillimore to Lord Clarendon, 24 Apr. 1866, in McNair, *International Law Opinions*, 12–13.

16 Alexander Hamilton thought the position of the Canadian authorities might have been tenable had Le Couteulx emigrated to and been naturalized in the United States after the British-French war had commenced: to Cheriot, 18 Nov. 1800, C series, vol. 1209.

17 See, *DCB*, vol. 5, 839.

18 Ryland to Mountain, 3 Feb. 1806, Christie, *A History*, VI: 84–6; same to Robert Peel, 27 June 1811, ibid., 226–7

19 Osgoode to Burland, 27 Oct. 1795, CO42, vol. 22

20 Osgoode to ——, 13 Oct. 1796, CO42, vol. 22. See re opinion on Dorchester, Mountain to Spenser, 26 Oct. 1804, Mountain Papers, vol. 5.

21 See, for example, Chapais, *Cours*, II: 99–106 and Manning, *The Revolt*, 19. Wade (*The French Canadiens*, I: 102–4) leaves the same impression, although he suggests in passing that the act may have owed something to Milnes's fear that the illiterate habitants were prey to demagogues.

22 See, for example, Arthur R.M. Lower, *Colony to Nation*, 3rd ed. (Toronto: Longmans, Green 1957), 155–7; Audet, *Le système scolaire*, *passim* but particularly xxiii–xxiv; Fernand Ouellet, 'L'enseignement primaire,' *Recherches sociographiques* 2 (1961), 174–5.

23 Mountain to Dorchester, 17 July 1795 quoted in Audet, *Le système scolaire*, 10, n 8. A French translation of Mountain's plan is printed on pp. 11–14 (hereafter Mountain's Plan).

24 Jonathan Sewell's Notebook (hereafter Sewell's Notebook), *c.* 1800, Sewell Papers, vol. 1, 7–15; Sewell to Ward Chipman, 19 Oct. 1799, Chipman

Papers, (letter 23 for 1799); Chartier de Lotbinière to Sewell, 14 Jan. 1800, Sewell Papers, vol. 4; Milnes to Portland, 10 June 1801, CO42, vol. 116. Sewell's Notebook contains a plan which is very similar to the provisions in the act of 1801. Almost certainly Sewell drafted the government bill which, after enactment, became the act: Audet, *Le système scolaire* , 87.

25 Sewell to Prescott, 12 May 1797, *RNAC* (1891), 76

26 Sewell's Notebook, *c.* 1800, 9; Milnes to Portland, 23 Feb. 1801, CO42, vol. 116; same to same, 10 June 1801, ibid. The teachers appointed to teach in the few royal schools established for Canadiens during the ten years after the passage of the act were Roman Catholic and French-speaking: see Audet, *Le système scolaire,* 136.

27 *Quebec Gazette,* 5 Aug. 1802. In 1805 Malherbe's school was brought under the administration of the Education Act and he was given a salary of £54 per annum: Audet, *Le système scolaire,* 136; Roy, *Histoire de la seigneurie de Lauzon,* III: 346–54.

28 The only clear reference to the connection between education and the economic development of the province I have found in the extant writings of those who helped formulate the policy behind the act of 1801 is Mountain's statement in 1795 that subsidized schools would stimulate the 'Industry' of the Canadiens: to Dorchester, 17 July 1795, quoted in Audet, *Le système scolaire,* 10–11, n 9.

29 Mountain's Plan; Milnes to Portland, 5 Apr. 1800, CO42, vol. 114; *An Inquiry into the Nature and Causes of the Wealth of Nations* [1776], ed. A Library of Universal Literature (New York: Collier & Son 1901), III: 170–1; Sewell's Notebook, *c.* 1800, 12

30 Milnes to Portland, 1 Nov. 1800, *Const. Docs., 1791–1818,* 252–3; Sewell to Milnes (draft), 16 Nov. 1799, Sewell Papers, vol. 3

31 Mountain to Dorchester, 17 July 1795, quoted in Audet, *Le système scolaire,* 10–11, n 9, *Quebec Herald,* 26 Jan. 1788; Osgoode to Burland, 27 Oct. 1795, CO42, vol. 22. See also Milnes to Portland, 5 Apr. 1800, CO42, vol. 114.

32 Richardson to Ryland, 1 Dec. 1799, S series, vol. 70; Sewell's report, 264; Sewell's Notebook, 21–3; Milnes to Portland, 1 Nov. 1800, *Const. Docs., 1791–1818,* 249–51. In the absence of a will, seigneurial real estate devolved on death as follows: the eldest son inherited the manor house and one-half of the seigneury, with the other children sharing equally in the remainder. Moveables and *roture* lands passed to all children equally.

33 A detailed study of this question is Frère Marcel-Joseph's, 'Les Canadiens veulent conserver le régime seigneurial,' *RHAF* 7 (1953–4), 46–56.

34 The act is SLC 1801, c. 3. An abstract of it was printed in *Const. Docs., 1791–1818,* 259–62.

35 Milnes to Portland, 16 Apr. 1801, ibid., 258
36 Sewell's report, 265; Milnes to Portland, 10 June 1801, CO42, vol. 117
37 For examples of this common view among the English at the turn of the century, see Ogden, *Tour through Upper and Lower Canada*, 24–5; Milnes to Portland, 23 Feb. 1801, CO42, vol. 116. Sewell was highly concerned in 1800 that opposition from the curés could destroy the projected education policy: Sewell's Notebook. 9.
38 Milnes to Portland, 1 Nov. 1800, *Const. Docs., 1791–1818*, 252–3; Portland to Milnes, 6 Jan. 1801, ibid., 256
39 A scholarly annotated edition of this document is provided by Jean-Pierre Wallot, 'Sewell et ... le clergé canadien,' in his *Québec qui bougeait*, 169 (proof of its secret nature at p. 179, n 13).
40 Francis Maseres, attorney general of Quebec, had entertained such an idea in 1768: Neatby, *Quebec: The Revolutionary Age*, 119–21
41 Ryland to ——, 23 Dec. 1804, Christie, *A History*, VI: 72–3; Mountain to Milnes, 6 June 1803, *RNAC* (1892), 20
42 Mountain to Spenser, 26 Oct. 1804, Mountain Papers, vol. 5; *Quebec Mercury*, 5 Jan. 1805
43 See, for example, Milnes to Hobart, 15 Aug. 1803, *RNAC* (1892), 16. Milnes took care to appoint at least some of the *parti canadien* MPPs to government posts, such as J.-F. Perrault as prothonotary of the King's Bench, Quebec, and notary Joseph Planté as clerk of the land roll (administrator of the seigneurial system).
44 Wallot, 'Sewell et ... le clergé canadien,' 177, 179, n 13; Milnes to Hobart, 15 Aug. 1803, *RNAC* (1892), 16; Hobart to Milnes, 9 Jan. 1804, ibid., 22–3. See also Christie, *A History*, VI: 86–90.
45 Document in Sewell's handwriting on the Royal Institution, n.d., Sewell Papers, vol. 14 (p. 7165); Richardson to Ryland, 1 Dec. 1799, S series, vol. 70: 'In my mind it [facilitating conversion of tenure] is one link of that chain of measures which good policy may dictate as a means of assimilating the Inhabitants to their fellow subjects in other parts of His Majesty's Dominions.'
46 White, *Selkirk's Diary* for 10 Feb. 1804, 219–20
47 It will be recalled that the reformers' joint agent, Adam Lymburner, had favoured payment of members in the paper he read to the Commons in 1791. *JHALC*, 1799 (17 May); *JHALC*, 1802 (13, 15 Feb., 8 Mar.).
48 *JHALC*, 1793–4 (4 Apr., 22 May 1794). The martial law motion was unsuccessful.
49 Critics (of both nationalities) pointed to the chicanery of lawyers, the multiple sources to be mastered, and the functioning of the Court of Appeals

where one district's judgments were often overturned by the chief justice and his colleagues from the other. English critics harped on archaism, while Canadien complainants (and a few English) stressed the English judges' ignorance of the civil system. (Sewell was an acknowledged exception.) Their constant attempts to anglicize it was another common Canadien theme. Both complaints had substance but cannot be explored in this book. See Sewell to Milnes, 28 Oct. 1805, S series, vol. 88; Chief Justice Henry Allcock, to Shee, 5 Dec. 1806, Q series, vol. 101; Cuthbert, *An Apology*, 7–9; Gray, *Letters from Canada*, 120–3; *Quebec Mercury*, 22 Mar., 28 Dec. 1807; *Le Canadien*, 27 Aug. 1808; Wallot, 'Plaintes contre l'administration de la justice'; Kolish, 'Impact of the Change in Legal Metropolis,' 14, 23 n 46; *DCB*, vol. 7, 783, 785.

50 Other factors were undoubtedly at play, such as the habitants' conservatism and the gradual demise of that segment of the Canadien bourgeoisie from import and export commerce. Too much should not be made of the latter since Canadiens continued prominent in the country merchant sector and in urban, real estate speculation.

51 Pothier, *Oeuvres*, III: 260, 305, 356–9. The refusal to compensate the buyer for merely useful expenditures was based on the idea that otherwise the buyer could easily frustrate the family's right of *retrait*.

52 *JHALC*, 1792–3 (7 Mar. 1793)

53 During the last decades of New France the *retrait* had become subordinated to the seigneur's right to repossess sold land for the price stipulated, the purpose of which was to protect against fraudulent lowering of the *lods et ventes* payable by the purchaser. Cole Harris contends that this change 'was contrary to an article in and violated the entire spirit of the Coutume de Paris,' indicating that 'family land did not mean to Canadians during the French regime what it did to Frenchmen': *Seigneurial System*, 75.

54 Issues of the *Quebec Mercury* for 9, 23 Feb. 1805

55 Un Canadien [Viger], *Considérations, passim*

56 J.-A. Panet's criticism in the Assembly of the education dispensed by the Seminary of Quebec (1808) seems to have been a rare and partial exception: see Wallot, 'La religion catholique et les Canadiens au début de XIXe siècle,' 217, n 101.

57 Trudel, *L'Influence de Voltaire au Canada*, 15–77; Hare and Wallot, *Les imprimés*, 317; *Le Canadien*, 17 Dec. 1808

58 These paragraphs are based mainly on a reading of *Le Canadien* and the Assembly *Journals* and on the following secondary sources: L.A.H. Smith, '*Le Canadien* and the British Constitution, 1806–1810'; Manning, *The Revolt*, ch. 3–5; Hare and Wallot, *Les imprimés, passim*; Ouellet, *Lower Canada*, 84–94, 103; Finlay, 'Bédard as a Constitutionalist.'

59 Harvey and Olsen, 'French Revolutionary Forms in French-Canadian Political Language'
60 For a useful detailed study, see Jean-Pierre Wallot, 'La querelle des prisons dans le Bas Canada (1805–1807),' in *Québec qui bougeait*, 47.
61 Milnes to Camden, 12 Apr. 1805, Milnes Papers, Entry Book
62 *Quebec Mercury*, 3 Apr. 1809
63 *Le Canadien*, 14, 21 May 1808
64 Ibid., 1806–10, *passim*; see also Creighton, *The Empire*, 157–9.
65 *Le Canadien*, 20 Nov. 1806

9 THE SHADOW OF NAPOLEON IN LOWER CANADA

1 Daniel Sullivan to Richardson, 21 May, 20 June 1803, S series, vol. 80; Milnes to Hobart, 1 June 1803 (with enclosures), CO42, vol. 121; Richardson to Ryland, 27 June, 22 Sept. 1803, S series, vols. 80, 81. On the alarmist reaction to the fires, see particularly Stephen to Jonathan Sewell, 9 June 1803, Sewell Papers, vol. 4; Alexander Henry to John Askin, 18 Aug. 1803, in Quaife, *Askin Papers*, II: 394; Labadie Journal, Aug. 1803.
2 Milnes to Hobart, 10, 24 June 1803, CO42, vol. 121, 122; Barclay to Hunter, 2 Dec. 1803, S series, vol. 82; Ryland to Richardson, 16 Jan. 1804, ibid.; Richardson to Ryland, 20 Feb. 1804, ibid., vol. 83
3 Richardson to Ryland, 17 May 1804, ibid.
4 Richardson to Ryland, 24 Dec. 1804, 9 May 1805, CO42, vol. 127; same to same, 27 Dec. 1804, S series, vol. 83; Turreau to Talleyrand, 3 Nov. 1806, LOC/France, vol. 59
5 Bord, 'Le Canada,' 100–1 (trans.)
6 Ibid.; Thomas Barclay (British consul general at New York) to Craig, 22 Nov. 1809, Correspondence from the British Minister to the United States; Daniel Sullivan to G.O. Radford, 24 Jan. 1810, C series, vol. 673; William Thorton (military secretary) to Major-General Drummond, 5, 18 Mar. 1810, ibid., vol. 1216; Ryland to McGill, 15 Mar. 1810, Civil Secretary's Letter Books, vol. 12
7 Turreau to Talleyrand, 3 Nov. 1806, LOC/France, vol. 59
8 Webster, 'Napoleon and Canada,' ch. 1; Nathan Schachner, *Aaron Burr* (New York: Barnes 1937), ch. 28
9 See, for example, Denaut to Pius VII, 26 Apr. 1803, *RANQ* (1931–2), 204; Plessis to Roux, 3 June 1805, 'Evéques de Québec,' vol. 3, AAQ; same to the Bishop of Nisibe, 8 Feb. 1810 *RANQ* (1927–8), 270; same to Burke, 18 Feb. 1810, ibid., 271; de Calonne to Craig, 17 Jan. 1809, S series, vol. 102
10 See de Gaspé, *Mémoires*, 202; Paul-Roch de St Ours to Baby, 3 June 1802,

quoted in Wallot, *Intrigues*, 107; same to de Lavaltrie, 17 Sept. 1804, Collection Baby, vol. 13; Chartier de Lotbinière to Jonathan Sewell, 8 May 1805, Sewell Papers, vol. 4

11 See, for example, *Courier*, 21 Jan. 1807, 21 Jan. 1808; *Séance de la société littéraire de Québec, tenue samedi, le 3e juin 1809* (Quebec: John Neilson 1809).

12 For a particularly good example, see J.-T. Taschereau to Jacques Viger, 12 Mar. 1810, in Viger's 'Ma Saberdache,' série bleu, MG24, L8, vol. 2, NAC. See also Christie, *A History*, I: 340.

13 *Le Canadien*, 13 Nov. 1806, 28 Mar. 1807, 8 Feb. and 24 Sept. 1808, 23 Sept. and 4, 11 Nov. 1809; *JHALC*, 1810, 2, 9 Feb.

14 Un Canadien [Viger] *Considérations*; *Le Canadien*, 11 Mar. 1809

15 That these public statements were not mere window dressing is indicated by a number of private letters written during the war by activists in the party, such as merchant-seigneur-MPP Jacques-Nicolas Perrault, then (1807) a follower of Bédard; Papineau's son, Louis-Joseph; and writer Jacques Viger, one of the editors of *Le Canadien* (1808–9). Reacting to a rumour in 1814 that Napoleon had committed suicide, Viger commented to a friend: 'Yes, Bonaparte is dead! this [*sic*] is the wisest act of an execrable Tyrant ... and the only excusable one.' Viger to J.-D. Mermet, 18 Feb. 1814, quoted in translation by Ouellet, *Economic and Social History*, 239; Perrault to Olivier Perrault, 21 Sept. 1807, Collection Baby, vol. 14; Louis-Joseph Papineau to Antoine Ménard, 22 Mar. 1809 [1810], ibid. Although he would later change his politics, Perrault regularly voted with Bédard during the fourth legislature (1805–8): Hare, 'L'Assemblée législative,' 379. In the letter cited above Perrault referred to Bédard as the finest of citizens and a 'profound thinker' (trans.).

16 *JHALC*, 1803, 3, 4, 5, 6, 9 Aug.

17 For example, in 1806, Bédard seconded the motion that the Better Preservation Bill be engrossed: *JHALC*, 1806, 22 Feb.

18 SLC 1804, c. 3; Richardson to Jonathan Sewell, 9 Feb. 1804, S series, vol. 83; *JHALC*, 1804, 27, 29 Feb., 9 Mar. Three years later a bill to discourage desertion among sailors and merchant mariners passed into law with ease: *JHALC*, 1807, *passim*; SLC 1807, c. 9.

19 SLC 1808, c. 1; *JHALC*, 1808, 14 Apr.

20 De Gaspé, *Mémoires*, 170–6; de Calonne to Craig, 17 Jan. 1809, S series, vol. 102 (trans.); *Quebec Mercury*, 23 Dec. 1811 (letter of 'A Canadian')

21 De Gaspé, *Mémoires*, 170–6; 'Camillus' [Henry], *An Enquiry*, 30; Roy, 'Napoleon au Canada,' *passim*; Elizabeth Frances Hale to Lord Amherst, 2 Feb. 1806, Hale Family Papers; *Quebec Gazette*, 16, 23 Jan. 1806; *Quebec Mercury*, 13 Jan. 1806; *Montreal Gazette*, 3 Feb. 1806

22 Cochran to his mother, 29 May 1814, Cochran Papers

23 Berczy to his wife, 18 Aug. 1808, Collection Baby, vol. 26, (trans.)

24 See Lt.-Col. Joseph de Longueuil (commander of the Canadien battalion of the Royal Canadian Volunteers) to Hunter, 26 Dec. 1799, C series, vol. 1208 ('insurmountable prejudice of the Canadien people for their country of origin' [trans.]). See also Milnes to Hobart, 24 June 1803, CO42, vol. 122; de Lotbinière to Jonathan Sewell, 8 May 1805, Sewell Papers, vol. 4; Thomas Dunn to Philip Ruiter, 26 Aug. 1807, Ruiter Papers, vol. 1.

25 Monk to Governor Prevost, 12 Dec. 1812, S series, vol. 126, (trans.)

26 Galarneau, *L'Opinion canadienne*, 333; *Quebec Mercury*, 26 Jan. 1807

27 Maulevrier, *Voyage*, 66

28 Gray, *Letters from Canada*, 334

29 Estimated from the censuses of 1790 and 1825

30 Stephen to Jonathan Sewell, 19 Mar. 1801, 21 June 1810, Sewell Papers, vol. 4. See also the 1805 letter from 'Les habitants du Canada' to the French authorities printed in Wallot, *Intrigues*, 139–41. Government officials, it appears, did not know of its existence.

31 De Lotbinière to Sewell, 8 May 1805, Sewell Papers, vol. 4 (trans.)

32 See, for example, Richardson to Ryland, 1 May 1803, extract enclosed in Milnes to Hobart, 1 June 1803, CO42, vol. 121; —— to R. Mathews, Quebec, 27 Jan. 1807, ibid., vol. 135.

33 7 Aug. 1807, S series, vol. 95 (trans.). For a similar incident involving a militia riot see, Sewell to Milnes, 26 Sept. 1803, Pardons, vol. 2. I am indebted to Patricia Kennedy of NAC for drawing my attention to this document.

34 In addition to the sources given in the following note see, for example, Milnes to Hobart, 1, 10 June 1803, CO42, vol. 121; same to same, 24 June 1803, CO42, vol. 122; Richardson to Ryland, 13 June 1803, S series, vol. 80; same to same, 5 Nov. 1804, ibid., vol. 84; same to same 9 Nov. 1807, ibid., vol. 96; David Ross to Arthur Davidson, 26 July 1805 (re rumours in the capital), Arthur Davidson Letters; Elizabeth Frances Hale to Lord Amherst, 2 Feb. 1806, Hale Family Papers (re rumours in the capital); Ryland to Mountain, 27 Apr. 1806, Mountain Papers, C series, vol. 5; Thomas Dunn to Philip Ruiter, 26 Aug. 1807, Ruiter Papers, vol. 1; Craig to D.M. Erskine, 13 May 1808, CO42, vol. 136; Stephen to Jonathan Sewell, 23 Aug. 1810, S series, vol. 110; *Quebec Mercury*, 18, 24 Nov. 1806, 21 Sept. 1807, 3 Apr. 1809; *Canadian Courant*, 12 Nov. 1810, 29 July 1811; and Gray, *Letters from Canada*, 367–8 (re common opinion in the colony). As early as 1801 Edward Edwards, proprietor-editor of the *Montreal Gazette*, worried lest Napoleon's 'intoxicating Success' in Europe encourage the French to 'look to British

America, they know the Canadians would not do much to prevent any attempt to attack us.' Retired fur merchant Alexander Henry (1806) was likewise 'much afraid Boneparte [sic] will over run the old World and then step over the water to pay us a Visit.' Edwards to John Neilson, 23 Apr. 1801, Neilson Collection, vol. 1; Henry to John Askin, 18 Jan. 1806, Quaife, *Askin Papers*, II: 500; Stephen to Jonathan Sewell, 26 May 1803, Sewell Papers, vol. 4.

35 Isaac to William Brock, 31 Dec. 1809, Tupper, *Brock Correspondence*, 74–5

36 Milnes to Hobart, 1 June 1803 (with enclosure), CO42, vol. 121; Isaac to William Brock, 31 Dec. 1809, Tupper, *Brock Correspondence* , 74–6; Stephen to Jonathan Sewell, 23 August 1810, S series, vol. 110

37 Erskine to Canning, 6 Mar. 1808, FO5, vol. 57; Craig to D.M. Erskine, 13 May 1808, CO42, vol. 136; Craig to Castlereagh, 15 July 1808 (with enclosures), ibid.; Mathews to Col. Gordon, 25 Apr. 1807 (with enclosure), CO42, vol. 135

38 Richardson to Ryland, 1 Mar., 5 Nov. 1804, S series, vol. 84; *Mercury*, 21 Sept. 1807 (emphasis in the original); Brock to Gore, 21 Sept. 1807, C series, vol. 1214

39 Francisco de Miranda was a Venezuelan patriot who in 1806 had unsuccessfully attempted to liberate his country from Spanish rule by organizing a military expedition from the United States. In the autumn of 1806 Aaron Burr led a small armed force down the Mississippi towards New Orleans. Although his ultimate objectives are unknown, many in the United States believed he intended to establish an independent republic in the American southwest.

40 Mathews to Colonel Gordon, 25 Apr. 1807, CO42, vol. 135. The growing 'insolence' referred to the recent establishment of *Le Canadien* and the exercise by the Assembly of the right to arrest for contempt.

41 See 'Mercator' [John Young] to ——, 28 July 1805, CO42, vol. 131; —— to R. Mathews, 27 Jan. 1807, CO42, vol. 135; Gray, *Letters from Canada* , 77; Ryland to Mountain, 17 Oct. 1807, postscript dated 27 Oct., Mountain Papers, vol. 5.

42 Hitsman, *Safeguarding Canada*, 77–9

43 For the serious desertion problem see, for example, Brock to the Duke of York, n.d., Tupper, *Brock Correspondence*, 35; Richardson to Ryland, 9 Feb. 1804, S series, vol. 83; William Smith Jr to Jonathan Sewell, n.d. (postmarked 14 Feb. 1804), Sewell Papers, vol. 4. On the unreliability of the Canadien militia see, for example, White, *Selkirk's Diary* (10 Feb. 1804); Gray, *Letters from Canada*, 343.

44 To R. Mathews (extract), in Mathews to Colonel Gordon, 25 Apr. 1807,

CO42, vol. 135; *Montreal Gazette* , 16, 23 Dec. 1818; see also *Canadian Courant*, 12 Nov. 1810.

45 Craig to Liverpool, 1 May 1810, *Const. Docs., 1791–1818*, 390–2. See also same to Castlereagh, 5 Aug. 1808, CO42, vol. 136; same to Bunbury, 21 Feb. 1810, CO42, vol. 141; *Quebec Mercury*, 4, 18 July, 1 Aug. 1808; *Montreal Gazette*, 5 Mar. 1810.

46 *Mercury*, 10 Mar. 1806; Ryland to Mountain, 27 Apr. 1806, Mountain Papers, Series C, vol. 5

47 Ryland's 'Observations,' May 1808, Christie, *A History*, VI: 117; 'Camillus' [Henry], *An Enquiry*, 11–12 (original emphasis). See also, for example, John Black's 'Observations' (*c*. October 1806), *Const. Docs., 1791–1818*, 323–5; Fleming, *Some Considerations*, *passim*; *Quebec Mercury*, 16, 23 Apr. 1810; Craig to Ryland, 9 Nov. 1810, Christie, *A History*, VI: 166–7.

48 'Camillus' [Henry], *An Enquiry*, 16. See also Ryland to Mountain, 3 Feb. 1806, Mountain Papers, vol. 5; same to Peel, 11 Feb. 1811 and enclosure, Christie, *A History*, VI: 193.

49 Elizabeth Frances Hale to Lord Amherst, 2 Feb. 1806, Hale Family Papers; Gray, *Letters from Canada*, 327–8; John Hale to Amherst, 26 May 1803, Hale Family Papers

50 White, *Selkirk's Diary* (10 Feb. 1804, 217). John Elmsley, a native of Middlesex was chief justice of Lower Canada from 1802 to 1805.

51 Sewell's observations on the state of the province. May 1810, *Const. Docs., 1791–1818*, 401

52 *Mercury*, 16 Mar. 1807; Cuthbert, *An Apology*, 20. Cuthbert cited only one example, that of an inn on the king's highway; Samuel Bridge's Journals, vol. 1, 11 July 1805 (emphasis added)

53 Ryland to Mountain, 26, 29 Oct. 1805, Mountain Papers, vol. 5; Black's 'Observations,' CO42, vol. 135 (p. 376). See also *Quebec Mercury*, 26 Jan., 5 Mar., 8 June 1805; *Quebec Gazette*, 8 Apr., 13 Oct. 1808.

54 Stephen to Jonathan Sewell, 30 Apr. 1810 Sewell Papers, vol. 4; Craig to Liverpool, 1 May 1810, *Const. Docs., 1791–1818*, 389. See also White, *Selkirk's Diary* (10 Feb. 1804); *Quebec Mercury*, 25 Apr. 1808; John Antrobus (merchant-overseer of roads for the District of Trois-Rivières) to Louis Foy, 14 June 1811, S series, vol. 113, (government should 'keep a very, very watchful Eye' on the Roman Catholic Church).

55 Milnes to Portland, 1 Nov. 1800, *Const. Docs., 1791–1818*, 250; Ryland to Plessis, 24 Apr. 1800, *RANQ* (1931–2), 167; Plessis to Ryland, 26 Apr. 1800, S series, vol. 70; Bishop Denaut to Milnes, 8 May 1800, *RANQ* (1931–2), 167

56 19 Mar. 1801, Sewell Papers, vol. 4

57 Craig to Liverpool, 1 May 1810, Q series, vol. 112. This portion of the dis-

patch is not printed in *Const. Docs., 1791–1818*. See also Ryland to Mountain, 3 Feb. 1806, Mountain Papers, vol. 5; Milnes to Shee, 14 June 1806, CO42, vol. 131.

58 According to Galarneau (*L'Opinion canadienne*, 192–3) fifty-one emigré priests entered the colony up to the end of 1811, of whom four died and nine departed prior to the Napoleonic War. Four more died between 1804 and 1811 inclusive.

59 Milnes to Sullivan, 21 Oct. 1803, CO42, vol. 123. Ryland to Richardson, 26 Dec. 1803, S series, vol. 82. Milnes and Ryland suspected that Desjardins, who actually became vicar general of Orléans, might work through his brother; Hale to Lord Amherst, 2 Feb. 1806, Hale Family Papers.

60 Another Sulpician, Dr Jacques-Guillaume Roque, who prior to the Revolution had been director of the Seminary of Angers, was the director of the Soeurs de Hôtel Dieu from 1796 to 1806 and in the latter year was appointed grand vicar and director of the Petit Séminaire de Montréal. Among the other emigré priests was Jacques de Calonne, brother of the pre-Revolutionary finance minister, who became chaplain to the Ursulines at Trois-Rivières. The Abbé Pierre-Joseph Malavergne, a native of Bordeaux, was chaplain of the Hopitale-Générale in Quebec from 1797 to 1809.

61 Milnes to Sir George Shee, 18 May 1806, CO42, vol. 131; Dionne, *Les Ecclésiastiques* , 105–13, 169–314. Only one emigré priest appears to have entered the colony (1813) from Europe after the war had begun: Galarneau, *L'Opinion canadienne*, 192–3. The Abbé de Calonne, a former resident of Prince Edward Island (since 1799) had to wait three years (1804–7) for permission to re-emigrate from London to Lower Canada: ibid., 215.

62 Jonathan Sewell to Craig, – May 1810, *Const. Docs., 1791–1818*, 405

63 Draft letter from Mgr. J.-H.-A. Roux to the governor, n.d., St Sulpice Papers, MG17, vol. 5 (p. 1676), NAC. Internal evidence indicates the letter was drafted sometime after Governor Craig's departure in 1811.

64 De Calonne to Craig, 17 Jan. 1809, S series, vol. 102; Galarneau, *L'Opinion canadienne*, 285; *DCB*, vol. 6, 105, 200, 667

65 See also Desjardin's letters to Abbé Robert: 28 Mar. 1803, 10 July 1805, 26 Jan. 1806, undated letter written in or after 1809, 21 Oct. 1809, 25 Mar. 1811. Archives of the Quebec Seminary, Lettres, carton T. These letters which deal, *inter alia*, with the grave problems faced by the French clergy and the writer's hopes for peace, contain no hint of political intrigue. See also Galarneau, *L'Opinion canadienne*, 206–9.

66 Fleming, *Some Considerations, passim*; Cuthbert, *An Apology, passim*

67 See ibid., 13–14; Henry, *An Enquiry*, 28; *Quebec Mercury*, 24 Nov. 1806; Lambert, *Travels*, I: 343–4.

68 *Montreal Gazette*, 18, 23 Dec. 1818

69 See Richardson to Ryland, 21 Sept. 1801, S series, vol. 74; Milnes to Hobart, 24 June 1803, CO42, vol. 122; Dunn to Philip Ruiter, 26 Aug. 1807, Ruiter Papers, vol. 1; Craig to Castlereagh, 4 Aug. 1808, CO42, vol. 136; Gray, *Letters from Canada*, 366–8; *Canadian Courant*, 3 Aug. 1807, 29 July 1811.

70 *Quebec Mercury*, 24 Nov. 1806. For similar responses to Viger's pamphlet of 1809, see ibid., 3 Apr. 1809 (editorial note and letter of 'Scevola').

71 White, *Selkirk's Diary* for 10 Feb. 1804, 217; Gray, *Letters from Canada*, passim; Christie, *A History*, I: 313; Ryland to Craig, 4 Aug. 1810, ibid., VI: 123–4; Craig to Castlereagh, 4 Aug. 1808, CO42, vol. 136; Un Canadien [Viger], *Considérations*, passim

10 THE GARRISON FINDS ITS LEADER

1 Ryland to Mountain, 17, 22, 25 Oct. 1807, Christie, *A History*, VI: 92–5. The best biographical account of Craig is Jean-Pierre Wallot's article in *DCB*, vol. 5, 205.

2 Têtu and Gagnon, *Mandements*, III: 71; Craig to Castlereagh, 1 June 1809, Q series, vol. 109; *DCB*, vol. 8, 843. See also Baynes to Brock, 4 Oct. 1810, Tupper, *Brock Correspondence*, 83; Christie, *A History*, I: 353–4.

3 Samuel Bridge's Journals, vol. 2, 13 Sept. 1809

4 Baynes to Brock, 4 Mar. 1811, Tupper, *Brock Correspondence*, 99

5 De Gaspé, *Mémoires*, 265–9; Christie, *A History*, I: 347; de Lotbinière to Jonathan Sewell, 8 June 1809 (draft), De Lery-Macdonald Papers, (trans.)

6 De Gaspé, *Mémoires*, 265–9. According to de Gaspé, Craig had once served as judge advocate and often presided in the provincial Court of Appeals.

7 Sir Henry Bunbury, *Narratives of Some Passages in the Great War with France (1794–1810)* ed. J.W. Fortesque (London: P. Davies 1927), 122

8 Creighton, *The Empire*, 161

9 See Craig to Castlereagh, 15 Aug. 1808, Q series, vol. 107; same to Bunbury, 21 Feb. 1810, CO42, vol. 141; same to Liverpool, 1 May 1810, Q series, vol. 112.

10 De Gaspé, *Mémoires*, 265, 269–73; Richardson to William Ellice, 30 Oct. 1811, Ellice Papers, MG24, A2, vol. 2, NAC. The opening of his first legislature (1808) was described in the newspapers as the most brilliant in the history of the colony: *DCB*, vol. 5, 207.

11 Manning, *The Revolt*, 77–8; Hitsman, *Safeguarding Canada*, 76; Craig to

Castlereagh, 9 Nov. 1807, Q series, vol. 106; same to same, 11 Jan., 8 Feb. 1808, ibid., vol. 107

12 This and the next paragraph are based principally on Ezekiel Hart to Philips and sons, 26 May 1808, Hart Family Papers, McCord Museum, Montreal; Thomas A. Coffin to J. Sewell, 5 Feb, 1808, Sewell Papers, vol. 4; Stephen to Jonathan Sewell, 29 Feb. 1808, ibid.; 'Proceedings Relating to the Expulsion of Esekiel Hart,' *Const. Docs., 1791–1818*, 351–4; *Le Canadien*, 2 March 1808; 13 Geo. II (1740), c. 7; 13 Geo. III (1773), c. 25; B.G. Sack, *History of the Jews in Canada* [c. 1945] (Montreal: Harvest House 1965), 69–79.

13 The debates were reported in detail in *Le Canadien*, 20, 27 Feb., 9, 12, 19 Mar., 2 Apr. 1808. Under the provisions of the bill, magistrates would have remained eligible for election.

14 Even two of Craig's closest advisers, Sewell and Richardson, were prepared to support legislation excluding judges from election in the districts where they acted: *Le Canadien*, 20 Feb., 12 Mar. 1808. A little over a year later Craig wrote that 'very many of the best meaning Men in the Province are of opinion that it would be better if the Judges were not under the necessity of counting [courting] the people, as they are obliged to on the occasion of their Elections'. to Castlereagh, 5 June 1809, *Const. Docs., 1791–1818*, 361.

15 Unless otherwise specified this section is based on the newspapers for May–June 1808; Hare and Wallot, *Les imprimés*, 137–44; Hare and Wallot, *Confrontations*, 117–28.

16 *Le Canadien*, 4 June 1808; Christie, *A History*, I: 275; Pierre-Georges Roy, *La famille Panet* (Lévis: J.-A.-K. Laflamme 1906), 55–8

17 Sewell had during the year (a particularly good one financially) received over £3,300 for work done in the period 1793–1801, his salary of £333.6.8, and £857.8.7 for the many prosecutions of the *Chesapeake* rioters of 1807: *Le Canadien*, 7 May 1808.

18 Ibid., 28 May 1808

19 Hare, 'L'Assemblée législative,' 381–3

20 Craig to Castlereagh, 11 Jan., 8 Feb., 6 Apr. 1808, CO42, vol. 136

21 11 June 1808, S series, vol. 99

22 *Le Canadien* later classified them as *ministérielistes*: Hare, 'L'Assemblée législative,' 381. Hare has Turgeon listed as such, but could not find any recorded vote by Faribault. The *DCB* article (vol. 8, 288) is inconclusive on political orientation. Faribault was the notarial and business agent of the seigneur Paul-Roch de St Ours and hence unlikely to have been drawn strongly to the *parti canadien*.

23 ' "*My friends, they are forging irons for you. I won't say any more, but watch out*" ' (emphasis in original).

24 Craig to Castlereagh, 5 June 1809, *Const. Docs., 1791–1818*, 361. See also Ryland's 'Observations Relative to the Political State of Lower Canada' of May 1808, Christie, *A History*, VI: 117; *DCB*, vol. 5, 651; Paul Roch de St Ours to Ryland, 20 June 1808, S series, vol. 99.

25 Craig to Castlereagh, 5 Aug. 1808, CO42, vol. 136; form letter of Ryland to the dismissed militia officers, 14 June 1808, Christie, *A History*, I: 276; *DCB*, vol. 6, 586

26 Craig to Castlereagh, 4 Aug. 1808, CO42, vol. 136; to same, 5 June 1809, *Const. Docs., 1791–1818*, 363; to Bunbury, 21 Feb. 1810, CO42, vol. 141; to Liverpool, 1 May 1810, *Const. Docs., 1791–1818*, 391

27 It can be extracted from four dispatches he wrote on the subject. Craig to Francis Gore (Lieutenant-Governor of Upper Canada), 11 May 1808, Q series, vol. 107; same to D.M. Erskine (minister to the United States), 13 May 1808, CO42, vol. 136; and to Castlereagh, 4, 5 Aug. 1808, ibid.

28 The successive Spanish kings in 1808 – Charles Bourbon, his son Ferdinand, and Napoleon's brother Joseph – were entirely dependent on the emperor. The beginning of the end for Napoleon in Spain came with the defeat of General Dupont at Baylen in July 1808 by an army of Spanish rebel regulars and peasants.

29 Erskine to Canning, 6 March 1808, FO5, vol. 57

30 Craig to Castlereagh, 5 Aug. 1808, CO42, vol. 136.

31 For Bédard's constitutional ideas see *DCB* , vol. 6, 41; Lawrence Smith, 'Le Canadien'; Wallot 'La pensée révolutionnaire' 276–81; Finlay, 'Bédard as Constitutionalist.'

32 Blackstone, *Commentaries*, I: 155. That Bédard had ideas which pointed to (but fell well short of) responsible cabinet government is well known. These ideas were broached in *Le Canadien* (1807), but not, apparently, in the House during our period. For impeachment, see Raoul Berger, *Impeachment: The Constitutional Problems* (Cambridge, Mass.: Harvard University Press c. 1973), particularly 1–2, 55–63 and references therein.

33 Smith, 'Le Canadien,' 98

34 Law officers to Bathurst, 30 Dec. 1815, *Const. Docs., 1791–1818*, 480–3. The law officers were responding to a question on privileges, phrased so as to suggest the Assembly's pretensions needed restricting (p. 483). The original text of the question (CO42, vol. 164, pp. 194–5) is definitely in the handwriting of Sewell (then in London), who had received permission to draft it for submission from the colonial secretary, Lord Bathurst: Henry Goulburn to Sewell, 14 Nov. 1815, Sewell Papers, vol. 5.

35 Goderich to Aylmer, 26 Jan. 1832, Christie, *A History*, III: 441–2 (denial of

Assembly's power to exclude members); *Kielley* v. *Carson* (1842), 4 Moo.
PC 63 (denial of Newfoundland Assembly's power to arrest for contempts
committed out of doors)

36 The stress on this was almost constant in *Le Canadien* from 1808 to 1810.
One of the leaders of the *parti canadien* (probably Bédard) stated in the
Assembly that the 'first duty of this House ... was to maintain its independence, even against the attempts of the first [branch, i.e., the executive] to
lessen it': *Le Canadien*, 26 Apr. 1809.

37 Craig to Castlereagh, 5 Aug. 1808, CO42, vol. 136. This was certainly not the
case. See, for example, *Le Canadien* , 26 Apr. 1809.

38 Craig to Bunbury, 21 Feb. 1810, CO42, vol. 141

39 Ryland to Peel, 11 Feb. 1811 and enclosure, Christie, *A History*, VI: 192–4.
See also, for example, Craig to Liverpool, 30 March 1810, *Const. Docs.*,
1791–1818, 374.

40 *Mercury*, 10 July 1809

41 See Manning, *The Revolt*, 83–5; Christie, *A History*, I: 278–88; ibid., 283–8;
JHALC, 1809 (14 Apr.–12 May, Appendix 23); Craig to Castlereagh, 5 June
1809, *Const. Docs.*, *1791–1818*; 360–3.

42 Minutes of the Executive Council, 18 Apr., 10 May 1809, *Const. Docs.*,
1791–1818, 356–9

43 Chartier de Lotbinière to Sewell (draft), 8 June 1809, De Lery-Macdonald
Papers; Christie, *A History*, I: 287

44 *Le Canadien*, 3, 4, June, 9 Oct. 1809

45 Harc, 'L'Assemblée législative,' 384–5

11 CRAIG'S 'REIGN OF TERROR'

1 Jackson to Craig, 17 Nov. 1809, Diplomatic and Secret Service reports; *Quebec Mercury*, 1 Jan. 1810; Burt, *United States, Great Britain and British North
America*, 269–78

2 See *DCB*, vol. 8, 387.

3 Thomas Barclay (British consul general at New York) to Craig, 22 Nov.
1809, Correspondence from the British minister to the United States; Daniel
Sullivan, to G.O. Radford, 24 Jan. 1810, C series, vol. 673; William Thorton
(military secretary) to Major-General Drummond, 5, 18 March 1810, ibid.,
vol. 1216; Ryland to McGill, 15 March 1810, Civil Secretary's Letter Books,
vol. 15

4 Isaac to William Brock, 31 Dec. 1809, Tupper, *Brock Correspondence*, 75–6; *Le
Canadien*, 2, 9 Nov., 16 Dec. 1809

5 Castlereagh to Craig, 7 Sept. 1809, *Const. Docs.*, *1791–1818*, 364–5; SLC 1831,
c. 57

6 The main sources are *JHALC*, 1810, *passim.*; Craig to Bunbury, 21 Feb. 1810, CO42, vol. 141; same to Liverpool, 30 Mar. 1810, Christie, *A History* , VI: 102–12; ibid., I: 292–306

7 Taschereau to Jacques Viger, 12 Mar. 1810, Viger's 'Ma Saberdache,' série bleue, MG24, L8, vol. 2, NAC

8 Ibid.; Craig to Liverpool, 30 Mar. 1810 Christie, *A History*, VI: 109–11

9 Although Craig did not expressly refer to this in the Bunbury letter, he later professed belief that if the precedent were allowed to stand 'they will successively vote every class of His Majsty's servants to be ineligible': to Liverpool, 1 May 1810, *Const. Docs., 1791–1818*, 397.

10 *JHALC*, 1810, 21 Feb.

11 Such had been the strategy of the *parti canadien* since the termination of the 1809 session. See *Le Canadien*, 17 June 1809. In Craig's view, serious inconvenience might well arise, especially with regard to Americans entering the colony, but there was, after all, the Better Preservation Act – its renewal had already passed the house – to rely on. Frenchmen, moreover, could be expelled from the province under the prerogative or held as prisoners of war in accordance with Sewell's 1800 opinion in the Le Couteulx case.

12 See *Le Canadien*, 3, 10, 14 Mar. 1810; Bédard's electoral address, as *Votre ami sincère: À tous les électeurs du Bas-Canada* (Quebec: *Le Canadien* 1810); Hare and Wallot, *Les imprimés*, nos. 233, 234, 236, 238, 242; various addresses to Craig from his supporters, S series, vol. 107.

13 *Les imprimés*, nos. 235, 237, 241; *Le Vraie-Canadien*, 10, 21 Mar. 1810

14 Ryland to James McGill, 15 Mar. 1810, Civil Secretary's Letter Books, vol. 15; Christie, *A History*, I: 307; Heriot to Edward Winslow, 19 Mar. 1810, Winslow Papers, vol. 10; Craig's instructions to Ryland, 10 June 1810, Ryland Papers, McGill University; Ryland to Peel, 11 Feb. 1811, Christie, *A History*, VI: 193

15 This section is based mainly on the Executive Council minutes for 17 and 19 Mar. 1810: Lower Canada State Book F.

16 Christie, *A History*, I: 314. The magistrate was probably either one Thomas Allison, who executed the later order to deposit the press in the court house, or John Mure who took most of the depositions.

17 *Const. Docs., 1791–1818*, 138–40

18 Brock to William Claus, 22 Mar. 1810, quoted in E.A. Cruikshank, 'The Administration of Sir James Craig,' *PTRSC* (1908), II: 81–2

19 Papineau to Antoine Ménard, 22 Mar. 1809 (1810), Collection Baby, vol. 14; Henry to Ryland, 26 Mar. 1810, S series, vol. 108; Webster, 'Napoleon and Canada,' 188–9; Bord, 'Le Canada,' 100–1; François-Louis to Louis de Salaberry, 21 Dec. 1810, *BRH* 42 (1936), 563 (in English).

20 Garneau, *History*, II: 259; De Gaspé, *Mémoires*, 266; Christie, *A History*, I: 314; Samuel Bridge's Journals, vol. 2 (26 Mar. 1810); Brock to Mrs W. Brock, 8 June 1810, Tupper, *Brock Correspondence*, 76; same to Irving Brock, 9 July 1810, ibid., 77–8

21 See S series, vol. 108 and particularly McGill to Ryland, 29 Mar. 1810. The third person arrested in the district was one Pierre Papineau.

22 Papineau to Antoine Menard, 22 Mar. 1809 [1810], Collection Baby, vol. 14; *Le Canadien*, 9 Oct. 1809; Christie, *A History*, I: 307–23; Garneau, *History of Canada*, II: 209, 258–62; Chapais, *Cours*, II: 191–203; De Bonnault, 'Napoléon et le Canada,' 38–9; Wade, *French Canadians*, I: 103–15; Galarneau, *L'Opinion canadienne*, 145–6; Jean-Pierre Wallot, 'Sir James Henry Craig,' *DCB*, vol. 5, 211: 'The Executive Council allowed rumours of treason and conspiracy to spread, although they had no substance. The pro-governmental papers rejoiced in them and pretended to believe them.'

23 Craig to Liverpool (secret), 24 Mar. 1810, quoted by Wallot, 'La pensée révolutionnaire,' 291. See also Craig to Liverpool, s.d., Christie, *A History*, VI: 101–12; same to same, 30 Mar. 1810, *Const. Docs., 1791–1818*, 372–8. The *Shorter Oxford English Dictionary* includes the following quotation dating from 1728: 'Sicilian Vespers ... a general Massacre of all the French in Sicily, in the Year 1282; to which the first Toll that call'd to Vespers was the Signal.'

24 *Const. Docs., 1791–1818*, 387–400

25 Ibid., 400–5

26 Craig to Liverpool, 1 June 1810, Q series, vol. 112

27 Ryland's unsuccessful mission of 1811–12 can be studied in detail in dozens of letters, enclosures etc. printed in Christie, *A History*, VI. Although not neglecting the commercial future of the colony, Ryland's lobbying gave overwhelming emphasis to security.

28 Craig to Ryland, 10 June 1810 Ryland Papers, vol. 1

29 A draft copy of the charge may be found in vol. 12 of the Sewell Papers, 5592–600.

30 These examples have been chosen to show how wide-ranging Sewell's concept was. He also classed as seditious other writings (e.g., calculated to excite disobedience to the laws), in terms which would have been perfectly acceptable in England.

31 *Montreal Gazette*, 9 Apr. 1810; Garneau, *History of Canada*, II: 261. Whether this censure was made to accommodate the *ministérieliste* members or, as Garneau thought, reflected 'a mere subterfuge' by a packed jury 'to give an air of impartiality' to its denunciation of *Le Canadien* has not been determined.

32 Stephen to Jonathan Sewell, 30 Apr. 1810, Sewell Papers, vol. 4; Craig to Liverpool, 6 Nov. 1810, Q series, vol. 113; Christie, *A History*, I: 346

33 The case is found in *Stuart's Reports* 1, under the title *In re Pierre Bedard* and reprinted in *Const. Docs., 1791–1818*, 379–87. I have used the former.

34 Ryland to Uniacke, 16 Apr. 1810, Civil Secretary's Letter Books, vol. 15; same to Perrault and Bowen, s.d., ibid.

35 The court could conceivably have taken judicial notice of a notorious fact, delayed the hearing until official returns could be filed by Stuart or treated Bowen's arguments on chronology as constituting admissions of fact.

36 Temple, held under mesne process, asked that his civil trial be delayed on the grounds that since his arrest he had been elected a member of Parliament and was entitled to privilege. The court rejected the motion on two grounds: that Temple had not filed an official certificate of his election; and in any case 'it was proper for the Parliament (when they convened) to discharge him because the Justices doubted if they have power to do that.' 1 Sid. 42 (Trinity Term, 13 Chas. 2 [1661], KB). I thank Professor DeLloyd Guth of the Faculty of Law, UBC for valuable assistance in translating the report from law French and in helping me understand the case. At most it was authority that the King's Bench lacked jurisdiction to effect the discharge unless ordered to by the Commons or through a writ of privilege issued by the lord chancellor on receipt of a warrant signed by the Speaker, the usual ways of proceeding at the time. See also May, *Privileges*, 97.

37 Blackstone, *Commentaires*, I: 164 (emphasis added)

38 14 East 1 at 137 (emphasis added)

39 Whether Sewell contemplated a possible argument drawn from Blackstone, only to reject it (e.g., because of Bédard's incarceration at the time of his election) is not known, but given his vast knowledge of British constitutional law and tendency to think in terms of general principles, such seems more likely than not. A modern British precedent denying privilege in internment situations (*Captain Ramsay's* case, 1940) is beside the point, for the Commons committee report expressly acknowledged that the evolution of responsible cabinet government had made Blackstone's definition of purpose irrelevant to the question at issue: Report of the House of Commons' Committee of Privileges, 1940 in *Captain Ramsay's Case*, Geoffrey Wilson, ed., *Cases and Materials on Constitutional and Administrative Law* (Cambridge: Cambridge University Press 1966), 278–80: 'In the struggle of Parliament against the Crown privilege was regarded as a protection of the Member of Parliament against an executive authority not responsible to Parliament ... The fact that the Executive is now responsible to Parliament ... is relevant when considering general statements such as that quoted [above] from Blackstone made at the time of or in relation to that conflict.' Captain Ramsay, an MP, had been imprisoned under the internment

regulation (18b) of the Defence Regulations authorized by the Emergency Powers (Defence) Act of 1939. The committee found no breach of privilege.

40 That Gibbs was supplied with a full dossier of the proceedings and evidence appears from Ryland to Craig, London, 15 Aug. 1810, Christie, *A History*, VI: 134–5.

41 Lord Liverpool to Craig, 22 Aug. 1810, report and dispatch, 160–2

42 Craig to Ryland, 6 Aug. 1810, Christie, *A History*, VI: 128–9; ibid., I: 322–4; ibid., II: 159, 179

43 SLC 1811, c. 7. The amendment required the consent of the houses to detentions under the act, as had been the case in England since 1689. In 1812, with Bédard back in the house and taking the lead on this question, the Assembly amended the Council's renewal bill so as to prohibit entirely the arrest of members of either house under the act and to pin responsibility squarely on the governor by requiring his warrant (not that of three or more Executive councillors) for arrests, bail, trial, etc. The Council did not agree to these amendments and the bill lapsed. See the proceedings of the Assembly, 11–16 May 1812, printed in *Const. Docs., 1791–1818*, 428–31. In 1838 internment was again authorized by statute, but this was done by ordinance of the appointed Special Council.

44 *Canadian Courant*, 29 July 1811

45 This judgment results from reading dozens of his letters (1792–1811) preserved in the 'Letters of James Dunlop 1773–1815,' Dunlop Papers, MG24, D42, NAC (originals in the Scottish Record Office, Edinburgh).

46 Dunlop to Lister (?), 16 June 1811, ibid. Christie, *A History*, I: 345; *Quebec Mercury*, 24 June 1811. Christie, *A History*, I: 343, reported that Craig 'is said to have expressed, at the moment of his departure, a reflection on the deception, and ingratitude of mankind; declaring that he had experienced more of these human imperfections in Canada, than in the whole course of his life before coming to it.' Christie was uncertain whether these remarks 'were intended to be general, or aimed at some of those immediately concerned with him in the conduct of public affairs.' One thing seems certain: they did not reflect a last-minute conversion to the view that his advisers had manipulated him with scare tactics. On his return to England Craig successfully recommended Ryland, representative of the garrison mentality *par excellence*, to a seat on the Legislative Council: Craig to Liverpool, 10 Dec. 1811, Christie, *A History*, VI: 305–6.

47 An example of Craig's sympathy was his use of the military in 1810 to build 'Craig's road' linking the Eastern Townships with the capital. The immediate motive was to obtain badly needed provisions for the city. In the longer term the motives were both commercial and political (to forge

permanent links between the people of the townships and the capital). It is interesting to note that Sewell was made responsible for finding Americans to settle along the road: Craig to Ryland, 6 Aug. 1810, Christie, *A History*, VI: 130.

48 Burt, *United States, Great Britain and British North America*, 252

49 These words are found on p. 392 (first full paragraph), p. 393 (last sentence of first full paragraph), p. 394 (point 11), p. 395 ('& the furtherance of its prosperity'), and p. 397 (last sentence of first full paragraph).

50 See, for example, Black's 'Observations,' 1806, *Const. Docs., 1791–1818*, 323–5; Fleming, *Some Considerations*; *Quebec Mercury*, 16, 23 Apr., 18 June, 3 Sept., 8 Oct. 1810; *Canadian Courant*, 12 Nov. 1810; Gray, *Letters from Canada*, 81–3.

51 Craig to Liverpool, 1 May 1810, *Const. Docs., 1791–1818*, 396. See also on a distinct issue, same to Ryland, 9 Nov. 1810, Christie, *A History*, VI: 166–7.

CONCLUSIONS

1 In general, see André Siegfried, *The Race Question in Canada* [1906 in French], trans./ed Frank H. Underhill (Toronto: Carleton Library/ McClelland & Stewart 1966), particularly 29–30, 94–5.

2 Philippe Sylvain, 'Quelques aspects de l'ultramontanisme au XIX siècle,' *RHAF* 25 (1971–2), 241

3 Brian Young, *George-Étienne Cartier: Montreal Bourgeois* (Kingston/Montreal: McGill-Queen's University Press 1981), 73–4

4 'Le Principe des Nationalités,' printed in English by Ramsay Cook, ed *French Canadian Nationalism* (Toronto: Macmillan 1969), 108

5 'Civil Code du Bas-Canada. Législation sur le marriage' *La Revue Canadienne* 1 (1864), 602, 654, 731. De Bellefeuille complained, for example, that some of the canonic prohibitions, such as adultery between intending spouses, were not written into law. See also André Morel, 'La codification devant l'opinion publique de l'époque,' in Jacques Boucher and André Morel, *Le droit dans la vie familiale* (Montreal: University of Montreal Press 1970), 40–3.

6 The codifiers were progressive in one area, that of fostering capitalism, by their removal of restraints on the disposition of property and removing the notion of equity (enforceable by the courts) from contracts.

7 For the similarities and differences between the codes, see Pierre-Basil Mignault, *Le droit civil canadien*, 9 vols. (Montreal: Whiteford and Théoret/C. Théoret/Wilson and Lafleur 1895–1916); Louis Baudouin, *Le droit civil de la Province de Quebec* (Montreal: Wilson and Lafleur 1953);

Castel, *The Civil Law System of the Province of Quebec*; John Brierley, 'Quebec's Civil Law Codification Viewed and Reviewed,' *McGill Law Journal* 14 (1968), 521. I have also made use of the codifiers' *Reports* and the English secretary's pamphlet: Thomas McCord, *Synopsis of the Changes in the Law Effected by the Civil Code of Lower Canada* (Ottawa: G.E. Desbarats 1866).

8 Quoted in Baudouin, *Droit civil*, 203, n 24. The codifiers adopted the old rule without comment.

9 The force of tradition was so strong here that the codifiers often rejected changes found in the Code Napoléon even when those changes were not particularly alien to the spirit of the *Coutumes*. Thus the Lower Canadian code contained no rule prohibiting widows from remarrying within ten months of the husband's death and article 245 allowed the parents only a right of 'moderate correction,' while the French code permitted the father to incarcerate his child without any due process whatever.

10 Cushing, *Appeal*, iii–iv; Girod, *Notes diverses*, 50 (trans.)

11 *Les Soirées canadiennes* 2 (1862), 356. Some years earlier the historian Garneau had written this of the crown's main witness: 'Black received "blood money," but it did him no good, as every one who knew, shunned him, as a traitor himself. Overcome by public contempt, and his mechanical capabilities failing him, he fell into extreme penury, and might be seen some years afterwards, eaten up with vermin, begging his bread on the streets of that city, wherein he erstwhile was recognized for a legislator': *History*, II: 230–1.

12 Girod, *Notes diverses*, 49–53; *Les Soirées canadiennes* 2 (1862), 353–98

13 O'Callaghan to Bartlett, 31 Mar., 12 Apr. 1871, John Carter Brown Library, Providence, Rhode Island; *Evening Bulletin*, 26 Apr. 1873

14 Wallot, 'La crise sous Craig,' 146. See also Andrew Cochran to his father, 14 Sept. 1812, Cochran Papers.

15 *Vie politique de Mr. —— Ex. —— Membre de la Chambre d'Assemblée du B.C.* (n.p. 1814 from internal evidence), 10–11

16 *Vindicator*, 6 Mar. 1832

17 Papineau's address to the protest meeting at Saint-Laurent, 15 May 1837, printed in Gérard Filteau, *Histoire des Patriotes*, 3 vols. (Montreal: Éditions de L'ACF 1938–9), II: 106. De Gaspé (*Mémoires*, 265) wrote that Craig's 'memory is still odious to French Canadians after a lapse of fifty-four years.'

18 See Wallot, 'La crise sous Craig' and that article's bibliographical review.

19 This change was not achieved until enacted by the Special Council in 1841 (c. 30, s. 35) in the same statute which established a province-wide system of land registry offices.

20 See particularly Montreal Merchants Report, 1787, 916–17; letter of a bi-ethnic Montreal committee to the Legislative Council's committee on commercial affairs and police, 23 Jan. 1787, *Const. Docs., 1791–1818*, 920. To have been passed a land registry law would have had to make registration cheap, of little or no prejudice to notaries, and give a guarantee that it would not grossly 'expose the secrets and situations of Families': Quebec Merchants Report, 1787, 905. A bankruptcy law was enacted by the Special Council (SLC 1839, c. 36). The commercialization of the civil law accelerated during the Union of 1840 down to codification in 1866 with, *inter alia*, the abolition of the seigneurial regime (1854), the *retrait lignager* (1855), the usury laws (1853, 1858) and *lesion* between adults (nullity of contracts involving real estate where a party had made a bad bargain). By 1866 freedom of contract had become a civil law value at least equal in importance in the code as protection of family members or paternalistic equity.

21 See, for example, the 'Ninety-Two Resolutions' of 1834, (nos. 76, 77) in Kennedy, *Documents*, 366–8; Fernand Ouellet, ed., *Papineau: textes choisis et presentés*, 2nd ed. (Quebec: Les Presses de l'université Laval 1970), 38–42; Creighton, *The Empire*, 273.

22 Durham to Glenelg, 9 Aug. 1838, *RNAC* (1923), 318; Gérard Filteau, *Histoire des Patriotes*, II, book 5, ch. 3, 4; George Moffatt and William Badgely to Durham, 5 Apr. 1838 (1923) *RNAC* (1923), 169. The evidence on this point is overwhelming.

23 SC 1874, c. 38, s. 4

24 *DCB*, vol. 8, 726; Christie, *A History*, II–IV, *passim*; *DCB*, vols. 4–8, *passim*

25 C.S. Kenny, *Outlines of Criminal Law*, 1st ed., (Cambridge: Cambridge University Press 1904), 271; Earl of Halsbury, ed., *The Laws of England*, 3rd ed., vol. 10 (London: Butterworth & Co. 1955), 562, note o; Alan Wharam, 'Casement and Joyce' *Modern Law Review* 41 (1978), particularly 682–3, 687–8, 690–3

26 Ironically, in the one case I have found where *McLane* was used, it had an effect favouring the prisoner. In *R. v. Frost* ([1839–1840] 4 St. Tr. [n.s.] 86, particularly at 463–64) counsel for the Chartist leader cited *McLane* and eight other cases to show that it had been constant practice in treason trials for more than half a century to give the prisoner the lists of witnesses and jurors at the same time as a copy of the indictment. The court held i) that simultaneity was a crown obligation; ii) it did not matter that the list of witnesses, which had been received after the copy of the indictment, was delivered more than ten days before arraignment; but iii) that Frost had waived his right to object by not pleading the point at trial. The procedural

slip up and its illegality did, however, result in Frost's sentence being commuted from death to transportation for life.

27 (UK) 11 & 12 Vict., c. 12. This turned several of the constructive treasons contained in the 1795 act into felonies, punishable by imprisonment for life. The 1352 and 1795 acts remained in force.

28 Further detailed investigation could, of course, conceivably uncover an instance or instances of the doctrine's use in the colonial courts.

29 These extensions appeared in addresses to grand jurors. See *Quebec Gazette*, 24 Mar. 1838 (Sewell, Quebec); *Toronto Patriot*, 13 Mar. 1838 (Robinson, Toronto); *British Colonist*, 29 Mar. 1838 (Macaulay, Hamilton); and *Toronto Patriot*, 5 May 1838 (McLean, Kingston).

30 Among many indicators of Osgoode's aristocratic leaning was his determined effort to keep mere merchants (whom he called 'Tare and Trett') off the councils: Osgoode to King, 3 Aug. 1796, CO42, vol. 22; same to same, 17 June 1799, Osgoode Letters, 156.

31 Creighton, *The Empire*, 153. There were of course reasons other than those deriving from security or economic concerns for desiring anglification: for example, simply to live or at least enable one's posterity to live at 'home' in familiar, not foreign, surroundings. See Ryland's biography, *DCB*, vol. 7, 766.

32 Papineau to Wilmot Horton, 16 Dec. 1822, *Const. Docs., 1819–1828*, 156. The bill is printed in ibid., 123–31. For an analysis of the politics, see Ormsby, 'Canadian Union.' Among those in London helping the Colonial Office draft the bill were two anglifiers: former Chief Justices Osgoode and Monk.

33 *DCB*, vol. 6, 645. See also 'Petition from Eastern Townships for Union,' 1822, *Const. Docs., 1819–1828*, 133–5; Creighton, *The Empire*, 22–19, 227–8, 405, n 21.

34 Richardson quoted in Christie, *A History*, II: 37; *Montreal Gazette*, 20 Feb. 1832; *Vindicator*, 21 Feb. 1832

35 Campbell, *Lives of the Chief Justices*, IV: 54–69

36 Sewell's 'Observations,' May 1810, *Const. Docs., 1791–1818*, 403, enclosing a copy of same to Milnes, 28 Oct. 1805, S series, vol. 88

37 Neatby, *Administration of Justice*, 175–95

38 Dorchester to Sydney, 9 June 1788, CO42, vol. 59

39 Allcock to Mountain, 22 Nov. 1805, Mountain Papers, vol. 4; Monk to Craig, 10 Aug. 1810, Christie, *A History*, VI: 112–17; Craig to Ryland, 10 Sept. 1810, ibid., 155–7

40 Sewell, 'Observations,' May 1810, *Const. Docs., 1791–1818*, 403–5

41 [Francis Maseres and William Hey], *Considerations on the Expediency of Procuring an Act of Parliament for the Settlement of the Province of Quebec* (Lon-

don: n.p., 1766) as reprinted in *Const. Docs., 1759–1791*, 257–69. S.M. Scott, 'The Authorship of Certain Papers in the Lower Canada Jurist,' *CHR* 10 (1929), 339; R.A. Humphreys and S.M. Scott, 'Lord Northington and the Laws of Canada,' *CHR* 14 (1933), 42; Francis Maseres, *A Collection of Several Commissions and Other Public Instruments* (London: W. & J. Richardson 1772; S. and R. Publishers reprint 1966), 129–32

42 Kennedy and Lanctot, eds., *Reports on the Laws of Quebec, 1767–1770* (Ottawa: King's Printer 1931); Burt, *Old Province*, I: 231

43 Upon, *Loyal Whig*, 173–7, 191–2

44 A.L. Burt, 'The Tragedy of Chief Justice Livius,' *CHR* 5 (1924), 196

45 London, 13 Mar. 1782, CO42, vol. 42

46 *Wolfe Tone's* case (1798) 27 St. Tr. 613 (rebels not triable by court martial); *Wright* v. *Fitzgerald* (1799) 27 St. Tr. 759; O'Higgins, 'Wright v. Fitzgerald Revisited'

47 *Elphinstone* v. *Bedreechund* (1830) 1 Knapp. 316

48 See, for example, *The Trial of Dr. Morrison M.P.P. for High Treason, on Wednesday, April 24, 1838* (Toronto: Donlevy & McTavey 1838); report of John Beverley Robinson on the treason trial of Charles Durand, 21 May 1838, RG1, E2, State Book K, 282–99; Robinson to Arthur, 6 Aug. 1838, John Beverley Robinson Papers; same to same, 5 Dec. 1838, C.R. Sanderson, ed., *The Arthur Papers*, 3 vols. (Toronto: University of Toronto Press 1957–9), I: 417; *DCB*, vol. 6, 116 (Justice William Campbell's handling of the trials of Robert Gourlay for seditious libel, 1818).

49 Edward Bowen to Jonathan Sewell, 2 Aug. 1814, Sewell Papers, vol. 5

50 *In re Daniel Tracey* (1832) *Stuart's Reports*, 478; Law Officers to Bathurst, 30 Dec. 1815, *Const. Docs., 1791–1818*, 480–3. The original text of the question on privilege (CO42, vol. 164, 194–5) is definitely in the handwriting of Sewell (then in London). See also Henry Goulburn (under secretary of state) to Sewell, 14 Nov. 1815, Sewell Papers, vol. 5.

51 See issues of the *Vindicator* and *La Minerve* , Feb.–May 1832.

52 Christie, *A History*, III: 390–1. For complaints about the political partizan-ship of the Bench, see the '92,' resolutions 76, 77, 84(3). The last complained that the unconstitutional but commonplace extra-judicial opinions invaria-bly favoured 'the administration for the time being.'

53 See *La Minerve*, 13 Feb. 1832 (quoting Papineau on non-violent separation); ibid., 16 Feb. 1832.

54 For the Montreal court during the Rebellion period, see my article, 'The General Court Martial of 1838–39 in Lower Canada: An Abuse of Justice' in Pue and Wright, eds., *Perspectives*, 267–73.

55 Stuart to Goldie, 15 Dec. 1838, S series, vol. 559. Stuart, this time, refused to

give an extra-judicial opinion on various legal questions related to the court martial on the grounds that the questions might come before him in litigation. The habeas corpus question had been likely to arise again in litigation before Stuart and it did, with the predictable result: *R.* v. *Teed*, reported in the *Quebec Mercury*, 16 Feb. 1839.

56 See my articles: 'L'insurrection appréhendée et l'administration de la justice'; 'Court Martial'; and 'The Drafting and Passage of the War Measures Act in 1914 and 1929: Object Lessons in the Need for Vigilance,' in Pue and Wright, *Perspectives*, 291.

Select Bibliography

The following lists include only those documents or works which have been of the greatest importance in writing this book. They are cited by short form only in the notes. Other documents or works which had some modest influence on particular questions are omitted altogether or referred to, with full citation, at the appropriate point in the text. The bibliography does not include references to court cases or statutes, which are cited in standard form in the notes.

Primary Sources

MANUSCRIPT SOURCES

Archives de l'archevêché de Québec, Quebec City
    Cartable, Évêques de Québec, vols. 1–2
    Registre des lettres, vols. 1–4
Archives nationales du Québec, Quebec City
    Papiers Fraser
    Records of the Court of King's Bench, 1793–8
    Sewell Family Papers
Archives of Ontario, Toronto
    Claus Papers
    Osgoode Collection
British Library, London, United Kingdom

Charles Yorke's 'Legal Precedents 1602–1752' in the Hardwicke Papers, Add. Mss. no. 36,117, vol. 769

Library of Congress, Washington, DC., United States
France, Affaires étrangères; correspondance politique, États-Unis, vols. 37–67, supplements, vols. 19, 28 – Mémoires et documents, Angleterre, vols., 18,588. These series consist of copies of documents located in the archives of the French foreign ministry, Paris.
Genêt Papers

Massachusetts Historical Society, Boston, United States
Jonathan Sewall (sic) Sr Papers

McCord Museum, Montreal
Arthur Davidson Letters, McCord Family Papers

McGill University, Montreal: Department of Rare Books and Special Collections
De Lery-Macdonald papers, particularly file 2/10
Herman Ryland Papers

National Archives of Canada, Ottawa
Manuscripts Groups

Manuscript Group 5: Ministère des affaires étrangères
Mémoires et documents, Angleterre (vol. 2)

Manuscript Group 8: Documents relatifs à la Nouvelle France et au Québec (XVIIᵉ–XXᵉ siècles)
C9: Court of Quarter Sessions, 1764–84
F13: Knowlton Family Papers
F80: St Ours seigneury

Manuscript Group 11: Public Record Office, London, Colonial Office papers
CO42 and Q series transcripts thereof to 1841. Colonial Office and Governors. General correspondence, Canada, 1700–1922

Manuscript Group 16: Public Record Office, London. Foreign Office papers
FO5 series. Foreign Office general correspondence, United States of America, 1793–1901

Manuscript Group 21: Copies of Documents in the British Library
Haldimand Collection, Add. Mss. 21,661–892

Manuscript Group 23: Late Eighteenth Century Papers. As with MG24, only the person of most importance in this book is listed in describing the papers.
C: Nova Scotia
    6. Charles Inglis
D: New Brunswick
    1. Ward Chipman Sr
    2. Edward Winslow

GI: Quebec and Lower Canada: government
   8. Reconquest of Canada, 1795–1796
GII: Quebec and Lower Canada: political figures
   10. Jonathan Sewell
   14. William Smith
   15. Alexander Gray (re: *Gray* v. *Grant*)
   17. Robert Prescott
   19. James Monk (vol. 2)
GIII: Quebec and Lower Canada: merchants and settlers
   1. George Allsopp
   2. Lindsay-(James) Morrison (vol. 1)
   7. John Richardson Letters
   13. Henry Cull
   18. Journal of Louis-Généreux Labadie
   23. John Nairne
HI: Upper Canada
   1. John Graves Simcoe
   10. William Osgoode (files 9–11)
Manuscript Group 24: Nineteenth-Century pre-Confederation Papers
  B: North American political figures and events
    1. John Neilson collection (vols. 1–2, general correspondence; vol. 35, family correspondence)
    3. Herman Ryland
    4. John Young
    16. Andrew Cochran
  I: Immigration, land, and settlement
    20. Journals of Samuel Southby Bridge
  L: Miscellaneous
    3. Collection Baby
Record Groups
Record Group 1: Executive Council, Canada 1764–1867
  E1: Quebec and Lower Canada State Minute Books
Record Group 4: Civil and Provincial Secretaries Offices, 1760–1867
  A1: S series (correspondence incoming to civil secretary)
  B16, vol. 11: Records of Criminal Offences in the Courts of King's Bench, 1765–1827
  B20: Pardons, 1766–1858
  B21: Prison Returns, 1800–1867
  B45: Declarations of Aliens, 1794–1811
Record Group 7: Governor General's Office

G1: G series (Despatches to Canada from the Colonial Office, 1784–1909)
G15 B: vol. 1: Correspondence from the British Minister to the United States, 1799–1807
G15 C: Civil Secretary's Letter Books, 1788–1829
G18 vol. 15: Diplomatic and Secret Service Reports, 1797–1822
Record Group 8: British Military and Naval Records
   1. C series, particularly vols. 14 (Aliens, 1796–1816), 673 (relations with the United States), and 1204–16 (British–Canadian correspondence, 1796–1811)
Providence City Hall, Providence, Rhode Island, United States
   Documents relating to the estate of David McLane
Public Record Office, London, United Kingdom
   State Papers domestic 34, vol. 9, item 61. Proceedings against William Gregg, 1707/08
   CO323, vols. 35–6. Imperial control of colonial legislation in the 1790s
Quebec Diocesan Archives (Anglican Church of Canada), Lennoxville, Quebec
   Jacob Mountain papers, C series
Quebec Seminary Archives, Quebec City
   Lettres, carton T
   Documents Faribault
Rhode Island State Archives, Providence, United States
   Real estate and other deeds signed by David McLane
Toronto Metropolitan Library
   W.D. Powell papers, vol. B30
University of Toronto: Thomas Fisher Rare Book Library
   Hale Family Papers (1799–1918)
University of Vermont, Bailey/Howe Library, Burlington, Vermont, United States
   Allen Family Papers
Vermont State Archives, Montpelier, Vermont, United States
   Stevens Collection: Allen Papers

PRINTED SOURCES

Collections of Correspondence
Brymner, Douglas. 'Ecclesiastical Affairs in Lower Canada,' *RNAC (1892), 16;* 'French Republican Designs on Canada,' *RNAC* (1891), 57
Christie, Robert. *A History of the Late Province of Lower Canada,* 6 vols. Quebec/Montreal: Thomas Cary and others 1848–55, vol. 6
Colgate, William, ed. 'Letters from the Honourable Chief Justice William Osgoode: A Selection from His Canadian Correspondence, 1791–1801,' *On-*

tario History 46 (1954), 77, 149. These documents are referred to in the notes as the Osgoode Letters.

Const. Docs., 1759–1791

Const. Docs., 1791–1818

Const. Docs., 1819–1828

Cruikshank, E.A., ed. *The Correspondence of Lieut. Governor John Graves Simcoe,* 5 vols. Toronto: Ontario Historical Society 1923–31

Cruikshank, E.A., and A.H. Hunter, eds. *The Correspondence of the Honourable Peter Russell,* 3 vols. Toronto: Ontario Historical Society 1932–6

Kennedy, W.P.M., ed. *Documents of the Canadian Constitution, 1759–1915.* Toronto: Oxford University Press 1918

Memoirs of the Life of Sir Samuel Romilly, 2nd ed. by his sons, 3 vols. London: John Murray 1840

Quaife, Milo M., ed *The John Askin Papers,* 2 vols. Detroit: Detroit Library Commission 1928/31

Rousseau, Jacques, ed. 'Lettres du Dr. J.M. Nooth à Sir Joseph Banks,' *Le Naturaliste Canadien* 26 (1933), 139

Roy, Antoine. 'L'Association Loyal de Montréal,' *RANQ* (1948–9), 253

Têtu, Henri, and C.O. Gagnon. *Mandements, lettres pastorales et circulaires des Évêques de Québec,* 4 vols. Quebec: A. Coté 1887–8

Tupper, Ferdinand Brock, ed. *The Life and Correspondence of Major General Sir Isaac Brock, KB.* London: Simpkin, Marshall 1847

Turner, Frederick Jackson, ed. 'Correspondence of the French Ministers to the United States, 1791–1797,' *AHAR* (1903), vol. 2

Upton, Leslie F.S., ed. *The Diary and Selected Papers of Chief Justice William Smith, 1784–1793,* 2 vols. Toronto: The Champlain Society 1963–5

Newspapers, Quebec/Lower Canada

The British American Register, 1803

The Canadien Courant and Montreal Advertiser, 1807–11

Le Canadien, 1806–10

Le Courier de Québec, 1806–8

The Montreal Gazette–La Gazette de Montréal, 1788–1811

Montreal Herald, 1811

The Quebec Gazette–La Gazette de Québec, 1788–1811

The Quebec Herald and Universal Miscellany, 1788–92

The Quebec Magazine–Le Magazine de Québec, 1792–3

The Quebec Mercury, 1805–11

The Times–Du Cours du Tems, 1794–5

Le Vraie-Canadien, 1810

Pamphlets

La Bastille septentrionale, ou les trois sujets britanniques opprimés. Montreal: Fleury
Mesplet 1791

'A British Settler' [John Fleming]. *Some Considerations on the Question; Whether
the British Government Acted Wisely in Granting to Canada Her Present Constitution.* Montreal: James Brown 1810

'Camillus' [John Henry]. *An Enquiry into the Evils of General Suffrage and Frequent Elections in Lower Canada.* Montreal: Nahum Mower 1810

Un Canadien [D.-B. Viger]. *Considérations sur les effets qu'ont produit en Canada,
la conservation des établissements du pays, les moeurs, l'éducation, etc. de ses
habitants.* Montreal: James Brown 1809

Canadian and English Committees for Constitutional Reform. *Aux Citoyens et
Habitants des Villes et des Compagnes de la Province de Québec.* [Quebec, 1785],
reprint by the Société bibliographique du Canada. Toronto 1951

'A Citizen of Quebec.' *Observations on a Pamphlet, entitled a State of the Present
Form of Government of the Province of Quebec.* London: J.F. & C. Rivington 1790

Cushing, Elmer, *An Appeal Addressed to a Candid Public.* Stanstead, LC: S.H.
Dickerson 1826

[Cuthbert, Ross.] *An Apology for Great Britain.* Quebec: John Neilson 1809

*Discours prononcé par Mr. Alexandre Dumas au Club Constitionnel, tenu à Quebec
le 30 mai, 1792.* Quebec: Samuel Neilson 1792

Du Calvet, Pierre, *Appel à la justice de l'État.* London: n.p. 1784

[Genêt, Edmond.] *Les Français libres à leurs frères les Canadiens.* Philadelphia or
New York: n.p. 1793

Judicial Decisions on the Writ of Habeas Corpus ad Subjiciendum. Trois-Rivières:
n.p. 1839

Lymburner, Adam. *The Paper Read at the Bar of the House of Commons by Mr.
Lymburner.* Quebec: William Moore 1791

– *A Review of the Government and Grievances of the Province of Quebec.* London:
J. Stockdale 1788

[Monk, James.] *State of the Present Form of Government of the Province of Quebec*
[1789], 2nd ed. London: n.p. 1790

[Neilson, John?]. *Mort tragique du Roi de France.* Quebec: John Neilson 1793

'Société d'amis de la patrie et de la constitution,' *Dialogue sur l'Intérêt du Jour,
entre plusiers Candidats et un Electeur libre et indépendant de la Cité de Québec.*
Quebec: William Moore 1792

Travel Literature

Campbell, Patrick. *Travels in the Interior Inhabited Parts of North America in the
Years 1791 and 1792.* Toronto: The Champlain Society 1937

Gray, Hugh. *Letters from Canada, Written during a Residence There in the
Years 1806, 1807, and 1808.* [London 1809]. Coles Canadiana reprint, Toronto
1971

Lambert, John. *Travels through Canada, and the United States of North America, in
the Years 1806, 1807, & 1808.* [1810], 2 vols. Edinburgh/Dublin: Doig &
Stirling/M. Keene 1813

La Rochefoucauld-Liancourt, François-Alexandre, Frédéric, Duc de. *Voyage dans
des États-Unis d'Amérique fait en 1795, 1796 et 1797,* 8 vols. Paris: Du Pont,
Buisson & C. Pouges 1799, vol. 2. A Mr Guillemard (no first name given) of
British and Huguenot origin accompanied the duke on his travels. Guille-
mard's journal of his own visit to Lower Canada in 1795 was paraphrased in
French by the duke and published in the *Voyage* (vol. 2, pp. 194–216).

*Le Compte de Colbert Maulevrier. Voyage dans l'intérieur des États-Unis et au Ca-
nada* [in 1798], ed. Gilbert Chinard. Baltimore: Johns Hopkins Press 1935

Ogden, John Cozens. *A Tour through Upper and Lower Canada.* Litchfield Conn.:
United States Congress 1799

Robertson, J. Ross, ed. *The Diary of Mrs John Graves Simcoe* [Toronto 1911].
Coles Canadiana reprint, Toronto 1973

Weld, Isaac. *Travels through the States of North America and the Provinces of Upper
and Lower Canada during the Years 1795, 1796 & 1797,* 4th ed. [1807]. Augus-
tus M. Kelley reprint, New York 1970

White, Patrick C.T., ed. *Lord Selkirk's Diary, 1803–1804.* Toronto: The Champlain Society 1958

Miscellaneous

Annual Register (London for 1797, 1806)

Barruel, Abbé Augustin. *Mémoires pour servir à l'histoire du jacobinisme,* 5 vols.
Hamburg: P. Fauché 1798–1800

Blackstone, Sir William. *Commentaries on the Laws of England* [1765–70], in four
books, ed. George Sharswood. Philadelphia: J.B. Lippincott 1859

Bord, Gustave, ed. 'Le Canada sous le premier Empire,' *Revue de la Révolution*
7 (1886), 101 (an account made by the French ambassador to Washington in
1811 or 1812 of his activities in relation to Lower Canada)

Bulletin des recherches historiques, various volumes containing a miscellany of
letters

Christie, Robert. *A History of the Late Province of Lower Canada,* vols. 1–5

Coke, Sir Edward. *The Third Part of the Institutes of the Laws of England* [1641].
London: W. Clarke & Sons 1809, pp. 1–19 on treason law. In the text and
notes I usually refer to this portion as Coke.

Cugnet, F.-J. *Traité de la loi des fiefs.* Quebec: William Brown 1775

De Lolme, Jean-Louis. *The Constitution of England* [1771 in French]. Chandos Classics reprint, London: n.d.

East, Sir Edward Hyde. *A Treatise of the Pleas of the Crown*, vol. 1. London: J. Butterworth & J. Cook 1803, pp. 37–138 on treason law. In the text and notes I usually refer to this portion as East.

Ferrière, Claude de. *Corps et compilation de tous les commentateurs anciens et modernes sur la Coutume de Paris*, 2nd ed; 4 vols. Paris: Nicolas Gosselin 1714

Fleming, John as 'A British Settler.' *Political Annals of Lower Canada*. Montreal: Montreal Herald & new Montreal Gazette 1828

Foster, Michael. *A Report of Some Proceedings on the Commission for the Trial of Rebels in the Year 1746, in the County of Surrey; and of other CROWN CASES: to which are Added Discourses upon a Few Branches of the Law* [1762], ed. by M. Dodson. London: E. and R. Brooke 1792, particularly pp. 183–220 on high treason. In the text and notes I usually refer to this portion as Foster.

Gaspé, Philippe-Joseph Aubert de. *Mémoires* [1866 in French], trans./ed by Jane Brierley under the title of *A Man of Sentiment: The Memoirs of Philippe-Joseph Aubert de Gaspé 1786–1871*. Montreal: Véhicule Press 1988

Girod, Amury. *Notes diverses sur le Bas-Canada*. Village Debartzch, LC: J.-P. Boucher-Belleville 1835

Hale, Sir Mathew. *Historia Placitorum Coronae/The History of the Pleas of the Crown* [c. 1670], vol. 1, ed. by S. Emlyn. London: E. & R. Nutt & R. Gosling 1736, usually referred to in the text and notes as Hale.

Hare, John, and Jean-Pierre Wallot, eds. *Les imprimés dans le Bas-Canada, 1801–1840*, vol. 1 1801–1810. Montreal: Les Presses de l'université de Montréal 1967

– *Confrontations/Ideas in Conflict (1806–1810)*. Trois-Rivières: Boréal Express 1970

Hawkins, William. *A Treatise of the Pleas of the Crown*, vol. 1 [1716]. London: Professional books 1973, ch. 17 on treason law. In the text and notes I usually refer to this portion as Hawkins.

Journals of the House of Assembly of Lower Canada, 1792–1811

Kennedy, W.P.M., and Gustave Lanctot, eds. *Reports on the Laws of Quebec 1767–1770*. Ottawa: King's Printer 1931

McNair, Lord Arnold Duncan, ed. *International Law Opinions*, vol. 2. Cambridge: Cambridge University Press 1956

Munro, William Bennett. *Documents relating to Seigniorial Tenure in Canada 1598–1854*. Toronto: Champlain Society 1908

Paley, William. *The Principles of Moral and Political Philosophy* [1785], 20th ed., 2 vols. London: J. Faulder et al. 1814

Perrault, Joseph-François. *Abrégé de l'histoire du Canada*, 5 vols. Quebec: P. & W. Ruthven 1832–36, vol. 3

Plessis, Joseph-Octave. 'Les dénombrements de Québec faits en 1792, 1795, 1798 et 1805,' RANQ (1948–9), 7

Pothier, Robert-Joseph. *Oeuvres de Pothier* [c. 1760s], 11 vols., ed. M. Bugnet. Paris: Cosse & Marchal 1861

Quebec Almanack, 1792–1811

Robison, John. *Proofs of a Conspiracy against All the Religions and Governments of Europe* [1797], 2nd ed. London: T. Cadell Jr & W. Davies 1797

Soward, F.H., ed. letter of John Richardson to Alexander Ellice, 16 February 1793 *CHR* 4 (1923), 260

Tremaine, Marie, ed. *A Bibliography of Canadian Imprints, 1751–1800*. Toronto: University of Toronto Press 1952.

Secondary works

BOOKS

Audet, Louis-Philippe. *Le système scolaire de la Province de Québec*, vol. 3. Quebec: Laval University Press 1952

Bailyn, Bernard. *The Ideological Origins of the American Revolution*. Cambridge, Mass.: Belknap Press of Harvard University 1967

Bédard, Théophile-Pierre. *Histoire de cinquante ans*. Quebec: L. Brousseau 1869

Bellamy, John G. *The Law of Treason in England in the Later Middle Ages*. Cambridge: Cambridge University Press 1970

– *The Tudor Law of Treason*. London: Routledge and Kegan Paul 1979

Borthwick, J. Douglas. *A History of the Montreal Prison from A.D. 1784 to A.D. 1886*. Montreal: A. Periard 1886

Brown, Philip Anthony. *The French Revolution in English History*. London: George Allen and Unwin 1918

Brunet, Michel. *La présence anglaise et les Canadiens*. Montreal: Beauchemin 1964

Bryant, Arthur. *The Years of Endurance 1793–1802*. London: Collins 1942

Burt, Alfred Leroy. *The Old Province of Quebec* [1933]. Carleton Library Press reprint, 2 vols. Toronto: McClelland and Stewart 1968

– *The United States, Great Britain and British North America*. New Haven: Yale University Press 1940

Campbell, John. *Lives of the Chief Justices of England*, vol. 4. Boston: Estes and Laurait 1873

– *Lives of the Lord Chancellors and Keepers of the Great Seal*, vol. 8. Jersey City: Fred D. Linn 1885

Chapais, Thomas. *Cours d'histoire du Canada* [1919–34], 8 vols. Montreal: Boréal Express 1972

Creighton, Donald. *The Empire of the St. Lawrence* [1937]. Toronto: Macmillan 1956

De Conde, Alexander. *Entangling Alliance: Politics and Diplomacy under George Washington.* Durham, NC: Duke University Press 1958

Dionne, Narcisse-E. *Les Ecclésiastiques et les Royalistes français refugiés au Canada à l'époque de la Révolution (1791–1802).* Quebec: n.p. 1905

Dozier, Robert R. *For King, Constitution, and Country: The English Loyalists and the French Revolution.* Lexington, Ky: University of Kentucky Press *c.* 1983

Emsley, Clive. *Crime and Society in England, 1750–1900.* London: Longman 1987

Fecteau, Jean-Marie. *Un nouvel ordre des choses: La pauvreté, le crime, l'État au Québec de la fin du XVIIIe siècle à 1840.* Montreal: VLB Éditeur 1989

Foss, Edward. *The Judges of England,* 9 vols. London: Longman, Brown, Green, and Longmans/John Murray 1848–64

Galarneau, Claude. *La France devant l'opinion canadienne (1760–1815).* Quebec: Laval University Press 1970

Garneau, François-Xavier. *History of Canada from the Time of Its Discovery* [1852 in French], 2 vols. trans./ed. Andrew Bell. Montreal: Richard Worthington 1866

Goodwin, Albert. *Friends of Liberty: The English Democratic Movement in the Age of the French Revolution.* Cambridge, Mass: Harvard University Press 1979

Graham, Gerald S. *Empire of the North Atlantic.* Toronto: University of Toronto Press 1950

Green, Thomas Andrew. *Verdict According to Conscience: Perspectives on the English Criminal Trial Jury 1200–1800.* Chicago: University of Chicago Press 1985

Greer, Allen. *Peasant, Lord, and Merchant: Rural Society in Three Quebec Parishes 1740–1840.* Toronto: University of Toronto Press 1985

Groulx, Lionel. *L'enseignement français au Canada,* vol. 1. Montreal: Granger frères 1931

Harlow, Vincent T. *The Founding of the Second British Empire 1763–1793,* vol. 2. London: Longmans, Green 1964, particularly ch. 10, section 2 on the Constitutional Act

Harris, Richard Colebrook. *The Seigneurial System in Early Canada: A Geographical Study.* Milwaukee: University of Wisconsin Press 1966

Hitsman, J. Mackay. *Safeguarding Canada 1763–1871.* Toronto: University of Toronto Press 1968

Holcombe, Lee. *Wives and Property: Reform of the Married Womens Property Law in Nineteenth Century England.* Toronto: University of Toronto Press 1983

Hurst, James Willard. *The Law of Treason in the United States.* Westport, Conn: Greenwood Publishing *c.* 1971

Ignatieff, Michael. *A Just Measure of Pain: The Penitentiary in the Industrial Revolution 1750–1850.* London: Macmillan 1978

Link, Eugene Perry. *Democratic-Republican Societies, 1790–1800* [1942]. New York: Octagon Books 1965

Mahan, A.T. *The Influence of Sea Power upon the French Revolution and Empire, 1793–1812.* 2 vols. London: Sampson, Low, Marston 1892

Manning, Helen Taft. *The Revolt of French Canada 1800–1835.* Toronto: Macmillan 1962

May, Thomas Erskine. *The Constitutional History of England since the Accession of George the Third 1760–1860.* 9th ed., 3 vols. London: Longmans, Green 1889

– *A Treatise on the Law, Privileges, Proceedings and Usage of Parliament* 19th ed. David Lidderdale. London: Butterworths 1976

Miller, John C. *The Federalist Era, 1789–1801.* New York: Harper and Row 1963

Moore, John Bassett. *A Digest of International Law,* vol. 3. Washington: Government Printing Office 1906

Munro, William Bennett. *The Seigniorial System in Canada.* New York: Longmans, Green 1907

Neatby, Hilda. *The Administration of Justice under the Quebec Act.* Minneapolis: University of Minnesota Press 1937

– *Quebec: The Revolutionary Age 1760–1791.* Toronto: McClelland and Stewart 1966

Nelson, William. H. *The American Tory.* Boston: Beacon Press 1964

Ouellet, Fernand. *Economic and Social History of Quebec 1760–1850* [1966 in French], trans. Institute of Canadian Studies, Carleton University. Toronto: Carleton Library *c.* 1980

– *Lower Canada, 1791–1840.* Toronto: McClelland and Stewart 1980

Radzinowicz, Leon. *A History of English Criminal Law and its Administration from 1750,* 4 vols. London: Macmillan 1948–68

Roy, J.-Edmond. *Histoire de la seigneurie de Lauzon,* 5 vols. Lévis: Mercier 1897–1904

Rudé, George. *The Crowd in History: A Study of Popular Disturbances in France and England 1730–1848.* New York: Wiley 1964

Sharpe, R.J. *The Law of Habeas Corpus,* 2nd ed. Oxford: Clarendon Press 1989

Shetreet, Shimon. *Judges on Trial: A Study of the Appointment and Accountability of the English Judiciary.* Amsterdam: North Holland Publishing 1976

Stephen, James Fitzjames. *Digest of the Criminal Law* [1877], 6th ed. by H. and H.L. Stephen. London: Macmillan 1904

Trudel, Marcel. *Louis XVI, le Congrès américain et le Canada (1774–1789)*. Québec: Éditions du Quartier latin 1949
– *L'Influence de Voltaire au Canada*, 2 vols. Montreal: Fides 1945
Turberville, A.S. *The House of Lords in the XVIIIth Century*. Oxford: Clarendon Press 1927
Twiss, Horace. *The Public and Private Life of Lord Chancellor Eldon*, vol. 1. London: Cary & Hart 1844
Underhill, Nicholas. *The Lord Chancellor*. Lavenham, Suffolk: T. Dalton *c.* 1978
Upton, Leslie F.S. *The Loyal Whig: William Smith of New York and Quebec*. Toronto: University of Toronto Press 1969
Wade, Mason. *The French Canadians 1760–1967*, rev. ed., vol. 1 Toronto: Macmillan 1968
Walker, David M. *The Oxford Companion to Law*. Oxford: Clarendon Press 1980
Wallot, Jean-Pierre. *Intrigues françaises et américaines 1800–1802*. Montreal: Éditions Leméac 1965
Wilbur, J.B. *Ira Allen, Founder of Vermont*, 2 vols. Boston: Houghton Mifflin 1928
Williamson, Chilton. *Vermont in Quandary*. Montpelier: Historical Society 1949

ARTICLES

Baillargéon, Georges. 'À propos de l'abolition du régime seigneurial,' *RHAF* 32 (1968–9), 365
Biggs, E.C. 'Treason and the Trial of William Joyce,' *University of Toronto Law Journal* (1947–8), 171
Brierley, John. 'Quebec's Civil Law Codification Viewed and Reviewed,' *McGill Law Journal* 14 (1968), 521
Briggs, Asa. 'The Language of "Class" in Early Nineteenth Century England,' in Asa Briggs and J. Saville, eds., *Essays in Labour History* (London: Longmans 1960), 43
Brunet, Michel. 'Les Canadiens et la France révolutionnaire,' *RHAF* 13 (1959–60), 467
– 'La révolution française sur les bords du Saint-Laurent,' *RHAF* 11 (1957–8), 155
Crowley, Terence. ' "Thunder Gusts." Popular Disturbances in Early French Canada.' *CHAR* (1979), 11
De Bonnault, Claude. 'Napoléon et le Canada,' *Revista de historia de America* 41 (1956), 31
Dechêne, Louise. 'La croissance de Montréal au XVIIIe siècle,' *RHAF* 27 (1973), 163

Fecteau, Jean-Marie. 'Régulation social et répression de la déviance au Bas-
  Canada au tournant du 19ᵉ siècle (1791–1815),' *RHAF* 38 (1984–5), 499
Finlay, John L. 'The State of a Reputation: Bédard as Constitutionalist,' *Journal
  of Canadien Studies* 20 (1985–6), 60
Gosselin, Amedée. 'Louis Labadie ou le maître d'école patriotique, 1765–1824,'
  PTRSC 7 (1913), 3rd series, 97
Graffagnino, J. Kevin. ' "Twenty Thousand Muskets!!!": Ira Allen and the
  Olive Branch Affair, 1796–1800,' *William and Mary Quarterly* 48 (1991), 409
Greenwood, F. Murray. 'L'insurrection appréhendée et l'administration de la
  justice au Canada: le point de vue d'un historien,' *RHAF* 34 (1980–1), 56
– 'The Chartrand Murder Trial: Rebellion and Repression in Lower Canada,
  1837–39,' *Criminal Justice History* 5 (1984), 129
– 'The General Court Martial of 1838–39 in Lower Canada: An Abuse of Justice,'
  in W. Wesley Pue and Barry Wright eds., *Canadian Perspectives on Law and
  Society: Issues in Legal History*. Ottawa: Carleton University Press 1988, 267
– 'The Treason Trial and Execution of David McLane,' *Manitoba Law Journal*
  20 (1991), 3
Greer, Alan. 'The Pattern of Literacy in Quebec, 1745–1899,' *Histoire
  sociale/Social history* 11 (1978), 293
Hare, John. 'L'Assemblée législative du Bas-Canada, 1792–1814,' *RHAF* 27
  (1973–4), 161
– 'La population de la ville de Québec, 1795–1805,' *Histoire sociale/Social History*
  7 (1974), 23
Harvey, Louis-Georges, and Mark V. Olsen. 'French Revolutionary Forms in
  French-Canadian Political Language, 1805–35,' *CHR* 68 (1987), 374
Havighurst, Alfred F. 'James II and the Twelve Men in Scarlet,' *LQR* 69 (1953),
  522
– 'The Judiciary and Politics in the Reign of Charles II,' *LQR* 66 (1950), 52, 229
Hay, Douglas. 'Contempt by Scandalizing the Court: A Political History of the
  First Hundred Years,' *Osgoode Hall Law Journal* 25 (1982), 456
– 'Property, Authority and the Criminal Law,' in Douglas Hay et al. eds.,
  Albion's Fatal Tree: Crime and Society in XVIIIth-Century England. New York:
  Pantheon Books 1974, 17
– 'The Meanings of the Criminal Law in Quebec, 1764–1774,' in Louis A.
  Knafla, ed., *Crime and Criminal Justice in Europe and Canada*, rev. ed. Water-
  loo, Ontario: Wilfrid Laurier University Press c. 1985
Knafla, L.A. 'The Influence of the French Revolution on Legal Attitudes and
  Ideology in Lower Canada, 1789–1798,' in P.-H. Boule and R.-A. Lebrun,
  eds., *Le Canada et la révolution française*. Montreal: Interuniversity Centre for
  European Studies 1989, 83

Kolish, Evelyn. 'Imprisonment for Debt in Lower Canada, 1791–1840,' *McGill Law Journal* 32 (1987), 602

– 'Some Aspects of Civil Litigation in Lower Canada, 1785–1825: Towards the Use of Court Records for Canadian Social History,' *CHR* 70 (1989), 337

– 'The Impact of the Change in Legal Metropolis on the Development of Lower Canada's Legal System,' *Canadian Journal of Law and Society* 3 (1988), 1

Lederman, L.R. 'The Independence of the Judiciary,' in his *Continuing Canadian Constitutional Dilemmas* (Toronto: Butterworths 1981), 109

Lyon, E. Wilson. 'The Directory and the United States,' *AHR* 43 (1937–8), 514

Moore, John Bassett. 'The Doctrine of Expatriation,' *The Collected Papers of John Bassett Moore*, 7 vols. New Haven: Yale University Press 1944, vol. 4, p. 388

Morel, André. 'La codification devant l'opinion publique de l'époque,' in Jacques Boucher and André Morel, eds. *Le droit dans la vie familiale.* Montreal: Les Presses de l'université de Montréal 1970, 27

O'Higgins, P.O. 'Wright v. Fitzgerald Revisited,' *Modern Law Review* 252 (1962) 413

Ojala, Jeanne A. 'Ira Allen and the French Directory, 1796: Plans for the Creation of the Republic of United Columbia,' *William and Mary Quarterly* 36 (1979), 436

Ormsby, William. 'The Problem of Canadian Union, 1822–1828,' *CHR* 39 (1958), 277

Riddell, W.R. 'Pierre Du Calvet: A Huguenot Refugee in Early Montreal: His Treason and Fate,' *Ontario History* 22 (1925), 239

Rogers, Nicholas. 'The Gordon Riots Revisited,' *CHAR* (1968), 16

Romney, Paul. 'Re-inventing Upper Canada: American Immigrants, Upper Canadian History, English Law, and the Alien Question,' in Roger Hall et al. eds., *Patterns of the Past: Interpreting Ontario's History.* Toronto: Dundurn Press 1988, 78

Roy, J.-Edmond. 'Napoléon au Canada,' *PTRSC* (1911), I: 69

St Georges, Lise. 'Pratiques de la communauté marchande du bourg de l'Assomption, 1748–1791,' *RHAF* 39 (1986–7), 323

Smith, L.A.H. '*Le Canadien* and the English Constitution, 1806–1810,' *CHR* 38 (1957), 93

Tousignant, Pierre. 'La première campagne électorale des Canadiens en 1792,' *Histoire sociale/Social History* 8 (1975), 120

– 'Problématique pour une nouvelle approche de la constitution de 1791,' *RHAF* 27 (1973–4), 181

Townshend, Charles. 'Martial Law: Legal and Administrative Problems of Civil Emergency in Britain and the Empire, 1800–1940,' *Historical Journal* 25 (1982), 167

Trudel, Marcel. 'La servitude de l'Église catholique du Canada français sous le régime anglais,' *CHAR* (1963), 42

Turner, Frederick Jackson. 'The Policy of France toward the Mississippi Valley in the Period of Washington and Adams,' *AHR* 10 (1904–5), 249

Wade, Mason. 'Quebec and the French Revolution of 1789: The Missions of Henri Mezière,' *CHR* 31 (1950), 345

Wallot, Jean-Pierre. 'La crise sous Craig (1807–1811): nature des conflits et historiographie,' in his *Un Québec qui bougeait.* Montreal: Boréal Express 1973

– 'La pensée révolutionnaire et réformiste dans le Bas-Canada (1773–1815),' ibid., 253

– 'La religion catholique et les Canadiens au début de XIXe siècle,' ibid., 183

– 'Plaintes contre l'administration de la justice,' *RHAF* 19 (1965–6), 551, and *RHAF* 20 (1966–7), 28

– 'Religion and French-Canadian Mores in the Early Nineteenth Century,' *CHR* 52 (1971), 51

– 'Sewell et son projet d'asservir le clergé canadien (1801),' in *Un Quebec qui bougeait,* 169

Webster, Stuart. 'Ira Allen in Paris 1800, Planning a Canadian Revolution,' *CHAR* (1963), 74

Wharam, Alan. 'Casement and Joyce,' *Modern Law Review* 41 (1978), 681

Williams, Glanville L. 'The Correlation of Allegiance and Protection,' *Cambridge Law Journal* 10 (1948), 54

Wright, Barry. 'Sedition in Upper Canada: Contested Legality,' *Labour/Le Travail* 29 (1992), 7

THESES

Cockerham, B.F. 'Levi Allen (1746–1801): Opportunism and the Problem of Allegiance.' MA, University of Vermont 1965

Greenwood, F. Murray. 'The Development of a Garrison Mentality among the English in Lower Canada 1793–1811.' PHD., University of British Columbia 1970

Kolish, Evelyn. 'Changement dans le droit privé au Québec et au Bas-Canada, entre 1760 et 1840: attitudes et réactions des contemporains.' PHD., Université de Montréal 1980. Evelyn kindly let me use a revised, unpublished version of this, entitled 'Le debat sur le droit privé.'

Noël, Françoise. 'Gabriel Christie's Seigneuries: Settlement and Seigneurial Administration in the Upper Richelieu Valley, 1764–1854.' PHD., McGill University 1965

Tousignant, Pierre. 'La Genèse et l'avènement de la Constitution de 1791.'
  PHD., Université de Montréal 1971
Vernon, Howard A. 'The Impact of the French Revolution on Lower Canada,
  1789–1795.' PHD., University of Chicago 1951
Wallot, Jean-Pierre. 'Le Bas-Canada sous l'administration de Craig, 1807–1811.'
  PHD., Université de Montréal 1965
Webster, Stuart. 'Napoleon and Canada.' PHD., University of Chicago 1961
Woodfin, Maude. 'Citizen Genet and His Mission. PHD., University of Chicago
  1928

Index

Picture Credits and Sources

National Archives of Canada: Smith (c1844); Haldimand (c3221, painting by Mabel B. Messer); Papineau (c10359, from *L'Opinion publique*, Montreal, 2 January 1873); Sewell (c111156); McGill (c2873, by Dulongpré); Prescott (c12562, painting by William Albrecht Ulrich Berezy Senior, Baron von Moll); Craig (c24888, painting by Garritt Schipper); plan of Quebec City, 1805 (c14814)

Archives nationales du Québec, photographer John Mylod: Mabane, Hertel de Rouville, Panet, De Bonne (from Pierre-Georges Roy, ed., *Les Juges de la Province de Québec* [Quebec City: Archives du gouvernement de la Province de Québec 1933])

Musée du Chateau Ramezay: Carleton (438, painting by Baron Eyvino H. de Dirjinck Holmfeld)

McCord Museum of Canadian History, Notman Photographic Archives: Monk (m22340)

The Law Society of Upper Canada Archives, Photograph Collection: Osgoode (p248)

Metropolitan Toronto Reference Library, J. Ross Robertson Collection: Ryland (t34681)

Cartography Department, University of Toronto and Murray Greenwood: Northeastern North America; Lower Canada (based on Holland, National Archives of Canada nmc18873); Montreal Island and Area

Helen Taft Manning, *The Revolt of French Canada, 1800–1835* (London: Macmillan and Company 1962): map of the region of the seigneuries

Public Record Office, London: Base of espionage operations (CO 42/108)

PUBLICATIONS OF THE OSGOODE SOCIETY